4-3-74

GOLF MAGAZINE'S

GREAT GOLF COURSES
YOU *CAN* PLAY

GOLF MAGAZINE'S

GREAT GOLF COURSES YOU *CAN* PLAY

A GUIDE TO GOLF COURSES AROUND THE WORLD

Edited by
ROBERT SCHARFF

and

GOLF MAGAZINE

CHARLES SCRIBNER'S SONS · NEW YORK

Printed in the United States of America
Library of Congress Catalog Card Number 72-2208
SBN 684-13431-4 (cloth)

CONTENTS

1799034

/v/

GOLF MAGAZINE'S

GREAT GOLF COURSES
YOU *CAN* PLAY

1

THE WIDE WONDERFUL
WORLD OF GOLF

You can play the most famous golf course in the world, the old course at St. Andrews in Scotland, for three dollars, or play on the same course as the King of Morocco for about the same green fee. No penalty is charged for strokes used in killing deadly snakes that wiggle across the fairways in India or for chasing wild birds that steal balls in Pakistan. There's a course in Egypt, near the pyramids, that is one giant sand trap—with no vegetation whatever—and layouts in Norway that are little more than a chain of fjords. There are courses in New Zealand that erupt with geysers or courses in Nepal seven thousand feet up in the shadow of the Himalayas.

Some of the most beautiful courses in the world are located in distant places. The Royal Golf Club de Belgique, once the royal hunting grounds of King Leopold II, has fifty varieties of trees lining its fairways. A bird watcher, instead of a birdie shooter, would find a paradise in the Delhi Golf Club in Calcutta, India. It is rich in vegetation, and beautifully plumed birds of endless varieties flit among its trees. The Wack Wack Golf and Country Club near Manila is regarded as one of the world's most beautiful and exacting.

Grazing cattle are used to keep fairways manicured in Hong Kong and Switzerland but Burma has gone modern—coolies with hand scythes mow the courses. In darkest Africa, natives fashion primitive clubs from tree limbs—with knots for club heads—and bat rocks into improvised holes. You can get a husky housewife to carry your clubs in Belgium or a smiling girl caddy in Japan. There is a golf course in Tahiti for those who become jaded with the local hobby of girl-watching.

Golf has gone worldwide, and it's still growing. The craze no longer is a Western addiction, confined to the British and their rebellious offspring in America. Half a hundred nations on every continent now have citizens—many of them high in government or leaders of industry and finance—who fret over their hook or slice. Just as it was once said—not entirely in jest—that high government decisions in the United States might depend on President Eisenhower's golf score, so it is said now of a prime minister in Malaysia, a prince in Scandinavia or a president in Pakistan.

A survey by *Golf Magazine* discloses that golf is now thriving in well over fifty countries, about the same number that signed the original United Nations charter. They range from Luxembourg, with its single Golf Club Grand-Ducal de Luxembourg, and Israel, with its Caesarea, to the United States, where there are more than nine thousand regulation courses, two hundred new ones being built every year and still not enough to accommodate the eager players, estimated at over ten million.

The biggest boom is in the Orient, spearheaded by Japan where the sport has become almost a religion. The largest vacuum lies behind

In many countries of the world women and girls are caddies. They range from a hefty Belgian woman (*left*) in a flowered apron to a diminutive Japanese girl in her colorful headpiece.

the Iron Curtain, where the Communists have branded it as "bour-geois," a game for the idle rich. There are no golf courses in the Soviet Union but, despite government frowns, golf is experiencing a revival in some of the satellite nations, Czechoslovakia particularly. At first, Czechoslovakian courses were confined almost entirely to personnel from foreign embassies. Recently the Czechs themselves have become more brazen and formed a small society which meets and competes regularly. Some of them use hickory-shafted clubs.

World interest in this sport, which some historians trace back to the Stone Age but which apparently was born in the Low Countries about the fifteenth century and flowered on the Scottish coastline a couple of centuries later, has been enlarged and intensified by international competitions. *Golf Magazine*'s mail survey, in which the associations were asked such intimate questions as the cost of club membership and lessons, the availability of golf carts and the trend toward expansion, disclosed a wide variance in both interest and economics. In many of the countries, golf is a game for the well-to-do, much too expensive for the average worker or ordinary citizen. These barriers are gradually being broken down, however, with growing participation by the middle class. In places such as Finland, Belgium, Mexico, Pakistan, Peru, and Brazil, there are no public courses—only private courses. Sweden has 130 private courses and only five for public use. The ratio in South Africa is even greater—295 to 11.

Golf cars are almost unheard of outside the United States. There are none in Britain, South Africa, many parts of the Orient, Belgium, Mexico, Sweden, Norway, and Denmark. They are plentiful in Canada, scarce but available in Germany, Venezuela, and Pakistan. Peru claims a total of four electric cars and Malaysia one, which is reserved for the prime minister.

Green fees range from two rupees a day, less than 50 cents, to play one of the courses in Ceylon, to as high as $15 a round in Japan. Public course fees are the most reasonable in South Africa, $1 a round, and in Britain, where the sport is made as available to commoners as to royalty. The Old Course at St. Andrews, the cradle of golf, is a municipally run course belonging to the township. For around three dollars a citizen may test the hazards of the Principal's Nose, the famous Road Hole, and Hell's Bunker. Today, any golfer can go on tour, just like the professionals. He can play thousands of the public courses and those operated by resorts. Also, if he belongs to a golf club, many of the private courses here and abroad will give him guest privileges as a reciprocal courtesy.

THE RESORT GOLF COURSE

Great golf resorts have sprung up everywhere, encouraged by the age of jet travel. Out of wastelands of lava ash, rice paddies, and swamps rose glittering hotels, championship golf courses, green oases, meccas for the universal sportsman. These are some of the great golf resorts of the 1960's and 1970's, places such as El Conquistador, Puerto Rico; Mauna Kea, Hawaii; Penina, Portugal; Doral in Florida; Sea Island, Georgia; Concord in New York; Harbour Town Links in South Carolina; and Boyne Country, Michigan.

Each, like a new child, has a personality of its own, but the common touchstone is golf. The resorts have commissioned architects like Robert Trent Jones, George Fazio, and Robert Von Hagge to mold the raw land into manicured golf courses, aimed at attracting vacationers from thousands of miles away.

To the golf courses have been added luxury hotels, some made with marble, Spanish tile, and burled woods. Servants are everywhere, but never there when you don't want them and always there when you do. For après-golf there is a variety of glistening beaches and pools, or you can go wandering through the many one-man-owned native shops. As dusk slips into evening there are native drinks and excellent cuisine. The novelty of foreign custom adds a new dimension for the golfer, and from this a new insight into the game, the land and even his home town.

If . . . if . . . if . . . if golf in the United States hadn't started as a society resort game, it might never have become firmly established here. Golf first came to the United States as a curious, alien invention like haggis. Its importers were wandering Scotch cowhands, lumbermen, farmers, bankers, industrialists and ship-jumping sailors. Then golf became the pet sport of American Society, just at the time American Society was creating its summer and winter resorts.

Golf was introduced to American society at Pau, France. In that community, southwest in the Basses-Pyrenees, winter seldom got colder than 50 degrees. It provided European nobility an escape from the goose pimples of icy palaces before the French Riviera became popular.

Pau had an 18-hole course built in 1856. There was little else to

One of the toughest and most beautiful golf courses in the world is Pebble Beach Golf Links. This famous resort course was the site of the 1972 United States Open.

do at Pau, so refugees from northern Europe's miserable climate and rich Americans took up golf.

In almost every direction you go looking for the beginnings of golf among Americans you wind up at Pau. W. G. Lawrence, who won the first American Amateur championship at Newport in 1894 with 188, against the aggressive Charles Blair Macdonald's 189, learned his golf at Pau. H. B. (Dickey) Martin, author of *Fifty Years of American Golf,* tells of talking to a gentleman in suburban Boston who told him about a young lady who was visiting friends at Wellesley, Massachusetts, in 1892. She got her hosts and their neighbors so stirred up about the game she had played at Pau that the result was a 6-hole course at The Country Club of Brookline. Arthur Hunnewell, Laurence Curtis, and Robert Bacon led the building of that course, in 1893, at a cost "not to exceed $50." The first shot played on it was Mr. Hunnewell's. It was an ace.

But to see the first real center of golf in the United States, look at Newport, Rhode Island, where the United States Golf Association

(USGA) National Open and National Amateur championships began in 1895. The first official golf championships of the United States were played at Newport because it was the fashionable resort capital of the nation.

Luckily for golf, a major enthusiast was Theodore A. Havemeyer, a sugar magnate and smartly groomed sportsman who picked up the bills for the players in the first USGA Amateur and Open championships. The pros could use the help.

The family angle was accented at that premier golf resort. The Newport Golf Club, which was established in 1890 and converted to the Newport Country Club in 1893, had two nines. The championship course, on which the USGA National Open and Amateur championships were played in 1893, was about 2,800 yards. There was a shorter course on which the women and children could play, and they did— plenty! And now we think that par-3 courses for women and children are something new. America's foremost golf resort was way ahead of us.

Of the five charter members of the United States Golf Association, three of them (Newport Golf Club, Shinnecock Hills Golf Club, and Chicago Golf Club) could be termed summer resort courses. The other two, St. Andrews Golf Club in Yonkers and The Country Club of Brookline, were mainly neighborhood clubs, with some townfolks commuting for golf. Perhaps Chicago Golf Club might not be considered in a resort area, 25 miles or so west of Chicago's Loop, but back in the '90's any territory to the windward of Chicago's stockyards was a resort.

A factor that popularized resort courses convenient to suburban homes was rapid-rail transportation. At Lake Forest, Illinois, where the fifth Amateur championship of the USGA was played at the Onwentsia Club in 1899, a Northwestern Railroad advertisement in a golf magazine, prior to the tournament, noted that train time from downtown Chicago to the north shore suburb was one hour. It still is, 69 years later.

Now, for travel, to golf resorts, you have planes or air-conditioned automobiles and lightweight clothing. Back when golf was growing up at the modish summer resorts, golfers didn't mind a veneer of cinders in an open-windowed Pullman. The enthusiasts were wearing wool coats and vests and pants hot enough to make a polar bear drip sweat on an iceberg. And while en route by rail to the golf course, they knocked off a dining-car snack of soup, steak, vegetables, pie, and several cooling beers or bourbons. Thus fueled, the athlete played 18 holes in less than three hours with the temperature in the nineties.

In the United States as in Europe, early golf resorts had the added therapy and entertainment of medicinal waters for drinking and bathing, and gambling casinos, although there wasn't much wagering action at the New England playgrounds.

One of the most popular resorts in Europe was Biarritz, not far from Pau and almost at the border of France and Spain. Sea bathing, mineral baths, medicinal waters, mild climate, gambling, fine hotels, and the distinguished patronage of Napoleon III and his empress, Eugénie, and others needed just one thing to make the Biarritz season continuous. That one necessity was the golf course, built in 1889, which in a manner of speaking, soon had an American offspring—the famed Shinnecock Hills.

W. K. Vanderbilt, Edward S. Mead, and Duncan Cryder, highly

The old Miami Biltmore in its heyday was the great resort course and was typical of the opulence associated with golf of that period.

solvent Americans, were watching Willie Dunn complete the construction of the Biarritz course and saw him hit a 125-yard shot across a ravine to a roughed-in green. Dunn fired so accurately that Vanderbilt, according to legend, told his compatriot, "This game beats rifle shooting—it would go in our country." Dunn was brought over to design the original 12-hole course at Shinnecock Hills, adjoining an Indian reservation. Indian burial mounds formed some of the bunkers.

Consider the headliners of American society and business who grabbed the ball and clubs of the immigrant Scots: Vanderbilt, Morgan, Wharton, Carnegie, Taft, Harriman, Worthington, Tallmadge, Stoddard, Chauncey, Parrish, Astor, Gould, Atterbury, Schieffelin, Flagler, Plant, Reid, Ten Eyck, Rockefeller, Havemeyer, Oelrichs, Bonaparte, Winthrop, Goelet, Van Cortlandt, Lorillard, Livingston, Hoyt, Curtis, Belmont, Keene, Chatfield-Taylor, Cabot, Root, Livermore, Mills, et al.

The discovery of golf by the American rich at the *haut ton* European resorts and its importation to Newport, Shinnecock Hills, The Country Club of Brookline, Tuxedo, and a few other private clubs led, without much delay, to installation of courses at Lake Champlain, Lake Placid, Saratoga Springs, and other New England summer resorts, where clients of the hotels were feeling the need of something more exciting than the scenery of the Berkshires, the White and Green mountains, a stern and rockbound coast, and rocking chairs on the porch.

The vague yearning was converted into a lively interest in golf by Harry Vardon and J. H. Taylor, the British pros who were the Palmer and Nicklaus of that era, coming over here in 1900 for a tour arranged by the Spalding company. In addition to fanning up a golf fire, Vardon and Taylor finished one-two in the USGA Open at Chicago Golf. In winning, Vardon set a record that still continues to cheer all golfers. He missed a two-inch putt, completely, when he carelessly whiffed it.

Courses began popping out on the dunes and marshes of the Jersey shore resorts. C. C. Worthington built the Buckwood Inn and the Shawnee course at his huge estate near the Delaware Water Gap. There the Shawnee Open was held annually. The idea of the PGA was conceived during one of those tournaments with Mr. Worthington and Rodman Wanamaker as the principal movers. Fred Waring owns the historic place now and has updated it completely.

The mid-South got very much into the golf-resort picture. Virginia Hot Springs, Asheville, Biltmore, and Pinehurst, which became to American golf approximately what St. Andrews was to British, lengthened the golf season. Pinehurst, started by James W. Tufts as a rest and cure refuge for tubercular employees of New England druggists, soon became the autumn and spring mecca of America's golf nuttiest. Tuft's son, Leonard, built the first course at Pinehurst, then Donald Ross was hired as professional and greenskeeper. Ross, a personable, skilled tutor from Dornoch, Scotland, had a feeling for golf-course design. Men who visited Pinehurst had Ross come to their home towns and design courses. He not only designed more than four hundred courses, but supervised their construction and trained men for the maintenance programs.

Pinehurst greens up to the mid-1930's were of sand mixed with used crankcase oil. It didn't stick to shoes, it held approaches fairly well, and if you dragged a square of carpet ahead of the line of putt, it made a good putting surface where there wasn't enough water to grow and maintain first-class greens. It was the Pinehurst type of green, a great improvement over other sand or clay greens, or the "putting browns" of early resort courses, that accounted for a rapid spread of golf at places where watering and other expenses of maintenance made golf too expensive to be popular.

John Reid and other canny Scots forefathers in the Apple Tree Gang of St. Andrews at Yonkers thought golf wouldn't get far in the United States, because to build an attractive course would cost maybe as much as $100 and to take care of it for a year, even with sheep doing most of the mowing and all of the fertilizing, might cost $50—and who was going to throw away money like that? The questioning Scots very soon heard who. In 1894, the Newport Country Club was incorporated and capitalized for $150,000. Stanford White was architect of the Shinnecock Hills Golf Club clubhouse, the first golf clubhouse built in the United States. It cost $150,000 and soon needed enlarging.

Railroad and steamship companies had much to do with the promotion of early American resort golf. Henry M. Flagler's Florida East Coast Railroad hotels and courses were established at St. Augustine, Ormond, Palm Beach, and Miami and established the Caribbean outpost resort chain with a course at Nassau. Alexander Findlay was the East Coast's big-name pro. They advertised him as "Golfer in Chief." In a corresponding job for Henry B. Plant's Florida West Coast Rail-

An aerial scene of Pinehurst Country Club, showing three of the four first tees of the four 18-hole golf courses. The first tee of the third course is near the flagpole at the left front of the clubhouse. The first tee of championship course number two is at the back right of the club, near the road. Number four first tee is between the row of trees, left center foreground. The first tee of the first course is just out of the photo, at the extreme lower-left corner. The Carolina Hotel is near the water tanks and the village of Pinehurst is right center.

road group of resort courses at Tampa, Belleair-Biltmore at Clearwater, Kissimmee, Winter Park, and Ocala was John Duncan Dunn. He had expert Northern pros down for winter teaching jobs. Among them were Laurie Auchterlonie, Jim Foulis, Willie Marshall, J. M. Watson, and J. S. Pearson.

In California, the Wilmington Transportation Company steamship line built a 9-hole course on Santa Catalina Island. Hotel Del Monte had a 2,208-yard, 9-hole course for guests. Hotel Green at Pasadena, hotels at Ojai Valley and the Coronado at San Diego had their courses. Generally, though, California was late in approaching its present richness in golf resorts. The explosion of golf resorts in the Palm Springs area definitely started a chain reaction of building deluxe resort hotel courses not only in California, but in Arizona, Hawaii, and New Mexico, and more recently in Mexico.

Johnny Dawson, one of the world's nicest guys and a near National Amateur champion years ago, conceived and promoted the Thunderbird Country Club at Palm Springs, which was the initial demonstration that the water underlying the barren Palm Springs desert acreage eventually would make the prophecies of Isaiah and the real estate salesmen come true: "The desert shall rejoice and blossom like the rose." With canopied golf cars hauling you around a Palm Springs, Arizona, or Florida golf course in the morning before the thermometer starts to blow its top, you can play golf, in Palm Springs, for instance, in July and August—months when Death Valley Scotty would have been scared to wander from the slim shade of a cactus. Dawson, whose vision, energy, and integrity accounted for creation, with resort golf as a catalyst, of fantastically high values out of wasteland, unquestionably has done more than any other man to make golf mean big money in the Southwest's winter playgrounds and residential areas.

Restlessness of the rich had a lot to do with extending resort-course geography and the golf season to 12 months. The case of Robert Todd Lincoln was typical. This son of the Emancipator spent hot summers playing at Ekwanok Country Club, Manchester, Vermont, and dropped into his law firm's shops at Chicago and New York now and then en route to Augusta, Georgia, where he was a fall, winter, and spring golfer. He had a lot of good company. At Aiken, South Carolina, across the river from Augusta, there were golf, horses, and hunting.

Caddies used to be an essential at resort courses. Schoolkids in New England in the summer, the hillbillies in the Virginias and at French Lick, the Negroes at Pinehurst, Augusta, and Florida, the migrant workers in southern California, all have virtually vanished and the golf cars have replaced them at the resorts. The cars are producers of substantial revenue for the resorts and help to pay salaries adequate to attract the kind of expert professionals who attract and serve golfers.

No authorities have ventured a creditable estimate of how much money the resort golf business means a year. It is so many times larger than the purses of the tournament circuit that the tourney pros seem to be playing for the tip money of the resorters. Pinehurst replaced its North and South Open years ago with a Senior Amateur tournament that now has a years-long waiting list. The North and South Open, when it was going, gave professionals special rates, and Pinehurst lost a lot of money on the party.

The many invitation tournaments of senior golfers at winter resorts usually have most available rooms and starting times taken a couple of months before the first shot is fired. Most of these senior contestants now have their wives along for distaff events and making certain that money is put into circulation.

There no longer is a "golf season." The resorts have made the season 12 months long. The summer golf resorts are jumping again and, according to veteran golf-ball salesmen, the winter resorts are getting more rounds played from November through March than were played in all of the United States in any one year up to about 1949.

CHAMPIONSHIP GOLF COURSE

Nowhere has the golf boom shown itself so conspicuously as in the resort hotel field. It seems no luxury resort hotel is constructed today without a golf course as an integral part of the plan. Older golf resorts continue to add new layouts and those hotels without golf facilities are scurrying to construct a course or make arrangements with nearby private clubs for playing privileges. The growth in golf resorts is not limited to any particular region of the country. They are springing up everywhere, including places never before considered resort areas. But what makes some golf resorts stand out among the others as America's greats? First, they offer play on golf courses that, in the opinion of experienced and well-traveled golfers, are meticulously maintained, present a stimulating challenge, and provide scenic surroundings that enhance the enjoyment of golf. The great golf resort also is known for the excellence of its accommodations, cuisine, and service. It provides additional activities and sports to assure that nongolfing members of a family may derive equal pleasure from the vacation.

We use the phrase "championship golf course" quite frequently. The term is so widely used that one would expect that it could be easily and precisely defined. But that is not the case. To say that a champion course is one on which a championship can be played is not enough. Championships have been played on both good and bad courses. One could assume that a course of extreme length would be classified as a championship golf course, but this also is not the case. Extreme length alone does not make a championship course. One could also expect that large greens would be a requirement, but this is not necessarily so. One would naturally expect that a profusion of trapping would also be required in a championship course, but this, too, is not always the case.

When one analyzes the characteristics of some of the well-known and accepted-as-great championship golf courses of the country, the points above are easily proved. Merion, near Philadelphia, is not a long golf course in the modern sense: only 6,694 yards. Augusta National, while having length, is not profusely trapped; there are only 23 traps on its full 18 holes.

Big greens alone do not make a great golf course. Merion's greens are small, averaging only about six thousand square feet, though some are smaller and some much larger, often being as large as nine thousand square feet. Pinehurst No. 2 has relatively small greens, as have Pebble Beach and the Olympic Club in San Francisco. Conversely, St. Andrews in Scotland, probably the most famous of all championship golf courses, has mammoth greens, almost acre-sized, primarily due to the fact that seven greens are in reality two greens each, being played with two pin settings, thus becoming different holes from the opposite directions.

Scenic beauty does not necessarily make a championship course, although it does add to the enjoyment and pleasure of playing the course. Consider the contrast between Pebble Beach along the blue Pacific, Augusta National in a natural horticultural amphitheater, and Pinehurst No. 2 in its pine-tree-framed sand dunes. All of these courses have in common one basic quality: *character*.

Character in the golf course sense is similar to character in the individual sense in that character is attributed to those who have strong individual points making them stand out over and above others. While great golf courses should necessarily have beauty, they should, above all else, have great playing value.

Great shot value and playing value are linked arm in arm. The tee shot must be hit straight as well as long within the scope of well-laid-down limitations. The perfect shot on a given hole can be considered as in the "white" area. When the shot takes on a degree of error, it goes into the "gray" area. If the shot becomes exaggerated in its degree of error, the color becomes a deeper tone of gray until the badly missed shot goes into the "black" area. The values of a hole should be emphasized so that the player can see at a glance what he must conquer to avoid penalty: traps, rough, out of bounds, water, trees, or just plain lack of position. The position of the trapping, the position of the ponds and creeks, the tilt or contour of the fairways, and the width as well as the narrowness of the fairways are all part of the formula making demands upon the player, rewarding for accuracy and penalizing for lack of it.

The green, of course, is the ultimate target. What is more enjoyable than to play a shot to a well-placed, beautifully designed green where the guarding traps as well as the contours are in harmony and a pin position demands the greatest possible shot! The variety of green design is infinite. Elevated greens, terraced greens, tilted greens, mounted contours, flanked trapping on the sides, direct trapping in the front, creeks or water ponds to carry—these many varied green designs contribute to the joy of playing a great golf course and to the miseries of failing to meet their demands.

Golf has an intriguing distinction from other games in that it puts no hardbound strictures on the configuration of its "fields." Baseball or football, for example, must be played on flat ground, whether in the mountains of Mexico or the meadows of Maryland, and it's always ninety feet between bases and one hundred yards from goal line to goal line. But no rule of golf states that a green or fairway must be a specific size or shape, a bunker so deep or shallow and located in a particular place, a par-4 just so many yards long. It is a rather open-ended proposition that stirs individual inventive juices and makes the building of courses extremely fascinating. This is not to say that the golf architect's creative engine has no governors. There are always financial considerations that affect how much earth can be moved. A client may insist on a certain clubhouse location, and this largely determines the basic routing of a course. The architect does not set the tee markers and cut in the cups, and this has a definite bearing on how his course actually plays. (More on this later.) There is still a limit to how far a man can hit a golf ball in the air, so you don't put a tee in Brooklyn, and its green on Staten Island.

Yet, while there are restraints, some obvious, some less so, there is still ample flexibility with which the architect can exercise personal judgment and aesthetic taste. For instance, a central precept of golf architecture is, "land dictates design." Thus, if given a hilly site, the architect should bring in a course that is essentially hilly. At the same time, if a dull spread of dead-level ground stretches out before him, the architect is free to push some of it into mounds that break up the horizon and become obstacles as well. In either case, the course builder controls the severity and placement of contours and convolutions. A golf course must have either 9 or 18 holes, and par for each is set by yardage. These are fixed quantities. But the latter leaves a good bit of room for architectural discretion. The designer can make the golfer slug long irons and woods to par 3's put at or near the 250-yard maximum, or arrange more accessible 160-yard short holes. One man may conceive par 5's as reachable with two very strong shots, another as full three-shot holes. In brief, the course builder can shape or re-shape terrain pretty much as he will and inject into a layout what he believes is a proper golfing challenge. *What he believes.* That is the crux of the matter, and, man being the complex creature he is, subject to myriad outside influences as well as to inherent characteristics, the design of every golf course will inevitably be an expression of many forces as they manifest themselves in the individual who builds it. By the same token, any evaluation of a golf course by those who play it must necessarily be highly subjective, because the same forces work on them.

One of the most celebrated of all golf courses was built by a man with the soul of a black humorist, and a touch of hangman, too. His name was George Crump, and he set out to build the "toughest golf course in the world." Why men are inclined to such a deed is an interesting study in itself. Anyway, Pine Valley (New Jersey) was Crump's get. His 18 holes run amid great areas thick with trees. This alone is not unusual in golf, but he capped his monument by leaving much of the south New Jersey sand and scrub in place, allowing it to sprawl seemingly everywhere, particularly in front of the tees. Even to better players, who can carry them easily, the mere existence of those arid wastelands jellies muscles and induces migraine. For the average golfer the place is a Pandora's box of evil jokes. Not only does his slice or hook put him in a timber trap, he gets the noose for the mere indiscretion of a straightway, but topped, shot, and probably also for thinking he can play the damned game in the first place. Perhaps Mr. Crump was a guilt-ridden self-flagellant, since he too was to play the course. Perhaps we all are, because for all its terrifying prospects, not a soul who has ever lunged at the dimpled spheroid will turn down a chance to "do" Pine Valley, which is how one man interpreted "tough."

George Crump was a Philadelphia hotel magnate, and an amateur architect. Pine Valley was his only course (actually, he died before its completion and H. S. Colt finished the last few holes), but most American courses built early in this century, when golf was first moving onto the national sporting scene, were designed by professionals, many of whom were immigrant Scots. Donald Ross (mentioned earlier) and Alistair MacKenzie are two of the most revered. Not surprisingly, they drew heavily if not exclusively on precedents set in the game's natal ground (as did even American-born course builders of the time). These layouts very often reflect instinctive elements of Scotch economy and subtle understatement. For example, before it was remodeled, the sixteenth hole at the Augusta National, a MacKenzie course, might have been directly transplanted from the grim environs of Carnoustie to the red clay soil of sunny Georgia. Bob Jones, who was in charge of designing the course at Augusta, sought to pattern much of his pet project after the British courses he loved, and with typical insight went to a designer blooded in that tradition. MacKenzie's sixteenth had a rough-hewn, unmanicured look, a small green with odd little humps called chocolate drops scattered about, and a narrow ditch, a burn really, angling casually in front of the putting surface. When Jones decided to redo the hole, he conceived changes that moved well away from the British motif and in our opinion gave to it a very American appearance. The burn was opened up so that water (tinted for color TV at Masters time) covers almost the entire fairway. The green was considerably enlarged, and the entire hole lengthened. It now has a kind of dramatic, eye-catching, well-groomed beauty that appeals more readily to American tastes.

Here again, Jones chose and instructed an architect, Robert Trent Jones, who could best perform what he, consciously or not, wanted. Born in England, but raised from the age of four in Rochester, New York, Robert Trent Jones is probably the first course designer of consequence who in his work expressed, and continues to express, a wholly American point of view. Generally speaking, as a nation we are much impressed by size. Size and a bit of glamour. These are important criteria for quality in our society, and Jones, with his archetypal long tees, massive greens, and sculptured bunkers, has built courses with a sweeping dimension and flair for visual excitement that bespeaks a national predilection. Where a MacKenzie might emulate the native parsimony of his homeland in representative North America landscape, Trent Jones takes that natural abundance and builds in its light.

A writer working on a TV golf show once described a Jones' bunker as having a "whirlygigging, Picasso-like" effect. Course building has come a long way since primitive days when bunkers were originally holes made by sheep burrowing into the soil for protection against chill sea winds. Jones' bunkers, and particularly his greens, more often than not originated as sketches on paper. These are not simple drafts-manlike drawings, either, but artistic renditions, full of shadings and soft curving lines.

Jones has remarked that he likes to have at least one hole on each of his courses that will remain eternally etched in the golfer's memory. One such is his 13th at The Dunes in Myrtle Beach, South Carolina, a par 5 that bends all the way around a huge pond. There is no short-cut route, and the merest slice off the tee or from the fairway is destined for dampness. A plaque commemorates the 22 that one hacker (the late Charley Bartlett) made on the hole. The seventeenth at Jones' new Firestone course is a par 3 with a narrow-necked peninsula green only some ninety feet deep. It requires at least a fairly long iron from a well-elevated tee, which makes the target area look like a garter snake sunning itself in the Straits of Gibraltar. Miss to the left and you've got a patch of grass no wider than a nymph's waist on which to land. Better a nymph's waist. A little long, or short, or right, and you buy your ball back in Bobby Nichols' pro shop. Such holes offer little to no margin for error, but they are optical knockouts, and Jones, as he has intimated, likes to take an occasional dip into the heady wine of the spectacular for the sake of itself.

Two of Jones' most famous trademarks are the 150-yard-long tee-way, and greens as big as aircraft-carrier landing decks. It would be easy, but not quite meet to say, that they derive solely out of his or a national obsession with bigness. Jones explains them primarily as his solution to turf maintenance. The tremendous growth of golf since World War II has brought so many players to tromp the greens that the traditional smaller tees and greens might be churned to mud under all those feet. Jones provides for wider spacing of tee markers and cups so that worn places have a chance to recover. A by-product, as Jones points out, is course variability. A 7,500-square-yard green offers pin placements that can change an approach shot by as much as three clubs. With the tee markers back to the "tips" a course plays a tough 7,000 yards or so—from up front a more comfortable 6,600 yards.

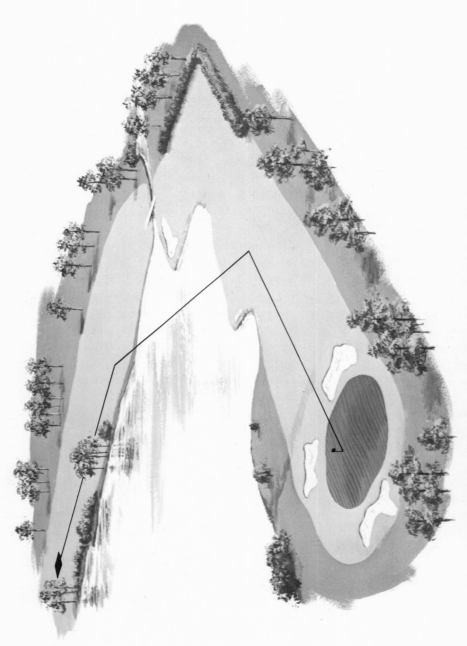

One of the most difficult holes in the world that you can play is the thirteenth at The Dunes Golf and Beach Club. It is 560 yards long and is a par 5.

Another great golf architect of our times is George Fazio. He was one of the finest players on the pro tour in the '30's, '40's, and early '50's. He won a number of events, including a Canadian Open, and was in a playoff with Lloyd Mangrum and Ben Hogan for the 1950 U.S. Open at Merion, which Hogan won. Fazio had, and still has, a wonderfully coordinated "classic" golf swing. Other pros seldom saw George off the course (he was always bored with the tour, except for the competition), but all liked playing with him so they might somehow learn to duplicate his perfect rhythm and simple swing mechanics. There's an appropriate parallel between Fazio's golf swing and his golf courses. There is no wasted motion. He feels the drive is not so much a force stroke as it is a controlled power shot and that the second shot, or the shot to the green, is the game's most demanding. So, he builds fairways that put a premium on accurate driving that will open up the greens for easier entrance, and smaller greens that require precision iron play. Should you hit a Fazio green you've made a good shot and you deserve a run at a birdie, not the ninety-foot something or other that is neither a chip nor a putt. George builds four or five teeing areas at varying angles to the fairway so course variability becomes more than that of mere distance. There's nothing really new in all this, and it is in some part a reaction to Trent Jones' innovations. Fundamental to Fazio's technique is the idea that the game of golf is not only a test of terrain and muscle, but a battle of the individual with himself to acquire the powers of concentration necessary for correct analyses of shots and a swing to pull them off consistently. That is usually battle enough.

With every golf course Fazio builds, a struggle is waged within himself. His Italian nature wants to sculpt an 18-hole Roman garden, while the British influence on him seeks a less flamboyant, more "natural" development of the land. The forces can make a rich combination, and courses such as Moselem Springs, the "Jackrabbit" at Demaret, and Burke's Champions, and the new Jupiter Hills, in Florida, indicate that George has fought the good fight and achieved an admirable balance, an important word in his design lexicon. He would be dissatisfied if a golfer remembered only a few holes in his 18-piece set. He's after a total picture, with no indifferent brush strokes. The sensation of playing a Fazio course is a quiet one, like viewing an Impressionist Monet rather than a Surrealist Dali.

The days of building golf courses on naturally attractive land for the private country club are almost ended. The real estate, even if available in this era of suburban sprawl, is so costly as to make such a luxury prohibitive. Almost exclusively, courses are now built for home-development complexes or resorts. In this situation the course builder gets the worst land available, the best being reserved for the more profitable "ranches" and hotels. You put houses and hotels on high ground *overlooking* golf courses. As a result, course building is beginning to tax the architect's ingenuity to an extreme. Bob von Hagge, given his earliest experience in golf design, his youth and personality, may be leading a new vanguard. Bob's first efforts, for the most part, have been in the southern tip of Florida. He's beginning to move out of this narrow realm, but tracts of swamp, old garbage dumps, and generally pancake terrain have up to now been his unaccommodating canvas. For him the "outside influence" is mostly a void, and his aim is to fill it; make something out of nothing.

An outstanding example is his Boca Rio course, near Boca Raton, which he feels is his best to date. Built on what had been a boggy city dump, he drained the water, trucked in all the topsoil, then proved that as far as he's concerned, design can also dictate to the land. He created an astounding number of fairway mounds that make Boca Rio truly unique to the area—the Troon of the Tropics. The mounds, none of which is as tall as a grown man, are cleverly placed so the golfer can always read the line of the hole. As Hagge defines it, in his sometimes tortured prose (a hole is never a *hole,* but an *examination,*) "I was able to . . . describe the shot problems and the correct tactical approach to the shots." Simply, it's a helluva position course. There are an extraordinary number of doglegs, and some people feel this weakens it as a potential or existing "great" course. But the term "great," while often used, is largely indefinable, so Boca Rio, measuring only some 6,600 yards from the back tees, is at least an excellent test of championship golf.

Von Hagge's architecture credentials are sound. His father built courses in Florida and Illinois in the 1920's. Bob made a mild, unsuccessful bid at the pro tour, and when finally settled down he went to work under the tutelage of Dick Wilson, considered one of the top course builders ever. Von Hagge worked with Wilson on a number of courses, including Doral's Blue Monster, and the PGA National's East course, where the 1971 PGA was held. Wilson's penchant for doglegs and "flash" bunkers that define the turns and the backs of greens are apparent in his disciple's own work. Von Hagge has brought the ace Australian tournament golfer, Bruce Devlin, into the business with him, which makes available another sound golfing voice, and has probably helped acquire commissions Down Under.

Von Hagge has gotten a reputation as something of a radical, at least in golf designing. Boca Rio may warrant this label in that he turned a trash heap into a golfing rose garden, so it can't be a denigrating assessment in that instance. The fact is that the mounding technique he used dates back to the style of C. B. MacDonald and the early 1900's. Some of his other ideas, though, might make the game's traditionalists uncomfortable. Bob remarks that there are things he wants to do on a golf course that "people aren't yet ready for." One is a course made entirely of artificial turf. "It had to come, didn't it? You roll it up once a year and redesign the whole thing. Plus, it will be less expensive. No green superintendents, no water bills, very little maintenance." There you have it. Course design by Von Hagge, wall-to-wall fairway by Mac Dosian, patterned greens in a modish psychedelic vein. Who can say never? Twenty years ago no one thought baseball would be played in a carpeted air-conditioned hall.

Many more men could, and should, be discussed here at length, but we've only got space to mention a few. Pete Dye was a million-dollar-a-year insurance salesman before turning to course building. A fine golfer himself, Pete hooks up with Jack Nicklaus on some projects, the most notable being the Harbor Town course on Hilton Head Island, which has gotten some deservingly good notices. A casual, easygoing person, Pete is moving with the fast-developing trend toward shorter courses. He also likes to shore up a green with old railroad ties, and throw a freight car over a creek to serve as a bridge. Some of it is gimmicky, but the gimmicks never intrude on the courses themselves, which are quite sound golf tests.

Joe Finger was an engineer and business executive for years, then built the first Houston Champions, and has been very busy since. He has laid out 18-hole courses for the Catskills' two top resorts, the Concord and Grossinger's. Many touring pros are getting into the course-building business, which should prove interesting, since they'll learn that, odd as it may seem, building courses and simply playing them are two very different pursuits.

GOLF ON THE GO

Every year it becomes easier for you and your wallet to take a vacation. The airlines are scheduling more jet flights to vacation areas around the world and are offering group plans and all-inclusive tours. There are special low rates on transporting golf bags. Even if you are limited to one season for vacation time, you'll have no problem in finding a suitable golfing spot. An increasing number of resorts operate year-round and golf facilities and privileges are available most of the time. The best areas for year-round activities are found in the western and southeastern United States, and the islands of Bermuda and the Caribbean. If time, besides money, is a big factor, take advantage of special golfer's package plans, which are growing in popularity. Many are planned for two- or three-day weekends and include room, meals, services, and golfing, along with the many other activities offered by the hotel. On the other hand, these packages are also planned for several weeks, and include many relaxing days on the fairways. Quality has kept pace with the quantity of golf courses. These top resorts have spared very little in order to provide courses of high championship caliber. Twenty-seven-hole courses are becoming a common sight, as are courses lit for night play, driving ranges, par-3 and pitch-and-putt courses. All these features plus unmatched hospitality, impeccable service, Nature's beautiful surroundings, and endless activities and sports are typical of the resorts presented in this book. Whether it's the call of the Wild West, the enchantment of the islands, or the grandeur of the mountains, there's a place somewhere to please the golfer on the go.

The next 19 chapters are devoted to golf courses you *can* play throughout the world. Of course, it is impossible, within the scope of this volume, to list all of the courses available for play on the face of the earth. Those included in this book are selected as representative of the courses in the area or country and are generally considerd to be the most challenging and interesting by our panel of experts. We apologize, in advance, if your favorite golf course has been omitted from any of our lists.

As a rule, only the courses that traveling or touring golfers can visit and play without problems were selected. In other words, we did not place in our lists such courses as Pine Valley, Oak Hill, Merion, Cypress Point, and others that don't welcome visitors. Golf courses in the United States, of course, fall into four basic categories: public, resort, semiprivate, and private. (The legends to these courses in Chapters 2 through 12 are as follows: Pub—public; R—resort; SP —semiprivate; and Pvt—private.)

While public or municipal courses which are often operated by city, county, or state governments are fairly numerous in the United States, they are usually very crowded, especially in and around major cities such as New York, Cleveland, Chicago, San Francisco, and Los Angeles. Any golfer who can play the green can play on a public course, but since most of them have reserved starting times, particularly on weekends, it is not wise for the tourist golfer to plan to play on them unless he is willing to wait. For this reason, we have limited our selection of public courses in this book to those that are a great challenge or interesting enough to be worth the wait to play. To play most public courses, it is wise to call or write in advance to find out about the reserved starting-time policy.

Resort courses are really the best bet for the touring golfer. These courses are generally owned and operated by resort owners. They are designed to accommodate the tourist and his needs, and usually have complete package arrangements for meals and lodging as well as for golf. Fine, well-kept resort courses can be found almost everywhere in the United States and are on the increase throughout the world.

Semiprivate courses in the United States have a regular golf membership, but permit the public to play at specified times under some other restrictions such as higher green fees. In our selection of semiprivate courses, we have chosen those which have a fairly liberal policy for the tourist golfer, but it is still wise to check their *exact* restrictions in advance. Generally, it's not wise to plan to play a semiprivate course on a weekend.

Almost every private golf club in the United States will admit guests of members and many of them will welcome the traveling golfer if he has proof of membership in another established club. If you are a member of such a club, it is wise to carry an identification letter from your club secretary as well as your membership card on any golf journey. Some hotels and motels have arrangements with both private or semiprivate courses to permit their guests to play at any time. The private courses listed in this book either fall in this category or they accept visiting golfers under certain conditions. Again, it is wise to write or call in advance before planning to play these courses.

The foreign courses mentioned in Chapters 13 to 20 are, for the most part, private courses. (Canadian courses described in Chapter 12 fall into the same four general categories as United States

courses.) But most visiting golfers can play them without any difficulty. The majority of the courses mentioned in these chapters will
accept you just on payment of green fees. Some clubs require a letter
of introduction. If you are a member of an established golf club in
the United States, a letter of introduction from your club secretary
or membership card is all that is needed. If you are not a club member, a letter from that country's tourist bureau or board, your transportation carrier, or the hotel where you are staying will usually
provide the necessary introduction needed to play on the course.

While it is always best to take your own clubs with you when
traveling, golf club rentals are generally available at most public,
resort, and semiprivate courses in the United States and at the majority of the courses mentioned in Canada, Mexico, Ireland, Scotland,
England, Japan, New Zealand, Australia, Morocco, Bermuda, the
Bahamas and the Caribbean, and on the European continent. As
previously stated, the costs of green fees and course facilities around
the world range from very high to very low. At most clubs, you find
caddies and/or golf carts available. Except in the United States and
Canada, motorized golf carts are, if available at all, at only the
more luxurious clubs.

Enough generalities, let's look more specifically at the great golf
courses around the world that you can play.

2

THE UNITED STATES: NEW ENGLAND

The visting golfer to the New England states will always have his hands full when he attempts to pick out his golf sites from road maps and travel brochures. His trouble will come from trying to whittle down his list of choices. For proud and proper New England, celebrated for its wintertime skiing, deep-sea fishing, sailing, historic landmarks, and Yankee cooking, is no less renowned for its lush golf facilities.

Some of the finest resorts offering golf privileges can be found here, particularly for the familyman-golfer. The hotels, lodges, and inns provide enough diversion for his wife and kids to keep the golfer from becoming conscience-stricken as he hacks his way around the fairways.

The architecture of the golf courses at most New England resorts are also of early design. The older courses feature a short 9 or 18 holes with small greens and very few sand traps. They rely on natural hilly, wooded terrain with God-created streams and lakes, rather than manmade hazards. The perimeters of many fairways are bordered by watermelon-sized field rocks that were tossed aside by farmers when the earth was first plowed. Except on courses where watered fairways exist, the sod is usually not as thick and lush as, for instance, on the richer farmlands of the Midwest. Golfers must learn to "pinch" the ball for best results from this thinner turf.

Today's golf boom, however, has encouraged some course modernization. Newer courses reflect the seven thousand-yard trend, triple tees, and expansive, undulating greens. Often this has meant bulldozing new fairways and leveling new greens from virgin timberlands. Those along the northeastern coastline, especially on Cape Cod, often flirt with the ocean waters on the first few holes, crank inland through the timbers, and then return for another bout with the sea breezes. Such planning also delights more amphibious vacationers who also enjoy water sports. The newer courses, too, have taken advantage of improved disease-resisting grass seeds, modern sprinkling, and drainage systems to offer the golfer the ultimate in manicured conditions.

CONNECTICUT

While Connecticut is one of the smaller states in the Union, it has over 150 regulation golf facilities. Thus, Connecticut is virtually loaded for golf, with excellent playing conditions at such points as Farmington, Canaan, Torrington, Stratford, Bridgeport, and Westport, but unfortunately most of the state's better courses are private. However, there are some good courses (listed below) you can play while in the Nutmeg State.

LOCATION	COURSE	HOLES/PAR/ YARDAGE	TYPE
Bridgeport	D. F. Wheller GC	18/72/6,580	Pub
		18/71/6,470	SP
Farmington	Tunxis Plantation CC	18/72/6,685	Pub
		9/36/3,238	Pub
Glastonbury	Minnechang GC	18/71/6,350	Pub
Groton	Shennecosset CC	18/72/6,512	Pub
Middlefield	Lyman Meadow GC	18/72/6,320	SP
Norwich	Norwich Inn GC	18/71/6,425	R
Southburg	Heritage Village CC	18/72/6,300	R

MAINE

The well-worn homily "As Maine goes, so goes the nation" might apply to golf as well as to politics. The first golf course in this country to be built by a resort was the one at Poland Spring, Maine, begun in 1894 when six holes were put up. The course was enlarged to nine holes in 1898 and eventually to 18 holes in 1915. Today, the Poland Spring Hotel draws golfers from all over the country. (Distinguished golfers who have trod its fairways include two former Presidents—McKinley and Harding—as well as such notables from the game as Bobby Jones and Harry Vardon. The course, 6,464 yards long with wide, well-clipped fairways, offers a true test of golf. The York Golf and Tennis Club at York, is another of the state's prized golf layouts. No less than Donald Ross designed the course, and though it is only 6,173 yards in length, it carries the Ross trademark of

Putting on the fourteenth green of Maine's popular Poland Springs golf course. The Poland Spring Hotel can be seen in the background.

deceptively difficult holes whose characteristics are at the mercy of capricious breezes blowing in off the ocean a mile away.

Most anywhere in Maine, golf facilities are available within a half-hour ride of the towns or cities. The state's 93 golf courses are more heavily concentrated in the Greater Portland area, but from York to Fort Fairfield picturesque links challenge the golfer. According to National Golf Foundation statistics, Maine ranks fifth nationally in golf holes per capita.

For untouched scenic beauty, few areas can approach the mountainous western part of Maine, where there are a good number of courses scattered among the verdant forests and blue lakes. Crossing into Maine on Route 2, the first stop is the Bethel Inn, where gracious accommodations are combined with a spotty 9-hole course in the Oxford Hills. Nearby is Evans Notch, a national wildlife area with a spectacular view of the Presidential Range. If you choose to enter the state farther south, there is a choice of four courses on the way to Bethel. Continuing north to the Rangely Lakes region, you may like to try your skill on the 9-hole, par-35 course at Oakdale in Mexico.

Rangely is the center of the famed Rangely Lakes region, with numerous hotels, lodges, and camps. Its two golf courses—Mingo Springs and Rangely Lakes—are 9-hole, par-35 layouts, two thousand feet above sea level.

Traveling north from Rangely, the golfer will enter the unspoiled Northern Lakes and Forests Region. Yet, even in this seeming wilderness he can find his favorite sport. There is Mountainview Golf Club at Jackman, a town known as the "Switzerland of Maine" because of its backdrop of mountains. And farther east at Moosehead Lake, there are two more courses. Surrounded by rugged mountains and virgin forest, Moosehead has been a vacationer's haven for many years. Greenville, at the foot of the lake, is the starting point for excellent roads that strike for many miles northward along both sides of the lake. At Greenville Junction, you can play Squaw Mountain Inn's sporty nine, while the family tries a climb to the top of Big Squaw Mountain for a magnificent view of the entire lake area. Opposite Rockwood and West Outlet, Kineo Mountain rises sheer and majestically from the heart of the lake, and at its foot lies the golf course at Mount Kineo Hotel.

There are many courses for the visiting golfer to play while in Maine. Here are the ones that we feel are the most challenging:

LOCATION	COURSE	HOLES/PAR/ YARDAGE	TYPE
Bangor	Penobscot Valley CC	18/72/6,353	Pvt
Bar Harbor	Kebo Valley GC	18/70/6,209	SP
Bethel	Bethel Inn GC	9/34/2,413	R
Greenville Junction	Squaw Mountain Inn CC	9/36/2,463	R
Kennebunk	Webhannet GC	18/70/6,200	SP
Kineo	Mount Kineo GC	9/36/3,100	Pub
Poland Spring	Poland Spring GC	18/71/6,464	R
Portland	Riverside Municipal GC	18/72/6,329	Pub
York	York G & TC	18/70/6,158	Pvt
Fort Fairfield	Aroostock Valley CC	18/72/6,565	SP

MASSACHUSETTS

Some people claim that Massachusetts is a 3,322-hole golf course. This is most likely true since there are more than 237 public and private golf courses in the Commonwealth and there are many good golfing areas.

The Berkshires, noted for summer music festivals at Tanglewood and the dance festival at Jacob's Pillow, for example, abound in fine golf terrain—with one important new addition. Jug End Barn, at South Egremont, which is host to skiers in winter, has added an 18-hole golf course. Designed by famed golf-course architect Alfred Tull, the Jug End course covers 6,250 yards of rolling, wooded terrain and plays to a par of 72. It is the first new golf course to be built in the Berkshires in more than a quarter of a century. Pittsfield, in the heart of the Berkshires, has three courses—Pontoosuc Lake, Berkshire Hills, and the Pittsfield Country Club—and there is golf to be found also at Lee, Great Barrington, Williamstown, Adams, North Adams, and Dalton.

A side trip east on Route 90 will take you to the choice golf area around Springfield, with some 15 courses all within a short drive of each other. And by continuing on this route, you may treat the family to a tour of Old Sturbridge Village, where life is seen as it was lived in the early 1700's in a town that has been completely restored.

In another of the state's major resort areas—Cape Cod—golf has always been among the many recreations available, but it was usually secondary to such attractions as boating, fishing, and lolling on the beach. Now, however, the happy combination of ideal climate, additional courses, and the increased popularity of the game everywhere has lured people here strictly to play golf.

The principal attraction of the Cape—for the golfer or anyone else —is its climate. The area is bounded on the north and west by Cape Cod Bay, on the east by the Atlantic, on the south by Nantucket Sound, and on the west by Buzzards Bay. This abundance of water gives the place a moderate climate that is conducive to outdoor pursuits almost the year round. In fact, there are no more than perhaps a half-dozen weekends on which it is too unpleasant to play golf. This means, of course, that it is possible to play on the Cape when the connecting Massachusetts mainland is covered with snow.

There is also something for every golfing taste. The Cape has 26 courses, including public, semiprivate, and private, and they offer the golfer a variety of terrains and playing conditions. There are eleven 18-hole layouts—including two at New Seabury—eleven 9-hole courses, and four 18-hole par-3 courses.

Six of the clubs are private, and it is necessary to be accompanied or introduced there by a member in order to play. Most of these courses remain open all year and properly introduced persons usually can play during the off-season. The private clubs are Oyster Harbors Club, Hyannisport Golf Club, Wianno Club, Eastward Ho! Country Club, and Woods Hole Golf Club.

Semiprivate clubs include Clauson's Inn and Golf Resort, formerly the Coonamessett Country Club, and Bass River Golf Course, Chatham Bars Inn, Country Club of New Seabury, Dennis Pines Golf Course, and the Cummaquid Golf Club. The latter, a 9-hole layout, was opened in 1895 and is the oldest club on the Cape. The public courses are listed in the chart at the end of this section.

These layouts vary greatly in price, difficulty, length, and condition, but they have one thing in common—the wind. It blows harder in some areas than in others, but it's always a factor, and, when it changes direction, the golfer sometimes thinks he is playing an entirely different golf course.

This is especially true at Eastward Ho!, which many consider the toughest course in the state. This rugged layout, which always seems about to fall into the Atlantic, is constantly swept by the wind, and veteran Cape Cod golfers know that what might be a 6-iron shot one day is likely to require a No. 2 or 3 the next day.

Sankaty Head Golf Club on Nantucket is an 18-hole, 6,675-yard layout thirty miles off the coast of Massachusetts. Designed by architect Donald Ross, Sankaty Head is a course for the golfer who still likes old designs. It has deep bunkers, heavy course rough, and small greens. The most interesting features of the course add to its challenge. It's very hilly and the winds always blow hard and never from the same direction. The course can play differently from one day to the next and there are abrupt changes of weather, even in summer. A second course on the island is the 9-hole, public Nantucket Golf Course. Nantucket was first settled in the late 1600's, but still retains much of the natural beauty and atmosphere of centuries ago.

One of the newer and tougher courses in Massachusetts is the Topsfield Country Club, located about twenty miles north of Boston on Route 95. This Robert Trent Jones course conforms to all PGA standards for professional play but offers a fair chance for lesser mortals. The front nine is basically flat with much water in strategic areas. The back side contains plenty of trees and rolling terrain for a change of pace. Bunkers are large and filled with a special mixture of limestone silica and white sand. Of all 18 holes, Jones' favorite is the 530-yard eighteenth, a downhill, dogleg par 5 with a large green protected by water.

Some of other really good courses that you can play while in Massachusetts are:

LOCATION	COURSE	HOLES/PAR/ YARDAGE	TYPE
Agawam	Crestview CC	18/71/6,485	Pub
Bolton	International GC	18/72/6,855	Pvt
East Dennis	Dennis Pines GC	18/72/7,029	Pub
Greenfield	CC of Greenfield	18/69/6,175	Pub
Hatchville	Coonamesset GC	18/72/6,480	R
Holden	Holden Inn & CC	18/70/6,424	R
Holyoke	Wyckoff Park CC	18/71/6,296	SP
Lynnfield	Colonial CC	18/71/6,825	SP
Martha's Vineyard	Island CC	18/70/6,018	R
Mashpee	CC of New Seabury	18/72/7,122	SP
Nantucket	Miacomet GC	9/37/3,337	Pub
Nantucket	Sankaty Head GC	18/72/6,675	Pvt
North Falmouth	Clauson Inn & CC	18/72/6,688	R
North Swansea	Swansea CC	18/72/6,855	SP
Pittsfield	Berkshire Hills CC	18/71/6,328	Pvt
Pocasset	Pocasset GC	18/72/6,309	Pub
South Egremont	Jug End GC	18/72/6,250	R
Southwick	Edgewood GC	18/71/6,570	SP
Southbridge	Bass River GC	18/72/6,218	Pub
Springfield	Franconia GC	18/71/6,411	Pub
Sutton	Pleasant Valley CC	18/72/7,280	SP
Topsfield	Topsfield CC	18/72/6,804	SP
Tewksburg	Trull Brook GC	18/72/6,350	SP
Williamstown	Taconic GC	18/72/6,550	SP

NEW HAMSPHIRE

Historic New Hampshire has a half-dozen vacation regions—White Mountains, Lakes, Dartmouth-Lake Sunapee, Monadnock, Merrimack Valley, and Seacoast. In every one the visiting or vacationing golfer can find a course to test his prowess. A total of 96 courses are sprinkled throughout this state, which boasts a population of a half-million. Many of the courses are members of the New Hampshire Golf Association, the remainder are connected with hotels.

Most famous of the latter is the 18-hole Mt. Washington course, an adjunct of the Mt. Washington House in Bretton Woods, largest hostelry in the state. Also in the White Mountain region are a number of other fine resort golf courses such as the Waumbek Inn Golf Club at Jefferson, where magnificent mountains seem to loom over every hole, and the Eagle Mountain House golf course farther east. At the north end of the White Mountains in Dixville Notch, you can enjoy excellent accommodations plus 18 holes of golf designed by Donald Ross at the Balsam Hotel & Country Club. At Portsmouth, Wentworth-by-the-Sea has a Donald Ross-designed 9-hole course that is slightly longer than three thousand yards. Actually, the most testing of the New Hampshire courses, most experts will agree, is the 7,200-yard Portsmouth Country Club, designed by Robert Trent Jones in 1957. Portsmouth is a private club but visitors are generally welcomed.

Over toward the Vermont border there is nothing flat about the Dartmouth College course, the only 27-hole layout in the state. The Hanover Indians have sent some magnificent teams into Ivy League intercollegiate competition over the years and the course has had much to do with the excellence of the collegiate golfers. The 18-hole Dartmouth course has a deep ravine down the middle, 75–100 yards wide, and several holes cross the ravine. The 9-hole course is in the ravine itself.

Just north, at Pike, is the Lake Tarleton Club and its magnificent 18-hole course set high in the White Mountains. The Club looks over 5,500 acres and five lakes and is the setting of the Festival of the Seven Arts.

The Lake Sunapee course to the South at New London is one of the most attractive in the state. It is operated by Henry Homans, who specializes in raising turf for other courses. Homans took over from a New York syndicate in the 1929 crash and has developed one of the most lush courses to be seen anywhere.

The Manchester Country Club in Bedford was designed by Donald Ross more than forty years ago. Its narrow, lush fairways are a stern test, and the whole course has been carved from a pine forest. Remember that on the western side of the state and in much of the central and southern areas, New Hampshire abounds in rolling countryside. The southern area is especially rich in colonial structures such as white meeting houses, churches and historic houses.

Further reminders of yesteryear are sixty covered bridges ranging from Massachusetts border all the way to Pittsburg and Stark in "Christmas Tree Country" up by the Canadian border.

Here are some of the courses that will give you "fits" if you decide to play them while in New Hampshire: **1799034**

LOCATION	COURSE	HOLES/PAR/ YARDAGE	TYPE
Bethlehem	Bethlehem CC	18/70/6,201	Pub
Bretton Woods	Mt. Washington GC	18/71/6,189	R
Candia	Charmingfare Links	18/71/6,700	SP
Concord	Beaver Meadow GC	18/72/6,600	Pub
Dixville Notch	Balsam Hotel & CC	18/72/6,600	R
		9/33/3,100	
Hanover	Hanover CC	18/70/6,100	Pvt
		9/36/3,000	
Jackson	Wentworth Hall GC	18/72/5,900	SP
Jefferson	Waumbek Inn & CC	18/72/6,104	R
Maplewood	Maplewood CC	18/72/6,209	SP
Melvin Village	Bald Peak Colony Club	18/72/6,190	Pvt
New London	Lake Sunapee CC	18/70/6,348	Pub
North Hampton	Sagamore Hampton GC	18/71/6,479	Pub
Pike	Lake Tarleton Club	18/72/6,226	R
Portsmouth	Wentworth-by-the-Sea Club	18/70/6,179	R
Province Lake	Five Chimneys GC	9/37/3,227	SP
Whitefield	Mountain View GC	9/35/2,915	R
Woodstock	Jack O'Lantern Club	9/36/3,026	R

RHODE ISLAND

Twenty-four private clubs and 24 public courses dot the landscape of the nation's smallest state. The Newport Country Club was the state's first course, incorporated in 1894. Narragansett, a chief resort town, boasts a championship layout at the Point Judith Country Club, near the ocean. Other courses decorating the locale include the Agawam Hunt Club, in Rumford, a 15-minute drive from downtown Providence; the Misquamicut Country Club, near fashionable Watch Hill; the Pawtucket Country Club and the Quidnesset Country Club, which opened this year and listed Sam Snead as an adviser and member of the board of directors. Among the state's public links facilities are: the Jamestown Golf and Country Club; the Louisquisett Golf Club, in North Providence; and the imposing Wanume-tonomy Golf and Country Club, in Middletown, which offers, in addition to a rugged 425-yard, par-4 fifteenth hole constantly caught in the throes of a crosswind, a spectacular view of Narragansett Bay.

"Little Rhody" offers a lot for tourists to see and do, but for visiting golfers, unless you are a member of the USGA club, there are really only four courses:

LOCATION	*COURSE*	*HOLES/PAR/* *YARDAGE*	*TYPE*
North Providence	Louisquisset GC	18/69/6,080	Pub
Portsmouth	Pocasset CC	9/35/3,000	Pub
Providence	Triggs Memorial GC	18/72/6,539	Pub
Westerly	Winnapaug CC	18/72/6,328	SP

VERMONT

Lovely, yet challenging golf courses—over fifty of them—spread over the rural Vermont countryside. Greens are gently silhouetted against lakes and ponds, and mountain scenery surrounds fairways near historic towns and villages.

Soon after entering the state in the west, at Bennington, you can

The beautiful view of the Vermont countryside that can be seen from one of the elevated tees on Equinox golf course.

try your skill at Mt. Anthony Country Club—a layout of 18 extremely hilly and picturesque holes. Farther north, in Manchester, a golfer can enjoy a stay at Equinox House & Lodges, which offers its guests a fine 18-hole test.

Several famous ski resort areas also turn into golf havens during off-season, and rates on excellent accommodations generally are reduced. Mt. Snow Country Club, two miles from the ski slopes, is spread across a high plateau, two thousand feet above sea level. The course is noted for its rolling, wooded terrain, long tiered tees, and large greens. In other well-known ski area, Stowe Country Club opens its course to guests of member hotels, lodges, and motels of the Stowe Area Association. The Stratton Mountain Golf Course, an 18-holer designed by Geoffrey Cornisch, is tied in with the famous ski resort Stratton Mountain Inn. The Sugarbush Golf Club is a Robert Trent Jones course in the heart of Sugarbush Valley—another of Vermont's famous ski areas.

Fox Run, a newly opened golf resort in Ludlow, has a 9-hole course laid out by Frank Duane. Hiking, horseback riding, and sightseeing excursions to the Vermont Marble Company Exhibit Halls in Proctor and the Calvin Coolidge Homestead in Plymouth Notch provide recreational fun for the entire family here. The Rutland Country Club and the Pittsford-Proctor Country Club have 18- and 9-hole golf courses open to the public. The terrain of the Rutland Club includes three water holes, and some holes that stretch up to 550 yards.

On the way up to Burlington, the main city on Lake Champlain, a tourist may stop at the Basin Harbor Club, seven miles west of Vergennes. The 18-hole woodland bordered course at the club is open to the public by reservation.

Golf in the Lake Champlain Valley of Vermont centers around Burlington and luxurious waterside clubs at Malletts Bay and Basin Harbor. Vacationers on the Champlain Islands can enjoy the golf links at country clubs in Alburg and St. Albans.

Golf courses in the northern lake region of Vermont are among the most picturesque in the northeast. The Orleans Country Club sits high on a hill above Lake Willoughby and Crystal Lake. The Newport Country Club is near the South Bay of beautiful Lake Memphremagog. As a diversion, there is marvelous salmon fishing in these waters and the rivers that flow into them.

In the central mountains of Vermont the pastoral Blush Hill golf course above Waterbury welcomes travelers. At Stowe, William F. Mitchell designed the 18-hole golf course at the country club. It is open to members and guests of many lodges and motels around the base of Mount Mansfield.

Should the visitor decide to come up the eastern side of the state he could make Brattleboro his first stop. There he will find a 9-hole course. The Crown Point Country Club at Springfield has an 18-hole

Mount Snow golf course is one of the many ski-golf areas that are becoming so popular in the New England states.

championship layout, and is open to the public any time. It also has a large (ten thousand sq. ft.) putting green. In Woodstock, another Robert Trent Jones–designed 18-hole course at the Woodstock Country Club lies between the spacious new Woodstock Inn and the more intimate Kedron Valley Inn of South Woodstock. Lake Morey Inn at Fairlee is host to the annual Vermont State Open Golf Tournament and shares a popularity with Bonnie Oaks golf resort at the northern end of Lake Morey. Water sports, tennis, and summer theater at nearby Bradford add to the vacation entertainment in that vicinity. Here are some of the more challenging courses in Vermont:

LOCATION	COURSE	HOLES/PAR/ YARDAGE	TYPE
Bennington	Mt. Anthony	18/72/6,640	SP
Burlington	Burlington CC	18/72/6,491	SP
Burlington	Rocky Ridge GC	18/70/5,985	SP
Fairlee	Lake Morey CC	18/69/5,400	R
Manchester	Equinox CC	18/71/6,750	R
Manchester	Manchester CC	18/72/6,724	SP
St. Albans	Champlain CC	9/36/3,200	Pub
Shelburne	Kwiniaska GC	18/72/6,837	SP
Springfield	Crown Point CC	18/72/6,580	SP
Stratton Mountain	Stratton Mountain CC	18/72/6,195	Pvt
Stowe	Stowe CC	18/72/6,645	Pvt
Vergennes	Basin Harbor Club	18/72/6,018	R
Warren	Sugarbush GC	18/72/6,741	R
West Dover	Mount Snow GC	18/72/6,482	R
Wilmington	Haystack G & CC	18/72/6,275	SP
Winooski	Marble Island G & YC	9/35/2,865	R
Woodstock	Woodstock CC	18/69/5,939	Pvt

3

THE UNITED STATES: MIDDLE ATLANTIC

Of all regions in the United States, the Middle Atlantic States of New York, New Jersey, Delaware, Maryland, Pennsylvania, and West Virginia contain the greatest concentration of golfing population. In other words, there is a higher number of players to course ratio. This means that courses, especially the public ones, are more crowded than elsewhere in the United States.

The bright side to this picture is the resort courses—there are excellent ones, especially in New York and Pennsylvania.

NEW YORK

There are over 575 regulation golf facilities in New York State of which about 115 could be considered resort courses. Let us start our vacation tour of the Empire State by looking at the better courses you can play while nongolfing members of your party go sightseeing nearby.

Beginning in the western part of the state there is Rochester, Walter Hagen's birthplace, with four fine public courses, Durand-Eastman, Genesee Valley East, and West, and Lake Shore. There are facilities at Geneseo, and Elmira, where the exacting municipal course is named after the city's most distinguished son, Mark Twain, and there are several courses in the Ithaca area, site of Cornell University, including the beautiful and tough University course.

In Niagara Falls there is Hyde Park, a pretty 18-holer that will test your accuracy off the tee. Up in the Thousand Islands and St. Lawrence area there is the fine Treadway Thousand Island Club.

Coming east on the Thruway there is a dip south once past Utica and you are on modest country roads en route to Cooperstown, site of the Farmer's Museum and Baseball's Hall of Fame. This is the hallowed spot where General Abner Doubleday did not invent baseball, although there is a field named after him to commemorate this bit of amiable fiction. The Otesaga Inn at Cooperstown, once a fashionable girls' school, has a fine course—the Cooperstown Country Club—available to the public. This is also Leatherstocking country, made famous by James Fenimore Cooper.

It is a two-hour run over to Saratoga Springs where there is another museum (thoroughbred), more sports action (thoroughbred racing and night-time trotting), and the newest golf course in the state, the state-operated 18-hole layout designed by Bill Mitchell, who laid out such courses at Atlantis at Palm Beach, Bon Air at Pompano, and Rolling Hills at Fort Lauderdale. Saratoga's terrain is a gently rolling one, cut out of pine country. An 1,800-yard, par-29 course is also here, and a 240-bed hotel and health club with mineral baths is adjacent to the course. Also located in Saratoga Springs is the MacGregor Country Club, an 18-holer, and the 9-hole Saratoga Golf Club, both private courses. To the north is Glens Falls, the insurance city which pioneered in the early days of the big open tournaments. For years, the fine Glens Falls Country Club course

																							Handicap	Net Score
Handicap	13	5	14	10	4	7	1	17	15		2	6	18	16	12	11	8	9	3					
Yardage	361	389	206	500	408	359	424	388	196	3231	400	560	132	357	294	475	375	180	550	3323	6554			
Men's Par	4	4	3	5	4	4	4	4	3	35	4	5	3	4	4	5	4	3	5	37	72			
WE + — O																								
HOLE	1	2	3	4	5	6	7	8	9	Out	10	11	12	13	14	15	16	17	18	IN	TOT			
THEY + — O																								
Women's Par	4	5	3	5	4	4	4	4	4	37	4	5	3	4	4	5	4	4	5	38	75			
Yardage	361	389	206	467	298	359	308	388	196	2972	312	442	132	357	260	410	242	180	550	2885	5857			
Handicap	11	4	17	2	13	8	10	6	15		7	3	18	9	16	5	12	14	1					

PLAYER_____ATTESTED_____DATE_____

U. S. G. A. RULES govern all play unless modified by the following:
   All fences and red and white stakes wherever placed are boundaries.
   A ball lying in Country Club Road or any part of macadam road embankment may be dropped without penalty
      not nearer hole.
   Lateral water hazards are identified by yellow stakes.
   Water hazards are identified by red stakes.
   Drinking springs and water boxes are deemed hydrants; a ball lying in or next to the same may be dropped two
      club lengths away not nearer the hole, without penalty.
   Artificially constructed cart paths, will be considered ground under repair—relief is to nearest point, not nearer
      the hole.
   A Ladies' and Gentlemen's Rest Room is located at the 11th tee.

The scorecard for the Cooperstown Country Club.

was a mecca for every major shotmaker in the country and is still worth a special trip to see and play.

Further to the north lies the Adirondack country with its lakes, famed courses and highly publicized outdoor facilities. Sagamore, at Lake George, is a course which attracts a myriad of visitors each year. The Top o' the World, a tough nine-holer, also at Lake George, offers an unparalleled view, as its name implies. There are easily accessible courses, all good tests of golf, beautiful Whiteface Inn's 18-hole layout at Lake Placid, Loon Lake, Saranac Inn, Rouses Point, and Boonville.

From the Adirondacks down to New York City, the Thruway follows the Hudson River Valley and there is good golf along the way. There need not be too much concern about finding yourself on the wrong side of the river. There are eight bridges spanning the strand which old Hendrik Hudson once thought led to the Northwest Passage to India.

There is a good 18-holer at James Baird State Park in Pleasant Valley, six miles outside Poughkeepsie. A round on this demanding layout can be combined with a visit a half-hour away to the estate where Franklin D. Roosevelt is buried in the rose garden of his Hyde Park home. The Hudson may be crossed at both Poughkeepsie and Rhinebeck at this point and a golfer can head west here for the Catskills. Available will be some fine golfing and incredible eating at the fabulous Catskill resorts.

The best-known of the Catskill resorts, of course, are Grossinger's and the Concord, those twin summits of Catskill luxury. Grossinger's, located about ninety miles from New York, introduced golf to the Catskills. Today, there is a 9-hole, 3,175-yard Vista course, which plays to a par 36, and the 18-hole "Big G" course.

One of the salient features of the Big G course is that you are playing downhill from the first tee through to the seventeenth tee; then it is uphill to a very sturdy par 4. Another feature is that all three of the par 5's can be reached in two. It is tempting for the big hitters, because none of the par 5's is more than 520 yards. But if you go for the green and miss, be prepared to take a penalty stroke. The fourth hole is the most spectacular. It measures 512 yards with a lake on the left and an island green.

The real strength of the course is its par-4's, of which there are seven over four hundred yards. The eighteenth is one of the strongest; it measures 435 yards from the blue tees and doglegs 265 yards out.

Even from the middle tees it is 230 yards around the dogleg—and then you have fly the ball that far because there are bunkers at the elbow of the dogleg. The Big G course measures 6,758 yards from the blue tees, 6,410 from the white, and plays to a par 71. Water comes into play on eight holes. This includes the shortest hole—the 145-yard second, which is over a brook. On the sixteenth, a 225-yard, par 3 where you are hitting to an elevated green there is water on the left and behind the green.

At the Concord, overlooking Lake Kiamesha, there are three Concord courses: "The Challenger," a 9-hole layout that is 2,216 yards

The picturesque raised fourteenth green of the Big G course at Grossinger, New York.

long and plays to a par 31; the "Concord International," which is 7,062 in length from the back tees, 6,250 yards from the front tees, and plays to a par 71; and the "Concord Championship," 7,790 yards from the back tees, 7,107 from the front, and playing to a par 72.

Do not be fooled by the 9-holer. Its par-3, 212-yard fourth hole would add spice to any regulation-length course. You must carry the green, which is located at the top of hill, with your tee shot, or risk having your ball roll back virtually to the tee. One of the more testing holes on the "International" is the par-4, 424-yard thirteenth. The elevated tee is about 100 feet above the fairway and your drive must carry a brook, which is about 150 yards out. From here, the fairway doglegs left and your uphill approach must thread a narrow gap of trees to an elevated green.

The "Championship" course is usually called the "Monster" and for good reason. Many of the tees are one hundred yards long and there are eighty bunkers. The average size of the greens is eleven thousand square, undulating feet. Water comes into play on nine of the holes. On five of these the drive has to be threaded either between water and water or water and sand. Most golfers do not make it. The average number of lost balls per round is three. In fact, the Concord probably is the only course in the world that has a skin diver. Periodically he dresses in a wet suit, fins and snorkel and digs balls out of the eight lakes. Last year he retrieved 30,000 balls, or $34,500 worth. One golfer playing the 154-yard fifth hole, straight over water, hit two brand new balls into the lake, and when he teed-up another brand new ball his partner asked, "Why don't you use an old ball?" "Around here," the golfer said, "they just don't get a chance to age."

On the first hole, measuring 417 yards from the regular tee, the fairway is guarded on the left by a long lake 200 yards out and on the right by a creek that snakes its way in front of the green. The drive has to land in a small area about 35 yards wide. The second hole is completely over water. On the third, a par 5 measuring 531 yards, a huge lake juts in and out of the right side of the fairway. If one hits a big drive of about 300 yards, he can gamble on his second shot and try to reach the green in two, but the ball will have to carry 225 yards completely over water. A golfer can play safe and lay up with an iron, and then hit another one across the water. But if he pulls or hooks the shot slightly, he is in the water on the left.

Such holes, along with the 586-yard thirteenth with a long narrow lake cutting the fairway diagonally, making the second shot a decisive one, has produced a plethora of bets around the New York metropolitan area that a seven handicapper could not break 85 his first time on the course. Once four Texans, none with a handicap over four, did not break 90. But there is a more positive side of the coin. Most golfers who have played "The Monster" several consecutive days gleefully admit that when they go back to their home course, they shoot five or six shots better. The reason is that the course is a complete 14-club course. It also demands mental keenness. Any temporary mental lapse and you wind up with an 8. It is like playing golf under tournament conditions.

Most of the credit for the creation of "The Monster" goes to its architect, Joe Finger, and consultants Jimmy Demaret and Jackie Burke. Finger was given carte blanche to do anything he wanted to build a championship course. "People are always aghast at how long the course is," Finger says, "but it wasn't designed to play at 7,790 yards. In fact there hasn't been an official round played there at that length. The long tees and the big greens are to give the course flexibility. If on a certain day there's a following wind on one hole, the tee markers can be set all the way back—so that the wind is no longer a factor. Naturally the reverse is also true. Long tee shots aren't the determining factor for scoring. The course was built so that a golfer who worked the ball well, drawing and fading it at will, would score well. Actually for the average golfer I would advise that he play the course from the front of the tees."

The city of Monticello is almost synonymous with the Catskills, and just three miles outside of Monticello stands Kutscher's Country Club, whose golf course now draws as many raves as their apple

The famed thirteenth hole on the Championship at The Concord. This is an extremely long hole playing 586 yards. A very long drive is required and should be placed on the right side of the fairway. A second long wood is required and must be kept on the right side in order to miss the lake that extends to the middle of the fairway. A third shot can require as much as a 5-iron and must be accurately placed to avoid the yawning traps that surround the green.

strudel. The course here stretches out to 7,157 yards, plays to a par 72 and has three tees on every hole. A beautifully landscaped layout over rolling terrain, it has woods separating each of the fairways. The hole that impresses the most on this William Mitchell-designed course is the par-5, 565-yard sixth hole. Woods bordering both lengths of the fairway make it mandatory that you keep your tee shot in play. The hole has a tricky dogleg and your second shot must carry water. The green is well-bunkered and is elevated, as are all of the greens at Kutscher's. All together, there are water hazards on four of the holes.

The Nevele Country Club is another challenging 6,500-yard, par-71 course in the Catskills. The first nine is relatively flat, with tricky, good-sized greens; the back nine has more roll to it, some devilish bunkering and a nice view of the mountains. The par-5 second hole is about as tough as any on the course. It doglegs from right to left, and at about two hundred yards out there is a mound that must be cleared on your tee shot. The hole then swerves left sharply and you have to shoot between a narrow gap of pines to reach the green.

There are many other excellent courses in the Catskills area. Tarry Brae, Tennanah Lake, Laurels, Stevensville, Lochmor, and Kass to name some of the leaders. There are other reasons—in addition to wonderful courses—why visitors to New York should consider a golfing tour of the Catskills. During the summer months, New York public links are almost as steamy as the city itself, and you will find the mountain air of the Catskills a lot cooler. However, if you still intend to try your luck on New York's overcrowded municipal courses, heed these gentle words of advice from one hard-bitten public linkster who has grown jaded after years of early rising and long hours of waiting to get on the first tee. "Stay away!"

If you must play in New York City, there are 13 municipal courses. There is one in every borough except Manhattan. The breakdown is Queens: (Clearview, Douglaston, Forest Park, Kissena); Brooklyn (Dyker Beach and Marine Park); the Bronx (Mosholu, Pelham, Split Rock, Van Cortlandt); Staten Island (La Tourette, South Shore, and Silver Lake). They are all listed in the phone book under Department of Parks.

Of course, in New York's metropolitan area there are almost one hundred courses, offering everything from mountain-goat inclines to short-side lies. On Long Island there are courses where you can play nine holes inland and another nine along the ocean. Bethpage should warrant a look if only to see a state facility that operates five excellent courses simultaneously. Bethpage's Black Course is one of the toughest in the country.

The story of golfing attractions in New York State needs no embellishing. Remember, they were playing golf there when a good many other states were still having trouble with their Indians. Here are some of the most testing courses you can play in the state:

LOCATION	COURSE	HOLES/PAR/ YARDAGE	TYPE
Akron	Dande Farms GC	18/71/6,425	Pub
Alexandria Bay	Thousand Islands GC	18/73/6,140	R
Amherst	Ransom Oaks CC	18/72/6,315	Pub
Batavia	Batavia CC	18/73/7,012	SP
Binghamton	Ely Park GC	18/71/6,410	Pub
Bolton Landing	Sagamore GC	18/72/6,754	R
Camillus	Pine Grove GC	18/72/6,653	SP
Chenango Forks	Chenango Valley GC	18/72/6,340	Pub
Churchville	Churchville GC	18/72/6,671	Pub
		9/36/3,195	
Commack	Commack Hills G & CC	18/71/6,809	Pub
Cooperstown	Cooperstown CC	18/72/6,554	R
Cooperstown	Otesago GC	18/72/6,372	R
Ellenville	Nevele CC	18/71/6,600	R
Elmira	Mark Twain CC	18/72/6,734	Pub
Endicott	En-Joie GC	18/72/6,966	Pub
Farmingdale	Bethpage State Park	18/71/6,246	Pub
		18/72/6,288	
		18/71/6,008	
		18/70/6,468	
		18/71/6,147	
Grand Island	River Oaks CC	18/72/6,400	SP
Grossinger	Grossinger CC	18/71/6,758	R
		9/36/3,288	
Hauppauge	Hauppauge CC	18/72/6,525	SP
Hurleyville	Lochmore GC	18/71/6,470	Pub
Kiamesha Lake	Concord Hotel & CC	18/72/7,790	R
		18/72/7,062	
		9/31/2,216	
Lake Placid	Craig Wood CC	18/72/6,544	Pub

LOCATION	COURSE	HOLES/PAR/ YARDAGE	TYPE
Lake Placid	Whiteface Inn GC	18/72/6,777	R
Lock Sheldrake	Lochmor GC	18/71/6,470	SP
Malone	Malone CC	18/72/6,485	SP
Margaretville	Kass CC	18/71/6,401	R
Massena	Massena CC	18/71/6,395	Pub
Montauk	Montauk G & RC	18/72/6,402	R
Monticello	Kutsher's Hotel & CC	18/72/7,157	R
Niagara Falls	Hyde Park GC	18/71/6,365	Pub
		9/36/3,275	
		9/35/3,135	
Pleasant Valley	James Baird GC	18/71/6,520	Pub
Pompey	Pompey Hills CC	18/71/6,675	SP
Rochester	Genesee Valley GC	18/69/6,078	Pub
		18/67/5,297	
Roscoe	Tennanah Lake GC	18/72/6,750	R
Saranac	Saranac Inn GC	18/72/6,535	Pub
Saratoga Springs	Saratoga Spa GC	18/72/7,110	Pub
South Fallsburg	Tarry Brae GC	18/72/7,200	Pub
Swan Lake	Stevensville	18/72/7,070	R
Syracuse	Drumlins GC	18/71/6,180	Pub
Ticonderoga	Ticonderoga CC	18/71/6,239	SP
Tupper Lake	Tupper Lake CC	18/71/6,129	SP
Warrensburg	Cronin's GC	18/71/6,313	R

NEW JERSEY

Golfing has become New Jersey's most popular seasonal recreational activity with the rapid development and improvement of some of the finest and best-maintained courses in the country within easy access of New York and New Jersey metropolitan centers.

One of the best-conditioned public courses in the country is only a 15-minute jaunt from the George Washington Bridge—River Vale Country Club in River Vale. Some 44 traps dot its lush fairways and 39 others surround its well manicured greens. A natural stream crosses six fairways and forms lakes on two.

In Monmouth County, the Jersey shore area, a former private club is joining the public ranks this season. It is the Jumping Brook Country Club in Neptune. The Rutgers University Golf Club in New Brunswick is also open to the public. This well-conditioned,

6,028-yard, par-71 course is one of the top layouts in the state. Another excellent course is Playboy Club Hotel at Great Gorge. As beautiful as they are rugged, the eighteen (6,920 yards, par 71) and 9-hole (3,350 yards—par 35) courses wend their often tortuous way across 170 acres of lush, rolling hill country that adds optical difficulty, particularly in judging distances, to the other natural and manmade hazards that dot the landscape. Three of the 27 holes were literally blasted through an old limestone quarry, and are among the most architecturally unusual in the world. Spring-fed lakes and luxuriant trees abound in the quarry area. Combined with limestone rock formations and cliff faces that often rise more than a hundred feet, these natural hazards make the quarry holes magnificent from the standpoint of beauty and challenge.

Golf-course architect George Fazio, who designed the courses at Great Gorge with touring professional Doug Sanders serving as consultant, made good use of the abundant water resources. Natural and manmade lakes provide 28 acres of water hazards on 13 of the 27 holes. To liven things up even more, the 27 holes and fairways are bunkered with a total of 83 traps of sugar-white sand. The golf facilities bear two distinct Fazio trademarks. They feature smaller than average greens and are designed to fit the terrain, leaving the natural beauty of the land totally unspoiled.

Of course, New Jersey has three of the really great private courses in the country: Baltusrol, Pine Valley, and Forsgate. Unfortunately, most of us will never play at these fine clubs, but we can play at the following good courses in the Garden State:

LOCATION	COURSE	HOLES/PAR/ YARDAGE	TYPE
Ashland	Mays Landing CC	18/72/6,857	Pub
Belleville	Branch Brook GC	18/71/6,100	Pub
Brigantine	Brigantine CC	18/72/6,753	Pub
Flanders	Flanders Valley GC	18/72/6,353	Pub
Franklin Lakes	High Mountain GC	18/71/6,620	Pub
Great Gorge	Playboy CC	18/72/7,059 9/35/3,350	R
Hackettstown	Musconetcong G & CC	18/70/6,601	SP
Hanover	Valley View GC	18/71/6,105	Pub
Lakewood	Lakewood CC	18/71/6,567	Pub

LOCATION	COURSE	HOLES/PAR/ YARDAGE	TYPE
Milton	Bowling Green GC	18/72/7,011	Pub
Neptune	Asbury Park G & CC	18/72/6,217	Pub
New Brunswick	Rutgers University GC	18/71/6,028	SP
Paramas	Saddle River G & CC	18/71/6,208	SP
River Vale	Park Vale CC	18/71/6,313	Pub
River Vale	River Vale CC	18/72/6,882	Pub
Somerville	Green Knolley C	18/72/6,537	Pub
Spring Lake Heights	Homestead G & CC	18/72/6,378	SP
Tuckerton	Atlantis CC	18/72/7,019	R
West Orange	Essex County CC (West Course)	18/72/6,511	Pub

DELAWARE

While there are some twenty regulation golf facilities in the state, only two 18-hole courses—Rock Manor Golf Club and Green Hill Golf Club—are public and both are located in Wilmington. There are two 9-hole courses—Old Landing Country Club and Henlopen Hotel Country Club—at Rehoboth Beach. This is the extent of public courses in Delaware. There are, however, several fine private courses, including the Wilmington Country Club, Newark Country Club, DuPont Country Club, Brandywine Country Club, and Rehoboth Beach Country Club.

One of the finest public golf facilities in the east is Baltimore's Pine Ridge course. Note how the five fingers of land extend out in Loch Raven.

MARYLAND AND WASHINGTON, D.C.

The Maryland and Washington, D.C., area has some of the best known private courses in the country—Chevy Chase Club, Congressional Country Club, Country Club of Maryland, Burning Tree Club, Baltimore Country Club—to name a few.

Baltimore has excellent public golf facilities, including the fine Pine Ridge course, cut through pines and with five fingers extending into Loch Raven. And for proof that Baltimore's Mount Pleasant is a superb test of golf, look at the players who have won the Eastern Open there—Lloyd Mangrum, Cary Middlecoff, Sam Snead, Dick Mayer, Tom Bolt, Bob Toski, Frank Stranahan, Arnold Palmer, and Art Wall. But, visitors to the nation's capital will not find too much public golf available. And remember that public courses, as in most large cities, are very crowded in this area.

In addition to the two Baltimore Public courses just mentioned, here are layouts that will surely put you to the test:

LOCATION	COURSE	HOLES/PAR/ YARDAGE	TYPE
Baltimore	Mt. Pleasant GC	18/72/6,802	Pub
Baltimore	Pine Ridge GC	18/72/6,820	Pub
Berlin	Ocean City CC	18/72/6,343	SP
Bowie	Bel Air G & CC	18/71/6,017	SP
Gaitherbury	Washingtonian GC	18/72/6,429 18/70/6,596	Pvt
Glenwood	Allview GC	18/72/6,365	Pub
Hunt Valley	Hunt Valley	18/72/6,588	SP
Ocean City	Ocean Pines G & CC	18/72/6,625	R
Sherwood Forest	South Sherwood Forest GC	18/72/6,082	SP
Wheaton	Northwest GC	18/72/7,217	Pub

PENNSYLVANIA

Pennsylvania boasts more than 500 golf courses, including almost 300 public, 243 private, and more than 30 resort courses, several of which feature fairway living.

As listed on page 397, three of the one hundred most challenging courses are listed among Pennsylvania's famous resort facilities. One of these is Fred Waring's Shawnee Inn & Country Club. The Shawnee has three championship nines—Red, White, and Blue, an 18-hole putting green and a practice fairway. All but three of the 27 holes are located on an island, surrounded by the Delaware River, and there are large rolling greens with numerous sand traps. Flowering red crabapple trees are used for 150-yard markers on the Red Course, white birches on the White Course, and blue spruce for the Blue Course. There are four sets of markers on each tee. No. 6 on the Blue nine is a distinct challenge. A 185-yard par 3, it is practically all carry over the Delaware River to an elevated rolling green surrounded by trees and dense woods. Few golfers play at Shawnee without trying to drive a ball across the Delaware, a belt of some 230 yards.

Also among the top one hundred toughest courses is Tamiment-in-the-Poconos. This grueling 18-hole, 7,110-yard course was designed by Robert Trent Jones and he best describes his creation: "When one reaches the third hole, the 20-mile view one gets from all directions is an inspiration. Not only does the beauty of this mountain-top course

An aerial view of the three 9-hole courses that make up the Shawnee Inn and Country Club.

thrill you, but the shifting winds play an important part and are a subtle factor in the playing value. The third is the beginning of a sequence of five holes from which one gets one of the finest views in the Poconos. There are two fairway traps on this hole that cause even the better golfers plenty of trouble. The receptive well-trapped green, that terminates the hole, is backed up by woods."

The seventeenth cost $30,000 and two years to build. The entire length of the fairway had to be raised six feet so the elevated green would be visible on the third shot. Jones sees it this way: ". . . played from an elevated tee, framed throughout the length of the hole by woods on each side, to an elevated green which nestles in the hillside. One can see the green from the tee, it stands out like a lighthouse beacon. The big drive will be downhill and your ego may be salved by the extra length you will obtain on your tee shot. Let it not deceive you, for the second shot is a powerful one. It is doubtful that even the biggest of hitters can get home in two, but the second shot will bring you to a bench directly in front of the green and from there on uphill, onto the green is an interesting pitch."

One of the standard jokes around the Tamiment pro shop concerns a new golfer who asked one of the Tamiment regulars if the course was tough, or one of "those driver and nine-iron layouts."

"Oh, it's a driver and a nine-iron type all right," replied the regular, "a driver, two fairway woods, and a nine-iron."

Both Shawnee and Tamiment also feature some of the finest lodging facilities and other recreational activities in the area, which is rapidly becoming a four-season resort area. Ten ski resorts round out the activities available in this beautiful mountainous region.

Among the older resort courses is the Hershey Country Club, a par-73, 6,988-yard test. Hershey was the scene for many years of the Pennsylvania Open, State Junior, State Ladies, and many other tournaments. The PGA also has been played on its fairways. Hershey also offers the golfer another challenge at the Park Golf Course, a par-71 championship course, that has played host to the National Public Links tournament. This is a demanding course that can present problems to those who stray off its narrow fairways or dunk a shot in Spring Creek, which crosses the course nine times. At "Chocolate town U.S.A." there also is the Hotel Hershey 9-hole course; and now open to visitors is the 9-hole Juvenile Course originally designed by the late Milton S. Hershey for use by some golf

Plenty of sand is a feature at the Hershey Country Club.

enthusiasts in Derry Township. The latest course in Hershey is a devilishly tough George Fazio design, adjacent to the original championship 18 which itself is rated in this book as one of the Keystone State's representatives among the one hundred most challenging course you *can* play.

As for other fine Pennsylvania resort courses, the Pocono Manor features two 18-hole courses of 6,460 and 6,855 yards, both par 72, to test the skill of golfers with high and low handicaps. A beautiful layout in a woodland setting, the Pocono Manor Inn offers lodging at its best. Actually this 4,000-acre mountain estate also includes trails, gardens, croquet, tennis, swimming pool, programmed entertainment, evening dances, horseback riding, hayrides, bowling, billiards, canoeing, trout fishing, and swimming in the blue waters of Lake Minausin. From November through the winter, there is ice skating, skiing, tobogganing and sledding.

Also in the Poconos is the Inn at Buck Hill Falls, a sprawling resort in the grand manner of a country estate. And an important part of the gracious atmosphere is the scenic 27-hole layout, a 6,665-yard, par-72 course plus a par-34 nine.

The White-Blue championship course and the shorter Red nine start and finish at the clubhouse. From its beautiful No. 14, the golfer may look forty miles across the hills to New Jersey, and yet enjoy a course that involves little climbing. Several of the holes run along Buck Hill Creek, only half a mile above one of the most spectacular waterfalls in the Poconos, Buck Hill Falls, which is on the estate.

Just next to picturesque No. 14 on the White-Blue course is the "tough hole," No. 13. With a slope bearing off to the left and a plateau in the middle, it is a par 5. Dogleg No. 6 on the White course is another test. All the holes are surrounded by woods and there are six water holes throughout the course.

Another stern resort test in the western edge of the Poconos is the Le Chateau Country Club, where architect Geoffrey Cornish created a demanding course of lakes, woods, and hills. This par-72, rolling course with eight water holes is 6,675 yards in length.

Among the courses in the mountains of southwestern Pennsylvania is the famous Bedford Springs Hotel links, a testing layout of 6,734 yards that boasts an unusual par 74. Bedford Springs is handy for golfers traveling the Pennsylvania Turnpike, just four miles south of the Bedford interchange.

One of the newer resort courses is Charnita, located at Fairfield, eight miles west of Gettysburg. Charnita has been famous as a ski area, and now offers a rolling 6,720-yard golf course with a par 71. This layout, at the foot of the mountainous ski area, is laced with plenty of natural and manmade hazards, including lots of water.

In the southeastern part of the state are two resort courses of championship caliber. East of Lancaster is the Host Farm Motel, in the heart of Pennsylvania Dutch country. Located along the famous old Lincoln Highway, Route 30, the Host Farm Motel features two courses, a par-72, 6,870-yard layout and a 9-hole, par-30 course of 2,680 yards. Fine food and lodging are offered visitors to the many attractions of "Dutch Country." Nearby is the nationally famous "Dutch Wonderland," considered one of the state's finest tourist attractions.

Closer to the Philadelphia area is the Downingtown Inn & Golf Club, featuring excellent accommodations, and a par-72, 7,052-yard course, which stretches through beautiful rolling, heavily wooded countryside. It is set on historic grounds with Revolutionary period farm buildings which have been restored to their natural state while the interiors have been modernized.

On this George Fazio-designed course, the seventh hole, a par 5 and 575 yards long, is a real challenge with two lakes and bunkered fair-

Plenty of trees, though fairly small, is a feature at Downingtown Inn and Golf Club.

ways. The tenth hole, a par 3, is loaded with trees and the green is heavily trapped; the golfer must "thread the needle" through that one. The eighteenth is 447 yards and it takes a real champ to make the par 4. But, on the ninth the golfer is confronted with a unique "psychological hazard." Only thirty feet from the green looms a massive plate-glass window. One hundred feet long and twenty feet high, this glass panorama offers diners at the clubhouse an exciting view of the course—and the golfers a lot to think about as they drive toward the green. "Some golfers get off a bad hit," said the local pro. "When they see the ball heading straight for that huge window, they grab their heads and look away."

But look again! When the ball hits, it simply bounces off while the diners inside laugh and wave. The glass is golf-ball resistant, and was imported from England at a cost of $25,000 especially for Downingtown Inn.

Although we have been dealing primarily with resort courses, you will find some of the finest public courses in the nation in Pennsylvania and they welcome tourists and vacationers. Many of the championship public courses are listed here among the courses you can play in Pennsylvania:

LOCATION	COURSE	HOLES/PAR/ YARDAGE	TYPE
Allentown	Twin Lakes CC	18/70/6,450	R
Bedford	Bedford Springs Hotel	18/74/6,734	R
Buck Hill Falls	The Inn at Buck Hill Falls	18/72/6,665	R
Bushkill	Fernwood GC	18/72/6,712	R
Cambridge Springs	Riverside Inn & CC	18/70/6,104	R
Carlisle	Cumberland GC	18/72/6,508	Pub
Champion	Seven Springs	18/72/7,065	R
Downington	Downington Inn & GC	18/72/7,052	R
Downingtown	Malvern GC	18/71/6,365	SP
Eagles Mere	Eagles Mere CC	18/72/6,750	R
Elizabeth	Seven Springs GC	18/71/6,700	Pub
Ellwood City	Del Mar GC	18/72/6,562	SP
Erie	Lawrence Park GC	18/72/6,337	SP
Gettysburg	Charnita	18/71/6,720	R
Gibsonia	Bakerstown GC	18/72/6,700	SP
Hellertown	Sandy Lakes GC	18/72/7,200	SP
Hershey	Hershey CC	18/73/6,988	R
Hershey	Hershey Park GC	18/71/6,116	R
Hershey	Park View GC	18/72/6,400	Pub
Lancaster	The Host Farm Motel	18/72/6,870	R
Lancaster	Overlook GC	18/70/6,223	SP
Langhorne	Langhorne G & CC	18/70/6,858	SP
Malvern	Malvern GC	18/71/6,365	Pub
Marshall's Creek	Mountain Manor Inn & GC	18/71/6,300	R
Mt. Union	The American Legion CC	18/74/6,700	SP
Pocono Manor	Pocono Manor Inn & GC	18/72/6,400 18/72/6,300	R
Shawnee-on-the- Delaware	Shawnee Inn & GC	9/36/3,435 9/36/3,310	R
Skytop	Skytop Club	18/71/6,370	R
Stroudsburg	Glenbrook CC	18/72/6,400	SP
Tamiment	Tamiment Resort & CC	18/72/6,870	R
Thorndale	Ingleside GC	18/72/6,795	SP
Titusville	Cross Creek Motor Lodge & GC	18/72/6,275	R
Tunkhannock	Shadowbrook CC	18/71/5,655	R
University Park	Penn State University GC	18/69/6,055	Pub
Wernersville	Galen Hall GC	18/71/6,400	R
White Haven	Le Chateau CC	18/72/6,675	R
York	Briarwood GC	18/72/6,734	SP

WEST VIRGINIA

West Virginia's natural terrain provides some of the most challenging golf courses in the country. Unfortunately, except for one, the courses are virtually unknown to all but local residents. That one is, of course, the Greenbrier, in White Sulphur Springs.

This lovely 18-hole layout, which draws its name from the Greenbrier Hotel, is only a small part of the large hunk of real estate (6,500 acres) that makes up one of the most picturesque watering places in the nation. If history rather than golf is your dish, you can trace much of this country's political and cultural growth by making a visit to White Sulphur Springs. Nestled snugly in the Allegheny Mountains of West Virginia, the town emerged as a spa for some of the country's most prominent families as far back as 1778. It has served as a retreat for 13 Presidents, including Andrew Jackson, Martin Van Buren, Millard Fillmore, Ulysses S. Grant, William Howard Taft, and Woodrow Wilson.

Actually, The Greenbrier is one of three golf courses located on the estate. (The other two are the Old White and The Lakeside.) The predecessor to The Greenbrier Hotel was the Old White Hotel, which was built in 1858, and except for the Civil War, when it was used interchangeably by both the Confederate and Union troops as a hospital, it remained in service until 1921, when it was condemned as a fire hazard. Meanwhile, the original Greenbrier, a magnificent 250-room Georgian structure, had gone up in 1913. In 1930–31, The Greenbrier was almost completely rebuilt into the handsome 600-room building that stands today.

The Greenbrier boasts five tennis courts, indoor and outdoor swimming pools, two hundred miles of riding trails, a stable of excellent horses, skeet and trap shooting ranges, horseshoes, archery, shuffleboard and eight automatic bowling lanes. A golfer eager to play a number of courses will find three challenging courses in one location. Even more unusual, all three have the first tees and the eighteenth greens meeting at the clubhouse. Some golfers are apt to jest that the mountain vistas with the colorful foliage are disconcerting because the golfer cannot keep his head down and concentrate fully on the game. However, the valley setting influences weather conditions and wind shifts enabling a golfer to play each course differently every day.

Reigning over the Old White, Greenbrier, and Lakeside courses is Sam Snead with his staff of professionals. Slammin' Sam has

An aerial view of the three championship courses at the Greenbrier—the granddaddy of resort golf courses.

been associated with The Greenbrier for many years, and one of the most thrilling moments in his career happened at The Greenbrier Spring Festival Tournament in 1959 when he scored a 59—the first time he broke 60 in full-tournament play. It was a round that included nine birdies and an eagle for a total of 59 on a par-70 course. In describing the Old White Course, Sam Snead rates the first hole as one of the most difficult starting holes to be found, while the second is a slight dogleg with the advantage of being on the right side of the green. The third is a 220-yard par 3 with a slanting green that favors a shot to the left side of the green. Nearly as difficult is the sixth hole, which is 435 yards and the longest par 4 on the course.

There is the problem of playing against a prevailing wind into a well-guarded green from right to left. Out-of-bounds on the right and parallel hazard on the left for the length of the fairway, the thirteenth hole requires accurate driving to make the 383-yard par 4, while the fifteenth hole has a yawning trap guarding each side of the green. The player with a short drive or slice will be in trouble on the sixteenth hole because of the lake in front of the tee. The approach shot is over a stream to a large, but well-guarded green. The hole is rated the toughest on the Old White course. Holes 17 and 18 also have water hazards—the seventeenth is 540 yards, par 5, with a stream in front of the tee, while the same stream runs directly between tee and green of the par-3 eighteenth hole.

For variety during a stay at The Greenbrier, there is The Greenbrier Course, a 35/35–70-par course with 11 holes recently redesigned. The first hole is a challenging par-4, 371-yard straightaway, requiring a well-played iron to the green on the second shot. One of the most beautiful holes of golf at The Greenbrier is the fifth (532 yards, par 5). From a high tee, the golfer looks at a long, wide and undulating fairway, with a slight dogleg to the right and heavy woods on both sides. A tough course overall, holes six, seven, nine, and sixteen are extremely difficult. From the championship tee on the eleventh hole, it is one hundred fifty-six yards to the green requiring an accurate chip shot across the stream at a very large, spacious green with bunkers parallel to it.

The Lakeside Course (34/36–70), as the name suggests, follows the flow of a winding stream emptying into Swan Lake and beyond. The first hole is short in yardage, but requires great accuracy for a par 4. Number two is 189 yards, par 3, with the inlet directly in front of the lake and to the right of the green, which is guarded by one large sand trap. A long iron or 3- or 4-wood is necessary to reach the green from the tee. The fourth hole is designed for the long hitter. It covers 580 yards, a par 5 with the fairway open all the way from tee to undulating green and slightly uphill for the last three hundred yards. There is a stream to the left of the tee, two fairway traps, and two traps at the green. Another difficult hole on the front nine of the Lakeside Course is the sixth, which is a par 4, 435 yards long, with a deep stream in front of the tee and to the left "out-of-bounds" extremely tight to the right. If the creek or out of bounds does not get you, the 435 yards will. There are two traps, one guarding each side of the green. The pros at The Greenbrier will tell you that the tenth hole is probably the easiest on the course for a birdie. It is straightaway, 458 yards par 5, with a wide open fairway sporting a few sand traps with some well-placed ones at the green. Holes 11 and 13 are tricky ones, but they are also fine holes to test abilities. The second toughest hole in the course is the fourteenth measuring 496 yards, par 5, with a slight dogleg to the right. Off the tee is wide open except for one sand trap and large trees to the left of the fairway. A pulled tee shot or hook spells trouble. It opens again until chipping to the green heavily guarded by sand traps. The fifteenth hole has an unusual sand trap— it is formed to the shape of the State of West Virginia, and has caused many a golfer to remark that he was "stuck in Wheeling." Number 18 is a very good finishing hole, 382 yards, par 4. There is a slight dog-leg to the right. The tee shot must be very straight because of trees to the right and left. The second shot is slightly uphill to a most beautiful green. The green is kidney shaped, tremendous in size with traps to the right and left and in front. The elevated green on this hole provides a panoramic view of the Greenbrier Estate.

Traveling west from Greenbrier brings you to Charleston, the chemical center of the nation. The city has two public courses, Meadowbrook, 18 holes, and Rock Branch Golf Course, a 9-hole layout with sand greens. There are five private courses, Berry Hills, Kanawaha and Sleepy Hollow, all 18 holes, and Edgewood and Southmoor, both nine holes.

The Parkersburg area, situated in the Ohio Valley, is another good golfing spot in West Virginia and is the site of three good 18-hole courses, Worthington, South Hills, and Par-Mar. Another fine course is in Wheeling—Oglebay Park, a municipal park of over one thousand acres, originally the beautiful country estate of the late Colonel Earl W. Oglebay. Waddington Farm, as it was known 35 years ago, was left to the city by the colonel for park and recreational purposes. Accommodations are available either at cabins or at the 81-room Wilson Lodge. The park has much to offer with an 18-hole layout open daily, a par-3 golf course open from May through October and a driving range. In addition, there are hay rides, sleigh rides, skiing, swimming, tennis, and fishing.

Here are the courses in West Virginia that are the best challenge:

LOCATION	*COURSE*	*HOLES/PAR/ YARDAGE*	*TYPE*
Beckly	Glade Springs GC	18/72/6,584	Pvt
Canaan Valley	Canaan Valley GC	18/72/6,625	R
Grafton	Tygarts Lake CC	18/72/6,330	Pub
Morgantown	Lakeview CC	18/71/6,855	Pvt
Pipestem	Pipestem GC	18/72/6,828	R
Wheeling	Oglebay Park GC	18/71/6,183	Pub
White Sulphur Springs	The Greenbrier		
	(Old White)	18/70/6,534	R
	(Greenbrier)	18/70/6,473	
	(Lakeside)	18/70/6,298	

4

THE UNITED STATES:
SOUTH

Scratch players and duffers alike can enjoy the beauty and challenge of over 1,500 courses in the southland states of Virginia, North
Carolina, South Carolina, Georgia, Kentucky, Tennessee, Alabama,
Mississippi, Louisiana, and Arkansas. No other region in the United
States has as great a variety of golf courses. The major concentration
of resort courses—some of the finest in the world—is in the four
Southern Atlantic States of Virginia, North Carolina, South Carolina,
and Georgia. In addition to the many great courses, the fine year-
round weather, many of the world's most avid golf fans, and that ever-
present southern hospitality make this section of the United States a
prime target for leisure-minded golfers.

VIRGINIA

Golf—as everyone knows—can be educational, and nowhere is this
more evident than in the State of Virginia. For instance, a tourist
playing the new Golden Horseshoe course at historic Williamsburg is
little more than a tee shot away from Jamestown, where astonished
Indians stood on the shore May 13, 1607, and watched the *Susan
Constant, Godspeed,* and *Discovery* drop anchor, bringing Captain
John Smith and the first permanent English settlers. It is virtually impossible to play a course anywhere in the Old Dominion without
coming into contact with history.

Just a few miles up from Chesapeake Bay and near the shoreline
of the historic James River there is the James River Country Club at
Newport News. A wedge shot from its main gate is the Mariners'
Museum. And just a few miles away at Yorktown one can walk
over the battle area where General Cornwallis surrendered to George
Washington. Follow the Colonial Parkway from Yorktown to Williamsburg and you will find two 18-hole courses and one 9-hole. In
this restored colonial capital the visitor can relive the history of early
America. Only fifty miles away is Richmond, with the classic capital

designed by Thomas Jefferson, and other historic landmarks like St. John's Church, where Patrick Henry declared in 1775, "Give me liberty, or give me death." Along almost every roadside there are historical markers, reminding passersby of a major battle, of an epic event, or of the birthplace of a president.

In the post–World War II years, Virginia has become a tourist mecca. The many outstanding golf courses have played their part, both as tourist attractions and as championship sites. Introduced to the Old Dominion little more than a half century ago, the royal and ancient game now vies with boating as the No. 1 participant sport. Indeed, in the last five years forty new courses have been opened and greater increases are anticipated. At this point Virginia boasts 180 courses, ranging from the flat terrain near the seacoast to the mountainous terrain of the Alleghenies.

In recent years, the opening of the Hampton Roads bridge tunnel over and under Chesapeake Bay has made possible greater recreational use and development of the eastern Virginia shore. Formerly cut off from Virginia's mainland and linked only to lower Maryland, the shore can now be reached from the Tidewater or Norfolk as well as from Newport News and Richmond. Consequently, the Eastern Shore, until now best known for its annual wild pony roundups at Chincoteague Island, is fast becoming a resort area, especially for boating, fishing and golf.

Golf in Virginia is keeping up with the national fever. For every 26,446 persons there is a course. The national average is 25,376 persons. Still, there is need for even more courses, so crowded is the membership in many private clubs. Incidentally, while most courses in Virginia are private, many of them grant reciprocal courtesies to visitors who are members of clubs affiliated with the United States Golf Association. This is especially true early in the week, although some of the clubs require visitors to be guests of members on weekends.

Golf is virtually a year-round sport in the Old Dominion. In central and eastern Virginia it is possible for those who do not object to occasional chilly breezes to play ten or eleven months. In the western or more mountainous region the courses are seldom closed more than three months a year. In the southern sector the playing time is even greater. There are only a few weeks when the courses are closed because of snow or unplayable conditions. Spring and fall, of course, are the ideal playing times. The spring foliage is matchless, especially during the dogwood time. Dogwood and wild flowers grow in abundance throughout the state and, happily, they were not thinned out during the growth of golf. The turning of the leaves in the fall presents a panorama of color that is breathtaking.

The late Fred Findlay, a Scot, was one of the pioneers of golf in Virginia. He came from the old country and designed a number of the better courses, including Farmington and the James River course of the Country Club of Virginia at Richmond. "Nowhere is the terrain better for golf or the scenery more beautiful than it is here," he often said.

Until his death, a few years ago at the age of 92, Findlay spent the greater portion of his days outdoors. He loved to paint and to fish. So, when he built a golf course, he always wanted to put it where there was plenty of water, and he believed in doing nothing to harm the scenery. "My mother would never forgive me if I did," he said.

Findlay is only one of the architects who left his mark on Virginia golf. The list includes the late Donald Ross, Sir Guy Campbell, Dick Wilson and Robert Trent Jones, among others. It is entirely possible that Sir Guy Campbell, whose relatives made quite a name for themselves with land speed records, built his last golf course in Virginia, The Tides Inn course near Irvington.

Two of the newer championship courses are the handiwork of Jones. They are the Golden Horseshoe at Williamsburg and the Lower Cascades at Hot Springs. In these Jones has built two contrasting courses. The Golden Horseshoe is in a setting of rolling woodland on the grounds of the palatial Williamsburg Inn, just a short distance from the colonial governor's palace and capital. Each hole on the Golden Horseshoe layout is equipped with four separate tees from which the golfer may play. This allows the course to stretch from a relatively short 5,370 yards from the front or ladies' tees to a mighty 6,743 yards from the championship tees. The fifteenth tee, for instance, measures a lengthy 135 yards from front to back. The hole is 630 yards long from the championship tees, making it virtually impossible for even the game's mightiest hitters to reach it in two strokes.

The Golden Horseshoe consists of eleven par 4's, four par 3's, and three par 5's, and tests the golfer's skill and accuracy with water hazards on six holes and doglegs on another six. Ten of the holes—the third, fourth, fifth, sixth, eighth, ninth, tenth, thirteenth, fourteenth, and fifteenth—were cut out of virgin woods. Many fairways are wide enough to allow the golfer to "let out a little shaft" on occasion, but he cannot let his drive stray too much off line or he will find his ball nestled up against one of the many trees that border the fairways. The course was so well planned that all who play it will notice its fairness. It is the type of course that encourages a golfer to try a risky shot, and if the shot is well executed, the player can expect to be rewarded. If not, he can certainly expect to pay the penalty!

Although every hole on the course has its own unique character and beauty, the four par-3 holes may become the most famous "foursome" in the country. Each involves a water hazard, and the golfer who

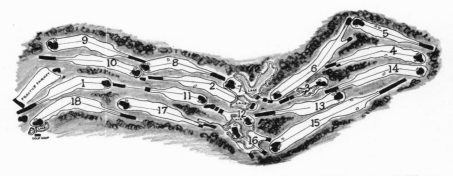

The course layout of the famed Golden Horseshoe Golf Course at Williamsburg, Virginia.

plays these holes in par figures will undoubtedly belong to a very select group. The par-3 third measures 110, 141, 161, and 176 yards from front to back. Trent Jones describes it as "tiny, watery, awesome." The golfer playing it for the first time will wholeheartedly agree. From a tee elevated some forty feet above the level of the green, the shot must carry over a water hazard that cuts across the front part of the green. This makes the hold play especially difficult when the pin is located toward the front. There is a sand trap in the front and another in the rear. A bank also at the rear gives support to the golfer who hits a shot that is too strong. It's much better to be long than short, so be sure to take enough club on this one!

The seventh is 100, 170, 185, and 210 yards from front to back. The back tees are located on a high bluff that overlooks a lake-filled valley below. The green is nestled in a hillside 25 feet above the water line. The hole is well-trapped and is probably one of the few holes where the golfer may not be disappointed to see his ball come to rest in one of the traps. At least he will be safely over the water! As is the case on all of the Golden Horseshoe's par 3's, do not be short.

On the twelfth hole, your shot must carry over 200 feet of water. The tees are a series of steps measuring 100, 165, 185, and 210 yards from front to back. The green is set in a corner of the water hazard, against a hillside covered with mature pine and oak. There are two large traps at the rear of the green. It is one of the most picturesque holes on the course. The sight from the elevated championship tee to the seemingly small green below will make some golfers wonder how it's possible to play this hole with only one ball! Fortunately, the hole does play progressively easier from the shorter tees, but the golfer will find an irresistible urge to try to conquer the hole from the championship tee.

There are few holes in the country as beautiful as the sixteenth. It's the shortest hole, measuring 100, 145, 155, and 165 from front to back. The green is manmade island, completely surrounded by water. The only access to the green is over a footbridge. The green is large, however, consisting of approximately 25,000 square feet of putting surface. Any golfer will be thrilled to get a par here. Jones believes this hole will rank with golf's best great short holes and that it will be a topic of conversation throughout the country. For those who have played the hole, it already is.

The Lower Cascades, like the two other courses at Hot Springs, takes advantage of the abundance of waterfall from the Cascades springs. The Lower Cascades was built only a year ago to take some of the play from the older Cascades, perhaps the best known of all Virginia courses. The new course is longer and more tiring, but hardly more exacting than other courses at the Homestead, one of the finest resorts in the world.

Long ago Hot Springs, the heart of Bath County, was famed for its health baths. Washington and Jefferson frequented them, as did many of their colleagues. When golf became popular, Hot Springs adopted the game, building a 6-hole course. When play became congested on it, it was enlarged to 18 holes. Later another course was built and then still another.

One of the three courses in Hot Springs, the Homestead—named after the venerable inn—was first, and while it is only a 6,040-yard, par-71 workshop, there is trouble enough there for everyone. For instance, the third hole measures only 300 yards, but on the left there are trees galore and on the right a Mount Vesuvius–like crater. The fourth and fifth holes are par 5's, but play from only 463 and 457 yards respectively. The sixth is a 167-yard par 3, where the green sits around a bay of traps that are yawning invitations to "jump right in." Hole seven would be a tough four on any course. The hole measures 413 yards and the green sits atop an elevated knoll. Hit to the left and you bounce into the trap, while a slice will send you down the green and maybe into a riding trail.

The back nine is even tougher hole for hole than the front side. No. 10 is 388 yards long and unless you bang out a drive of at least 245 yards you are faced with a downhill lie for which these Hot Springs courses are famous. The twelfth is an uphill 404-yard monster and is easy only if you can swat a ball 285 yards straight. Anything less and you have an uphill lie to cope with. The thirteenth is the longest par 4 on the course—445 yards—and don't be too awed with the beauty, or the woods will get you. The par-4 eighteenth, which stands in the shadow of that Homestead tower, isn't distressingly long —373 yards—but you hit to an elevated green that has traps and trees on either side and trees just past the green. Aside from the lies and the sensational views, however, the Homestead is a fairly modest golf course. It does claim a footnote to golf history—the first tee has been in continuous use since 1892, and a sign proclaims that "no other tee in the U.S. has been used for a longer period."

The Lower Cascades course, unlike the other two, is a *comparatively* flat course. It is the longest—6,895 yards from the back tees— and it features the long Jones tees and jumbo undulating greens. The saying at the Lower Cascades is "if the traps and trees don't get you, the greens will." All roll a variety of ways and are enough to turn a man against his favorite putter.

The Cascades course is the Homestead's classic championship layout. All 18 of the Cascades holes (ask a fellow who has played one) are noted for both beauty and toughness. The opener is 413 yards and is a tight piece of landscape and is generally rated as the second toughest par hole on the course. A hook lands you into some of the largest oaks you have ever seen, while a slice can cost you a trap (if you are lucky) or more woods. The fairway is tight—devilishly tight—and if the course is damp, even the best hitters need a wood or long iron for the second shot.

Sam Snead once drove the 308-yard par-4 third but few players are willing to gamble with a wood, since the fairway is too narrow for such nonsense. A long iron and eight-nine or wedge makes more sense than the wooden club gamble.

The fourth is a downhill 210-yard par-3 hole that is flanked by woods and traps. The fifth is a 586-yard "giant killer" that few have ever reached in two. The sixth is a dogleg that requires at least a 235-yard drive. Anything else and you don't even see the green. Seven stretches 444 yards (all uphill) and eight is a par-3, 148-yarder that is enveloped with large traps on either side. Nine is a 411 par-4 hole where, unless you hit over the rise (a drive of 270 yards), you cannot see the green and could have an uphill shot. Your best bet is to take

The ninth hole on The Cascades course at the Homestead.

aim at the bull's eye target hung in the big pine in back of the green, take a deep breath, swing, and hope for the best.

Ten is 374 yards and comparatively easy if you hit the long ball and hit it straight—but what hole is not? The eleventh measures two hundred yards and plays to three. Once in a while there is a hole-in-one, but more frequent are the rumbles of the ball batting against the rocks in the water hazard to the right or against the tall timber to the left. The twelfth is rated the prettiest, of course, and is one of the most beautiful golf holes in America. For all of its 481 yards are encircled by beautiful trees that in the evening cast some of the prettiest shadows ever seen on any golf course. The white course twelfth is 414 yards and calls for par 4, but it's a par 5 from the blue markers. Cascades caddies call this hole the "bear hole." A high bank is on the right and, more often that not, if you slice your ball comes back to you courtesy of the unseen bear. But hook and the devil gets you as your ball rumbles among the rocks and trees.

The thirteenth, 414 yards and par 4, was once rated as the prettiest thirteenth on the course and only the twelfth can rival this thing of beauty for sheer golfing joy. The long uphill 424-yard par-4 fourteenth is rated as the toughest hole to par. It is not only long but is flanked by trees, and an assortment of five traps guard the entrance and outer limits of the green.

Number 15 is a 234-yard par 3 that forces the golfer to shoot straight through some trees, and then once in the fairway hope for a slight hook that will guide the ball to the green. The sixteenth is a lake-fronted par-5 534-yarder that few golfers have ever hit in two shots. Traps are down in the fairway 240 yards out and flank the lake. After two shots and in front of the lake you might be distracted by the leaping trout on the third shot and land right in the middle of the stream. The seventeenth is a curving 504-yard par 5 that requires a slight hook. Get too far to the right and the trout stream will get you, while a too vigorous hook could plop in the trees.

A fine finishing par-3, 200-yard eighteenth awaits you. A lake ends but fifty yards from where the green begins and trees and traps breed plenty of trouble. That hole all but epitomizes golf at the Homestead—a great hole on a great course at a great resort.

Another fine resort course in Virginia is the one at the Tides Inn. This course is very challenging and requires several unusual playing tricks. For example, it is fairway, trees, greens, and water, with very

The second hole at the Tides Inn International "18."

little rough but not too much room for spraying shots, with water staring you in the face at ten holes. Another unusual feature of the Tides International course is the character of the par-5 holes—two of which can be played without a single wood shot. On the 535-yard third, "The Monster," a dogleg with two water crossings, better players use a 4-iron, a 5-iron and an 8-iron to the green; on the double dogleg twelfth, 533 yards, they generally use two 3-irons and a 7-iron, depending on the wind. Another par 5, the short 472-yard sixth, is considered the toughest hole on the course. If you do not clear a rise to get within sight of the green for your third shot, swing away and pray for a miracle; even if you do see the pin, what you are looking at is the narrow length of a sliver of a green—with water on both sides of it and also behind it. As veteran traveling golfers say, "the approach to the sixth green demands a better shot than any other on this fine course."

The beginnings of golf in Virginia are not recorded. Some hold that the "humblin" game of the Scots was first played in the Commonwealth in the Tidewater area by visiting Scots and Englishmen whose ships had anchored in Hampton Roads. Still others contend that the game was first played in the state at Hot Springs. The latter group has supporting evidence for, by 1892, the Bath Country Club boasted a 6-hole course that covered part of the acreage of the present Homestead course.

Transplanted Easterners and visiting Europeans, of course, were among the first to play the Scots' game. Initially, it had a slow growth. In 1900 there were only six 9-hole courses in the state. Two of them were in Richmond—the Hermitage, then situated on the present site of the Broad Street railway station, and the Richmond Wheel Club, from which emerged the Country Club of Virginia, chartered in 1908. The Wheel Club later was renamed the Lakeside Wheel Club and now is part of the Jefferson–Lakeside Country Club.

Richmond had the lead in clubs from the start and it does today, having 10 clubs with a total of 12 courses, all 18 holes. There are three other clubs little more than a good brassie shot away. But, today golf flourishes throughout Virginia. Virtually every town of any size has its own course. However, the following are considered among the best tests of your golfing skills:

LOCATION	COURSE	HOLES/PAR/ YARDAGE	TYPE
Bayce	Bayce Mountain GC	18/71/6,230	R
Fredericksburg	Sheraton Fredericksburg GC	18/72/7,150	Pub
Hot Springs	The Homestead		
	(Upper Cascades)	18/71/6,732	
	(Lower Cascades)	18/72/6,895	
	(The Homestead)	18/71/6,040	R
Irvington	Tides Inn CC	18/72/6,482	R
Jefferston	South Wales CC	18/72/7,039	R
Newport News	James River CC	18/71/6,322	Pvt

LOCATION	COURSE	HOLES/PAR/ YARDAGE	TYPE
Newport News	Newport News GC	18/72/6,882	Pub
Norfolk	Lake Wright GC	18/70/6,254	R
Norfolk	Ocean View GC	18/70/6,320	Pub
Norfolk	Stumpy Lake GC	18/72/6,200	Pub
Portsmouth	Bide-A-Wee Golf Assoc.	18/72/6,331	Pub
Reston	Reston North GC	18/71/7,005	SP
Richmond	Oak Hill CC	18/70/6,273	SP
Richmond	Laurel GC	18/71/6,023	SP
Roanoke	Blue Hills GC	18/71/6,420	SP
Roanoke	Ole Monterey GC	18/71/6,712	SP
South Boston	Greens Folly CC	18/72/6,812	SP
Staunton	Ingleside Augusta GC	18/72/6,609	R
Suffolk	Suffolk GC	18/72/6,245	SP
Virginia Beach	Bow Creek G & CC	18/72/6,493	SP
Virginia Beach	Cavalier G & CC	18/69/6,065	Pvt
Virginia Beach	Kempville Meadow G & CC	18/72/6,900	SP
Virginia Beach	Red Wing Lake GC	18/72/6,387	Pub
Virginia Beach	White Sands G & CC	18/71/6,505	SP
Williamsburg	Golden Horseshoe GC	18/71/6,778	R

NORTH CAROLINA

"Geographically, topographically, climatically—North Carolina appears to have been designed by St. Andrew himself as a golfing state." In this way the late O. B. Keeler, perhaps the most knowledgeable golf journalist the game has ever known, described the setting for one of golf's unique and exciting adventures. His vivid discourse still fairly shouts an invitation to the hundreds of thousands of vacationers who annually make their way to North Carolina. In the words of that famous scribe: "There is every kind of golfing terrain in the Old North State; the golfing pilgrim may suit his fancy down to the last steep pitch of the crafty run-up approach; he may play his game over hill and dale, and across lakes and streams. He may wallop away along fairways flat or rolling, and bordered by piney woods or noble oaks or gigantic clumps of laurel and rhododendron.

"He may select an emerald bowl in the mountains, if he has a flair for scenery and the altitude agrees with him; or he can find an English countryside, set about with green pastures and placid herds."

Variety, then, is the keynote in North Carolina's golf adventure story. There is no season of the year when golf is not being played somewhere in the state. There's winter golf in the sandhills and summer golf in the mountains; year-round golf at courses extending from the shores of the Atlantic to the ruggedly handsome high country of the Great Smoky and Blue Ridge mountains. Spaced generously in between, etched from great pine forests and rolling foothills, are more than three hundred golf courses offering a delightful variety of climate and terrain.

Indeed, North Carolina has combined the best of two worlds—the challenge of championship golf and the leisurely comfort of vacation living—to add new dimensions to this time-honored and increasingly popular sport. Accommodations range from luxurious golf resorts, many ranking among the world's finest, to efficient and modestly priced hotels and motor inns.

World-famous North Carolina golf can be enjoyed at scores of

The clubhouse and eighteenth green at Mid-Pines in Southern Pines, North Carolina.

outstanding courses by payment of a modest greens fee, while most private clubs require visiting golfers to be in the company of a member. Many of these courses extend playing privileges to guests of nearby hotels and inns.

It is not surprising that Pinehurst, nestled in the perpetual greenery of the North Carolina sandhills, is the focal point of Tar Heel golf. It is here that golfers the world over have tested their skills over the hallowed acres of Pinehurst Country Club. It is the only private golf club in the world with five 18-hole courses, and in the height of the season it is not unusual for one thousand rounds to be played daily on these five courses.

Of the five courses, Pinehurst's storied No. 1 is one of the greatest courses in the world and is a great monument to the architectural genius of Donald Ross, its designer. To fully appreciate the magnificence of No. 2, one must go out and battle it. One must walk the fairways where the great and the near-great have walked. One must see the silent magic of the course at work as it graciously rewards the good shot and—sometimes discreetly, often harshly—punishes the poor shot.

Pinehurst No. 2 can play as short as 5,915 yards or as long as 7,007 yards. Playing back tees gives one the thrill of coming to grips with a great course at its greatest. As they progress around its gently rolling fairways, golfers find at once two unyielding requisites— distance and accuracy. Bunkers blanketed with clumps of tall, thick growth lie in wait at strategic points to gobble up wayward tee shots. Sand traps yawn menacingly around the greens. To stray just a touch off the fairway is to face a shot from packed sand and sparse, course grass. To stray farther is to be confronted with the task of hitting between trees from a thick bed of pine needles.

Seven of the ten par-4 holes on No. 2 measure 419 yards, or longer, from the championship tees. Where distance is lacking, there is increased emphasis on accuracy. For example, the 340-yard third hole gives a man a breath after he has strained 427 yards on the first and 448 on the second. While he does not have to bend his driver double on this one, though, he cannot rest. There is out-of-bounds on the left, woods on the right. There are sand traps short of the green on the right and guarding the green on the left and across much of the front. Serious tree trouble waits in the rear. The need for finesse continues on the rolling putting surface.

The par-3 holes range from 156 to 211 yards and all are truly formidable. The shortest of the one-shotters, the ninth, is the most heavily guarded.

The par 5's, with the exception of the 593-yard tenth hole, present comparatively good chances for birdies. Long hitters can reach three of them in two shots. The tenth is one of the finest holes on the course and is undoubtedly one of the best par 5's in the country. It has all of the testing qualities of the other holes for some 450 yards, and then it begins to take on a decided individuality. It doglegs sharply to the left, taunting the long hitters. A bunker lies ready to strike at the corner of the dogleg. As the fairway bends around the trees, it plunges headlong into an elevated green whose undulations are not the least of the hazards in the area. Harsh and demanding in places, teasing and inviting in others, this great hole leaves an indelible impression on all who come that way. Many a golfer has left the tenth muttering curses at his scorecard.

And no one who has challenged Pinehurst No. 2 can forget the 440-yard fifth hole—at once a beauty and a beast. The fairway slopes to the left, doglegging around rough and trees. A deep sand trap borders the green on the left. Beyond that, there is a sharp dropoff into trees. On the right, a giant trap lies in wait for those who shy too sharply from the pitfalls on the left. The last half of the battle is uphill—literally and figuratively.

Pinehurst has served to spark the development, in close proximity, of one of the finest complexes of golf facilities to be found anywhere. Seven additional courses are located within 15 minutes' driving time of the Pinehurst Country Club. Among these are the Mid Pines, Whispering Pines, and Pine Needles courses near Southern Pines, the long-established Southern Pines Country Club, Knollwood Fairways, Foxfire, and the fabulous Country Club of North Carolina courses. The Pinehurst-Southern Pines area has long been recognized as a winter resort area, but recent air-conditioning of hotels and inns have extended the season to year round.

If any area can challenge the Sandhills as the golf capital of North Carolina, it is the mile-high mountain country of western North Carolina. The grandeur of the scenery, together with the comfort afforded by natural "air conditioning," has made it a favorite summer respite for golfers from far and wide. Old-timers say this land is so strikingly vertical that you have to "lie down and look up to see out."

Asheville, high in the Blue Ridge Mountains of southwestern North Carolina, is best known for its Beaver Lake and Country Club of Asheville courses. Playing privileges at both these courses are available to guests of the nearby Grove Park Inn and Motor Lodge. To the south of Asheville are Hendersonville, Sapphire, Cashiers, Highlands, Lake Toxaway and Tryon, each with outstanding championship courses. Waynesville and Maggie Valley, still further westward, also offer exceptional golfing facilities. Just to the east of Asheville is Black Mountain, which has the game's longest hole—745 yards, par 6. The longest par-5 hole in the country is Beaver Lake's 690-yard No. 13.

Long-established and traditional favorites in North Carolina's northern mountain region around Boone are the Linville and Blowing Rock courses. The 6,634-yard Linville Golf Club course is located on the grounds of picturesque Eseeola Lodge. Five newcomers have been added to the golfing scene around Boone in recent years. These include three scenic masterpieces, Grandfather, Boone Golf Club, and nearby Hound Ears. Beautiful mountain courses are also located at Roaring Gap, Spruce Pine, Lenoir, and Newland. Many of North Carolina's mountain courses are situated at altitudes of more than three thousand feet, and yet many are relatively flat for such rugged terrain.

The mushrooming development of golfing facilities in the sandhills and western North Carolina has been closely paralleled in the urban areas of the state. Charlotte, the state's largest city, has 11 golf courses. Best known of these are the private Myers Park and Charlotte Country Club courses. Quail Hollow, a recent addition, is regarded by many as perhaps the toughest test in the lower Piedmont section of North Carolina. Other favorites here include Cedarwood, Sunset Hills, Eastwood, Larkhaven, Greenbrier Hills, and Hillcrest golf courses.

Established landmarks in historic Winston-Salem are Old Town and Forsyth, while Pine Brook is noted as the area's pioneer in the successful use of bent grass greens. Grandview, Winston Lake and Reynolds Park each offer outstanding 18-hole courses that may be enjoyed by visiting golfers.

To the southeast of Winston-Salem is High Point, the nation's largest furniture market, which claims a very promising championship course in the private Willow Creek Golf Club. Two 18-hole public courses—Blair Park and Sumner Hills—and the 9-hole Fair-

Most of North Carolina features plenty of pines, and as you look over the list of challenging courses you can play in the "Tar Heel State" you will note how many of the courses carry tree names, like the Pine Needle Country Club shown above.

field Golf Club, further enhance the area's popularity among local and visiting golfers.

The annual visit of pro golfers keeps interest at a high pitch in Greensboro, home of the annual Greater Greensboro Open. The GGO is played over the par-71, 7,034-yard Sedgefield Country Club course. Two recent additions to the Greensboro golf facilities are the Forest Oaks and Carlson Farms courses. Other favorites include Starmount Country Club, Greensboro Country Club, and the city-owned Gillespie Park golf course.

Among the many fine courses located in the fast-growing area around North Carolina's Research Triangle are the private Carolina Country Club at Raleigh, Wake Forest Country Club, MacGregor Downs at Cary, and Durham's Hope Valley course. The Raleigh Golf Association offers 27 holes of championship golf. Visitors are also welcomed at Durham's Hillandale, Wofford, and Lakeshore golf courses. Also integral parts of the Research Triangle are Duke University at Durham and the University of North Carolina at Chapel Hill, both of which operate championship caliber campus courses.

While visitors to North Carolina will find an abundance of courses to challenge their golfing proficiency, we have selected the following as the state's most trying:

LOCATION	COURSE	HOLES/PAR/ YARDAGE	TYPE
Asheville	Beaver Lake GC	18/72/6,556	SP
Banner Elk	Beech Mountain GC	18/72/6,560	R
Black Mountain	Black Mountain GC	18/71/6,387	SP
Blowing Rock	Blowing Rock CC	18/70/6,180	SP
Blowing Rock	Hound Ears Lodge & GC	18/72/6,359	R
Boone	Boone GC	18/71/6,388	R
Boone	Seven Devils Resort	18/71/6,542	R
Canton	Springdale CC & Lodge	18/72/6,700	R
Cape Carteret	Star Hill CC	18/71/6,837	SP
Cashiers	High Hampton Inn & CC	18/71/5,904	R
Clemmons	Bermuda Run GC	18/72/6,427	Pvt
Clemmons	Tanglewood Park GC	18/71/6,400	SP
Fayetteville	Cypress Lake GC	18/72/7,240	Pub
Garner	Eagle Crest GC	18/71/6,253	Pub
Greensboro	Green Valley CC	18/71/6,191	SP
Greensboro	Sedgefield CC	18/71/7,034	Pvt

LOCATION	COURSE	HOLES/PAR/ YARDAGE	TYPE
Hayesville	Chatuge Shores GC	18/72/6,792	Pub
Highlands	Highlands CC	18/70/6,147	Pvt
Kitty Hawk	Duck Woods GC	18/72/6,559	SP
Kitty Hawk	Sea Scape GC	18/71/6,122	SP
Linville	Grandfather G & CC	18/72/6,852	R
Linville	Linville GC	18/71/6,700	R
Maggie Valley	Maggie Valley CC	18/71/6,431	SP
Pinehurst	Foxfire G & CC	18/71/6,644	SP
Pinehurst	Pinehurst CC (#1)	18/70/6,129	R
	(#2)	18/72/7,051	
	(#3)	18/71/6,044	
	(#4)	18/70/6,172	
	(#5)	18/71/6,461	
Raleigh	Eagle Crest GC	18/71/6,253	Pub
Roaring Gap	High Meadows GC	18/72/6,650	R
Roaring Gap	Roaring Gap CC	18/70/6,200	Pvt
Sapphire	Sapphire Valley GC	18/72/6,890	Pvt
Stanford	Carolina Trace G & CC	18/72/6,995	SP
Southern Pines	Mid-Pines Club	18/72/6,628	R
Southern Pines	Pine Needles CC	18/71/6,905	R
Southern Pines	Southern Pines CC	18/71/6,426	SP
		9/34/2,700	
Southport	Oak Island G & Beach Club	18/72/6,608	Pvt
Waynesville	Waynesville CC Inn	18/71/6,015	SP
Whispering Pines	Whispering Pines CC	18/72/7,151	SP
		18/71/6,590	
Wolf Laurel	Wolf Laurel	18/72/6,548	R

SOUTH CAROLINA

Of over 140 courses in South Carolina, more than 90 are open to the public. The state's courses range from the seacoast upward through the mountains. South Carolina also has several highly competitive championship courses. "The Monster," the thirteenth hole of the Dunes Golf and Beach Club's course at Myrtle Beach, is known as one of the best in America. The links of Pine Lakes International, oldest course on South Carolina's Grand Strand, has a "rated" seventh hole.

The Grand Strand is one of the finest golf areas of South Carolina. It is a part of the state's Golf Coast, reaching between the borders of

North Carolina and Georgia, along which 26 courses are located. The Grand Strand, of course, is an ideal place for resort golf. All of the usual resort pleasures are available to the golfers and their families. There is the natural lure of the Atlantic. There is the wedding of golf and sand, which the great architect Donald Ross proclaimed a blessed one. And there is the breeze off the Gulf Stream that cools the climate during the summer and warms it during the winter, making the seasons less severe than they are inland. The mean air temperature between 10 a.m. and 4 p.m. along the Grand Strand is 54.1 in January, 59.7 in February, 61.3 in March, 69.0 in April, 74.2 in May, 79.4 in June, 82.4 in July, 83.0 in August, 78.7 in September, 71.7 in October, 61.6 in November, and 54.6 in December.

Golf is played the year round on the Strand, although December and January can turn up some uncomfortable days. There were ten days last year when temperatures dropped below freezing. The most popular golfing months are March, April, September, October, and November. The best months are in the fall, when the courses are in peak condition and the weather is perfect.

The types of golf courses available for play are as varied as the

The resort course on Flipp Island is one of South Carolina's most interesting.

moods of the sea. Generally they are cut out of pine forests, well-trapped, and liberally splashed with water. The basic grasses are rye in cool months and various refined strains of Bermuda in the warmer months. The soil is, of course, sandy, making for some demanding recoveries for those who stray off the fairways and beyond the intermediate rough. The sand is firm for the most part, though. Thus, on the Grand Strand, you can get any kind of golf you are after, ranging from the leering challenge of the famous Dunes Golf & Beach Club at Myrtle Beach to the sweet and simple courses that produce scores that sound good back home. Experts are generally agreed that there are three courses in the Carolinas that rank with the nation's best—Pinehurst's great No. 2 course, the beautiful and ferocious Country Club of North Carolina at Pinehurst and the Dunes.

The Dunes is the only Strand course that is actually located at the ocean's edge. At its simplest, it is not an easy course and was never intended to be. At its toughest, it is virtually unmanageable for the very best players. In its normal state, it is a good, stiff challenge, but an enjoyable one. The par is 72, both from the championship tees, which can go to about 7,000 yards, and from the regular tees, which play about 6,400 yards.

The oldest course along the Strand is the elegant Pine Lakes International Country Club, which has more of the country club air about it than the others and is a center of social activity. As for the golf course, it features ten picturesque lakes that come into play, but on the other hand lets you off with only three fairway traps. The course features the deepest traps along the Strand. It can play very comfortably or very hard, depending upon how you want it. Pine Lakes plays, 6,700 yards and 6,300, with a par 71. It is located near the downtown area of Myrtle Beach.

The third member of the "old" trio of golf courses that have served the Grand Strand area for many years is the Surf Golf and Beach Club at Ocean Drive Beach. This is an extremely popular facility used for some forty-thousand rounds of play in 1967. It is a lush course featuring Tifton 328 grass, basically a green grass, throughout—on tees and fairways as well as on greens. It has water in play on 15 holes, but most of it is only for the truly wayward and it has an interesting character named Oscar residing in the pond along the tenth fairway. Oscar is an alligator about eight to ten feet long. The Surf plays 6,700 yards and 6,300 yards.

The first course to evolve from the flood of northern golfers was

Myrtlewood Golf Course in Myrtle Beach. It opened November 1, 1966, and has proved to be highly popular. It plays only 6,300 yards and 6,000 yards, which makes it an ego-builder and a speed course. It has only splash traps, which do not require a lot of blasting. It does have many little lagoons knifing into the fairways, though. Myrtlewood is unique among Strand courses in that it is not built on sandy soil, but on clay. It is built where a swamp once lay before the Intracoastal Waterway drained it.

Litchfield Country Club, at Litchfield Beach, measures 6,800 yards and 6,200 yards and has no parallel fairways. This layout, carved out of the woods, is a scenic one, with plenty of water. Doglegging fairways put the long driver to a stiff test of accuracy.

Sea Gull Golf Club at Lawley's Island ranks among the best on the Strand as a pleasure to play and to view. It has wide fairways, averaging eighty yards in the landing area, and huge greens, averaging ten thousand square feet. The front nine is built on rolling terrain that is not characteristic of this area, but the back nine is flat. The third hole is unusual. It is a 525-yard par 5 for men, a 330-yard par 4 for ladies. The men play across water to the green, the ladies play to a separate green short of the pond. Sea Gull measures 6,900 and 6,300.

Robbers Roost Golf Club at Ocean Drive rates alongside the Dunes as the most scenic of all the Strand courses. Robbers Roost, which has a pirate theme in the naming of its holes, plays 7,000 and 6,500 yards. It is planted throughout with Tifton Dwarf grass, assuring a lush playing surface, and is set among giant pines, holly trees and towering cypress. Its trees stretch one hundred yards, its fairways are wide, there are eight water holes, and the course is heavily trapped.

Possom Trot Golf Club at Crescent Beach is situated on some of the highest ground on the Grand Strand. It is long, playing 7,000 and 6,500 yards, but has wide fairways, big greens and not a great deal of water. It is built on rolling ground and it, too, offers a carpetlike playing surface, with Tifton 328 grass on tees and fairways, Tifton Dwarf on the greens. It is situated in a forest of small pines.

A close neighbor of Possum Trot is Beachwood Golf Club, a relatively short but well-trapped course. It has strong, multilevel tees, not a great deal of water but an abundance of pine trees.

Quail Creek Golf Club is 11 minutes inland from Myrtle Beach. It has a wide variety of tees. Choose your own poison. There are challenge tees that stretch the course to 7,300 yards, the championship tees that bring it down to 6,800 and the regular tees that reduce it to 6,400. It is located on flat, wooded land and features water on five holes.

Nine of the ten Grand Strand courses are open to everyone with only the Dunes restricted. To play at the Dunes a visitor must be a patron of one of a dozen motels or be introduced by a member. Green fees are nowhere exorbitant; neither are the charges for golf cars.

Each of the ten courses has something to offer to every golfer. Myrtlewood and Beachwood are the easiest, not because they lack challenging and alluring hazards, but because they present them on a reduced scale. Pine Lakes, Surf, and Litchfield demand a good deal of accuracy from the tees. Quail Creek, Sea Gull, Robbers Roost, and Possum Trot for the most part permit room for maneuvering, but a well-placed tee shot always will pay off by leaving a better angle of approach. All will give the best golfers a severe test if he chooses to operate from the championship markers. Actually, the Myrtle Beach area seems to abound in memorable par 5's with Robbers Roost boasting two on its second nine. Both wind through forests of towering pines and evergreen live oaks with water presenting strategic hazards.

The 544-yard thirteenth at the Dunes justifiably is notorious. The drive skirts water on the right, the second must carry across an arm of a lake and the water remains on the right nearly up to the closely bunkered green. So few eagles have been scored there than an awed visitor presented the club with a plaque enshrining forever the names of those fortunate enough to have recorded threes. It bears only a half-dozen names. So well known has the thirteenth become that the first question asked of a visitor returning from Myrtle Beach is not "How did you play?" but "What did you do on thirteen?" The hole requires no further identification.

Further down the coast and just off the shore lies Hilton Head, which was an isolated giant of an island as recently as 1955. The island was reached only by boat; there were no paved roads or electricity. Natives on the island who spoke, and still speak, a lilting sing-song dialect called Gullah were little concerned with the world of the twentieth century. They shrimped, gathered oysters and grew choice vegetables which they took by boat to nearby Savannah— sometimes a week's round trip, depending on the winds.

Today the oyster-shell roads and the great wooden-wheeled ox carts that were used have been replaced by a network of paved roads and sleek cars from all over America. The lush, semitropical landscape has been preserved, but nestled in it, along the ocean, are six 18-hole courses and three 9-hole courses, all open to guests of the different golfing complexes. According to planners and developers on the island, the next five years will see 16 full-length courses on Hilton Head. Today all the courses are of the seaside variety yet they lack that chilled-to-the-bone bleakness of the British links. Also, there are no awesome holes where the golfer has to hit over turbulent waves that can swallow with one swoop a golf ball, golfer and caddy.

At the lower tip of the island, is Sea Pines Plantation with three courses: the Harbour Town Golf Course, the Ocean Course and Sea March Course of the Plantation Club. In the middle are Palmetto Dunes, the Hilton Head Golf Club and Adventure Inn Golf Course. (The latter is a par 3 lighted for night play). Near the upper tip is the Port Royal Inn and Golf Club with an 18-hole Barony course, a 9-hole Robbers Row Course and another nine, the Spanish Wells Golf and Country Club, which is strictly private for residents of the community. Here the rolling, sandy terrain is ideal for golf courses. Even after a sub-tropical shower the turf is very playable. Many of the holes resemble those in the Sandhill area of North Carolina. Tall pines and oaks line the fairways, and the rough is more sandy than grassy. From the back tees, the 18-hole Barony Course plays to 6,901 yards. Most of the fairways are comparatively wide and well bunkered, as are the entrances to the greens. With the sandy soil and closely cut grass, the long pitch-and-run shot can be used. The most treacherous and most beautiful hole at Port Royal is the seventeenth, a 425-yard par 4. A stream guards the right side of the fairway and a lagoon fronts the elevated green that tilts toward the fairway. A well-placed drive will favor the left side of the fairway, while the second shot might look like a long way to the green, it is advisable to use one club less. The eighteenth hole is a deceiving 215-yard par 3 over water. It heads toward the clubhouse, the center of the Port Royal Inn and Golf Club.

Palmetto Dunes, designed by Robert Trent Jones, measures 7,207 yards from the blue tees, making it the longest layout on the island. From the middle tees, though it will play to a scant 6,550 yards. All the Jones trademarks are featured: large undulating greens, long tees, wide fairways, and wiry Bermuda rough that can be allowed to grow to make the fairways as narrow as subway tracks. Ten holes are adjacent to lagoons, providing an unusual trial for golfers. The

Two reasons why Harbour Town Links is one of the one-hundred toughest golf courses: (*top*) its sand traps (note board bankings) and (*bottom*) its water holes.

other holes weave through dense woods and over the gently rolling terrain which is typical of Hilton Head. Of particular interest is the fourth green, which is identical to the original eighth at Augusta National. Working from the Augusta National plans and from his own intimate knowledge of the course, Jones has recreated a unique challenge for golfers.

The Hilton Head Golf Club course, designed by George Cobb who also did the Port Royal courses, is one which is laid out half in dunes forest, half in swamp forest. While the fairways are quite wide, almost everything doglegs. It plays 7,002 yards from championship tees, but only 6,320 yards from the middle tees.

The Harbour Town Course was designed by Pete Dye and Jack Nicklaus, who know championship courses like Fred Astaire knows dance floors. The course uses some of those classic touches of British links: pot bunkers, 100-yard fairway traps and boards banking many greenside traps. It plays to just under 7,000 yards from the championship tees and 6,500 from the club tees.

Neither the Sea Marsh nor the Ocean course of the Plantation Club is as demanding as the Harbour Town course. Even from the back tees, they measure 6,443 and 6,617 yards respectively. While most courses pride themselves on fierce, long par 4's as their unbending backbone, the Sea Pines courses offer some of the most exciting and challenging short par 4's of any resort. If you do not think a 289 yard, par 4 dogleg left with a narrow green the size of an elephant's ear is demanding, just play the second hole on the Sea Marsh course.

In addition to Hilton Head and Grand Strand, other South Carolina courses that will challenge the golfer's mettle are the one at the inland resort of Santee; the Spring Lake at York, a difficult par 72; the Bonnie Brae at Greenville, which requires every shot in a player's repertoire; the intriguing resort course at Fripp Island; and Persimmon Hill at Johnson, one of the state's best courses. Here is a rundown of major challenging links in South Carolina:

LOCATION	COURSE	HOLES/PAR/ YARDAGE	TYPE
Aiken	Highland Park CC	18/70/6,050	SP
Aiken	Midland Valley CC	18/72/6,823	SP

GREAT GOLF COURSES YOU *CAN* PLAY/88

LOCATION	COURSE	HOLES/PAR/ YARDAGE	TYPE
Aiken	Palmetto CC	18/72/6,550	SP
Anderson	Pine Lake GC	18/70/6,400	SP
Charleston	Charleston Municipal GC	18/72/6,400	Pub
Charleston	Seabrook Island GC	18/72/6,975	SP
Columbia	Coldstream CC	18/71/6,430	R
Florence	CC of South Carolina	18/72/6,611	Pvt
Florence	Oakdale CC	18/72/6,700	SP
Fountain	Fountain Inn-Simpson-ville CC	18/71/6,400	Pvt
Fripp Island	Fripp Island CC	18/72/6,538	R
Greenville	Bonnie Brae GC	18/72/6,515	SP
Hilton Head Is.	Hilton Head GC	18/72/7,003	R
Hilton Head Is.	Palmetto Dunes GC	18/72/7,207	R
Hilton Head Is.	Port Royal Plantation Inn & GC	18/72/6,901	R
Hilton Head Is.	Sea Pines Plantation Club		
	(Sea Marsh)	18/72/6,443	R
	(Ocean)	18/72/6,617	
	(Harbour Town Links)	18/72/6,885	
Johnston	Persimmon Hill CC	18/72/7,070	SP
Loris	Carolinas CC	18/72/6,500	R
Myrtle Beach	Azalea Sands GC	18/72/	R
Myrtle Beach	Dunes G & Beach Club	18/72/7,008	R
Myrtle Beach	Myrtlewood GC	18/72/6,350	R
Myrtle Beach	Pine Lakes International CC	18/71/6,609	R
Myrtle Beach	Quail Creek GC	18/72/6,877	R
N. Myrtle Beach	Bay Tree Golf Plantation		
	(Gold)	18/72/7,130	R
	(Green)	18/72/7,074	
	(Silver)	18/72/6,888	
N. Myrtle Beach	Beachwood GC	18/72/6,220	R
N. Myrtle Beach	Cypress Bay GC	18/72/6,502	SP
N. Myrtle Beach	Eagle's Nest GC	18/72/6,950	SP
N. Myrtle Beach	Possum Trot GC	18/72/6,966	R
N. Myrtle Beach	Robbers Roost GC	18/72/7,128	R
N. Myrtle Beach	Surf G & Beach Club	18/72/6,850	R
Pawleys Island	Litchfield CC	18/72/6,886	R
Pawleys Island	Sea Gull GC	18/72/6,900	R
Santee	Santee-Cooper CC	18/72/6,890	R
York	Spring Lake CC	18/72/6,919	SP

GEORGIA

Georgia's wonderful variety of topography is the basic ingredient for adventure in golfing. Courses throughout the state were designed by taking nature's contours and developing them into exciting, different holes. The mountain area of northern Georgia offers hilly courses. The seashore area to the south includes a chain of history-steeped islands, festooned with broad white sand beaches. Many holes open to broad vistas overlooking the ocean. The vast plateau of middle Georgia offers yet another type of course. Georgia holes are well-trapped with lakes, marshes, forests. Fairways are manicured; greens, velvety scenery, superb. You will use every shot in your bag on the state's courses. More than eighty are open to tourists, not to mention the long list of private clubs, many of which honor memberships in the nation's leading golf clubs.

Golf is an adventure in Georgia—and it is something else. It is a way of life, for you can play golf at least three hundred days a year in Georgia—more if you don't mind a nip in the air and a bit of dampness now and then.

Much of Georgia's enthusiasm for golf is attributable to one man, Bobby Jones. He played in the United States Amateur championship when he was only 14. By shooting a 74 on the first two qualifying rounds, then winning two matches against the nation's best adults, the Atlanta boy established himself as a national golf prodigy and laid the foundation for the game's most illustrious career.

Jones won the top four titles—U.S. Open and Amateur and British Open and Amateur—in the same year and ended his career with 13 major championships. He became the golfing idol of every nation where the game is known. His honors are many. A few years ago he was made a Burgess of St. Andrews, Scotland, the Cradle of Golf. Only one other American, Benjamin Franklin, was given this recognition.

After Jones got Georgia off to a fine start in golf by his own success, he did one other significant thing to make golf the game for Georgia. With Cliff Roberts, he collaborated on construction of the Augusta National Club and launched the Masters tournament. The Masters has become the elite golf tournament of the world, attracting major pros and amateurs by invitation from all over the globe.

Georgia is loaded with fine courses, such as Peachtree, Sea Island, Atlanta Country Club, and Augusta Country Club, to name a few.

Mossy oaks of the famed old Retreat border fairways of the Sea Island golf course beside the Atlantic Ocean surf.

Augusta Country Club is so great that if the Masters had been played there, it would be just as accepted and just as famous as Augusta National. And there are many other Georgia courses that are just as great. It is just that kind of golfing state. In fact, hardly a town of seven thousand population is without its own course. While the state has many courses of note, perhaps the best known ones for winter golfing are: Sea Island, the Savannah Inn and Country Club, Jekyll Island, Sea Palms (on St. Simons Island), Callaway Gardens, and Kingwood.

Sea Island has three 9-hole courses—Plantation, Retreat, and Sea Side. The clubhouse, rebuilt from the ruins of a barn still standing from the days when the course was the site of a plantation, blends the old with the new. Golfing privileges on these courses are offered to guests of the Cloister. A devoted staff nurses greens and fairways to perfection.

Sea Palms is designed for people who like superlative golf and unhurried life. This new addition to the Georgia golf scene has Tifton Bermuda greens and fairways in a woodland setting. George W. Cobb designed Sea Palms. It is one of the seven layouts in the United States that have both greens and fairways of rare Tifton grass. Playing from the blue tees, expert golfers have a 6,700-yard challenge. White tees are somewhat less demanding, and afford the average player a rewarding game. The lady golfer has a choice of tees—one for the low handicapper and another on most holes, some forty to fifty yards out, for the 100 and above shooter. The alternate tee also enables the player to avoid water and sand hazards.

A few miles from Sea Island, also situated on the seacoast, is Brunswick Country Club, built in the marsh area of Glynn County in the Golden Isles region. It is a long course with many bunkers filled with beach sand and sharply breaking doglegs, making it both demanding and picturesque. This course is kept in impeccable condition, using rye grass during winter and spring and Bermuda during the hotter summer months. This makes playing on good fairways and greens a year-round reality.

Almost three-quarters of a century ago, a group of America's wealthiest men organized a club in coastal Georgia. One of its major purposes was golfing, and hoes were patterned after the sand-dune courses of Scotland. Today that course at Jekyll Island has become a championship challenge. It now has 45 holes (some old, some new). The addition of the Pine Lakes course last winter brought Jekyll a new title—"Golf Island." This challenging course of 18 tree-lined, lakeside holes gives the island three courses with different layouts for each. Players do not cross water in tours of Pine Lakes, but it is not an easy course. Greens are large, with many traps, and the length of holes (6,407 yards, par 72) is arranged to provide a true test for golfers of every ability. For variety, Jekyll Island has a 6,476-yard, par-72, 18-hole championship course with some unsettling water crossings. For a taste of golf as the millionaire pioneers of Jekyll Island knew it, the 9-hole seaside course with its grassed dunes and miniature greens provides a challenge in St. Andrew's style. Motel guests have their choice of the three courses to play at no added cost other than their room charges during winter (ending March 31).

On Wilmington Island, ten miles east of Savannah, is the Savannah Inn and Country Club's par-72 championship golf course. Designed by Donald Ross in 1927 and completely modernized by William Byrd, the course is becoming a must for vacationing golfers in Georgia. It stretches 7,100 yards from the men's tees. Contoured fairways and raised greens, enhanced by strategic placement of 76 bunkers and 10 water holes, make it one of the finest coastal courses in the country. The course is set on 154 acres of Tifton Bermuda grass and is completely irrigated with four artificial lakes and a stream. Live oaks with Spanish moss, palm trees, and pines add scenic beauty.

Callaway Gardens, 75 miles southwest of Atlanta in the Pine Mountain region, has 63 holes of golf, including a wealth of water hazards. The Gardens emphasize azaleas, holly, and nature trails. Courses are designed so that golfers can see blossoms in almost any direction. Greenhouses are stocked with broad assortments of flowers. There is fishing, boating, and water skiing, but golf takes top billing among tourists.

The full course built at Callaway is Lake View, which now measures 6,009 yards and plays to a par of 70. The first nine, built around a mountain, is the older part of the course and the most inviting to tourists. The back nine winds around a lake, is surrounded by hills, and is longer and tighter. A few years back Mountain View, which measures 7,040 yards and is a par 72, was added. Then in 1970, Garden View—a 6,392-yard, par-72 test was added: the newest layout takes the golfers past the arbors of muscadine grapes used for making the Garden's famous Muscadine Sauce. There is a 9-hole par-3 course also.

One of Georgia's newest mountain golf resorts is Kingwood, nestled in the Blue Ridge Mountains just two hours from Atlanta near Clayton. Though fairly new, the course is well-matured. The lush greens have been groomed until they are some of the greatest anywhere. The atmosphere of the resort reflects the freshness of the crisp mountain air. Kingwood is a private resort course, which is surrounded by beautiful mountain homesites overlooking the course.

In Atlanta, vacationers may play the fine Bobby Jones Municipal Golf Course, located just four miles from the heart of the city, along the banks of Peachtree Creek. This is one of the busiest courses in the state. The area is hilly (as hills go in Georgia) thus making the course interesting for anyone.

Radium Springs Golf Course, located in the southwestern part of

The fifth at Lake View, Callaway Gardens: 152 yards, par 3. The 90-yard carry over Mountain Creek Lake against the usual crosswind requires a well-hit 5 or 6 iron. If that doesn't give you enough problems, the green is surrounded on three sides by sand traps, so only a well-placed shot will permit the ball to run onto the green.

the state a little south of Albany on the Thomasville road, provides another interesting test for golfers. The course is short at 6,366 yards with a par 72. It is wide open, with small, interesting greens. Many holes run along the banks of the Flint River and fairways are lined with oaks, tall as a cathedral and draped with moss.

Near Thomasville is the Glen Arven Country Club, an old course that makes severe demands. Accuracy is at a premium since there is an abundance of bunkers. However, the golfer will appreciate the beautiful fairways and well-manicured greens.

One of the state's most unique courses is the new one at Stone Mountain, about 16 miles east of Atlanta. Only nine holes are ready for play now, but others will be open soon. All fairways and greens are made from turf placed atop the granite base and carefully conditioned and beautified for golfing. Stone Mountain is a 3,600-acre park surrounding the world's largest granite monolith, which rises 683 feet. A monument to Confederate leaders was completed in 1972. The park has a Memorial Hall which is a Civil War Museum, an activated relief map called the "Battlarena" that relates the story of the Civil War in Georgia, an 18-building complex typical of an ante bellum plantation, a scenic railroad, an antique automobile museum, a game ranch, a marina, and a carillon with a full schedule of concerts the year round.

Throughout Georgia there is an enthusiasm for golf that has continued to grow. Scottish Highlanders brought the game to Darien almost two hundred years ago. The land, the climate and the people were right for its growth. Scratch players and duffers tend to agree that golfing in Georgia is an exciting challenge, especially on any of these courses:

LOCATION	*COURSE*	*HOLES/PAR/ YARDAGE*	*TYPE*
Albany	Radium CC	18/72/6,366	SP
Atlanta	Adams Park GC	18/72/6,455	Pub
Atlanta	Bobby Jones Municipal GC	18/71/6,300	Pub
Atlanta	Browns Mill GC	18/72/6,800	Pub
Atlanta	East Lake #2 GC	18/72/6,800	Pvt
Atlanta	Fairington G & TC	18/72/6,400	Pvt
Atlanta	Indian Hills CC	18/72/6,635	Pvt
Atlanta	Mystery Valley GC	18/72/6,628	Pub
Atlanta	North Fulton GC	18/71/6,600	Pub
Brunswick	Brunswick CC	18/72/6,500	SP
Clayton	Kingwood Inn & CC	18/70/6,200	R
Cumming	Canongate-on-Lanier GC	18/72/6,300	SP
Decatur	Fairington G & TC	18/72/6,530	SP
Gainesville	Chattahoochee GC	18/72/6,535	Pub
Jekyll Island	Jekyll Island Championship C	18/72/6,476	R
Jekyll Island	Pine Lakes GC	18/72/6,407	R
Jekyll Island	Oceanside GC	9/36/3,257	R
Marietta	Indian Hills CC	18/72/6,754	SP
Palmetto	Canongate GC	18/72/6,365	SP
Pine Mountain	Callaway Gardens (Gardens View) (Lake View)	18/72/6,392 18/70/6,009	R

LOCATION	COURSE	HOLES/PAR/ YARDAGE	TYPE
Pine Mountain	(Mountain View)	18/72/7,040	
(cont.)	(Sky View)	9/31/2,096	
Rutledge	Hard Labor Creek State Park	18/72/6,651	Pub
St. Simon Island	Sea Palms G & CC	18/72/6,644	R
Savannah	Beacon Park GC	18/72/6,260	Pub
Savannah	Savannah GC	18/70/6,291	SP
Savannah	Savannah Inn & CC	18/72/7,009	SP
Sea Island	Sea Island GC	9/36/3,321	R
		9/36/3,371	
		9/36/3,506	
Snapfinger	Snapfinger GC	18/72/6,400	SP
Stone Mountain	Stone Mountain State GC	18/72/6,831	Pub
Thomasville	Glen Arven CC	18/72/6,350	SP

KENTUCKY

Kentucky has over 150 golf courses, but over two-thirds of them are private. There are, however, several fine public courses in the state, principally in Paducah, Owensboro, Frankfort, and Louisville. There are a few resort facilities, too, the leading ones being Village Greens Golf Course and the Park Mammoth Golf Club. At the latter you can take in the cavelands before or after playing golf. Here are the most interesting or challenging courses that you *can* play while in Kentucky:

LOCATION	COURSE	HOLES/PAR/ YARDAGE	TYPE
Burnside	General Burnside State Park	18/70/6,002	R
Fort Knox	Anderson GC	18/72/6,507	SP
Gilbertsville	Village Greens GC	18/72/6,745	R
Owensboro	Ben Hawes GC	18/71/6,820	Pub
		9/35/3,062	
Park City	Park Mammoth GC	18/70/6,950	R
Springfield	Lincoln Homestead GC	18/71/6,180	SP

TENNESSEE

Like Kentucky, Tennessee has over 150 golf clubs, but about three-fifths of them are private. Among the two-fifths that are open to the public, there are many good ones around the state at such

Often called one of the most intimidating holes in golf, the par-5, 569-yard first hole of the Azalea Nine at the Lakewood Golf Club surrenders its few rewards only to those who plan every shot. A dogleg right with out-of-bounds along the entire left side of the fairway and dense woods on the right, this monster requires a teeshot over a long, narrow lake to the sloping fairway. For those big hitters who want to cut off yardage, a fairway trap 225 yards out guards the right side. The key to the hole, however, lies in the pinpoint accuracy of the second shot. Fairway traps on the right and a landing area only 35 yards wide leave small margin for error, and still requires a good 150 yards to a green guarded by four mammoth traps. Starting with a par here makes any round a success.

locations at Chattanooga, Memphis, and Gatlinburg. The Gatlinburg course, nestled in the Great Smoky Mountains, has a very interesting par-3 hole—No. 12. It is only 150 yards long, but requires very good club judgment, since a 170-foot drop straight down extends the carry of the ball and there is danger of hitting out of bounds over the green. Trees on the left and right also spell trouble for the misdirected tee shot.

ALABAMA

Most of the great courses that you can play in Alabama are located along the Gulf Coast. Golf is a way of life in this area—an experience that natives happily enjoy and generously share with their visitors.

Naturally, the weather is a major factor in the game's popularity. Generally, even in the months of January and February, the temperatures are mild and pleasant. Only when those rare "cold snaps" hit for brief periods do golfers on the Gulf Coast find even a light sweater necessary. This mild climate has made the area perfect for some of the best courses and some of the most luxurious resorts in Dixie.

At Point Clear, just across Mobile Bay from Mobile, is the Grand Hotel, with its Lakewood Golf Club. Long popular with Midwesterners and Easterners, as well as others closer by who like a little something extra, this renowned resort golf course presents the exciting challenge to the good golfer, and a real thrill to the hacker.

Like most Gulf Coast courses, Lakewood is reasonably flat. But ancient, moss-draped oaks and stalwart pines stand alongside rather tight fairways on this course, which boasts 13 dogleg holes. Well-trapped and featuring the Tifton Bermuda greens that are so familiar to the area's courses, this layout is acknowledged as one of the toughest in the South. In fact, your fingers and toes will more than suffice to count the number of times par has been broken on this 6,723-yard par-70 course.

Because this Grand Hotel-Lakewood complex has grown so popular with the golfing set, an additional nine holes, laced with manmade lakes and live streams, has been added. This new par-35 nine, comprising 3,302 yards, has been named the "Magnolia" course, while the two nines of the "old 18" are called "Azalea" and "Dogwood." They are aptly named for the magnificent blooms that abound at the club.

On an island just off the southern tip of Alabama is another course that is perhaps among the world's most unique. It is the Isle Dauphine

Country Club—available for play by visitors to Dauphin Island. One side of this quaint and picturesque layout winds along the shore of the Gulf. The other is laced among giant sand dunes that reach several stories up. It is not unusual to tee off from atop a towering sand dune overlooking the vast expanse of the Gulf and the scenic beauties of the island. There are, as might be expected, many "water holes" in this majestic island queen. Nonetheless, the fairways are tightly adorned by the loblolly and slash pine trees that are as much a part of the South and the Gulf Coast as corn pone and hominy, grits and white gravy.

LOCATION	COURSE	HOLES/PAR/YARDAGE	TYPE
Dauphin Island	Isle Dauphine CC	18/72/7,000	SP
Decatur	Point Mallard GC	18/72/6,820	Pub
Dothan	Olympia Spa & CC	18/72/6,636	R
Huntsville	Jetport GC	18/72/6,470	SP
Mobile	Langan Park GC	18/72/6,383	Pub
Mobile	Skyline CC	18/72/6,575	SP
Pell City	Pine Harbor Champions CC	18/71/6,720	SP
Point Clear	Lakewood GC (Azalea)	9/35/3,292	R
	(Dogwood)	9/35/3,421	
	(Magnolia)	9/36/3,302	
Talladega	Alabama International CC	18/71/6,646	R
		18/71/6,682	

MISSISSIPPI

Mississippi's three centuries of history include the legend and lore of pirate days on the Gulf, the ante bellum era, steamboats on the river, Delta plantations, Civil War battle sites, parks, and—of course—golf courses. But, like Alabama, Mississippi's best area for visiting golfers is along the Gulf Coast. This semitropical area offers a lush green playground for golfers during the colder months of fall, winter, and spring.

It is also one of golfdom's great bargains for the vacationing golfer and his family who want to prolong the season or just get away for a week or so of excellent golf. With ten 18-hole courses and three par-3 courses open to visiting golfers, the region offers a variety of play. Recent years have seen much activity in the growth of luxury resort hotels and motels offering excellent golf packages as an incentive to lure golfers to the area.

The Sun Course at Broadwater Beach Hotel and Country Club in Biloxi has water on fourteen of the eighteen holes.

Most of the Mississippi coastline's more enchanting resort golf courses are in a closely related stretch that requires travel only from Ocean Springs to the Biloxi-Gulfport area.

At Ocean Springs, the quite novel—for the South, anyway—

Gulf Hills Dude Ranch and Country Club offers ranch-type life combined with golf. The course here, although not like those in the Smokies or the Adirondacks, is hilly enough to be a little different from the average course in the area.

Just a few minutes drive and you reach the Broadwater Beach Hotel's 18-holer, which is located just behind this huge and grandiose resort. Or, if you are a boat owner, you can dock in front of the hotel at its $1,000,000 marina.

In a low, flat area not too far from the water's edge is the apparently rustic but meticulously manicured course. The Spanish moss hangs in the trees here the same as it did when the French and Spanish settlers first visited the area. The oaks are huge and the magnolias, the jasmine, the honeysuckle, the azaleas, the camellias all lend natural beauty and color to the golf course. Broadwater Beach is quite proud that its course is one of the oldest in the South. As the old Great Southern Golf Club, it was originally constructed in 1908. Very tight and with numerous doglegs, its 6,100 yards require great ball control. Its fourth hole overlooks the Gulf and photographs of it have appeared in many national magazines. Their newer Sun course is truly a championship test.

Lying between the Broadwater Beach and Gulf Hills is the Edgewater Gulf Hotel and its 6,314 par-72 layout. This also is a flat, but interesting course, with the usual tight fairways, comparatively small greens, and great natural beauty. A creek crosses a number of fairways, putting a premium on club selection. And here is a fact that might attract several golfers to the Edgewater Gulf. The 143-yard fifth hole has had forty holes-in-one in the past ten years.

The St. Andrews on the Gulf course can be stretched to 7,100 yards but normally plays shorter. It is part of a prestige real estate development that encompasses apartments, a marina, and other sports activities.

Hickory Hill Country Club, located on the Singing River near Pascagoula, is some distance from the hotels and beach resorts but offers a real championship challenge of 7,049 yards from the blue tees. Sunkist and Lakeside round out the list that golfing vacationers will surely want to try.

While on the subject of a golf vacation anywhere along the Gulf Coast, remember that it should be a thoroughly enjoyable experience regardless of whether you are a scratch player or a high handicapper.

As in most sections you will find conditions that vary somewhat from those to which you may be accustomed in your own area.

The two major differences are in bunker play and in the need for great accuracy with your drives. The traps can be a problem because they generally consist of fine, powdery river sand. When you first play them you are inclined to dig too deeply because you do not meet the resistance of heavier grades of sand. This can be counteracted most easily by acquiring a wedge that has a thicker flange. Such a club will give you more bounce action instead of digging too deeply.

Wind, even in the beach area, is not a great factor. The principal reason is that most fairways are cut through sheltered trees. However, while this cuts down any interference from wind, it necessitates more accuracy off the tees and with longer fairway shots to keep from wasting shots cutting wood. Fairways in the main are of Bermuda grass and you will find that the ball sits up well.

It almost never is too cold to play along the Gulf Coast. However, it can get fairly brisk, and it is a good idea to have a windbreaker available for early morning or late afternoon play. Also, when it comes to warming up before you tee off, you will find relatively few practice ranges in this region. Your best solution is to get a weighted head cover for your driver. Wear a sweater and swing your driver vigorously for a few minutes before you head to the first tee. Here are the major tests of your golfing ability in the Magnolia State:

LOCATION	*COURSE*	*HOLES/PAR/ YARDAGE*	*TYPE*
Bay St. Louis	Diamondhead GC	18/72/6,547	R
Biloxi	Broadwater Beach GC	18/71/6,100	R
Biloxi	Edgewater Gulf Hotel & CC		
	(Sea Course)	18/72/6,314	R
	(Sun Course)	18/72/7,190	
Biloxi	Sun Kist CC	18/72/6,530	Pvt
Gulfport	Banyan View CC	18/71/6,622	Pub
Hattiesburg	University of Miss. GC	18/72/6,400	SP
Jackson	Livingston Park GC	18/72/7,049	Pub
Ocean Springs	Gulf Hills Dude Ranch & CC	18/72/6,294	R
Ocean Springs	St. Andrews on the Gulf	18/72/6,724	R
Pascagoula	Hickory Hill CC	18/72/6,632	SP

LOUISIANA

Of Louisiana's over one hundred golf courses, the ones most visited by out-of-staters are those open to the public in the southern portion of the state. There are several excellent courses available, especially in Baton Rouge and New Orleans.

ARKANSAS

Arkansas has about one hundred courses of varying length and diffi-culty. Predominantly a state of small cities and rural communities, most of even the smallest towns have their own golf courses or are within a short drive of at least one.

Perhaps Arkansas's most renowned "cultural" center is Hot Springs, a thriving resort less than an hour southwest of Little Rock. People come to the spa from all over the country to take hot baths and play the horses. They also come to play golf (there are 81 holes of golf in Hot Springs) or to play golf between bathing and races. The little 9-hole layout (run by the Jockey Club), nestled in the middle of the Oaklawn track oval, in some way demonstrates the mixture of ponies and pitches. However, the Hot Springs Country Club is considered the focal point of competitive Arkansas golf activity. The tight, medium-length Arlington layout (only 18 of the Hot Springs Country Club's 45 holes) is the spa's best known.

Its 6,865 yards are tree- and sand-studded (45 bunkers in all), and require above all accurate drive placement. Otherwise the first shot is likely to bounce off the side of one of the many hard and grassy slopes into a ditch, an artistically positioned stand of trees, or some other such bogie-hangout. A poor drive is a good way to do bad things to a golf score.

Picturesque holes are the order of the day at Arlington. Take No. 8, a medium-length 3-par over a lagoon to a well-trapped green. Or take No. 17, a short 3-par down a lane of trees to a trap-encircled green. Beauty often serves to make par 72 tougher.

Hot Springs Country Club's No. 1 course (the Arlington is No. 3) is 6,923 yards of ticklish pars, the tickling done by rolling greens, 35 sand traps, and six holes bordered by out-of-bounds stakes. Par 72, while perhaps easier than Arlington's, is no laughing matter.

A short nine holes (par 35) gives the youngsters and other people a less frequented place to try their talents, and even it has heavy timber, small greens, and numerous ditches meandering around.

Hot Springs' other top-flight layout, the Belvedere Country Club course, certainly doesn't lack "local color." Traps on the various holes are colored according to the par of each (red sand on the 5 pars, white on the 4 pars, and blue on the 3 pars). It is definitely colorful (the only course in the United States with such permanently colored traps), and golfers who forget where they are after hitting several shots in a trap and not getting out, have only to glance at the sand to figure out how many over par they are already.

The 6,700-yard course has three ball-eating lakes and, speaking of water, has the only completely automatic watering system in the state. The roughs are also watered, another rarity, and the course can be expected to be in great shape constantly. Fairways are Tiffway 419 (at their best, they are like rugs), and the greens are Penn-Cross bent.

There is a golf boomlet at the moment throughout the state, which is planning for increased facilities. Dawn Hill, for instance, located about ten miles from the Oklahoma border in the northwest corner of the state, is one of Arkansas's finest. This golf course, a 6,390-yard, par-72 layout, has been called "sufficiently difficult to be interesting," with a spring-fed stream called Flint Creek winding through it and coming into play on six holes. Dawn Hill may be the only course in the United States where it is sensible to carry a fishing pole in your golf bag. Where Flint Creek flows by the eleventh green, there is a pool in which you can see sizable bass. Since the course is rarely crowded, there usually is time to make a few casts in passing.

Another resort course—which backers claim is the best nine holes in Arkansas (and Arkies are honest, remember)—is the Red Apple Country Club on Eden Isle near Heber Springs, north of Little Rock. Most of the course is hilly with tree-lined fairways. It measures 3,220 yards. Par is 36.

Two of the newer—and better—courses in Arkansas are part of real estate developments. Bella Vista Country Club in the northwest corner of the state, and Cherokee Village Country Club, on the northeast border, are basically for those who buy property. But tourists can arrange to play by paying green fees and agreeing to look at property.

Since Arkansas's terrain varies so much—from the flat delta land along the Mississippi River to the emerald mountains of the Ozarks —it is possible to find almost any kind of golf course within its boundaries. Here are a few of the courses that will really give you a challenge:

LOCATION	COURSE	HOLES/PAR/ YARDAGE	TYPE
Bella Vista	Bella Vista Village CC	18/72/7,080	SP
Fayetteville	Paradise Valley GC	18/72/7,198	Pub
Hardy	Cherokee Village CC	18/72/7,051	Pub
Heber Springs	Red Apple CC	9/36/3,376	R
Hot Springs	Belvedere CC	18/72/6,700	SP
Hot Springs	Hot Springs G & CC	18/72/6,923	SP
		18/72/6,865	
Hot Springs	Hot Springs Village CC	18/72/6,770	R
Little Rock	Rebsamen Park GC	18/72/6,207	Pub
		9/35/2,797	
Little Rock	Riverdale CC	18/72/6,661	SP
Siloam Springs	Dawn Hill CC	18/72/6,390	R

Tips on the South. When playing southern, you'll find that the soil is a bit harder, being sand and clay, with Bermuda grass and rye grass the standard types.

In the Northeast, both the turf and the soil are soft, and you have no difficulty driving the clubhead through. Even with a tight lie, you can "go after" the ball without fear of a mis-hit. This is because you don't have to worry about hitting it absolutely flush. But in the South the great percentage of tight lies, with a concretelike soil, demand great concentration on hitting the ball squarely. Thus instead of a descending swing, you must concentrate on staying with the shot. The key here is to concentrate on keeping your head fixed, so that your arc doesn't move and cause you to drive the clubhead into unyielding soil or bounce up and belly into the ball.

The greens, which will be either Bermuda or rye or a combination of both, will almost always be slower than they are in the North. While they may appear fast, you will find that you are leaving most of your putts short unless you become a bit more aggressive with your putter. On the greens you will have to contend with a minimum of break, because the coarse blades of grass keep the ball from sliding off too much.

The rough in the South is not as deadly as it is in the North, because, for the most part, you will find tall pines or palm trees where the foliage starts growing out at a good height. Under such conditions, you will find it possible much of the time to make fairly successful recoveries.

In Florida, on the whole, you will find a rough much less demanding. At times your lie can be even better than on the fairway, because the grass is so thick and wiry that the ball tends to sit right up on top. We've seen instances where it sat up so well that you could take a driver if you wanted to. There are courses in Florida, however, where there is a great deal of sand in the rough. Under such conditions, once again, be certain that you keep your head still and plant your feet firmly. It is also a good idea to use one more club than usual—say a 5-iron instead of a 6.

5

THE UNITED STATES: FLORIDA

Florida, Uncle Sam's green-thumb playground that juts into the blue-green Atlantic and the Gulf of Mexico, could well be called the winter resort golf capital of the world. Not only has the Sunshine State more than three hundred golf courses from Pensacola to Key West, but among those three hundred are some of the finest golf resorts anywhere.

Though central and south Florida garner a large majority of sunseeking linksters during the winter months, there are a couple of resorts in the northern part of the state that offer a good starting point for our section on Florida.

NORTHERN FLORIDA

When Henry Flagler built his marvelous Ponce de Leon Lodge Hotel in St. Augustine just before the turn of the century, few golfing buffs (and there were only a few in those days) would have predicted that the entire northern portion of Florida would become one of the most attractive golf meccas in the country.

Pensacola now boasts a total of eight fine courses. The Osceola, Pensacola's original course, has been refurbished into a fine layout, and a few years ago Doug Ford took a beautiful site on Perdido Bay and turned it into the superb Perdido Bay Inn and Country Club. A testy course that measures 6,915 yards with a par 72, Ford's course features Ormond hybrid Bermuda grass and is open to members, guests, and out-of-town visitors. This course is a real buster, so bring your long irons.

Other top courses in Pensacola include the Scenic Hills Country Club, 6,972 yards, par 72; the Pensacola Country Club, 6,412 yards, par 72; the C.E.R.A. Golf Club course, 6,550 yards, par 71; the Naval Air Station course, 6,464 yards, par 72; and the St. Regis Golf Club, a fine 9-holer at nearby Cantonment.

Moving eastward along the strip, we come to Panama City, a fabulous new playground for the nation's tourists. Panama City has had a country club since 1926, actually, but it did not receive too much recognition outside Bay County. Now that thriving seashore resort has, in addition to the private Panama City Country Club, the semi-public Signal Hill Golf and Country Club. Signal Hill is located right off U.S. Highway 98, which is the throbbing ribbon of commerce along the white beaches. It features a full 18-hole course of 6,004 yards with a par 68. Another interesting semiprivate course is the long 18-hole Bay West Lodge and Golf Course.

North of Panama City is the little city of Marianna, on U.S. Highway 90. And right near Marianna is Florida Caverns State Park, with a 9-hole golf course that was constructed along the lines of venerable old St. Andrews in Scotland.

The Ponte Vedra Club's famous island ninth hole.

Florida's capital city, Tallahassee, once had only an 18-hole municipal course. Since 1956, however, the Capital City Country Club has been converted into a private course and is rated one of the toughest in the southland. As a matter of fact, CCCC's par-3 sixteenth hole, a 227-yarder, has been classified as the toughest 3 par in the state, and that takes in more than four hundred courses.

Tallahassee now has an 18-hole, par-56 course, Oak Valley, which is lighted for night play and Florida State University has a fine 9-hole layout that will test the skill of any golfer. The long private Killearn Country Club course is just north of Tallahassee.

Jacksonville, Florida's Gateway City on the northeast coast, where golfers used to have to stand in line from dawn to dusk to get to play on two municipal layouts, now has no fewer than eight fine courses. Jacksonville Beach, which did not know what a golf course looked like right after World War II (except for classic Ponte Vedra, just south of Jacksonville Beach), now has three outstanding clubs. They include Selva Marina, a championship course of 6,906 yards, par 72; the Jacksonville Beach Golf Club, an excellent public course of 6,395 yards and a par 72; and, of course, beautiful Ponte Vedra.

Jacksonville no longer has any municipal courses, but semiprivate layouts include Brentwood Golf Club, the Dunes Golf and Country, the Pine Tree Golf Club, and the Hyde Park Golf and Country. Private clubs that grant playing privileges to guests include the famous Timuquana Country Club, University Country Club and Duclay Golf and Country Club. However, the following are the best courses that we *all* can play while in northern Florida:

LOCATION	COURSE	HOLES/PAR/ YARDAGE	TYPE
Gulf Breeze	Santa Rosa Shores CC	18/72/6,970	SP
Jacksonville	Baymeadows GC	18/72/6,800	SP
Jacksonville	Brentwood GC	18/72/6,340	Pub
Jacksonville	Pine Tree GC	18/72/6,698	SP
Jacksonville Beach	Jacksonville Beach GC	18/72/6,395	Pub
Panama City Beach	Bay West Lodge & GC	18/72/6,990	SP
Panama City Beach	Signal Hill CC	18/68/6,001	R
Pensacola	Perdido Bay Inn & CC	18/72/6,411	R
Ponte Vedra Beach	Ponte Vedra Club	18/72/6,735	R
St. Augustine	Ponce de Leon Lodge & CC	18/71/6,226	R
Tallahassee	Killearn G & CC	18/72/6,316	Pvt

CENTRAL FLORIDA

As we head south, the number of golf facilities increases. Daytona Beach, for instance, features the Daytona Golf and Country Club, a 6,369-yard, par-72 course, and the Oceanside course, measuring 6,262 yards long and also plays to a par 71. Tomoka Golf and Country Club is built on the highest ground in the Daytona Beach area and looks like many northern golf courses with rolling terrain and fairways lined with pine trees.

Leesburg, just north of Orlando, has two fine courses. The Floridan Country Club, just five minutes off the Sunshine Parkway, is 6,250 yards and has a par 70. The Silver Lake Golf and Country Club is just east of the city on Highway 441 and has 6,412 yards, a par 72.

At nearby Eustis, on State Road 19, is the Pine Meadows Golf and Country Club, which is 6,531 yards in length. Mount Dora Golf Club is just right for short shooters, having 5,755 yards and playing to a par 70.

At Ocala, surrounded by Florida's famous thoroughbred horse breeding farms, is the old established Ocala golf course, one of the finest in the state, and the plush Golden Hills Turf and Country Club.

Another big golfing center in north-central Florida is, of course, Orlando. This booming metropolis features 14 fine courses, running the gamut from public to semiprivate to private. Leading courses include the Bay Hill Club, a 7,124-yard beauty, playing to a par 72; Rio Pinar Country Club, 6,812 yards, par 72; the famous Dubsdread Country Club in downtown Orlando, a 6,485-yard, par-72 course; and the Land O'Lakes Country Club, 6,200 yards, par 72.

Other leading courses in the Orlando area are the Mid-Florida Country Club, 6,624 yards, par 72; Orange Hill Country Club, 6,600 yards, par 71; and Rocket City Country Club, 6,340 yards, par 72.

Lakeland, between Orlando and Tampa, features three 18-hole layouts, including the Cleveland Heights Golf and Country Club, a 6,334-yard course with a par 72. The William Hutcheson golf course is a fine 18-hole layout that visitors can play.

On the west coast we have at Tampa Rocky Point Golf Club, a long 7,143-yard, par-72 affair; Rogers Park Golf Course; Loch Raven Golf Club, and Silver Lake Golf and Country Club. Also nearby are the Apollo Beach and Surf Club, and at Sun City, the fine Sun City Golf Club.

At St. Petersburg and Clearwater you will find such fine courses as

Airco Golf Course, Pasadena Golf Club, Seminole Lake Country Club, Sunset Golf Course, and Belleview Biltmore. The latter has two courses: the West Course measures 6,367 yards and has a par 71, while the East Course is par-70, 5,896 yards. Of course, one of the finest courses in central Florida is at the Innisbrook Golf and Country Club. Actually, there are three courses at Innisbrook: a championship Island Course, the shorter Sandpiper Course, and a par-60 executive course.

At the Paradise Country Club, the Crystal River and Kings Bay provide plenty of water worries to the visiting golfer.

The Island Course is not what one would expect to find in central Florida. In fact, it is much more reminiscent of the Carolinas, for elevation ranges from seven feet to sixty feet, and the rolling hills of the course with fairways fringed with Spanish moss, bearded strands of cypress, pine, and live oak make it unique. A reminder that one actually is in Florida is thrown in for spice where two of the fairways are bordered by citrus groves. Ten of the 18 holes of the Island Course play either along or across water. Interestingly, the Innisbrook resort property of some nine hundred acres has approximately sixty fresh-water lakes scattered through it.

Up the coast, at Crystal River, there are fine courses at the Plantation Hotel and Paradise Country Club. There are many good courses in central Florida, but for challenging golf we would suggest any of the following:

LOCATION	COURSE	HOLES/PAR/ YARDAGE	TYPE
Avon Park	Avon Park GC	18/72/6,537	Pub
Clearwater	Belleview Biltmore GC	18/71/6,367	R
		18/70/5,896	
Clearwater	Clearwater CC	18/72/6,112	SP
Clearwater	Cove Cay G & TC	18/70/5,796	SP
Clearwater	Pelican CC	18/72/6,582	SP
Cocoa Beach	Cocoa Beach GC	18/72/6,842	Pub
Crystal River	Paradise CC	18/72/6,805	SP
Crystal River	Plantation Hotel CC	18/72/6,838	R
Daytona Beach	Daytona Beach G & CC	18/72/6,369	Pub
		18/71/6,262	
Deltona	Deltona G & CC	18/72/6,689	Pvt
Doctor Phillips	Bay Hill Club	18/72/6,347	R
		9/36/3,448	
Dunedin	Dunedin CC	18/72/6,660	SP
Howey-in-the-Hills	Mission Inc. & CC	18/70/6,122	R
Lake Buena Vista	Walt Disney World GC	18/72/6,550	R
		18/72/6,410	
Lakeland	Cleveland Hts. GC	18/72/6,312	SP
Lakeland	William L. Hutcheson GC	18/72/6,540	Pub
Leesburg	Silver Lake G & CC	18/72/6,403	SP
Longwood	Mid-Florida GC	18/72/6,221	SP
Ocala	Silver Springs Shores CC	18/71/6,745	SP
New Smyrna Beach	Sugar Mill GC	18/72/6,550	SP
Orlando	Alhambra G & CC	18/72/6,750	Pub
Orlando	Cypress Creek GC	18/72/6,465	SP
Ormond Beach	Ormond Beach CC	18/71/6,133	SP
Ormond Beach	Tomoka Oak G & CC	18/72/6,725	SP
Sandord	Mayfair CC	18/72/6,490	SP
St. Petersburg	Airco GC	18/72/6,100	SP
St. Petersburg	Bardmoor CC	18/72/6,800	SP
		9/36/3,285	
St. Petersburg	Pasadena GC	18/71/6,226	SP
St. Petersburg	Seminole GC	18/72/6,504	SP
St. Petersburg	Sunset GC	18/71/6,288	SP
Sun City Center	Sun City GC	18/72/6,875	SP

LOCATION	COURSE	HOLES/PAR/ YARDAGE	TYPE
Tampa	Peble Creek G & CC	18/72/6,417	Pub
Tampa	Quail Hollow GC	18/72/6,739	SP
Tampa	Rocky Point GC	18/72/7,143	SP
Tampa	Rogers Park GC	18/71/6,677	Pub
Tampa	U. of So. Florida GC	18/72/6,962	SP
Tarpon Springs	Innisbrook G & CC	18/72/6,745	R
		18/72/6,328	
		18/71/7,065	
Tarpon Springs	Tarpon Springs GC	18/71/6,455	SP
Titusville	Royal Oak CC & Lodge	18/71/6,615	R
Williston Highlands	Williston Highlands GC	18/72/6,446	SP
Winter Haven	Willow Brook GC	18/72/6,421	Pub

SOUTHERN FLORIDA

For the most part southern Florida in winter is just like springtime in the North. Winter rates prevail on most courses in this region of the state and these rates, on courses where everyone is welcome to play, will range from a low of $3.50 to a high of about $10 or $18, depending upon the locale. Southern Florida's "in-season" arbitrarily begins December 15 and runs until Easter, give or take a week or two. Do not let those large daily rates for American or Modified American Plans scare you. You will save money. While rates for European Plans (no meals included) are less, it costs more paying separately for each meal. Much time and aggravation can be saved if you accept the fact that you must reserve a tee time. At most resorts and second-home complexes two days in advance is average.

Golf courses are all over southern Florida. In fact, many of the new courses have been constructed on seldom-used islands, such as the magnificent Longboat Key golf course near Sarasota and the new Marco Island resort course down in the heart of the famous Ten Thousand Islands. It was but a few years ago that the Ten Thousand Islands, on the western reaches of the Everglades, attracted nothing, but pioneers and hardy fishermen. Nowadays it is not at all unusual to see golfers in their sportiest attire mingling with the fishermen and the natives as they pursue their favorite pastime among the deep foliage of Everglades country.

The well-known resort areas, such as Miami, Palm Beach, Hollywood, Fort Lauderdale, Sarasota, Naples, etc., have gone into "average golfer" business with gusto. Sure, there are still the exclusive clubs where only the well-heeled can play. There are probably more of these clubs than ever before, but the increase of really fine courses for tourist play has outstripped blue-chip outfits.

The biggest boost occurred ten to fifteen years ago. It was then that resort layouts like Doral in Miami, the Diplomat in Hollywood, St.

Doral Country Club
MIAMI, FLORIDA
U.S.G.A. RULES APPLY

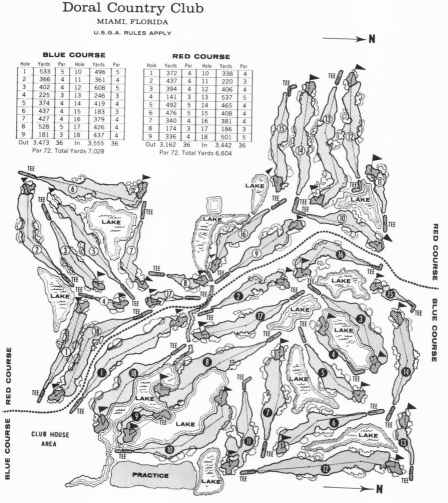

BLUE COURSE

Hole	Yards	Par	Hole	Yards	Par
1	533	5	10	496	5
2	366	4	11	361	4
3	402	4	12	608	5
4	225	3	13	246	3
5	374	4	14	419	4
6	437	4	15	183	3
7	427	4	16	379	4
8	528	5	17	426	4
9	181	3	18	437	4
Out	3,473	36	In	3,555	36

Par 72, Total Yards 7,028

RED COURSE

Hole	Yards	Par	Hole	Yards	Par
1	372	4	10	338	4
2	437	4	11	220	3
3	394	4	12	406	4
4	141	3	13	537	5
5	492	5	14	465	4
6	476	5	15	408	4
7	340	4	16	381	4
8	174	3	17	186	3
9	336	4	18	501	5
Out	3,162	36	In	3,442	36

Par 72, Total Yards 6,604

The layout of two of Doral Country Club's three famed courses.

Lucie Hilton Inn and Country Club at Port St. Lucie, Lehigh Acres near Fort Myers, and several other spots dotting the region began offering magnificent golf courses, plush accommodations, nearby beaches and other attractions, all at a price the whole family could afford. In addition, many resort cities such as Miami and Palm Beach established municipal courses that would rank as first-rate private layouts nearly anywhere in the world.

The flood of golfers each winter has even reached the Florida Keys. An old established course, Ocean Reef, caters to the yacht-club set and homeowners on upper Key Largo, but Key West has a fine course for visitors and natives alike, and the Sombrero Country Club at Marathon is a lengthy layout that is still having growing pains.

Par-3 courses in Florida have become a way of life. There is hardly a community worthy of the name that does not boast a fine par-3 course, and many of them are lighted for night play. Night play is beginning to attract some attention for full-sized courses, too. As a matter of fact, there are two full-sized courses lit for night play in Miami—the Colonial Palms and Miami Lakes. In addition, the Doral Country Club has nine holes lighted and there are two par 3's for night play in Greater Miami.

It was not too many years ago that "weekenders," those golfers just looking for a place to whack it around on Saturdays and Sundays, were pretty much out of luck. The municipal courses were few and far between, and what courses were in operation were not exactly ideal. Operation was casual, at best, and though the price was right, in most cases golf was a chore. This has all changed. Now, nearly every city in southern Florida has at least one municipal course, with the larger metropolitan areas boasting two, three, or even four. And these courses are meticulous. They are of championship caliber and green fees are reasonable.

The surge in municipally owned courses, of course, came about in the main because of population growth. In the past decade running a municipal golf course has changed from a liability to a profit. Well-known pros are beginning to come into the picture as home pros, and the courses more than fill the need of native Floridians as well as tourists.

Another aspect of Florida golf that separates the Sunshine State from most other vacation regions is the golf-club community. These are beautiful courses that are constructed as a part of a housing development. Most of them in southern Florida aim for the middle-income group with homes in the $25,000–$45,000 price range. These courses also are open to public play in most instances, or are on the basis of guest play with members.

Several of Florida's famous resort hotels, such as the Breakers in Palm Beach and the Hollywood Beach Hotel, have their own courses or have specific arrangements with a nearby country club where their guests can play without charge or for a small fee. Perhaps Florida's most famous resort hotel of long standing is the Boca Raton Hotel and Club. Whether you play Boca from the 6,735-yard championship tees or from the 6,277-yard members' tees, par is 36/35—71 (ladies' par is 37/36—73 over 5,769 yards) and with the prevailing wind right off the ocean from the east or southeast, it does not take you long to realize that the apparent easiness of the layout is a delusion. The course has *328* Bermuda greens and St. Lucie Bermuda

Palm trees and water add charm—but trouble—to Boca Raton Hotel course.

fairways, but when the wind whistles some of the world's finest amateurs have found the kitten to be a tiger.

Several golf clubs, such as DeSoto Lakes in Sarasota, feature small lodges and cottages for their customers' convenience, and the St. Lucie Country Club and Villas at Port St. Lucie are most attractive.

Attempting to list every course in southern Florida available for play by visitors would be like trying to write the Old Testament on the head of a pin. As with other states and parts of Florida, the following listing of resorts, top semiprivate and municipal courses indicate the availability of some of Florida's leading courses in various sections of the state.

LOCATION	*COURSE*	*HOLES/PAR/ YARDAGE*	*TYPE*
Broward County			
Fort Lauderdale	Bonadventure CC	18/72/6,515	SP
Fort Lauderdale	Lago Mar CC	18/72/6,750	Pvt
Fort Lauderdale	Oak Ridge CC	18/72/6,517	SP
Fort Lauderdale	Plantation GC	18/72/6,925	SP
Fort Lauderdale	Rolling Hills Lodge & CC	18/72/6,550	R
Fort Lauderdale	Sunrise CC	18/72/6,900	SP
Hollywood	Diplomat Hotel & CC	18/72/6,552 18/72/6,702	R
Hollywood	Fairways GC	18/72/6,840	SP
Hollywood	Hollywood Beach Hotel & CC	18/70/6,479 18/72/6,350	R
Hollywood	Hollywood Lakes CC	18/72/6,238 18/72/6,660	SP
Hollywood	Orange Brook GC	18/72/6,311	Pub
Lauderhill	Inverrary CC	18/72/6,444 18/71/6,715	SP
Plantation	Jacaranda CC	18/72/7,194	SP
Pompano Beach	Crystal Lago CC	18/72/6,884	R
Pompano Beach	Palm-Aire Lodge & CC	18/72/7,120 18/72/6,650 18/72/6,896	R
Pompano Beach	Pompano Beach GC	18/72/6,753 18/72/6,275	SP

LOCATION	COURSE	HOLES/PAR/ YARDAGE	TYPE
Pompano Beach	The Woodlands CC	18/72/6,955	SP
		18/72/6,750	
Dade County			
Biscayne Village	Adventura GC	18/72/6,377	SP
Coral Gables	Biltmore GC	18/71/6,563	Pub
Homestead	Redland G & CC	18/72/6,700	SP
Key Biscayne	Key Biscayne GC	18/72/7,294	SP
Miami	CC of Miami	18/72/7,100	Pvt
		18/72/6,927	
		18/72/6,821	
Miami	Diplomat GC	18/72/6,964	SP
Miami	Doral CC	18/72/6,324	R
		18/72/6,726	
		18/72/7,028	
		18/72/7,258	
Miami	Fontainebleau CC	18/72/7,121	Pub
Miami	Kings Bay Y & CC	18/72/6,834	Pvt
Miami	Lejeune GC	18/72/6,400	Pub
Miami	Miami Lakes Inn & CC	18/72/7,039	R
Miami	Palmetto GC	18/71/6,669	Pub
Miami	North Dade CC	18/72/6,337	SP
Miami Beach	Bayshore GC	18/72/6,893	Pub
Miami Beach	Normandy Shores GC	18/71/6,055	Pub
Miami Springs	Miami Shores G & CC	18/71/6,730	SP
Palm Beach County			
Boca Raton	Boca Raton Hotel & CC	18/71/6,500	R
Boca Raton	Boca Raton West GC	18/72/6,165	R
		18/72/6,400	
Boca Raton	Boca Teeca G & CC	18/72/6,165	R
Boca Raton	Sandalfoot Cove G & CC	18/72/6,874	SP
Boca Raton	Southern Manor CC	18/71/6,835	SP
Boca Raton	University Park CC	18/72/7,240	SP
Boynton Beach	Cypress Creek CC	18/72/6,808	SP
Delray Beach	Delray Beach CC	18/72/6,987	SP
		9/32/3,270	
Delray Beach	The Hamlet	18/72/6,840	SP
Lake Worth	Palm Beach National G & CC	18/72/6,639	SP

LOCATION	COURSE	HOLES/PAR/ YARDAGE	TYPE
Lantana	Atlantis CC	18/72/6,625	R
		9/36/3,325	
North Palm Beach	North Palm Beach CC	18/72/6,311	SP
Palm Beach	Breakers Ocean GC	18/70/6,008	R
Palm Beach	Royal Palm Beach GC	18/72/6,651	SP
West Palm Beach	Breakers West GC	18/72/6,388	SP
West Palm Beach	The President CC	18/72/6,660	SP
		18/72/6,150	
West Palm Beach	West Palm Beach G & CC	18/72/6,745	Pub

Southern Area and Keys

Boca Grande	Gasparilla Inn & CC	18/72/6,660	R
Cape Haze	Rotonda West GC	18/72/6,381	R
Cape Coral	Cape Coral G & CC	18/72/6,332	SP
Englewood	Englewood CC	18/71/6,412	SP
Fort Meyers	San Carlos Park GC	18/72/6,700	SP
Fort Myers	Cypress Lakes CC	18/72/6,430	Pub
Fort Myers	Fort Myers CC	18/71/6,105	Pub
Fort Pierce	Indian Hills G & CC	18/72/6,250	SP
Key West	Key West CC	18/72/6,300	SP
Lake Placid	Placid Lakes G & CC	18/71/6,844	R
Lehigh Acres	Lehigh Acres CC	18/71/6,710	R
Lehigh Acres	Mirror Lakes CC	18/72/6,722	R
Marco Island	Marco Island GC	18/72/6,651	R
Naples	Golden Gate G & CC	18/72/6,477	R
Naples	Lely G & CC	18/72/6,201	SP
Naples	Naples Beach Club	18/72/6,470	R
Naples	Palm River G & CC	18/72/6,650	SP
North Key Largo	Ocean Reef Club	18/72/6,449	Pvt
		9/36/3,313	
North Port Charlotte	CC of North Port Charlotte	18/72/6,688	SP
Palm Sola	Palma Sola GC	18/71/6,352	SP
Port Charlotte	Port Charlotte CC	18/71/6,643	SP
Port St. Lucie	St. Lucie Hilton Inn & CC	18/72/6,717	R
		18/72/6,429	
Sarasota	Bobby Jones GC	18/72/6,388	Pub
		18/72/6,080	

LOCATION	COURSE	HOLES/PAR/ YARDAGE	TYPE
Sarasota	DeSoto Lakes GC & Lodge	18/72/6,927	R
Sarasota	Longboat Key GC	18/72/6,890	R
Sarasota	Rolling Green GC	18/72/6,550	SP
Sarasota	Sarasota GC	18/72/6,900	SP
Sebring	Harder Hall Hotel GC	18/72/6,793	R
Sebring	Kenilworth Lodge & GC	18/72/6,622	R
Stuart	Martin County G & CC	18/71/6,441	Pub
Venice	Lake Venice GC	18/72/6,902	Pub

6

THE UNITED STATES:
MIDWEST

The Midwest ranks as number one in the nation in the number of public courses. But this region has few resort-type courses. Outside of Michigan, Minnesota, and Wisconsin, courses of this type are very rare indeed.

Let's look at the range of courses available to the tourist golfer in the Midwest.

ILLINOIS

The Chicago–Cook County area contains more public and semi-private courses available to golfers on a green-fee basis than any other major city in the United States. But still, it's not wise for the touring golfer to plan to do too much golfing in the Chicago area. Like most major cities, Chicago's public courses are crowded.

There are, however, many excellent layouts to be played while in Ilinois. Here are some of the better courses you can play:

LOCATION	COURSE	HOLES/PAR/ YARDAGE	TYPE
Carterville	Crab Orchard GC	18/70/6,285	SP
Bensenville	White Pines GC	18/70/6,331	SP
		18/70/6,234	
Bloomingdale	Indian Lakes CC	18/72/6,995	SP
		18/72/7,040	
Flossmoor	Cherry Hills CC	18/72/6,412	SP
		9/33/2,464	
Glenwood	Glenwoodie CC	18/72/6,667	SP
Hoffman Estates	Hilldale GC	18/72/6,397	SP
LaGrange	Timber Trails CC	18/71/6,396	SP
		18/70/6,035	
Lemont	Cog Hill G & CC	18/71/6,332	SP
		18/72/6,309	
		18/72/6,431	
		18/72/6,540	

LOCATION	COURSE	HOLES/PAR/YARDAGE	TYPE
Lisle	Woodridge GC	18/71/6,396	SP
Mt. Prospect	Old Orchard CC	18/70/6,035 18/71/6,875 9/35/2,857	SP
Mt. Vernon	Indian Hills GC	18/72/6,034	Pub
Mundelein	Countryside GC	18/73/6,545	SP
Northbrook	Sportsman CC	18/72/6,514 18/72/6,232 9/35/3,091	SP
Oak Brook	Midwest CC	18/71/6,380	SP
Orland Park	Silver Lake CC	18/72/6,320 18/70/6,005	SP
Palos Park	Palos CC	18/72/6,780 18/72/6,451 9/36/3,189	SP
Prospect Heights	Rob Roy GC	18/71/6,300	SP
Rockton	Macktown GC	18/72/5,935	R
Schaumburg	Golden Acres CC	18/72/6,500 9/36/3,200	SP
St. Charles	Pheasant Run Lodge GC	18/72/6,826	R
Wadsworth	Midlane Farm CC	18/72/7,130	SP
Wheaton	Arrowhead GC	18/72/6,500	SP

INDIANA

French Lick, Indiana was the site of one of the United States' early plush resorts. While the hotel had its ups and downs until 1955 when the Sheraton Hotel chain purchased it, today the old structure has been completely renovated and a second 18 has been added to the one built in the early 1900's.

The state of Indiana has over fifty municipal courses, of which 35 are 18-hole layouts. The Raber Public course in Elkhart, Shady Hills GC in Marion, American Legion GC in New Castle, La Fontaine GC in Huntington, Rozella Ford GC in Warsaw, South Shore GC in Syracuse, Lake Hills G & CC in St. John, Pheasant Valley CC in Crown Point, and the Indiana University GC in Bloomington are all public courses worthy of a stop. A complete rundown of the better courses that you can play while in Indiana follows:

LOCATION	COURSE	HOLES/PAR/ YARDAGE	TYPE
Bloomington	Indiana University GC	18/71/6,834	Pub
Columbus	Otter Creek GC	18/72/7,054	Pub
Elkhart	Elkhart Lodge & CC	18/72/6,345	SP
Fort Wayne	Elks CC	18/72/6,545	SP
French Lick	Sheraton CC	18/72/6,777	R
French Lick	Sheraton Valley CC	18/72/6,068	R
Indianapolis	Coffin GC	18/70/6,825	Pub
Indianapolis	Speedway "500" GC	18/72/7,179 9/36/3,486	SP
LaPorte	Beechwood GC	18/72/6,674	Pub
Santa Claus	Christmas Lake G & CC	18/72/6,500	Pub
West Lafayette	Purdue University GC	18/71/6,856 18/71/6,432	Pub

IOWA

In the tall-corn state of Iowa, there are approximately 260 courses, but only about 50 of them are 18-hole layouts. Fortunately, over half of these courses are public and are open to the visiting golfer. Here are the ones considered most challenging:

LOCATION	COURSE	HOLES/PAR/ YARDAGE	TYPE
Cedar Rapids	Ellis Park GC	18/72/6,515	Pub
Davenport	Emels GC	18/72/7,000	Pub
Iowa City	Finkbine GC	18/72/6,600	Pub
Spirit Lake	Okaboji V GC	18/71/6,215	R

KANSAS

The Midwest's western tier—Kansas, Nebraska, South and North Dakota—are not exactly crowded with challenging courses. True, the Sunflower State has over 180 golf courses, but only a few can be considered interesting enough for the tourist golfer. It's important, however, to keep in mind that many of Kansas' southern courses are open year round. This is also true in southern Missouri.

Kansas golf courses that you may wish to try are:

LOCATION	COURSE	HOLES/PAR/ YARDAGE	TYPE
Great Bend	Lake Barton GC	18/72/6,300	SP
Manhattan	Stagg Hill GC	18/72/6,327	SP
Olathe	St. Andrews CC	18/72/6,698	SP
Piper	Dub's Dread GC	18/73/8,101	Pvt
Wichita	MacDonald GC	18/71/6,825	Pub

MICHIGAN

Michigan, practically surrounded on three sides by Lake Erie, Lake Michigan, and Lake Huron, features courses which are perhaps more heavily wooded than most of the layouts in the Midwest. This is especially true of northwestern Michigan in the Boyne Country resort area.

Golf at Boyne Country is a pure golfing experience. And the Boyne Country courses have been made tough on purpose. Liberties have been taken with the courses' basic design to lift them out of the realm of the ordinary. Every hole is a challenge.

Boyne Highlands, near Harbor Springs, was designed by Robert Trent Jones. Because the tees range in length from 100 to 220 yards, the tee markers are all placed in sequence so that the course length can be 5,600; 6,000; 6,400; 6,600; and 7,200 yards. The tremendous flexibility of the tees has two basic advantages. No one can say the course is too long when he can choose the length he prefers to play. Second, everybody, from his particular driving position, can arrive at the same target area from the tee, with relatively comparable shots to the green.

Boyne Highlands is unique in that it has Pencross bent grass for tees, fairways, and greens. This newest seed bent was developed from a mutation of three parent strains by Dr. Bart Musser at Penn State. Simplifying general course maintenance is an automatic, electronically controlled watering system which waters the entire course in six hours.

Jones has come up with some water holes at Boyne Highlands that he compares to the famous No. 16 at Augusta National, No. 4 at Baltusrol, and No. 18 at Denver's Cherry Hills. Calling for demanding shots over 606-yard No. 9 (played from the back tee), and the closing hole, No. 18 where after a downhill drive of 300 yards, the player is faced with a 165-yard shot across water, unless he takes an alternate route.

The greens are masterpieces of mounds and swells, blending in with the flow of curving lines, creating approximately 10 to 15 possible cup changes on each hole, ranging from easy to difficult. "Even without varying wind conditions, because of the extreme length of the tees and the many cupping areas on the greens, the course has hundreds of possible changes," says Jones. "It'll take care of the duffers as well as the ego-saturated amateurs and the country's top pros," says Jones.

Another 18-hole championship golf course in the Boyne Country golf complex is the Boyne Mountain course, which was designed by William Newcomb, an imaginative Ann Arbor golf architect. This course has all of the unique features and benefits of a true mountain course without the climbing. A player can shoot from a high tee downhill. No. 1 tee is approximately one and a half miles to No. 18 and

Water and natural growth create problems for the golfer visiting Boyne Mountain course.

The famed Grand Hotel on Mackinac Island.

the club house. And the player approaches each tee downhill through a network of narrow, wooded mountain trails. Each fairway and green has its own separate setting with a completely new identity and challenge. Since the Boyne Mountain course fairways are continuous, there is no adjacent fairway play.

While the Boyne Mountain course is championship length, the emphasis is on strategic play. Each hole demands a carefully placed drive. The position of the drive determines the difficulty of the next shot. The scores recorded on the mountain course will reflect the player's ability to play strategic golf.

This mountain course makes a radical departure from classic trap design to offer the most intriguing variety of traps possible. The sand ranges from coarse to fine. Many of the traps are smooth, but the golfer may also find deep-furrowed or wide-raked traps, or some which are purposely unmaintained.

Land contours on the course were left relatively undisturbed to preserve the natural setting of Boyne Country. The course's topography with its gullies, gently sloping hills, and the beautiful vista of the Deer Lake Valley extending southwestward makes it one of the most scenic courses in the United States. The well-trapped greens, eight holes over mountain lakes, and intersection of three thousand acres of rolling mountain timberland will make it equal, if not superior to, the Boyne Highlands course.

One of Michigan's most famous resort centers is Mackinac Island. Known as the horse and buggy summer capital, this island is tucked between the upper and lower peninsulas of the state. There are two 9-hole courses on the island. The Grand Hotel Golf Course is 3,000 yards long and the municipal course is 3,300 yards. The island is marked by its nineteenth-century tempo. All autos are banned, and transportation is by horse and carriage, foot and bicycle. Main Street is lined with charming shops and curio stores, and there's even a boardwalk a few minutes from downtown.

Here are some of the other courses you may wish to play while paying a visit to the state of Michigan:

LOCATION	*COURSE*	*HOLES/PAR/ YARDAGE*	*TYPE*
Alto	Saskatoon GC	18/72/6,500	SP
Boyne Falls	Boyne Mountain Alpine GC	18/72/6,627	R
Carleton	Carleton Glen GC	18/71/6,350	SP
Dearborn	Warren Valley GC	18/72/6,246	Pub
		18/71/6,072	
Fenton	Tyrone Hills GC	18/72/6,700	SP
Harbor Spring	Boyne Highlands GC	18/72/6,450	R
		18/72/6,900	
Jackson	Casades GC	18/72/6,700	Pub
Lake Orion	Bald Mountain GC	18/71/6,206	SP
Mackinac Island	Grand Hotel	9/34/2,710	R
Pinckney	Push Lake Hills GC	18/73/7,110	R
Pontiac	Pontiac CC	18/72/6,315	SP
St. Clair	St. Clair Inn & CC	18/71/6,210	R
Wayne	Birch Hill CC	18/70/6,370	Pub

MINNESOTA

In the central portion of the land-of-sky-blue-waters, excellent lakeside and rolling-hill courses add a new dimension to the vacationing golfer's world. While most of the courses are 9-hole layouts, they can be quite challenging.

The Madden Lodge and Inn golf course located in Minnesota's lake country.

Minnesota's range of courses can best be shown by three typical courses. First, the *hilly* Detroit Country Club at Detroit Lakes, two hundred miles northwest of Minneapolis, is a tight, lush 9-hole layout. It's here that the hills gradually flatten out before one reaches the prairie lands of North Dakota. Then in Brainerd, less than one hundred miles north of Minneapolis, is Madden Lodge & Inn, where golfers can lower their handicaps on a *flat* 18-hole layout with small greens and grass bunkers. Finally the Bemidji Town & Country Club, rising above Lake Bemidji, is 120 miles northeast of Duluth and is one of the oldest and best groomed *lakeside* courses in Minnesota. Most of this state's courses can be classified as hilly or lakeside.

In the Minneapolis-St. Paul area, there are several excellent public courses including Keller Municipal Golf Course and Dellwood National Golf Course. Duluth, on the western tip of Lake Superior, is also an excellent golfing area with a satisfying number of courses open to the touring golfer.

LOCATION	COURSE	HOLES/PAR/ YARDAGE	TYPE
Albert Lea	Albert Lea CC	9/35/2,950	SP
Albert Lea	Green Lea GC	18/73/6,415	Pub
Alexandria	Alexandria GC	18/72/6,375	SP
Bemidji	Bemidji T & CC	18/72/6,309	SP

LOCATION	COURSE	HOLES/PAR/ YARDAGE	TYPE
Brainerd	Madden Inn & GC	18/72/6,150	Pub
Detroit Lakes	Detroit Lakes CC	18/71/6,009	Pub
Duluth	Lester Park GC	18/72/6,382	Pub
Hopkins	Eden Prairie GC	18/72/6,372	SP
Mankato	Mankato GC	18/72/6,195	Pvt
Falcon Heights	University of Minnesota GC	18/71/6,100	SP
St. Paul	Highland Park GC	18/72/6,350	Pub
St. Paul	Keller GC	18/72/6,557	SP
Rochester	Maple Valley G & CC	18/72/6,975	SP
St. Cloud	St. Cloud CC	18/72/6,700	SP
Worthington	Worthington CC	18/71/6,200	SP

MISSOURI

Missouri has more than two hundred regulation courses, but over half of these are private. The public courses, especially in Kansas City, are worth a stop. The Swope Park and Minor Park courses are very challenging and are kept in good condition. There are several semiprivate courses in the Missouri Ozarks and a very fine one at Excelsior Springs —about 28 miles from Kansas City.

The following are some of the more interesting Missouri courses that you can play:

LOCATION	COURSE	HOLES/PAR/ YARDAGE	TYPE
Belton	Southview GC	18/72/6,160	Pub
Chesterfield	River Valley GC	9/36/3,307	Pub
Excelsior Springs	Excelsior Springs GC	18/72/6,418	SP
Florissant	Paddock CC	18/72/6,300	SP
Kansas City	Minor Park GC	18/70/6,210	Pub
Kansas City	Swope Park GC	18/72/6,255 9/36/3,015	Pub
St. Louis	Forest Park Municipal GC	18/70/6,016	Pub

NEBRASKA

As previously noted, the Midwest's western tier, which includes Nebraska, isn't crowded with superior golf courses. Of the state's 140 courses, only about six 18-hole layouts are open to the touring golfer. In addition there are approximately 65 9-hole courses, several of which are worth a stop.

LOCATION	COURSE	HOLES/PAR/ YARDAGE	TYPE
Alliance	Municipal GC	18/72/6,812	Pub
Elkhorn	Chapel Hill CC	18/72/7,150	SP
Lincoln	Homes Park GC	18/72/6,449	Pub
Omaha	Benson Park GC	18/72/6,410	Pub
Omaha	Miracle Hill	18/70/6,344	Pub
Scottsbluff	Riverview GC	18/70/6,224	SP

NORTH DAKOTA

On a trip across the state of North Dakota, the following courses are worth a stop:

LOCATION	COURSE	HOLES/PAR/ YARDAGE	TYPE
Fargo	Edgewood GC	18/72/6,330	Pub
Grand Forks	Grand Forks CC	18/72/6,980	SP
Minot	Minot CC	18/72/6,475	SP
Wahpeton	Bois de Sioux CC	18/72/6,520	SP

OHIO

In total numbers, Ohio is the "big" golf state in the Midwest. There are approximately five hundred regulation golf facilities in the state and over three hundred of them will welcome the traveling golfer. There are good public and semiprivate courses in and around Toledo and Cleveland along Lake Erie, Akron and Youngstown in the northeastern section, centrally located Columbus, and Cincinnati and Dayton in the southwest.

Ohio also has several excellent resort courses. For example, at state park facilities at Newbury, Oxford, and Glouster, there are good little courses, and the resort area around Warren has two excellent courses: Avalon and Avalon Lakes. The latter, designed by Pete Dye, measures 7,001 yards from the championship tees and is a par 71. As further evidence of its championship caliber, the greens average about 10,000 square feet with large teeing areas averaging about 5,000 square feet. The greens and collars were stolonized from Toronto Bent grass, assuring the best quality putting surface. The fairways and tees were all seeded with Highland and Penn Cross bent with bluegrass and fescues used predominantly in the roughs. Gaping sand traps, 65 in number, are filled with pure white silica sand of the finest grade.

The shorter Avalon Course plays at 6,102 yards. It is a sporty course with many doglegs, lateral hazards as well as two lakes which must be conquered. It is well known throughout Ohio as one of the better municipal courses. Other Ohio courses that are good for the touring golfer are:

LOCATION	COURSE	HOLES/PAR/ YARDAGE	TYPE
Akron	Good Park GC	18/70/6,210	Pub
Alliance	Tannenhauf GC	18/72/7,006	SP
Bowling Green	Riverby Hills GC	18/72/6,830	SP
Canton	Tam O'Shanter GC	18/71/6,350	Pub
		18/70/6,178	
Columbus	Minerva Lake GC	18/70/6,010	SP
Galena	Blackhawk GC	18/71/6,524	Pub
Granville	Granville Inn GC	18/71/6,638	R
Hinckley	Hinckley Hills GC	18/70/6,580	SP
Hinckley	Ironwood GC	18/70/6,466	SP
Huron	Thunderbird Hills GC	18/72/6,162	SP
Lima	Tamarac GC	18/72/6,457	Pub
Lima	Westview GC	18/72/6,280	SP
Mansfield	Possum Run GC	18/71/6,200	SP
Mansfield	Twin Lakes GC	18/72/6,276	SP
Marion	Mar-o-del GC	18/72/6,632	Pub
Newark	Licking Springs GC	18/72/6,290	SP
North Olmstead	Springvale CC	18/72/6,230	SP
Olmstead Falls	Homelinks GC	18/72/6,200	SP
Peninsula	Brandywine CC	18/72/6,400	SP
Sidney	Shelby Oaks CC	18/72/6,590	Pub
Toledo	Sunningdale CC	18/71/6,490	Pub
Warren	Avalon Lakes GC	18/71/7,001	Pub
		18/71/6,102	

SOUTH DAKOTA

While there are about ninety regulation golf courses in the state, only ten of them contain 18 holes. And many of the 9-hole courses have sand greens which can prove rather trying for the touring golfer. However, Elmwood Golf Course in Sioux City is one of the most difficult in the country, particularly the back-nine with its tree-lined fairways and its traps located to make approaches hard.

Another fine test is the Elks Country Club in Pierre. This course has the largest greens in South Dakota with the average about eight thousand square feet and three with thirteen thousand feet each. With the large greens and 54 traps, the course is a championship test for pros and amateurs. Other courses worthy of a stop while in South Dakota are:

LOCATION	COURSE	HOLES/PAR/ YARDAGE	TYPE
Pierre	Elks CC	18/72/6,980	SP
Rapid City	Arrowhead CC	18/71/6,100	Pvt
Sioux Falls	Elmwood GC	18/72/6,600	Pub

WISCONSIN

Wisconsin has the greatest number of fine resort courses in the Midwest. Resort courses are located in Door County, on a peninsula that extends into Lake Michigan; in the Dells area in the south-central section; and on the Illinois border around Lake Geneva. Near Lake Geneva is the Playboy course designed by Pete Dye and Jack Nicklaus. It's beautiful and a genuine challenge to play.

There are many other fine challenges in Wisconsin, including the following courses:

LOCATION	COURSE	HOLES/PAR/ YARDAGE	TYPE
Bailey's Harbor	Maxwelton Braes CC	18/71/6,050	Pub
Delavan	Lake Dawn GC	18/71/6,110	R
Egg Harbor	Alpine Lodge & GC	18/71/6,200	Pub
Elkhart Lake	Quit-Qui-Oc GC	18/71/6,100	Pub
Ephraim	Peninsula State Park GC	18/71/6,450	R
Genoa City	Nippersink Manor CC	18/71/6,356	R
Green Lake	Tuscumbia CC	18/72/6,030	SP
Green Lake	Lawsonia Links	18/72/6,620	SP
Janesville	Janesville GC	18/72/6,415 9/36/3,096	Pub
Lake Geneva	Hillmoor CC	18/72/6,486	SP
Lake Geneva	Playboy Club	18/72/6,700 18/72/6,800	R
Lake Delton	Dell View CC	18/69/6,000	R
Land O'Lakes	Gateway GC	9/36/3,310	R
Madison	Cherokee CC	18/72/7,055	SP
Madison	Odana Hills GC	18/71/6,447	Pub

LOCATION	COURSE	HOLES/PAR/ YARDAGE	TYPE
Milwaukee	Brown Deer GC	18/71/6,591	Pub
Mishicot	Fox Hill's CC	18/71/6,500	Pub
New Richmond	New Richmond GC	18/72/6,400	SP
Port Washington	Port Washington CC	18/72/6,273	Pub
River Falls	River Falls GC	18/72/6,800	SP
Sheboygan	Riverdale CC	18/71/6,130	Pub
Twin Lakes	The Red Barn CC	18/70/6,100	SP

Midwest Playing Tips. The bent-grass fairways are in general very lush, and are similar to those in New England and the Middle Atlantic States. Here again, in certain sections, you will find a great many up-hill and downhill lies, and it is well to refresh yourself on how to play these types of shots (see the section on playing in the Middle Atlantic States). We are inclined to think of the Midwest as flat country. But most of the better golf courses have been planned around streams and lakes.

The rough on most Midwestern courses has also been planned to try your patience. You can get tall trees, but the underbrush is thick and tenacious and, when in doubt, you'd best concentrate on getting the ball safely back into play.

One of the major Midwestern dangers is the abundance of clover in the fairways. A heavy clover lie can cause some trouble if not properly played. Actually, the difficulty here is that you will hit a "flier," a ball which skips and runs because it has nonstop action. The clover is "greasy," and when it gets smashed between the face of the club and the ball, it can give you a lot of crazy, mixed-up action, shooting off at a tangent or "flying" right on over the green. So you must concentrate on hitting the ball before you take your divot so that the scored face of the club can do its work without interference. But if it looks impossible to hit the shot without catching the clover, the best thing to do is to play a little short of the green, allow for some run, and hope for the best. That is, if a lie is so bad in the clover that you feel you can't help but hit a flier, take one club less to allow for the additional run. Also, try to uncock the wrists sooner than usual, giving you almost the feeling that you are hitting from the top. This will enable you to avoid a cutting action and come into the ball at a shallow level.

7

THE UNITED STATES: MOUNTAIN STATES

Golf in the so-called mountain states—Colorado, Idaho, Montana, Nevada, Utah, and Wyoming—is available to the traveling golfer in endless variety—mountain, lakeside, desert, lush, dry, short and easy, long and tough. In certain spots in this region you can play golf in the morning and then travel a very short distance to ski in the afternoon.

COLORADO

What is your latest technique for getting distance on your tee shots? A new grip? A new stance? A box of Wheaties? How about a trip to Colorado? In the altitude of the highest state in the Union, a well-hit golf ball will travel as much as thirty yards farther than one hit as well on other courses. No, this is not a tale from the nineteenth hole. It is true. And as tempting as it sounds, it is only one of the many benefits offered by the state.

Colorado, one of the largest ski areas in the country, could easily be classified as a golfing mecca also. No less than 65 public and semi-private courses are sprinkled throughout the state, most playable on an average of 26 sunshiny days a month from June through August in temperatures averaging 70 degrees. And if that is not enough to please you, the sun shines more than three hundred days a year, humidity is extremely low, insects, heat waves, and cloudy spells are rare, and leisure activity and resort living are abundant. This should satisfy even the fussiest golfer.

Virtually every area in Colorado has one or more golf courses available. In the Denver-Boulder area alone, there are 36 courses of all types. In summer, you can golf high in the Rockies (Grand Lake GC is the highest grass greens course in North America at nine thousand feet). Visitors may be surprised to learn that golf is possible and pleasant on the eastern slope from Fort Collins to Trinidad up to three hundred days a year. About two-thirds of the state's courses are always open to the public, others accept guests.

One of the world's most famous resort areas—the Broadmoor—is about 15 minutes from downtown Colorado Springs. There are actually two courses at the Broadmoor, the East Course and the West Course. In fact, the Broadmoor offers almost every type of recreational and social facilities to its guests, including riding, indoor ice skating, all-weather tennis courts, and indoor golf-driving range. The opening of its International Center, which seats 2,400, has turned the resort into the convention and theatrical center of the area.

Travel west from Colorado Springs on Route 82 to Aspen, and you will cross the Continental Divide at Independence Pass between the twin peaks of Mount Massive, 14,418 feet, and Mount Elbert, 14,431 feet. Aspen, overflowing with skiers in winter (it is the site of the world's longest—three miles—and highest chairlift), is just as charming in the summer. The Aspen Country Club, a 9-hole course, is open to the public. Accommodations in and near the town are excellent, the restaurants offer fine continental cuisine, and browsing in the shops can become a favorite pastime.

The layout of East and West Courses at Broadmoor.

Denver is a city of parks (99 within city limits) and golf courses (over a dozen). Case Municipal, City Park Municipal, Park Hill and Wellshire Municipal are all 18-hole public courses. Cherry Hills, Denver CC, Green Gables, and Lakewood, all 18 holes, are open to outside players on introduction by members. Columbine, Meadow Hills, Rolling Hills, all 18 holes, and Valley CC, nine holes, are open to members of other bona fide golf clubs.

West of Denver, in the heart of the fast growing, luxury homes complex of Hiwan Village-Hiwan Hills in Evergreen, is the 18-hole Hiwan Golf Club. Architect J. Press Maxwell, who also designed the Kissing Camels course in Colorado Springs, calls Hiwan "one of the very best" of the 52 in America he has created.

Three of the 18 holes share a water hazard in the form of a mountain lake, one of a chain of eight lakes which supply water for the underground sprinkling system that feeds the greens and fairways. Winding through (but not up) the beautiful pine-covered slopes of the Colorado mountains, this exacting layout can be varied from 6,500 to 7,100 yards. The seventh hole, a dogleg to the right, is considered the most challenging. A powerful drive off the tee needs position as well as length for a 2- to 5-iron to the green. The green is cut into a bank. Anything short will roll into the water, anything long will go into the woods. The course and chalet-type clubhouse, built from some of the three thousand trees uprooted to make way for the twisting, rolling fairways, is open to nonmembers on a guest card basis. There is tennis and swimming with plans for a stable and trap shooting in the near future.

After thirty miles northwest of Denver in Boulder are two public courses, the nine-hole Mountain View and 18-hole Municipal. Northeast of Denver, the Sterling CC in Sterling offers 18 holes with grass and sand greens and natural fairways. Open to the public on payment of green fees, Sterling is open to vacationers at no charge.

While many of Colorado's courses may prove challenging to a visiting golfer, we feel the following will test you most:

LOCATION	COURSE	HOLES/PAR/ YARDAGE	TYPE
Boulder	Lake Valley GC	18/70/6,365	Pub
Boulder	University CC	18/70/6,597	Pub
Denver	Los Verdes GC	18/72/6,716	SP

LOCATION	COURSE	HOLES/PAR/ YARDAGE	TYPE
Denver	Meadow Hills CC	18/72/6,729	SP
Evergreen	Hiwan GC	18/70/6,673	Pvt
Golden	Applewood GC	18/71/6,383	Pub
Colorado Springs	Broadmoor GC	18/72/6,531	R
		18/72/6,309	
Colorado Springs	Kissing Camels CC	18/70/7,054	Pvt
Vail	Vail GC	18/71/6,156	Pub

IDAHO

Of Idaho's fifty golf courses, the one at Sun Valley is possibly the best known. This famous ski resort has a championship par-71 layout measuring 6,227 yards. The course is open for play from approximately May 15 to October 21, during which time the average daily maximum temperature is 73. The days are moderately warm, nights so cool that there is an occasional frost. The air is remarkably free of pollen. Accommodations are numerous, and the visitor has his choice of the luxurious Sun Valley Lodge, comfortable Challenger Inn or popular Chalet-Dormitories.

A second shot from the rough on Sun Valley's 312-yard, par-4 hole will have to carry a creek in front of the green.

Here are some of the better known Idaho courses that you may wish to try:

LOCATION	COURSE	HOLES/PAR/ YARDAGE	TYPE
Boise	Plantation GC	18/72/6,522	SP
Coeur d'Alene	Coeur d'Alene GC	18/72/6,248	Pub
Idaho Falls	Pinecrest GC	18/70/6,689	Pub
Pocatello	Riverside GC	18/72/6,219	Pub
Sun Valley	Sun Valley	18/71/6,227	R

MONTANA

Montanans like their golf. You can find the size and type course to suit your fancy in the state's 54. Well over half are public or open to visitors. Wherever you visit ask the local chamber of commerce to help arrange your golfing. Some private clubs invite visitors too.

Most Montana golf courses are set in scenic locations, some are dramatic. All are convenient to towns. Mountain valleys predominate in the western half of the state, and rolling plains in the eastern half. As previously stated, you will get longer drives in the high, dry air. Perspiration is at a minimum. You feel great golfing in Montana's "Big Sky" country and any one of these courses will give you a test:

LOCATION	COURSE	HOLES/PAR/ YARDAGE	TYPE
Billings	Yellowstone CC	18/72/6,725	Pvt
Bozeman	Valley View GC	9/36/3,330	SP
Great Falls	Municipal GC	18/72/6,955	Pub
Kalispell	Kalispell GC	18/71/6,010	Pub
Missoula	Missoula CC	18/72/6,454	SP

NEVADA

Golf is popular in sunny, dry Nevada, where most of the leading courses are open the year round (about the only golfing region in the Rocky Mountains that can make that claim). With the exception of a *few* private clubs, the welcome mat is out to visitors at courses ranging from compact, tricky 9-holers to spectacular championship layouts. Most of the spectacular courses in Nevada, however, are located at three gambling centers—Las Vegas, Reno, and Lake Tahoe, where golf is popular too.

Until 1969, the tour made two stops each year in Las Vegas— for the Tournament of Champions in the spring, and the Sahara Invitational in the fall. In fact, back in the early 1960's, tour officials gave some serious consideration to a bid to hold a third tournament in Las Vegas for what would have been the biggest purse on the circuit. Nothing came of it, but it shows just how much people in Las Vegas think of golf as an attraction.

The Desert Inn, Paradise Valley, Sahara-Nevada, Dunes, Tropicana, and the International Hotels on the Strip all have adjacent courses, and the city operates Las Vegas Municipal on the other side

The fifteenth tee at the Desert Inn Country Club at Las Vegas.

of town. The terrain in the Las Vegas region of Nevada dictates a general flat course and most play about the same. Because of this, let us pick up the Desert Inn—or DI as it is generally called—as an example.

If you are playing well and the weather is favorable, the DI is not particularly difficult. But you still have to be a good enough shot-maker to keep the ball in play. You not only have rough but, on more than half of the holes, out-of-bounds stakes that can be reached with shots that are not all that badly hit.

When the pros played the Tournament of Champions at the Desert Inn, the par 5's made the biggest difference in the scoring. All four measured well over 500 yards, but in the thin desert air they were reachable in two under mild wind conditions. The first hole is one of the par 5's and one on which everyone wanted an opening birdie. It is not a worrisome type of hole for the pros, but it is one that can scare a middle-to-high handicap amateur to death if he tends to slice. Out-of-bounds beckons all the way down the right side. Probably the most difficult holes at the DI are the ninth and eighteenth, both long par 4's (440 and 452 yards, respectively) that require long, accurate tee shots. They are parallel holes, their fairways separated by a concrete-bottomed pond at tee shot range. To get home with second shots, you almost have to hit a driver, and you cannot play it too safely away from the water, either. The ninth, which runs along one edge of the course, has out-of-bounds along that boundary no more than thirty yards from the right edge of the narrow fairway. The eighteenth is protected to the left at tee shot range by traps and trees, as well as the usual heavy rough. The average player should be well contented with bogeys on these two holes. And probably on the most difficult of the par 3's—No. 7—as well. When he was the director of golf at the DI, the late Bo Wininger thought the seventh was the toughest hole on the course, period. A pond guards the left front and side of a green which is slightly smaller than the others. A trap protects the right front. It measures 222 yards and, depending on the wind, requires, as Bo used to say, "Anything from a driver to a three-iron—and devout prayer." It is surely a wood shot from the back tee for most nonpros. But all in all, most important for scoring at the DI and all Las Vegas courses, no matter who the golfer, is accuracy off the tee. You must be in the fairways off the tee or you will be headed for bogeys or worse.

At Lake Tahoe, the elevation (over six thousand feet) certainly helps your driving. Two of North America's most beautiful golf courses—Edgewood—Tahoe GC and Incline Village GC—are located on the Nevada side of the lake. The latter is a Robert Trent Jones course with nine water hazards on the front and four on the back. The Edgewood-Tahoe GC covers over two hundred acres with small lakes and stream throughout, as well as over fifty sand traps filled with white Monterey sand. The greens at both courses average about ten thousand square feet. There are four other courses at Lake Tahoe; three on the California side—Lake Tahoe CC (18 holes), Bijou CC (9 holes), and Tahoe Paradise GC (18 holes)—and one on the Nevada portion—Glenbrook GC.

Reno's newest and most popular course is the Robert Trent Jones Lake Ridge layout. This public course of over seven thousand yards of rolling terrain, is speckled with lakes, streams, and sand traps. And like the Las Vegas courses, the emphasis is on accurate tee placement. Greens are the new Pencross bent, a smooth hybrid grass that holds a shot.

From the tungsten ore "greens" (the greens are made of crushed tungsten concentrate) at Sandy Bottom to the championship fairway of the great resort courses just described, you will enjoy golf nearly everywhere in Nevada. You can bet on it!

LOCATION	COURSE	HOLES/PAR/ YARDAGE	TYPE
Henderson	Black Mountain G & CC	18/72/6,397	SP
Lake Tahoe	Incline Village GC	18/72/6,656	P
Las Vegas	Desert Inn CC	18/72/7,209	SP
Las Vegas	Dunes "Emerald Green" CC	18/72/7,240	R
Las Vegas	Bonanza CC	18/71/7,125	SP
Las Vegas	Las Vegas GC	18/72/6,735	Pub
Las Vegas	Paradise Valley	18/72/7,143	SP
Las Vegas	Fairway to the Stars	18/70/6,335	Pub
Las Vegas	Sahara-Nevada CC	18/71/6,761	SP
Las Vegas	Tropicana CC	18/70/6,647	Pub
Las Vegas	Winterwood GC	18/71/6,395	Pub
Reno	Lake Ridge GC	18/72/6,378	SP
Reno	Brookside GC	18/70/6,500	SP
Reno	Washoe County GC	18/72/6,550	Pub
Stateline	Edgewood-Tahoe CC	18/71/7,200	Pub

UTAH

There are fewer than fifty courses in Utah, but there are several interesting ones for visiting golfers. One of these is the Wasatch Mountain State Park course five miles from Heber City. This lush and tough championship 18-hole, par-72 layout is set in an exquisite canyon. There is plenty to do in the park when not playing golf—fishing, hiking, horseback riding, camping. And this is an ideal spot for the golfer-camper, since the Pine Creek Campground is right off the course. Incidentally, this course—like many in the mountain states—does not have sand traps. It depends on natural terrain—water, hills, rocks, trees—for its hazards.

A short distance from Wasatch Mountain State Park, we find a most interesting 3,500-yard, par-36, 9-hole course at Park City. This layout offers a challenge to all skills. Other courses that you can play and that will prove challenging are as follows:

The Grand Teton mountains form a beautiful background for the Jackson Hole Golf and Tennis Club in Jackson, Wyoming.

LOCATION	COURSE	HOLES/PAR/ YARDAGE	TYPE
Heber	Wasatch Mountain State Park GC	18/72/7,005	Pub
Logan	Logan City G & CC	18/72/5,711	SP
Ogden	Ben Lomond GC	18/72/6,166	Pub
Ogden	Patio Springs CC	18/72/6,600	Pvt
Park City	Park City GC	18/72/6,400	R
Provo	Timpanogos GC	18/72/6,700	Pub
Salt Lake City	Bonneville GC	18/72/6,522	Pub
Salt Lake City	Forest Dale GC	9/36/2,996	Pub
Salt Lake City	Rose Park GC	18/72/6,436	Pub

WYOMING

While Wyoming has more golf courses (approximately forty) than Nevada (about thirty), they do not compare in beauty or size. In fact, Wyoming has only two resort-type courses—the Jackson Hole G & CC and the Old Baldy Club in Saratoga. The majority of Wyoming courses are small, 9-hole affairs. But there is one thing to say about these courses, they can be quite interesting to play, especially the one at Jackson Hole.

LOCATION	COURSE	HOLES/PAR/ YARDAGE	TYPE
Jackson	Jackson Hole G & CC	18/72/6,780	SP
Saratoga	Old Baldy Club	18/72/6,600	R

8

THE UNITED STATES:
SOUTHWEST

In the southwestern states of Arizona, New Mexico, Oklahoma, and Texas, there are over 725 regulation golf courses, and new courses are sprouting up at a dizzy rate. Most of this region is 365-golf-days-a-year country and is the home of some of better resort and private courses in the nation.

ARIZONA

In central and southern Arizona, each golf course is an exciting oasis. It is a proud wintertime boast in these regions that "here, everyone plays in the 70's." They may be talking Fahrenheit rather than strokes, but the climate plus the booming popularity of golf has turned the

The ninth green at the Paradise Valley Country Club.

desert of Arizona into a patchwork of green. The state already has more readily accessible golf courses than most areas of the country. And new ones are being built at a steady rate.

With over 65 courses in the Scottsdale, Phoenix, and Tucson areas alone, holiday seekers with a month to spare can play on a different course every day of their vacation and still not play them all. Each layout, too, offers a different challenge. Fairways in Paradise Valley, Estrella Mountain and Carefree wind through desert washes between giant cacti, while several resort courses such as the Wigwam, San Marcos Hotel, and Arizona Biltmore are carefully manicured layouts in garden settings.

Although the resort courses are primarily for guests, the general public may play them for reasonable green fees. Generally, they are integral parts of the resort, often adjacent to accommodations.

The private country clubs, which generally honor membership in other USGA clubs, are among the most luxurious in the country. Ultra-modern clubhouses not only have all the creature comforts but highly scenic views.

Arizona also boasts some of the finest public courses. These are run either by the city governments or, in some cases, by the counties. Phoenix alone has two municipal courses at Encanto Park, another at Maryvale, and a fourth at red-rock Papago Park. The latter two are 18-hole layouts while Encanto Park has both a 9- and an 18-hole course.

A great many people come to Phoenix just to see Camelback Mountain. Those who stay at either the Paradise Inn, the Jokake Inn, or the Royal Palms Inn have, so to speak, a front-row seat from which to view the Mountain. They can play golf on Paradise Inn's Valley Country Club, which is located on the southeast slope of the mountain. The Inn is completely encircled by the green fairways of the 6,341-yard, par-71 golf course with seaside bent greens. One of the unique features of this course is that a guest can step out on the fairway from his hotel cottage, or hotel-room doorway and begin to play on the tee nearest him. He can use his own pullcart, or phone the pro shop and an electric cart will be waiting for him at his tee.

There is one hole at Valley that has no rival in the Phoenix area. It is No. 13, a 135-yard par 3, which has a green elevated almost exactly as high in feet as the hole is long in yards. Naturally, this makes the surface of the green invisible to the player. On another hole, a 365-yard par 4, there is a drop from the tee of nearly two hundred feet to where the ordinary drive will land on the fairway. Short drivers really love this hole for good reason.

Located on some 250 peaceful acres at the foot of Mummy Mountain in Paradise Valley, the Camelback Inn provides a beautiful desert setting and luxurious accommodations. Golf is at adjacent 6,687-yard Camelback Country Club, a 6,317-yard, par-71 layout. The Inn itself also has an 18-hole pitch-and-putt, par-54 course, called "Quail Hollow."

Another Scottsdale resort, Mountain Shadows, offers an unusual layout. Eighteen holes are distributed along 2,865 yards of colorfully landscaped desert. While this is mostly a par-3 layout (two holes, measuring around three hundred yards each, are par 4) it should not be mistaken for a pitch-and-putt exercise. It is a golf course that will test the skill of even the low-handicap golfer. Lakes, a waterfall and a winding stream highlight the striking beauty of this course, and it is interesting to note that the glittering white sand in its traps was imported from Capistrano. Needless to say, deserts don't often boast of importing sand.

The eighth hole at the Mountain Shadows Hotel Course is short (only a 100 yards), but the water can give you problems.

On 150 acres of beautifully landscaped grounds surrounded by Mc-Dowell and Camelback Mountains is Scottsdale Country Club. Modern accommodations overlook the green fairways of its 18-hole championship course. Four water holes make it an unusual desert attraction, and the scenic solitude of the course makes golfing more enjoyable. The greens are small and testy. Like many other resorts in the desert, the Scottsdale CC offers a special package plan for the vacationing golfer.

In addition to these three resort layouts, Scottsdale boasts seven other fine courses. It is no wonder that Scottsdale has become a prime resort area and one of the largest cities in Arizona. Yet, this fantastic growth has not spoiled its Western charm. Picturesque porch-fronted shops may still be found lining its streets in contrast to the sprawling ultra-modern resort structures.

The Desert Forest Golf Club, located in Carefree, just north of Scottsdale, is probably one of the few golf courses in the world with its own airport. Its 6,929-yard, par-72 layout is one of the most interetsing courses in the country.

Another aristocrat among Valley golf resorts is the Arizona Biltmore. Midway between Camelback and the center of Phoenix, it is a luxurious 1,200-acre holiday estate. The grounds, gardens and 18-hole, par-72 course are kept in impeccable condition.

At Chandler, 24 miles southeast of Phoenix, is the famous San Marcos Resort and Country Club. This exacting, 6,755-yard, par-72 course is at the doorstep of a handsome, modern lodge. The layout also features 50 lanais along the fairways.

About ten miles west of Phoenix, the Wigwam Inn in Litchfield Park offers its guests play on two magnificent 18-hole courses of the adjacent Goodyear Golf & Country Club. Thirteen lakes make the club a veritable desert oasis. Incidentally, while the accent is on golf, the Wigwam, too, is a complete resort.

To the northwest of Phoenix is the much-publicized retirement community, Sun City. Its par-72 course, designed for the golfer in the 85–110 range is one of the busiest courses in the area (more than forty thousand rounds played last year) and one of the best. Near Sun City, is the Wickenburg Country Club, and its 3,461-yard, 9-hole layout. This is a semiprivate club which opens its doors to the guests of Rancho de los Caballeros.

The brisk, clear air of the Arizona northlands is an exciting stimu-

This aerial view of the par-5, 610-yard tenth hole at the Goodyear Golf and Country Club was taken from the landing area of the tee shot. From this point it is a long wood to the area between the lake on the left and the traps on the right, and then a 5- to 8-iron to an elevated green.

lant to the golfer. Spectacular scenery makes your first round on any one of the northern Arizona courses a memorable adventure. At Page you are on the brink of Glen Canyon; Clarksdale and Lake Montezuma are in the picturesque Verde Valley. Winslow and Kingman give you views of high plateau and distant mountains. This is BIG country. Payson, Williams, Coconino, and Antelope Hills are in delightful rolling country close to the mountains. Other courses are cut out of the forest. You play on fairways right in the middle of the world's largest stand of ponderosa pine. Some of the courses, like Pinetop, Flagstaff, and Alpine, are over seven thousand feet high.

Golf is a way of life for many people in southern Arizona. There is hardly a day that is not good for a game. You can start right on the border at Bisbee, where a bad hook on No. 1 might put your ball in Mexico; play close to sea level in Yuma; putt on greens equaling the world's finest in historic Tubac. Meadow Hills, at Nogales only two years old, already boasts fairways that are green all year round.

The 4,000-foot-plus altitude at Nogales, Douglas, Bisbee, Ft. Huachuca, and Wilcox offers cool playing when weather is hot in lower valley towns. Yuma lights Arroyo Dunes—so that golfers can enjoy playing in the coolness of summer nights. Tucson, center of the Sun Country's oldest resort area, has a wealth of intriguing courses. The fairways of Tucson Country Club wind along a natural wash whose underground waters nourish a colorful forest of Palo Verde, mesquite, ocotillo, and cacti. It has been the setting for many national and regional tournaments. Skyline is high up on the side of the Catalina Mountains. Oro Valley and Tucson National are on high rolling desert irrigated by underground flow from Canyon Del Oro, made famous years ago as the setting for Harold Bell Wright's *Mine with the Iron Door*.

Arizona golf courses are not as the average visitor expects and, in fact, the biggest percentage have rolling fairways, heavily tree-lined, giving them an eastern flavor. While most clubs keep up a tree-planting program, many courses are cut right through the natural cactus growth of the desert. Often the real conversation pieces among visitors as well as natives are the large saguaros. When in bloom, the mesquite, Palo Verde, and big cottonwood trees are incredibly beautiful.

The permanent fairway grass is Bermuda, which, during the off-season, is overseeded with winter rye, giving the course a lush, green look. Although this broad-leaf grass looks like eastern turf, it plays quite differently. In Arizona the golfer must learn to hit all the ball with both woods and irons, a good habit for the vacationing golfer to take home with him.

Arizona wind is only an occasional hazard, although the golfer sometimes finds himself hitting into headwinds simply because the courses are so wide-open. On those rare windy days, the shot will play three or four clubs longer.

The rarefied air, coupled with the mountains and canyons in the background, make judgment of distances deceptive. As a rule, the visitor sees the hole closer than it really is, and the result is under-clubbing. A good tip for the vacationing golfer is to take one more club than you think you need. In those areas that are surrounded by mountains, reading the greens is also a problem, partly because of

Beautiful Skyline Country Club at the foot of the towering Santa Catalina Mountains is truly one of the showplaces of the Southwest. Pictured here is the eighteenth green with a yawning waterhole stretching the entire breadth, ready to receive any short shots.

optical illusions that show a putt breaking just the opposite of the true break.

All in all, golf in the Arizona desert requires only a slight adjustment, and this unique country of sunshine, light air, good golfing facilities, and western hospitality is sure to make you anxious to return. As for the courses of Arizona, especially the ones mentioned below, they will offer a real challenge:

LOCATION	COURSE	HOLES/PAR/ YARDAGE	TYPE
Carefree	Desert Forest GC	18/72/6,929	SP
Casa Grande	Francisco Grande GC	18/72/6,957	SP
Chandler	San Marcos Hotel GC	18/72/6,775	Pvt
Goodyear	Sierra Estrella GC	18/70/6,600	Pub
Lake Havasu	Lake Havasu G & CC	18/72/6,382	Pub
Litchfield Park	Goodyear G & CC	18/70/6,107 18/72/7,105	R

LOCATION	COURSE	HOLES/PAR/ YARDAGE	TYPE
Mesa	Apache Wells CC	18/72/6,500	SP
Mesa	Golden Hills CC	18/71/6,560	R
Mesa	Mesa CC	18/71/6,255	SP
Nogales	Kino Springs GC	18/72/6,520	R
Phoenix	Arizona Biltmore GC	18/72/6,370	R
Phoenix	Encanto GC	18/70/6,245	Pub
Phoenix	Maryvale GC	18/71/6,135	Pub
Phoenix	Moon Valley CC	18/72/6,600	SP
Phoenix	Papago Park GC	18/72/6,690	Pub
Phoenix	Thunderbird CC	18/71/6,375	SP
Scottsdale	Century CC	18/72/6,576	SP
Scottsdale	Indian Bend CC	18/71/6,483	SP
Scottsdale	Camelback Inn CC	18/72/6,687	R
Scottsdale	McCormick Ranch GC	18/72/6,350	R
Scottsdale	Mountain Shadow CC	18/56/2,865	SP
Scottsdale	Pima Inn & GC	18/71/6,491	SP
Scottsdale	Roadrunner GC	18/71/6,341	Pvt
Scottsdale	Scottsdale Inn & CC	18/70/6,100	R
Scottsdale	Paradise Valley CC	18/71/6,341	Pvt
Scottsdale	Valley CC	18/72/6,050	SP
Scottsdale	McCormick Ranch GC	18/72/6,350	R
Sun City	Sun City GC		
	North	18/71/6,476	SP
	South	18/72/6,941	
Tucson	Forty Miner CC	18/72/6,917	SP
Tucson	Randolph GC	18/72/6,893	Pub
		18/70/6,418	
Tucson	Skyline CC	18/70/6,344	R
Yuma	Yuma G & CC	18/71/6,277	SP

NEW MEXICO

Golf is definitely on the upgrade in New Mexico. There are over 55 courses in the state—an increase of thirty in the last thirty years. All the major cities have courses available to the visiting golfer. The state's largest city, Albuquerque, has the most, as well as the most challenging. Situated atop a hill overlooking the city of Albuquerque and the Sandia Mountains, Panorama G & CC offers visitors a breathtaking view and a golf course that rates with the best in the Southwest. Measuring 7,196 yards from the back tees and playing to a par 72, the course covers some two hundred acres of rolling fairways and well-conditioned greens. Five manmade lakes figure heavily on each nine.

New Mexico lays claim to the highest course on the North American continent (and one of the sportiest)—Cloudcraft. The first tee is at 8,650 feet and some spots on the course are over 9,000. Here are some of the better New Mexico courses that you can play:

LOCATION	COURSE	HOLES/PAR/ YARDAGE	TYPE
Albuquerque	Los Altos GC	18/71/6,250	Pub
Albuquerque	Panorama G & CC	18/72/7,196	SP
Albuquerque	Paradise Hills G & CC	18/72/7,185	Pvt
Albuquerque	University of N. M. GC	18/72/7,062	SP
Cloudcraft	Cloudcraft Lodge GC	10/38/2,718	Pub
Las Cruces	New Mexico State University GC	18/72/7,100	Pub
Los Alamos	Los Alamos GC	18/72/6,512	Pub

TEXAS

Certain misconceptions to the contrary, Texas is all kinds of places, and thus, it has all kinds of golf courses and all kinds of golfers. As a matter of fact, Texas has produced more truly good golfers than any other one state in the country. Not even Californians deny that.

The geography of Texas changes abruptly in all directions so the golf courses change, too. In the metropolitan Fort Worth–Dallas area, you have rich Bermuda fairways and sprawling bent greens, forests of oak trees, elms and hackberrys, and occasional rivers. Here you have the best collection of courses in the state, the best known of which is Colonial Country Club in Fort Worth, site of the annual National Invitation Tournament. Colonial is a long, narrow, well-kept par 70, which practically every accomplished player puts in his "top five."

Drive a hundred miles east of Dallas and you come to towering pine trees that would almost (but not quite) match those along the slopes of the gorgeous Augusta National. Go 190 miles south of Fort Worth and you are in Austin, the state capital, with its multiple hills and "Colorado atmosphere" only ten minutes from downtown. And then if you go only 50 miles west of Fort Worth, you invade the dusty oil region. Finally, all along the coastal areas there are layouts whose style is architecturally comparable to those found in Florida.

There is one unifying characteristic about all these areas of Texas: the weather. It is hot in the summer and cold in the winter. It is also cool in autumn and pleasantly warm in the spring. But, except in a few isolated places, it may never be so cold that a true outdoorsman cannot play nine holes. A New Englander might consider a 25-degree day in the Panhandle a fine day for golf, because the sun undoubtedly would be shining.

Texas has a great many golf courses. Hardly any town of five thousand is without a golf course of some kind. It may have sand greens. It may have bent or emerald rye or Bermuda. It may have dirt fairways. But it has a course.

If there is a golfer somewhere who wants to see this weird golf land before he believes it, here is a suggested tour: Go first to Fort Worth and play Colonial, a course that most pros place with Merion, Pebble Beach, and Augusta National for combined toughness and enjoyment. Then go to Midland to see luxury in the flatland, a 7,000-yard course of firm, green footing with goliath greens of bent. And by all means test the Champion's course in Houston, a masterpiece of woods, moss, willows, ravines, and lovely demanding contours. Then, finally, play at Pecan Valley near San Antonio and you would see four radically different courses. This is actually the thing which Texas golfers can brag about the most—variety. And if not variety, then climate. If not climate, then availability. Or tradition.

LOCATION	COURSE	HOLES/PAR/ YARDAGE	TYPE
Arlington	Lake Arlington GC	18/71/6,900	SP
Amarillo	Tascosa CC	18/72/6,790	SP
Austin	Lakeway Inn & GC	18/72/6,395	SP
Austin	Morris Williams GC	18/72/6,597	Pub
Beaumont	Tyrrell Park GC	18/72/6,535	Pub
Brownsville	Valley International CC	18/70/6,114	R
Corpus Christi	Corpus Christi CC	18/71/6,790	Pvt
Corpus Christi	Padre Island	18/71/6,990	R
Dallas	Tenison Park GC	18/72/7,000 18/71/6,900	Pub
Fort Worth	Meadow Brook GC	18/71/6,431	Pub
Friendswood	Sun Meadow GC	18/72/6,500	SP
Galveston	Galveston CC	18/72/6,291	SP

LOCATION	COURSE	HOLES/PAR/ YARDAGE	TYPE
Galveston	Galveston Municipal GC	18/72/6,101	Pub
Great Prairie	Great Southwest GC	18/71/6,500	SP
Hilltop Lakes	Hilltop Lakes GC	18/72/6,316	R
Houston	Memorial Park GC	18/72/6,438	Pub
Houston	Sugar Creek GC	18/72/6,840	SP
Houston	Tejas GC	18/72/6,500	SP
Kerrville	Kerrville Hills CC	18/72/7,000	SP
Laredo	Casa Blanca GC	18/72/6,683	Pub
Longview	Longview CC	18/72/6,310 9/35/2,780	SP
Lubbock	Meadowbrook GC	18/72/6,696 9/35/3,254	Pub
San Antonio	Pecan Valley GC	18/72/7,007	SP
San Augustine	Fairway Farms GC	18/71/7,352	SP
San Marcos	Spring Lake GC	9/35/3,820	R
West Columbia	Columbia Lakes CC	18/72/7,198	R

OKLAHOMA

Oklahoma has over 140 regulation golf courses, but like Texas, unfortunately, many of its finer courses are private. The exception to this is Checotah's Fountainhead State Park, one of the most challenging courses in the United States. Basically, however, Oklahoma offers vacationing golfers many of the same kinds of facilities as are found in Texas.

LOCATION	COURSE	HOLES/PAR/ YARDAGE	TYPE
Afton	Shangrila G & CC	18/72/6,435	R
Burneyville	Falconhead CC	18/72/6,468	R
Checotah	Fountainhead GC	18/72/7,200	R
Moore	Broadmoore GC	18/70/6,600	SP
Norman	University of Oklahoma GC	18/72/6,574	SP
Oklahoma City	Hillcrest G & CC	18/70/6,800	SP
Oklahoma City	Lake Hefner GC	18/70/6,800 18/70/6,500	Pub
Oklahoma City	Lincoln Park GC	18/72/6,721 18/70/6,143	Pub
Tulsa	Shamrock CC	18/72/7,245	SP

9

THE UNITED STATES:
CALIFORNIA

California is politically one sovereign state, but the golf courses in the north and the south are entirely different.

The climate and geography of southern California make it an ideal habitat for the golf-minded. Golf in southern California embraces seaside links, mountain meadowland, and flat desert courses. This great variety is located in a very small area. And unless he has picked a desert course in August, the golfer can be reasonably certain the course won't be closed because of weather. (Most desert courses shutter their first tees in the hot summer months.) The golfer in southern California will discover that green fees or guest privileges are reasonable and are comparable to those in other sections of the United States. So are club-membership initiation fees and dues.

The climate in southern California is quite different from that of any part of the country except that bordering California. It is milder and more uniform than that of states at corresponding latitudes. Southern coastal temperatures rarely exceed 90 degrees. It is not humid. From the heavy rain belt of northern California the annual precipitation decreases southward until at San Diego, 16 miles from the Mexican border, the average yearly rainfall is a mere ten inches. Thus, nearly all golf courses must have complete watering systems.

Los Angeles' annual rainfall averages 15 inches and the mean temperature is 62.4 degrees. Until smog became a problem, there was a 72 per cent possibility of sunshine every day of the year in Los Angeles and 179 clear days. With smog, there is a 70 per cent possibility you won't see the sun unless you are an early riser. Golfers have complained little about the smog, however, but then, golfers are one of the hardier breeds.

Weather bureau records show that southern California, including coastal regions, averages more than 200 clear days a year. In the extreme south the average may run to 250 or more such days. Inasmuch as golf's physical benefits are fresh air, sunshine, and exercise,

Golfers at Sunol Valley's Palm Course are enjoying the extra hours of playing time afforded them by the excellent lighting system. It is the world's longest completely lighted course.

it's hardly surprising that southern California is an area of tremendous golfing interest.

Northern California is filled with lush courses, most of them featuring heavy, holding fairways and perfectly carpeted greens. In no way do they compare with the Bermuda grasses and sunbaked "highways" of the southern part of the state, a region where the ball rolls for prodigious distances. And, as in parts of Texas and the eastern seaboard, the winds blow hard in northern California, especially around Monterey and San Francisco where so many outstanding golfers play nationally known layouts.

Fortunately for the golfing tourist, he has much to pick from. From the tranquil lowlands of the San Diego area to the windswept cliffs of the Monterey Peninsula, there is enough golf to satisfy anyone's competitive taste. The visiting golfer can start his tour in San Diego county, but you have to be serious about the game to get the most out of a golfing vacation there. With over seventy courses in the county and a season that never ends, the problem is simply that there are too many other things to do in this most pleasant of southern California cities. For example, you might be sizing up a putt at Coronado and discover that an aircraft carrier anchored out in the bay is directly in your line of sight. That's a distraction. Or to get in a round at Balboa Park, you have to bypass one of the world's great zoos. (A mid-town advertisement exclaims, "Good gnus travel fast. Visit the zoo!" In San Diego they're as proud of the zoo as they are of native golfer number one, Billy Casper.)

What San Diego can mean to the golfer is a year-round golf vacation with plenty of side attractions. The golf is as varied as anyone could wish—ranging from Torrey Pines, a challenging 36 holes built above the ocean just north of La Jolla, to the inland courses like Singing Hills near El Cajon, a spread of three 18-hole courses, bright and green, surrounded by the sand-brown hills that are typical of the region. Accommodations are available at plush spas like La Costa, or in the twenty thousand motel, hotel and resort rooms in the city itself.

Most of the area's courses are open on a daily fee basis and only one or two won't honor memberships in other clubs. And in San Diego, even the municipal courses are consistently in good condition. Torrey Pines, for example, is usually the site of the San Diego Open.

Torrey Pines plays around the Pacific Ocean and its breezes control your play.

Torrey Pines uses its South course for the tournament. On this par 72, and rated 72, No. 12 is generally rated the toughest hole, a 453-yard slight dogleg to the right that plays uphill all the way and into the prevailing stiff breeze off the Pacific Ocean. The green is bunkered along the right side to catch anyone looking for a short cut, and a fairway bunker on the left side about 250 yards out can mean trouble for the golfer looking for good position for a safer second shot into the open side of the green.

Although most courses in the San Diego area can't match the setting of Torrey Pines, they're equally interesting. Coronado is just a few minutes from downtown San Diego, and located about three blocks from the Del Coronado Hotel, a comfortable 399-room hotel that was built in 1888. As a luxury hotel of another era, it's still a popular year-round vacation hotel and is more typical of the New England coast or Atlantic City than southern California.

The Coronado course, a municipal operation, is a par-72, 6,540-yard layout. The best of the new holes at Coronado is probably No. 8, a 400-yard par 4 that requires a delicate approach to a green almost surrounded by water.

It's impossible to examine each of the fine courses in the San Diego area, but the posh and impressive La Costa is worth a visit if for no other reason than to see a complete, golf-oriented resort. The course itself is a par-72, 7,299-yard bit of rolling countryside that is well trapped and laced with enough water to catch the careless. Accommodations can be had in the lodge, individual haciendas, or one of the resort's condominiums. Complete spa facilities are available, including whirlpool baths, saunas, massages, and so forth.

Just a few miles north of the San Diego area is Rancho Santa Fe, a course that many professionals consider one of the four best courses in the state of California. Rancho Santa Fe, in fact, was the site of Bing Crosby's famous pro-ams for many years until he moved his headquarters to Pebble Beach. The course has been improved since then, which means pars are now even more difficult to get. Visitors can either stay at the inn at Rancho Santa Fe itself or rent one of the lovely detached cottages. Aside from the golf, there is tennis, swimming in the pool or at any of a dozen nearby beaches.

Right next door, at Escondido, is the Pauma Valley course, built by the triumverate of John Dawson, Jimmy Hines, and Robert Trent Jones. It's a sporty course laid out in a spectacular setting; before going out to play it, you should obtain a guest card. Another nearby course at Fallbrook is Rancho Bernardo, right in the heart of avocado country.

Out of deference to the touring golfer, the Los Angeles area is being skipped here; conditions are simply too crowded there and there are no resort courses to speak of. Some new courses are being built, and systems of speeding up play on courses are being tried, but for the time being, the vacationer is best advised to continue up the shoreline—unless he wants to join long lines.

Twenty-seven miles from Los Angeles Harbor is the island of Santa Catalina and the Catalina Island Golf Club. Built in 1895, the layout was one of the first four golf courses in southern California. Most of the holes on this interesting 9-hole course have two sets of tees, so white markers are used for the first nine, and red markers for the second, giving varying distances for each side. While neither tee arrangement is over three thousand yards, this course puts great demand on accuracy. The long ball hitter must be doubly careful because of extremely narrow fairways. The tee shot must be precisely placed to have a clear shot at the greens. Many of the holes are doglegs and a ball hit too far will carry through the corner into trouble. It would be wise to use long irons and fairway woods off the tees.

Continuing north up the coast of California and going by Ventura, you reach Ojai, where there are two excellent courses. The Ojai Valley Inn and Country Club boasts a formidable 6,800-yard course nestled in a green, sheltered valley surrounded by towering mountains. It's an undulating course with bumpalong fairways and tricky greens. Here, summertime temperatures remain between 70 and 90 degrees, and at an altitude of 1,000 feet, the valley is free of smog and dampness.

The sleepy Spanish town of Santa Barbara is waking up to the golf boom. The Montecito Golf Course, built on the side of a hill, gives the golfer a slight touch of vertigo and a wonderful view of the red rooftops and Spanish architecture. In addition to Montecito, the tourist will find several other good courses.

Forty miles north of Santa Barbara is a little Danish town called Solvang. Here, against the background of the Santa Ynez Mountains, is the Alisal, one of the West's most renowned resorts. The Alisal has always been a guest ranch with excellent riding facilities; but since

The ninth hole of the San Luis Bay Inn and Golf Club course lies at the entrance to a picturesque canyon studded with ancient oak and sycamore. The course is threaded with small creeks which empty into water hazards and then on into the ocean.

the installation of a magnificent 6,434-yard, par-72 golf course in the oak-and-sycamore studded foothills, it has become the answer for families.

Just before reaching San Luis Obispo, at Avila Beach, you find the San Luis Bay Club. This par-71, 6,529-yard course has a fine course plus excellent resort facilities.

Farther up the coastline, just a few miles from the old William Randolph Hearst estate, is Morro Bay. Here, you say good-bye to those 250-yard screamers you hit in the tranquil air down below. The Morro Bay Golf Course, overlooking the sea, is a primer in playing the winds and should be a must on your itinerary—if only to contemplate Mr. Hearst's San Simeon castle.

No California golfing odyssey could be complete without a visit to the bubbling Monterey Peninsula. Here, no less than ten full golf courses await you. In addition to the testy layouts, your adversaries are the wind and fog that prevail throughout much of the summer. You have your choice of playing Pebble Beach, Cypress Point, Spyglass Hill, Carmel Valley, Monterey Peninsula, Corral de Tierra, Laguna Seca, Del Monte, Rancho Canada, and Pacific Grove. Except for the rather exclusive Cypress Pine course, visitors are welcomed.

Whenever two or three golfers are gathered together and start talking in superlatives about golf courses, someone is sure to mention Pebble Beach. This famous, fabulous, 6,747-yard, par-72 course on

The layout course of famed Pebble Beach Golf Links.

the Monterey Peninsula's rocky cliffs has some of the most photogenic—and photographed—golf holes in the world. But while beauty alone would make them famous, they are great because of their playability. This, after all, is the mark of a truly distinguished hole. An oceanside course, Pebble Beach boasts no fewer than seven great holes; most courses can boast no more than two, three at the outside. The holes in question are those which are bordered by the Pacific Ocean. Exposed, as they are, to the capriciousness of the winds, they can change character while the same foursome is still on the tee. On days when the wind is blowing from right to left off the ocean on the famous seventh hole, you actually have to aim your short-iron shot out over the ocean and allow the wind to carry it back onto the miniature green. The hole has been played with everything from a 2-iron on up, including a putter. And who but the irrepressible late

Walter Hagen would have thought of that? The Haig is supposed to have knocked it on short with his blade and got down in two to make his par. By contrast, the remaining holes at Pebble Beach—the first five and holes 11 through 16—are played inland through a forest, and they are no less demanding than the seaward holes. Most golfers would sooner play badly at Pebble Beach than score well at a course of less formidable character.

Wind, fog, mountain, or valley—whatever the golf challenge you seek, the California coast has it. If you plant your first tee in the fertile turf around San Diego county and hole your last putt on the swirling greens at Monterey, you will probably have run the full gamut. Perhaps the greatest challenge you'll come up against is trying to get all of it in one or two vacation weeks.

But, of course, there are plenty of other excellent golf courses away from the coastline. For instance, Apple Valley, some one hundred miles east of Los Angeles, ranks as one of the most interest-

While on the Monterey Peninsula you have a choice of playing wind-swept ocean courses, such as Spyglass Hill and Pebble Beach, or the picturesque inland courses, such as Carmel Valley Country Club shown here.

ing in the West. At an altitude of three thousand feet, the summers remain consistently cool, yet, the dryness of the desert leaves the winters warm. Plush accommodations are available at Apple Valley Inn and championship golf is available on the 7,000-yard layout designed by the late William P. Bell. About 25 years ago two enterprising Californians named Newt Bass and Bud Westland bought a plot of several thousand acres of desert, abounding with grotesque Joshua trees, chaparral and sagebrush, in the foothills of the San Bernardino Mountains. Their idea was to create a grazing area for their cattle. But, upon learning that the land contained an underground reservoir, they decided instead to create a year-round resort community with an emerald golf course, complete with water hole as its hub.

Going still further east of Los Angeles will bring you to Palm Springs, often called the "Winter Golf Capital of the World." This famous resort city is hot and dry, but the area does not want for water. It gushes from underground lakes and from Mt. San Jacinto which is nearly solid granite. When it rains on the mountain—or the snow up there melts—the water pours into Palm Springs, sometimes quite literally. Three golf courses have at least one fairway that crosses the wash (a wide ditch) which controls flash floods. Every 11 years or so, these fairways are sacrificed—along with anything else in the wash at the time. "It's the ultimate in water hazards," observed a local assistant pro. "Think of trying to concentrate on a 7-iron shot with a wall of water bearing down on you!"

Because its winter weather is warm and dry—the "season" runs from late December through April—and because of its water supply and its proximity to the West Coast, Palm Springs has been a fairly chic resort area since the 1930's when Charlie Farrell built the Racquet Club and those Hollywood picture show people moved in and turned the place into a kind of commune for the rich and celebrated. It has remained that way for the time being. About four thousand private swimming pools (one for every five of the city's 22,500 residents) help compensate for the absence of an ocean. But *golf* is what has made Palm Springs.

"In the two decades since Johnny Dawson opened Thunderbird CC in 1951, golf has been responsible directly and indirectly for the most apparent progress in the Greater Palm Springs area," cites *Palm Springs Life,* a slick city magazine. But the sport was a long time coming.

The first golf course in Palm Springs was constructed in the front yard of oil millionaire Tom O'Donnell in 1925. The 9-hole layout, at the foot of Mt. San Jacinto, survives today as O'Donnell GC, a prestigious little private club in downtown Palm Springs. It was the only course in Greater Palm Springs until Dawson, a top amateur player, decided he missed the old first-class back-East-type country club with a real 18-hole championship course.

The year 1951 is now called by *Palm Springs Life* the time when a "whole new era for the Greater Palm Springs area began. The place took off on a golf binge and has been on it ever since."

Thunderbird was followed by other well-known clubs—Tamarisk, Eldorado, Indian Wells, Bermuda Dunes, and La Quinta. Then came San Jacinto (now called Whitewater), Palm Springs Municipal, and Westward Ho! The tide continued. The Riviera and Biltmore hotels were erected with adjacent small courses. (Only the luxurious Canyon Hotel has its own private 18-hole layout.) Desert Air, Seven Lakes, Marrakesh, and Del Safari have also materialized.

Some of the water on the famed Canyon Country Club course at Palm Springs, California.

Then, in the spring of 1971, Mission Hills opened for play—the first of several land development and real-estate-oriented courses in the area. Other new projects include Mission Lakes, Desert Island, Palm Springs Mobile CC, and Palm Desert Greens—the first two being championship layouts, the latter two shorter executive courses wending their way between widely spread house trailers.

Some who live in Palm Desert can golf in both their front and backyards. Here, residents of a Manitou Springs Estate home are shown on the third fairway of Indian Wells golf course. The community, which lies halfway between Palm Springs and Indio, is in the center of the valley's twenty-eight golf courses.

Altogether, the Palm Springs area now contains 28 golf courses, not including the 9-hole layout on publishing heir Walter Annenberg's estate. But it has been suggested that 28 courses are not enough. Palm Springs *is* a wealthy community—the city magazine reportedly has a readership with a per capita income of $36,000— and it is true that except for a few recent additions, most of the best courses are private. However, a number extend reciprocal privileges to members of other membership clubs, to guests at hotels without courses, or for open public play at specified starting times.

For the general public—notably weekenders from nearby and vacationers planning longer stays—there are eight fine public courses, one semipublic course, and two driving ranges. Palm Springs municipal boasts a championship course, a strikingly modern clubhouse, and a first-rate pro shop.

Speaking of public courses, San Francisco boasts of one of the best 18 in the United States at Harding Park. There are five other public layouts in San Francisco—two are full 18's, two are 9, and one can best be described as a par 3—but like other major city municipal courses, they are generally very crowded, especially on weekends.

It is impossible to cover all of California's over six hundred golf courses in this chapter. However, here is a list of better courses that visitors to the Golden State can play:

LOCATION	COURSE	HOLES/PAR/ YARDAGE	TYPE
Alameda	Alameda GC	18/72/6,529	Pub
		18/72/6,417	
Apple Valley	Apple Valley GC	18/71/6,420	Pvt
Avalon	Catalina Island GC	9/32/2,264	SP
Avila Beach	San Luis Bay GC	18/71/6,529	R
Azusa	Azusa Greens GC	18/70/6,463	SP
Berkeley	Tilden Regional GC	18/71/6,364	Pub
Bermuda Dunes *	Bermuda Dunes CC	18/72/6,488	Pvt
Bonita	Bonita GC	18/70/6,007	SP
Borrego Springs	DeAnza Desert CC	18/72/6,400	SP
Bonsall	San Luis Rey GC	18/72/7,300	SP
Burlingame	Crystal Springs GC	18/71/6,112	SP
Carmel	Carmel Valley G & CC	18/72/6,756	SP
Carmel	Rancho Canada GC	18/72/6,613	Pub
		18/71/6,404	

LOCATION	COURSE	HOLES/PAR/ YARDAGE	TYPE
Cathedral City *	Mission Hills G & CC	18/72/6,454	Pvt
Chino	Los Serranos G & CC	18/71/6,921	Pub
Coronado	Coronado Municipal GC	18/72/6,450	Pub
Costa Mesa	Costa Mesa GC	18/72/6,704	Pub
Culver City	Fox Hills CC	18/72/6,640	Pub
Death Valley	Furnace Creek GC	9/36/3,300	Pub
El Cajon	Cottonwood CC	18/73/7,100	SP
El Cajon	Singing Hills CC	18/72/6,500	SP
Escondido	Circle R Ranch and GC	18/70/6,300	R
Fallbrook	Pala Mesa Inn & GC	18/72/6,400	R
Fallbrook	Rancho Bernardo GC	18/72/6,736 18/72/6,400	R
Fresno	Riverside GC	18/72/6,565	Pub
Galt	Dry Creek Ranch GC	18/72/6,489	R
Gilman Hot Springs	Massacre Canyon Inn & CC	18/72/6,978	R
Hayward	Hayward GC	18/72/6,680	Pub
Hesperia	Hesperia G & CC	18/72/7,100	Pvt
Indian Wells *	Indian Wells Cove GC	18/72/6,615	Pvt
Indian Wells *	Indian Wells North Cove GC	18/72/6,650	Pvt
Indio *	Westward Ho! GC	18/72/6,640	SP
La Jolla	Torrey Pines GC	18/72/6,316 18/72/6,723	Pub
Lakeside	Lakeside GC	18/72/6,506 9/36/3,253	SP
La Quinta	The La Quinta CC	18/72/6,433	Pvt
Livermore	Las Pasitas CC	18/72/6,790	SP
Milpitas	Spring Valley GC	18/72/6,395	Pub
Monterey	Del Monte G & CC	18/72/6,173	SP
Monterey	Laguna Seca GC	18/71/6,500	R
Monterey	Pebble Beach Links	18/72/6,747	R
Monterey	Spyglass Hill GC	18/72/6,810	SP
Morro Bay	Morro Bay GC	18/71/6,200	Pub
Mt. Shasta	Lake Shastina GC	18/72/6,620	Pub
Napa	Silverado CC (North) (South)	18/72/6,613 18/72/6,559	Pvt
Newport Beach	Rancho San Joaquin GC	18/72/6,580	SP
Oakland	Lake Chabot GC	18/72/6,365	Pub

LOCATION	COURSE	HOLES/PAR/ YARDAGE	TYPE
Oakland	Lew F. Galbraith GC	18/72/6,750	Pub
Ojai	Ojai Valley Inn & CC	18/71/6,351	SP
Palm Desert *	Del Safari CC	18/72/7,002	Pvt
Palm Desert *	Palm Desert CC	18/70/6,400	SP
Palm Springs	Canyon CC		
	(North)	18/72/6,763	Pvt
	(South)	18/71/6,700	
Palm Springs	Palm Springs GC	18/72/6,500	Pub
Palm Springs	Whitewater CC	18/71/6,164	Pvt
Palo Alto	Palo Alto GC	18/71/6,378	Pub
Pasadena	Brookside GC	18/72/6,533	Pub
		18/70/5,828	
Pauma Valley	Pauma Inn & GC	18/71/6,384	Pvt
Ponway	Valle Verdi CC	18/72/6,900	SP
Rancho La Costa	La Costa GC	18/72/7,114	SP
Rancho Mirage *	Desert Air CC	18/71/6,835	SP
Rancho Santa Fe	Rancho Santa Fe GC	18/72/6,610	R
Rancho Santa Fe	Whispering Palms G & CC	18/71/6,493	SP
Rialto	El Rancho Verde CC	18/72/6,700	SP
Salinas	Laguna Seca GC	18/71/6,500	R
San Bernardino	Spring Valley Lake GC	18/72/6,392	SP
San Diego	Balboa Park GC	18/72/6,187	Pub
San Diego	Stardust CC	18/72/6,400	Pvt
		18/72/6,975	
San Francisco	Harding Park GC	18/72/6,482	Pub
San Jacinto	Soboba Springs CC	18/72/6,726	Pvt
San Jose	Almaden GC	18/72/7,035	SP
San Jose	Oak Ridge GC	18/72/6,548	Pub
San Jose	Pleasant Hills GC	18/72/6,486	Pub
San Marcos	Lake San Marcos CC	18/72/6,497	SP
Santa Barbara	La Cumbre G & CC	18/71/6,338	Pvt
Santa Barbara	Montecito GC	18/72/6,447	SP
Santa Maria	Santa Maria GC	18/72/6,300	SP
Santa Cruz	Pasatiempo GC	18/71/6,245	SP
Santee	Carlton Oaks CC & Lodge	18/72/6,416	R
Santee	Fletcher Hills CC	18/72/6,459	Pub
Solvang	Alisal Ranch–Resort GC	18/72/6,434	R
Sunol	Sunol Valley GC	18/72/6,671	SP
		18/72/6,341	

LOCATION	COURSE	HOLES/PAR/ YARDAGE	TYPE
Temecula	Rancho California	18/72/6,800	R
Valencia	Valencia GC	18/72/6,700	SP
Walnut Creek	Walnut Creek GC	18/72/6,975	SP
Warner Springs	Warner Springs GC	18/72/6,500	R
Watsonville	Pajaro Valley G & CC	18/72/6,252	Pub
Yorba Linda	Yorba Linda Ranch & CC	18/72/7,200	Pvt

* In Palm Springs area

10

THE UNITED STATES: PACIFIC NORTHWEST AND ALASKA

Whether you golf mainly for pleasure or are a serious devotee, you will enjoy playing on the many fine and scenic courses of the Pacific Northwest. Lush, tree-bordered fairways, close-cropped greens, challenging and scenic water hazards combine to make golf in Oregon and Washington not only a test of skill but a pleasurable outing.

OREGON

Most of Oregon's 119 golf courses are located in the Willamette Valley, nestled in the western part of the state between coastal ranges and the mighty Cascade Mountains, which separate the higher sandy plains from the Pacific Ocean.

Portland, a city of 500,000 with a metropolitan area of more than 800,000, lying at the end of the valley on the Columbia River, is the golf capital of the state. It supports over forty courses, at an average of twenty thousand per capita, which is close to the national average. The rest of the state's two million people play on about seventy other courses with a per capita use of only seventeen thousand. So, in spite of the golf boom, crowded conditions are not yet a problem in the Northwest.

Golf courses in Oregon, (and western Washington, too) are among the most beautiful in the world. Douglas fir, native to the Northwest, is abundantly used to line gently rolling fairways. Fairway greenery completely isolates the golfer from the distraction of civilization during his four-hour round of 18 holes. Gigantic evergreens, growing often to a height of over one hundred feet, create a unique serenity and make golf a humbling experience for even the most expert player, not as a game, but in the realization of nature's magnificence.

Oregon's climate allows golf and other outdoor recreation the year round. Just enough rain falls during the summer to keep Oregon green and inviting while much of the rest of the nation suffers from drought.

From Portland it is: (1) an hour's drive to the Pacific Ocean; (2) an hour's drive to the snow-covered peaks of majestic Mt. Hood, the West's most popular ski resort; (3) an hour's drive to some of the most breathtaking mountainous scenery in the world; (4) an hour's drive to some of the most desirable fishing streams in the country; (5) two hours' drive to the sandy deserts of eastern Oregon.

The Hood River Golf Course above the city of Hood River looks invitingly toward the Cascade Mountains and Oregon's highest peak, Mt. Hood, 11,245 feet in elevation.

Golf is taking on a new look in Oregon and is being incorporated into the many developments now underway. Realizing the drawing power of the game, developers are building communities around a golf course. Woodburn Senior Estates, located just thirty minutes south of Portland on the state's major expressway, and King City, a senior resident city right outside of Portland, are examples.

Driving 15 minutes from Portland toward the Oregon coast, one finds a "first" in the state's rapid development schedule. This satellite city known as Somerset West, only three years old and still in its embryonic stage, is the Northwest's first, largest and most comprehensive planned community, involving seven thousand acres, with ten major residential divisions, all with their own personality. Rock

Creek Country Club, which was designed and built at almost twice the cost of a regular commercial golf course, is centered within the gently rolling hills of Rock Creek, the first residential community of Somerset West.

Coastal temperatures are ideal for year-round golf, rarely climbing above eighty in summer and never below freezing in winter. Nearly all of the 16 coastal golf courses are protected from sharp ocean winds by inlets and bluffs, allowing just enough breeze to cool the hot summer's day. It is not uncommon to find light alpacas worn on Oregon beach courses.

The spirit of Oregon coast golf is retained as Salishan Lodge and Golf Links, located at the head of Siletz Bay near Lincoln City. This multi-million-dollar project, including golf course, residential sites, and lodge, has incorporated the natural terrain into its design. Lovely houses on oversized lots, bordering the golf course and overlooking the vast expanse of the Pacific, blend beautifully into the surroundings. Salishan's ten-acre lodge facility, with interconnected buildings accommodating more than one hundred guests, features a three-level dining room with an unobstructed view of Siletz Bay and the Pacific Ocean; a coffee shop overlooking Salishan Bay and the golf course; a cocktail lounge; a special board room for meetings; a gallery room for exhibitions and banquets; a convention hall for audiences of up to three hundred; a heated swimming pool; sauna baths; and children's play areas.

Salishan Golf Links, an 18-hole championship caliber test, was literally carved from nature: at a cost of more than a half-million dollars. The rolling, winding fairways, lined with thick coastal underbrush, shrubs, and evergreens, demand the most of every shot. A variety of strokes is required over the rugged terrain with hardly any two shots the same. Several holes playing westward give a feeling of shooting right out over the ocean.

Although climate is suitable for year-round golf, the active season extends only from March through November, during vacation and tourist seasons. The grandeur of the Pacific demands that coastal areas be tourist and vacation havens, with very little industry. Vacationers maintain beach homes for weekend retreats and summer vacations, leaving them idle during off-seasons or leasing them out. Home owners visit the beach each summer from throughout the nation.

One of Oregon's most popular mountain resort courses is Bowman's Mt. Hood Golf Club. It is just 45 minutes from downtown

Portland, deep in the Cascades, yet just 1,400 feet high. The challenging 6,428-yard course is laid out on a gently rolling Alpine meadow with several small lakes, streams, and plenty of towering firs. Another Cascades Mountain resort is Sunriver Lodge, which has a 7,019-yard championship course at the base of Mt. Bachelor.

So, as you can see, there are beautiful and challenging courses in Oregon. Some of the most interesting are:

LOCATION	COURSE	HOLES/PAR/YARDAGE	TYPE
Clackamas	Pleasant Valley GC	18/72/6,500	Pvt
Cornelius	Forest Hills GC	18/72/6,244	SP
Gearhart	Gearhart GC	18/72/6,147	SP
Gleneden Beach	Salishan Golf Links	18/72/6,437	R
Hillsboro	Meriwether National GC	18/72/7,042	SP
Portland	Colwood National GC	18/72/6,422	Pub
		18/72/7,050	
Portland	Rock Creek CC	18/72/7,100	SP
Portland	Rose City GC	18/71/6,503	Pub
Portland	West Delta Park GC	18/72/6,555	Pub
Salem	McNary GC	18/72/6,718	Pub
Sunriver	Sunriver Lodge & GC	18/72/7,019	SP
Wemme	Bowman's Mt. Hood GC	18/70/6,428	R

WASHINGTON

The state of Washington has 51 private golf clubs and approximately 101 golf clubs open to the public either as public fee or municipal courses. Eastern Washington courses have, for the most part, only about a nine-month season. Unlike the western part of the state, eastern courses need constant sprinkling to prevent burning out, and cold midwinter weather closes them down completely.

Western Washington, like Oregon, has an abundance of rich, rolling courses. In this portion of the Evergreen State, only July and August are considered "dry" for the Northwest. In this sixty-day period, there is a 10–15 per cent probability of rain. The heaviest rains come in November, December, January, February, and March —but again it must be emphasized that "heavy" means only steady; northwestern rain, for the most part, comes in light drizzles.

The result, of course, is turf unmatched anywhere in the world. The courses have lush fairways and soft greens. Washington courses, and it is generally true of those in Oregon, too, are generally shorter

Located south of Olympia, Washington, just off the old Pacific Highway in Tumwater and bisected by the beautiful Deschutes River is the Tumwater Valley 18-hole championship golf course.

than those found in other parts of the country. Sand traps are not as popular here as they are in other places. There are more tree-roughs and water hazards. Northwest fairways are *usually* wider than in other parts of the country. But in spite of this, Washington does have courses, such as the following, that can be quite challenging:

LOCATION	COURSE	HOLES/PAR/ YARDAGE	TYPE
Anacortes	Simiek Beach GC	18/72/6,700	Pub
Olympia	Tumwater Valley GC	18/72/6,441	Pub
Redmond	Sahalee CC	18/72/6,555	Pvt
Spokane	Indian Canyon GC	18/72/6,277	Pub
Tacoma	Spanaway GC	18/72/6,825	Pub
Union	Alderbrook Inn & GC	18/73/6,376	R
Walla Walla	Veteran's Memorial GC	18/72/6,400	Pub

ALASKA

Even the sophisticated traveler may be in for a surprise in northern Alaska when, laden down with the standard equipment of fishing tackle and hunting gear, he stumbles upon the Fairbanks Golf and Country Club, just a hundred miles below the Artic Circle.

There, where glaciers, polar bears, Eskimos, and jagged mountain peaks are the advertised attractions, where mainly miners and trappers formed the sparse population till recent years, where things grow only five months of the year, it comes as a decided shock to find a regulation 18-hole course, which, if not the pride of the greenskeeper, is certainly the joy of the members.

With pride rather than prudence they claim that theirs is the northernmost course in the world, a fact that might be disputed by golfers in northern Sweden or by Lapps who have been photographed in native costume within the Arctic Circle (see page 309). Be that as it may, it is understandable that, owing to its geography, the Fairbanks Golf and Country Club layout is subjected to conditions not found in more southern climes—conditions that unquestionably would prove a decided challenge to the visiting golfer who is used to the velvety greens and fairways of his home club. However, the very fact that this sub-Arctic course does have conditions—or, shall we say, obstacles—not found on other courses should entice the average golfer and certainly provide him with plenty of material for locker-room discussion back home.

The Fairbanks nine has proven to be anything but easy. (It is rated by USGA as 70 par.) It is not designed for the weekend golfer who has only a slight acquaintance with a straight ball. In the first place, the course is well over six thousand yards in length, has no less than six par-5 holes and a couple of rather tricky doglegs. Add to this fairways that are quite narrow and bordered with thick stands of birches and spruce trees and you realize that you have to know quite a bit about the game before you can chalk up much of a score.

A stranger to the Fairbanks course will also find that playing a wood or an iron off the fairways is not quite the same as it is elsewhere. For the first month of the season, the turf is practically nonexistent. Many a player who has hit a drive straight down a fairway has groaned after seeing his ball hit a hard formation of ground and scud under the trees. Later on, some turf does appear, especially on two or three holes away from the trees, and it even has to be mowed periodically. For the most part, however, bare areas are more prevalent than those with turf, and golfers find that they have to be extremely careful, especially when approaching the greens.

It is the greens which puzzle the newcomer most. Unlike the beautiful, lush greens on courses several thousand miles to the south, the greens at the Fairbanks course are made of sand mixed with just the right amount of crankcase oil. This has been necessary because severe winters and lack of water in summer has made grass greens not only impractical but prohibitively expensive. Actually, after a few rounds, you find that sand greens, after all, are not so tough. For one thing, you soon learn that you can pitch a ball almost directly to the pin and expect it to stop there. As for the actual putting, an iron roller is provided at each green for smoothing a path to the cup. Three-putting is thus a rarity, especially in view of the fact that a previous putt often leaves a path that can serve as a guide.

There are a few special rules for the sand greens. Though unwritten, they are strictly adhered to by local golfers. For instance, it is necessary to roll only one path to the cup. By moving the ball over to this path and not nearer the cup, players speed up the game considerably. Also, it is good manners to leave a smooth path for oncoming golfers.

One of the remarkable things about the Fairbanks nine is that anyone would bother to build a course there in the first place, in view of the short playing season, to say nothing of obstacles indigenous to a course so far north. Fairbanks golfers are the first to admit that their season, which gets underway usually around the first week in May, only to shut down directly after the first of October, leaves a lot to be desired. However, they are also quick to point out that when the season does roll around, they have it all over golfers elsewhere. They can play just about any time of the day or *night* they want to.

With 24-hour daylight for a good portion of the season, it is not uncommon to see several foursomes negotiating the course at a time when the average golfer elsewhere is either deep in slumber or just pulling in from a night on the town.

Besides the Fairbanks course, there are only two other courses in Alaska: a military installation course at Anchorage (open to the public) and the Million Dollar Golf Course, operated on City of Juneau land by the Juneau Sandblasters Golf Club and open to guests. It is a 2,300-yard, 9-hole, par 32.

11

THE UNITED STATES: HAWAII

Some Hawaiians will tell you that the famed Captain James Cook, who met an untimely death in the 1700's at the hands of the natives of what were then called the Sandwich Islands, was a golfer. If this is true, the British seafarer arrived at that mid-Pacific paradise a couple of centuries too soon. What a time he would have there today!

Our fiftieth state has become a fabulous place for golf, because of its fine courses and its splendid scenery. One of every fifty people in Hawaii plays golf. But, more important to the economy of the islands, so do many of the million or more tourists who vacation there. There are over 40 courses on six of Hawaii's eight major islands, 27 of them on the island of Oahu, where Honolulu, Waikiki, Diamond Head, Pearl Harbor, and most of the state's 820,000 citizens are located.

Hawaii, of course, provides golf settings of almost unbelievable beauty and variety, plus the world's finest golfing weather. There are beautiful ocean courses such as Waialae Country Club in Honolulu, Mauna Kea Beach on the island of Hawaii, or the Royal Kaanapali on Maui. There also are lush inland courses with tropical mountain settings, such as Oahu Country Club. Or you might enjoy playing Hawaii Country Club in central Oahu, where the sweet scent of the surrounding pineapple fields hangs heavy in the air. On the jewel-like island of Kauai, known as the "Garden Isle," is the Wailua Golf Course, rated by many touring golfers as the best-kept, most beautifully manicured municipal course in the world.

Of Oahu's many golf courses, two better known are Waialae Country Club and Makaha Valley Inn. The latter is more or less off by itself on the western side of the island in a beautiful location. It has 36 holes roaming over the lower slopes of the Waianae Mountains and down to the sea and its own inn-hotel and other facilities. Makaha Valley is one of the newest resort complexes in the islands and its beaches are a paradise for the surfers. Waialae is a private country club in Honolulu—and a good course. It has limited guest privileges. Waialae lies on flat terrain but the ocean is nearby and the usual stiff winds increase its challenge.

In Honolulu, there are the Hawaii Kai, 18-hole "executive" course; Moanalua Golf Club, a fine 9-hole semiprivate course, and the Oahu Country Club, a sporty mountainside, par-68 course gracing the slopes of Nuuanu Valley.

Just outside Honolulu, near the foot of the majestic Pali Cliffs is the championship Pali Golf Course. This outstanding 18-hole, 6,920-yard course offers special rates to high school students and anyone wishing to play late in the afternoon. Another excellent layout located thirty minutes out of Honolulu is the Mid-Pacific Country Club, with a men's par 72 and a women's par 75.

Waikiki, noted for its fabulous beaches, is a golfing center as well. The beautiful Ala Wai Golf Course on the fringe of the city borders the Ala Wai Canal and has a par 71.

There was a time not so very long ago when golfers on a holiday in the fiftieth state rarely ventured outside the Honolulu area on the island of Oahu. Here was the largest concentration of lush courses, plus all the civilized comforts of ultramodern hotels. The neighboring islands—Hawaii, Kauai, Maui, Molokai, Lanai—for the most part were left to the hearty beachcombers willing to "rough it." These islands were difficult to reach, the small hotels were uncomfortable, the food hardly gourmet. Today all this has changed. The Neighbor Islands have been "discovered" and a good share of the credit belongs to golf. Fast, efficient airlines now link the islands with frequent flights that enable the golfer to play the excellent courses in the Honolulu area plus the newer challenges on the other islands—all during a short vacation. And it can be done without great strain on the pocket.

Hawaii, the largest "Neighbor Island," is the home of five volcanoes, two of which are still active. The soaring, often snow-capped, peaks of Mauna Loa and Mauna Kea, spire almost fourteen thousand feet above sea level to provide a breathtaking background to lava-crusted slopes, fern jungles, black-sand beaches, and acres of sugar cane. Hilo, the "Orchid Capital" of the island, is just a quick hour's ride by plane from Honolulu. The four courses on this island, located in the Hamakua–Hilo Volcano area, vary in terrain and climate, situated as they are on the coastal hills and volcanic slopes. Char-

Clouds hang low over the Ala Wai Golf Course, which is located across the Ala Wai Canal from Waikiki Beach.

acterized by large and attractive greens, the Hilo Municipal Course is situated six miles from the slopes of the volcano Mauna Loa. About one hundred miles south of Hilo is the Volcano Golf Course, an impressive 18-hole, par-72 layout, set in the unspoiled scenic wilderness of Hawaii National Park. The Hamakua Country Club, a cleverly designed 9-hole course, is forty miles northwest of Hilo, and guests may use clubs without charge.

On the island of Hawaii, there is one of the greatest seaside courses in the world, Mauna Kea Beach. In fact, the rolling terrain of this club is reminiscent of British seaside courses near Dover, but playing conditions on and around the greens at Mauna Kea are quite different. For instance, British seaside courses have fast-running fairways. The greens have subtle rolls but are otherwise easy to read. Mauna Kea, with a championship length of 7,016 yards, is planted in a thick-bladed, heat-resistant grass which gives up little roll. The ball must be pitched onto greens with strong grain that must be carefully judged. On these greens, the first putt is often an important one.

This is an arid area with only eight inches of rainfall a year. An automatic underground watering system operates on time clocks to keep the fairways and greens in luxuriant condition. Built on a base of volcanic mudrock, Mauna Kea is lined with kiawe bush, palms, and other tropical plants.

Mauna Kea was designed by Robert Trent Jones and it has a number of characteristics that have become his trademarks: long tees, averaging 75 yards, which provide a fair test for all classes of golfers; fairway bunkers with graded slopes that enable the golfer to make up for his original mistake if he can hit the ball clean and true out of the sand; and dogleg holes that invite the bold player to carry the angle and hit straight for the green but severely penalize a poor shot.

Many of the tees are elevated, with the ninth and eighteenth rising to a height of two hundred feet. The ocean is visible from every green, and several greens and tees face Mauna Lao and Mauna Kea, the island's two active volcanoes. Actually, Mauna Kea has two of the most spectacular holes in Hawaii—or anywhere, for that matter. The third hole is much like the famous sixteenth at Cypress Point on Cali-

The third hole at Mauna Kea is one of the most famous holes in the world.

fornia's Monterey Peninsula. It is a heavily trapped par 3, stretching 215 yards from the championship tee. The tee shot must carry 190 yards across a small peninsula and two covers of pounding surf. Another par 3, the eleventh, has you hitting from a highly elevated tee down to a green that has the ocean at its back door.

Island-hopping to nearby Maui, the tourist-golfer can sample any of the four courses open to the public. On the west side of the island at Kaanapali Beach are the rolling fairways of the Royal Kaanapali Golf Course. This course has two nines of such startlingly different char-

The first tee at the Royal Kaanapale golf course. Note that the fairway dog-legs to the left to a green some 426 yards away.

acter that one might almost believe they had been picked up in two separate places and dropped on the island's shore. But regardless of the player's preference both nines offer challenges worthy of his finest game, and each, in its special way, rewards the visitor with beauty. The total length is more than 7,100 yards. Par is 72. The first nine plays to the sea, and a 2,000-foot manmade lagoon winds through three of the holes. The course is laid out over gently rolling, lush fairways of Tifton grass, which is a species of Bermuda, and they are brushed by sea winds that come up so suddenly they can make a golfer want to switch clubs right in the middle of his swing. The winds follow you up into the hills on the back nine, which twists over a layer of volcanic rock. Eventually, you reach a spectacular vantage point, with the West Maui Mountains facing you in the distance and the con-voluting fairways stretching out before you. To say you are playing a different nine is to state the obvious.

Adjacent to the Royal Kaanapali is the Kaanapali Kai Golf Club, an 18-hole executive course.

Kahaului Harbor and Airport are centrally located to the Maui Country Club and Municipal Course. Maui Country Club is a top-flight 9-hole, 3,225-yard layout, and Warehu Golf Course, an exciting par-73 arrangement. Holes 1, 2, and 3 at this municipal course border the ocean and even the low-handicap player will be tested on this hilly and windy course. Problem spots are hole six, carrying over a swamp, and the ninth tee, set on a hill three hundred feet above sea level.

To digress for a moment, it is very important to know how to handle the tradewinds, which blow from the southeast at an average speed of 12–15 mph. When hitting *into* the trades you have to keep the ball low or overclub substantially—say, a 6-iron when you might normally hit a 7 or an 8. Of course, you do not *always* hit into the wind, so just as often it is to your advantage to try a 3-wood off the tee to get the ball up into the trades for more carry. Crosswinds? They can make a hook or a slice worse just as they do in the other 49 states.

There are two 9-hole courses on the island of Molokai, while Lanai has but one. On Kauai, oldest of the island chain, the tourist will find three courses worth testing. Narrow fairways, natural rough, and some of the best cocos bent greens in the Islands vividly describe the lovely Wailua Beach Golf Course. Overlooking Kalapaki, there is the 9-hole public course, the Kauai Surf Golf & Country Club. Farther inland is the Kukuiolona Golf Course, a well-conditioned, completely grassed hilltop west of Lihue.

There are more than enough beautiful and well-kept public and semipublic courses in Hawaii for the average vacation stay in the Island State. As on the mainland, a guest card is usually required on the private courses. But Hawaiian club members are just as friendly as any you will ever meet, and such courtesies are by no means unobtainable. Of course, if you are a retired serviceman, you should have no problem on Hawaii's unusually fine military courses. (There are ten military courses on the island of Oahu, but they are noted on the chart below.)

To be sure of playing where you plan to play, however, the first and best thing to do is to check well in advance with your travel agent or the manager of the hotel where you are staying.

LOCATION	COURSE	HOLES/PAR/ YARDAGE	TYPE
Island of Kauai			
Kalapaki Beach	Kauai Surf G & CC	9/35/3,175	Pub
Kalaheo	Kukuiolono GC	9/35/2,947	Pvt
Lihue	Wailua GC	18/72/7,028	Pub
Princeville	Princeville-at-Hanalei GC	18/72/6,530	SP
		9/36/3,260	
Island of Oahu			
Waikiki	Ala Wai GC	18/71/6,400	Pub
Pearl Harbor	Pearl CC of Hawaii	18/72/7,077	SP
Kahuku	Kiulima GC	18/72/6,575	R
Kunia	Hawaii CC	18/69/5,937	SP
Hawaii Kai	Hawaii Kai GC	18/56/2,690	Pub
Kahuku	Kahuku GC	9/35/2,725	Pub
Makaha	Makaha Valley Inn & CC	18/72/7,252	R
		18/71/6,092	
Lanikai	Mid-Pacific CC	18/72/6,421	Pvt
Waipahu	Ted Makaleva GC	18/71/6,295	Pub
Waipio	Mililani GC	18/70/6,460	Pub
Nuuanu	Oahu CC	18/71/5,955	Pvt
Waimanalo	Olomana GC	18/71/6,250	Pub
Pali	Pali GC	18/72/6,570	Pub
Waialae-Kahala	Waiolae CC	18/72/6,608	Pvt
Island of Molakai			
Kalae Heights	Ironwood Hills GC	9/35/2,804	SP
	Maunaloa GC	9/36/2,981	Pvt
Island of Lanai			
Lanai City	Cavendish GC	9/36/3,090	Pub
Island of Maui			
Sprecklesville	Maui CC	9/37/3,225	Pub
Kaanapali Beach	Royal Kaanapali GC	18/72/7,179	R
Kaanapali Beach	Kaanapali Kai GC	18/64/4,270	R
Waiehu	Waiehu GC	18/72/6,565	SP
Wailea	Wailea	18/72/6,600	SP

LOCATION	COURSE	HOLES/PAR/ YARDAGE	TYPE
Island of Hawaii			
Honokaa	Hamakua CC	9/33/2,505	SP
Kaumana	Hilo CC	9/36/2,854	SP
Hilo	Hilo GC	18/72/6,467	Pub
Kona	Keauhou-Kona GC	18/72/6,705	SP
Kawaikei Harbor	Mauna Kea Beach GC	18/72/7,016	R
Hilo	Volcano GC	18/72/6,411	Pub
Kamuela	Waikoloa Village GC	18/72/6,715	SP

12

CANADA

Canada has some of the most beautiful and challenging golf courses in the world. The first organized golf club in North America is near Montreal. Except in British Columbia on the Pacific coast, golf in Canada is played for a relatively short season from mid-May to mid-October. As in the United States, we'll mention, as a rule, only the courses that the tourist can play without special dispensation. Incidentally, most private Canadian clubs will accept members of comparable U.S. clubs as guests.

Let's start our tour of Canadian golf on the eastern coast.

THE MARITIME PROVINCES

For most tourists, the Canadian Maritime Provinces of Nova Scotia, New Brunswick, and Prince Edward Island suggest deep-sea fishing, big-game hunting, and menacing icebergs. Rarely, if ever, do we think of this eastern corner of Canada in terms of golf. This is a mistake, because some of the most picturesque and challenging courses on the North American continent can be found here. At latest count there were approximately 45 golf layouts ranging from sporty 9-holers to championship 18-hole tests, skirting the sea and/or ranging through forests.

Nova Scotia's best known layout is the Cape Breton Highlands Golf Links. It is an understatement to say that this is one of the great adventures in golf. The course, generally known as "Keltic" after the government-owned lodge nearby, is actually the "Everest" of golf courses—you play it because it's there!

The mountainous metaphor is not an accidental one; it is rather an attempt to convey a feeling of Keltic's challenge. It is a fiendishly difficult course to play.

To begin with, the setting is superb, combining seaside, valley, and mountainous terrain in almost perfect proportion. In laying out the individual holes, golf course and landscape architect Stanley Thompson sought to use every natural nuance, and placed tees and greens in only the most perfect positions. He also paid little attention to the usual practice of placing tees adjacent to the greens they follow. The result is a golf course whose actual walking length is half again as long as the 6,600-yard scorecard length.

The test begins promptly at Cape Breton Highlands. The first hole, a 415-yard par 4, runs up between walls of pines, along a rising fairway studded with little hills, to a wide but shallow green. The second hole is a 450-yard par-4 dogleg right. The top of the down-sloping fairway affords a wonderful view of Ingonish Bay. And that's the way the course goes; it's a great test of golf, and a beautiful picture every-

The Keltic Golf Course in Cape Breton Highlands National Park is one of the most difficult golf courses in North America.

where you look. But don't look up at the wrong time or the trees will get you.

Each hole at Cape Breton is named. (Naming holes is a Scottish tradition, and some names suggest that the Scots think of golf not only as a game but also as part of their heritage.) The seventh hole at Cape Breton is called Killiecrankie, Gaelic for long narrow pass. A battle famous in Scottish history was fought at a place called Killiecrankie. The golfer can expect to fight his way through Cape Breton's Killiecrankie, a 585-yard par 5. The fairway is a slender aisle between steep banks of evergreens. There are big mounds in the tee-shot landing area, and if you're behind one you need a lofted club to get the ball up fast over it. Further on, the mounds diminish, but the fairway climbs through an alley of bunkers. The third shot, with anything from a 3-wood to an 8-iron, depending on the wind direction, is to a two-level green with traps massed on the left, the side to which the green slopes. It's a tough hole, one of the best in the game and one which any golfer would like to try.

Deer help to keep the grass short on this course, which is part of a national park and game preserve operated by the Canadian government. It plays to 6,600 yards and a par 72 but is far more challenging than its statistics indicate. The first nine stretches out in a near-straight line, with no parallel holes. You return to the club house in the opposite direction. Throughout the course between green and tee you walk on tree-shaded paths. Of course, Keltic is not only a course for the scratch golfer, but it could easily be described as the duffer's paradise. After all, who could possibly be expected to score here? Besides, the scenic wonders are indescribable. If there is such a place as God's country, this is surely it. Playing at Keltic is not unlike competing in the Boston Marathon. For all but a very few, the object is not winning —the idea is to finish.

On the northeastern shore of the Nova Scotia mainland, approximately 65 miles from Yarmouth, is the old established resort community of Digby, overlooking the Annapolis Basin, which opens into the Bay of Fundy. A mile from town is the Digby Pines Golf Course, which has been attracting American and mainland Canadian players since the early 1930's. At 6,140 yards, Digby Pines is, as its name suggests, flanked by tall pine trees. Rolling fairways, well-trapped greens, and picturesque but formidable water hazards, make it one of the most interesting courses in the area. The 175-yard second hole is a par 3 of real distinction, calling for a tee shot to carry a creek and pond that bisect the hole all the way to the green. Behind the green is a large, overgrown mound that is very reluctant to give up a golf ball, so a precise tee shot is imperative. Actually, the trees from which the course derives its name border almost every fairway, and there is no lack of sand and/or grass bunkers. Straight driving is the name of the game at The Pines, and failure to keep the ball in play provides an opportunity to see a bit more of the surrounding countryside than is absolutely necessary. This course, as well as the Digby Motor Hotel, are operated by the Nova Scotia Government.

At the Acadian settlement of Truro, there is one of the first golf courses (built 1903) in the province. Originally only a 9-hole layout, it has been expanded to a full 18 holes in the past decade. Each year it is the site of many of Nova Scotia's premier golf tournaments, and low scores on Truro's lush layout are never easy to come by. Typical of the course is the 170-yard second hole. Looking toward the green from the tee you feel you are looking at a theater stage. A tall stand of elegant old spruce trees form the sides of the proscenium arch, effectively "curtaining" the entrance to the putting surface. Your tee shot must find the keyhole opening, or you're in the bordering woods. Truro is terribly tight and tough.

The capital city of Nova Scotia—Halifax—will serve as an excellent base from which to visit the three fine courses of Halifax County. The 1,300-odd members of the Halifax Golf & Country Club have developed something of a "Utopia" for the modern urban golfer. They have not one course, but two—and while this is not itself such a rarity, the nature and location of the two courses is. Both courses are operated under the name Ashburn Golf Course, and the older of the two layouts is located within the city limits of Halifax. It is a narrow, hilly, well-wooded course, with a number of natural water hazards. On its shortish dimensions (5,322 yards) the emphasis is on accuracy, and members find the course ideal for a fast midweek round.

When you are not pressed for time, play the "New Course" at Kinsac Lake. New Ashburn is the largest course in Nova Scotia at over 7,100 yards, and it is an impressively beautiful place to play. The course has been carved out of what was once a virgin lakeside woodland, and everything possible has been done to retain the scenic majesty. Tall trees border every fairway, and the frequent glimpses of Spruce and Kinsac Lakes makes it hard to believe that the course lies in a not very distant "suburb" of a big Canadian city. Most distinctive of New Ashburn's many interesting qualities, is the huge double green that serves the sixth and eleventh holes. This throwback to a bygone golfing era is, somehow, not at all anachronistic in this setting, but rather a "tipping of the hat" to a centuries-old heritage. There is one further item at New Ashburn that can safely be said to be uniquely Canadian. As you trudge up the eighteenth, directly in the center of the fairway, totally obstructing the entry to the green, looms a large, lonely evergreen.

Also in the suburbs around Halifax and Dartmouth is the Oakfields Country Club. It is as wide open as New Ashburn is wooded, but it is no less difficult. Its lakeside setting ensures a bit of a breeze at all times, and it is a fair and often trying test of golf. It also possesses what has to be one of the most unusual golf holes in the world. As you approach the fourth tee, after playing three interesting though hardly startling holes, you are faced with quite a sight. The scorecard clearly states that there is supposed to be a 329-yard par 4 to play at this point, and while there is in fact a tee, there does not seem to be either a green or a flagstick. There's not even a direction flag. All that you see is a 200-yard square, totally encircled by trees. It looks very much like someone's idea of a practical joke. But the caddies at Oakfield are used to a stranger's initial disorientation here, and are quick to end your disquiet. "Just hit for the middle of the square," they'll say, assuring you that this is not golf's version of the "Twilight Zone." Sure enough, tucked in the left corner of the square is a funnel-like opening that is obscured from view until you are almost on top of it. Beyond, there is even a putting green and a pin.

Another course worth playing in Nova Scotia is the Lingan Country Club, just outside of Sydney. It is the kind of course where bogeys are the rule and pars are mighty hard to come by. The Nova Scotia golf pros unanimously regard it as one of the hardest courses to score on in all of the Maritimes, and you'll find little reason to disagree with them. The course measures 6,700 yards and you play every foot of it. The distances on the scorecard are deadly accurate, and your driving had better be also. You get a real sense of the length when you encounter your first ladies par 6 at the fifth hole! Lingan is definitely not for the timid.

There are excellent golf courses in the other Maritime Provinces, too. For instance, for Americans who choose to come by car from Maine, the destination most likely will be St. Andrews-by-the-Sea in New Brunswick, some twenty miles from the United States border town of Calais via Route 1. As should be expected of any community called St. Andrews, there must be golf worthy of the name. St. Andrews offers two courses, both operated by the Canadian Pacific's Algonquin Hotel. For the serious player, the 18-hole Algonquin Hotel Golf Course offers an interesting test along with breathtaking views of Passamaquoddy Bay, famous for spectacularly high tides, a phenomenon of the coastal waters adjoining the Bay of Fundy. Designed more than a half-century ago by Donald Ross of Pinehurst, the course plays to par 71, and ranges from 5,871 to 6,314 yards, depending on tee placement. But even at the shorter length, Algonquin is no pushover. Sprayed shots will find the many strategically placed bunkers en route to, and surrounding, the cleverly contoured greens. There are out-of-bounds, heavy rough, and innocent-looking trees to remind the wild swinger that golf is a game of skill and intelligence. For sheer beauty and golfing pleasure, the par-4 fifth is a memorable experience. A 405-to-433-yard dogleg to the left, the hole opens up on a breathtaking view of the Bay. The fairway drops sharply to a well-trapped green surrounded by forest and sea. Under violent storm conditions, the waters at high tide have covered the green and the nearby sixth tee. The three par 3's—the third (172 yards), seventh (125 yards), and fifteenth (198 yards)—are a challenge to the sharpshooter, who hits from elevated tees to tightly trapped greens with lots of trouble in between. The par-5 second from the 480-yard back tee is tempting for the long hitter hoping to get home.

New Brunswick has 15 other excellent golfing facilities, including the beautiful 9-hole Alma Golf Club in Fundy National Park and the championship 18-hole Riverside Golf and Country Club at Rothesay, east of St. John. One of the most challenging courses in eastern Canada, Riverside has been the site of the Canadian Open, the Canadian PGA, and the Canadian Amateur.

A 55-minute ferry ride from Cape Tormentine, New Brunswick, will bring the golfer, his car and his clubs to Prince Edward Island. This smallest of the Canadian provinces offers man-sized golfing thrills and the best ocean swimming north of Cape Cod. The golfer's goal is the Green Gables Colf Course, also known as "The Links," located in Prince Edward Island National Park at Cavendish, on the north shore. A showplace of the National Parks system, Green Gables is a 6,410-yard, par-72 seaside links which has been in operation since the late 1930's. It takes its name from the Green Gables farm house immortalized by Island-authoress Lucy Maud Montgomery in her classic best-seller, *Anne of Green Gables*. The cottage is a lovely tourist attraction overlooking the par-4 ninth hole. Called "Green Gables," the 435-yard ninth is a tree-lined dogleg requiring a well-placed drive and a near-perfect second shot over a pond and on to a steep plateau green, which is backed by three traps.

All the holes are picturesquely named. The par-3, 185-yard second, known as the "Dryad's Bubble," is bedeviled by a pond in front of the heavily trapped elevated green. The 545-yard fifth, longest hole of the course, overlooks the Gulf of St. Lawrence and the dunes bordering the beach. This par 5 is called "Gulf View."

The first nine are inland holes, characterized by tree-lined, rolling fairways and tightly trapped greens. The back nine starts with the 315-yard dogleg tenth, a relatively easy par 4 if you keep your drive or approach shot away from the heavy rough and pond skirting the left side

One of the finest 18-hole golf courses in Canada is Green Gables, set in the rolling countryside near Cavendish, Prince Edward Island. The golf course centers around the old farm home, now a museum, known to children the world over as the home of Anne of Green Gables, created by Prince Edward Island authoress Lucy Maud Montgomery.

of the fairway. Then from the eleventh through the sixteenth, you have to contend with tidal ponds and channels, sand dunes, and unpredictable sea breezes that can, and often do, reach gale proportions. Playing conditions in this exposed seaside area are rarely the same from day to day, or even from morning to afternoon.

While most of the golf traffic, which is light by U.S. standards, is centered on Green Gables, there also are two other attractive 18-hole establishments, the Belvedere Golf Course at the Island's capital of Charlottetown, and the Town and Country Club at Summerside. Two par-3 courses round out the selection.

Here is a breakdown of the most challenging courses of the Maritime Provinces:

LOCATION	*COURSE*	*HOLES/PAR/ YARDAGE*
New Brunswick		
Alma	Fundy National Park GC	9/35/3,095
Edmundston	Edmundston GC	18/72/6,663
East Riverside	Riverside CC	18/71/5,960
Four Falls	Aroostook Valley CC	18/72/7,000
Fredericton	Fredericton GC	18/70/5,934
Fredericton	Mactaquac Provincial Park GC	18/72/7,030
St. Andrews-by-the-Sea	Algonquin Hotel GC	18/72/6,314
Newfoundland		
St. John	Bally Haly G & CC	18/71/5,941
Nova Scotia		
Corner Brook	Blomidon G & CC	18/71/6,011
Digby	Digby Pines GC	18/71/6,140
Halifax	Oakfields CC	18/72/6,975
Ingonish Beach	Cape Breton Highlands Links	18/72/6,600
Kinsac Lake	New Ashburn CC	18/72/7,100
New Glasgow	Abercrombie G & CC	18/72/6,450
Sydney	Lingan CC	18/72/6,711
Truro	Truro GC	18/70/6,380
Prince Edward Island		
Cavendish	Green Gables GC	18/72/6,410
Charlottetown	Brudenell G & CC	18/72/6,500
Charlottetown	Belvedere G & CC	18/72/6,372

QUEBEC

Variety is the keynote to golf in tourist-conscious Quebec. La Belle Province offers the vacationing golfer everything from picturesque mountain layouts in the colorful Laurentians to sporty short courses overlooking the mighty St. Lawrence River at the gateway to the Gaspe Peninsula.

There are actually three separate seasons for golf in Quebec. Because of the long winter, the majority of courses open in the middle of May. There follows a month of play when even the long hitters have difficulty reaching the par-4 and -5 holes in respectable figures, for the fairways are not yet dry. But by June 15 all courses have reached peak playability, which lasts for the next three months.

Perhaps the most picturesque season is the fall, when untold thousands of maples are brightly colored and the crisp air gives the golfer that good-to-be-alive feeling. This applies to the Laurentian Mountain area in particular.

The Laurentians, one of the oldest mountain ranges in the world, feature outstanding golf courses ideally located for the traveling tourist and easily accessible by train, plane, car, bus, or water. The mountain range extends from west to north of Montreal. A thirty-mile Autoroute, the province's super highway, leads the vacationer into the Laurentian foothills from Montreal to St. Jerome. For the next fifty miles, Route 11 provides pleasant driving to almost all of the resort golf courses.

Only 39 miles north of Montreal is the Shawbridge Golf and Country Club in Shawbridge, where nonmembers are admitted on weekdays, but on weekends only if accompanied by a member. The St. Sauveur Golf Club at Saint Sauveur has nine holes, and the Mont-Gabriel Golf Club in Piedmont has 18 holes. Both courses are open to the public.

Possibly the best-known resort course in this general area is the Gray Rocks Golf Club in St. Jovite. Its par-71, 18-hole course, considered one of the most beautiful in all of Canada, is surrounded by seven peaks of the Laurentians and thousands of pine trees. The course is long on the front nine, short and tricky on the back nine. The 360-yard, par-4 fourth is one of the most difficult. From an elevated tee, the fairway drops fifty feet to an out-of-bounds on the right and evergreen-covered roughs on the left. The fairway doglegs to the right to a steep climb of 75 feet, and the green sits up in a huge bowl. A long tee shot is required, and the second shot to the green is always longer than it appears because of the elevated green. If played too short, the ball will roll back to you and you can try again.

The fourteenth, a par 3 of 155 yards, is typical of the difficult back nine. The hole is built entirely on a steep hillside, sloping from right to left. The green is small with a big bank in the back, but none on the left. Should you overshoot the green, miss the green on the left, or be too short—well, you can guess the result. The hole has no fairway, only rough with steep inclines from right to left. The trick is to play to

TROU	1	2	3	4	5	6	7	8	9	SOR.	10	11	12	13	14	15	16	17	18	REV.	Total	Hdcp.	Net
BLEU	350	325	145	525	330	150	440	300	175	2740	320	495	200	505	340	180	305	300	430	3075	5815		
ROUGE	320	315	135	500	320	140	430	290	160	2610	305	485	175	495	325	165	290	290	420	2950	5560		
JAUNE	290	300	120	430	310	125	420	275	150	2420	290	400	130	425	320	150	280	210	390	2595	5015		
NORMALE	4	4	3	5	4	3	5	4	3	35	4	5	3	5	4	3	4	4	4/5	36/37	71/72		
TOLÉRANCE	5	9	15	1	7	17	3	11	13		10	4	14	2	8	18	12	16	6				

EVALUATION DU TERRAIN:
BLEU 69
ROUGE 69
JAUNE 66

Date _____
Pointeur _____
Témoin _____

One of the most scenic and challenging golf courses in eastern Canada is Club de Golf Lac Beauport. This is an aerial view of the course and its scorecard.

the right of the green on the high side and hope that the ball will drib-
ble down on to the green.

The Laurentian area is, in general, a summer vacationland for
Montreal's millions. Hundreds of lakes dot the mountain area and provide excellent boating, sailing, swimming, and water skiing. The better-
than-average golfer will find all he can handle at the Lachute Golf
Club, fifty miles northwest of Montreal. Lachute boasts two 18-hole
courses that can be extended to seven thousand yards at a par 72.
Both layouts wind through thick cedar and pine wooded areas which
place a premium on accuracy off the tee. And there are water holes,
doglegs, uphill par 4's and just about every type of hole imaginable
to test every club in the bag.

Also in the Laurentian area are such private courses as: Hillsdale
(27 holes), Cedarbrook (18 holes), Green Valley (18 holes), and
Rosemere (18 holes).

Unlike many metropolitan areas in the United States, the Montreal
district has few public courses compared to the number of private ones.
The city of Montreal maintains a 36-hole course, six miles from the
heart of town, where for a two-dollar greens fee, the golfer can enjoy himself with a minimum of travel. As with most public courses,
the earlier you tee off the better.

Further along Sherbrooke Street is the Anjou Golf Club, an 18-hole
layout where weekday greens fees compare to those of the Municipal.
In the southern section of the city is the LaSalle Golf Club, an 18-
holer; and across the St. Lawrence are the Bellevue and Beauchateau
Golf Clubs, both 18 holers.

In the past five years, some of Montreal's finest golf clubs have
moved because of the population swing to the suburbs. Royal Montreal
Golf Club, one of the oldest clubs in North America, has been shifted
to a site on Ile Bizard, some twenty miles west of the city. Here the
Royal Club has 45 holes, and either the Blue or Red courses offer the
toughest golf test in the province.

Adjacent to Royal Montreal are two other newly relocated courses:
the 36-hole Elm Ridge Golf Club and, 12 miles to the south at Cedars,
Summerlea's thirty-sixer.

Murray Bay, ninety miles below Quebec City on the St. Lawrence
River, has long been referred to as the "Newport of the North." Built
in the early 1930's by Herbert Strong, the mighty Manoir Richelieu
course is inevitably ranked among the great. The hilly layout has two

escalators, with a view of the mighty St. Lawrence River from the heights of the north shore, and is the ultimate in rugged-terrain golf. "The Manoir" belongs to the Canada Steamship Lines and is a first-class resort hotel.

Situated between Montreal and the Canadian capital, Ottawa, is the storied Seignory Club. Here is another Canadian Pacific product and one of the most unusual resorts in Canada. The Seignory course is not exhaustingly long, is in superb condition, and its accompanying log-style lodge is one of the luxury watering spots of North America.

The ancient capital of the New World, Quebec City, has a number of enjoyable layouts. Outstanding is the resort course at Lac Beauport, 13 miles from the picturesque Citadel City. Royal Quebec, one of the oldest courses in America, is situated at Boischatel, close to the trenches occupied by Wolfe's Highlanders in 1759.

There is plenty of water at Le Chateau Montebello Golf Course.

As was stated in Chapter 1, there are two schools of golf-course architecture: the penal and the strategic. Since so many courses today have been lengthened and tightened beyond all resemblance to their original layouts, it often takes a practiced eye to tell the difference between the two schools. At few clubs is the distinction as noticeable as it is at Royal Quebec, which has 18 holes of the penal school ringed by nine of the strategic. That is, the back nine of the 18 was laid out forty-odd years ago by Willie Park, a Scottish architect of the penal school, then very much in vogue, which treated courses as though they should be obstacle courses. Park's greens have rolls as steep as staircases or as obvious as Indian burial mounds. Traps in the form of gigantic horse troughs have been placed every which way, sometimes merely to break the monotony of a fairway or to catch wild shots rolling from parallel fairways. For the most part, these traps have been drawn back from the perimeters of the greens in order to leave plenty of room for chipping and pitching. When this course was laid out, chipping and pitching were looked upon not so much as recovery shots but as integral parts in the process of scoring a British "bogey." In America, the term "bogey" has come to mean a score that is one over par for a hole. In its original form "bogey" was another form of "par," often one stroke higher than the par we use today, and represented the score which a not-quite-first-rate player might be expected to take for a hole. In those days of hickory shafts, you weren't expected to drill long second shots to the center of the green or even onto the green, and so a deft chip or a pitch was your best chance of breaking "bogey."

The new championship nine at Royal Quebec—used as the front nine for the match—was built just a few years ago by Howard Watson, a member of the newer strategic school. This treats the game as a contest of qualified risks, rather than a steeplechase, in which weaker shots will almost inevitably punish themselves but in which hazards must be placed to entice the stronger player. Watson's subtly undulated greens cover an area half again as large as that used by Willie Park on the older, back nine. His bunkers are formless, almost impressionistic in shape, and yet are so natural and so logically placed that they look as though they have always been there, the course somehow ingeniously built to fit them rather than the other way round. Many of them are stuck flush against the greens, or more nearly where the steel shaft precisionists of today are apt to miss the greens, if they miss them at all.

Here are the leading courses you can play while in Quebec:

LOCATION	COURSE	HOLES/PAR/ YARDAGE
Montreal Area		
Laval	Club de Golf Islemer	18/72/6,420
		9/35/2,898
Montreal	La Prairie GC	18/72/6,575
Montreal	Meadowbrook GC	18/72/6,420
Montreal	Club de Golf de LaVille de Montreal	18/72/6,700

LOCATION	COURSE	HOLES/PAR/ YARDAGE
Southern Quebec Province		
Bromont	Club de Gold de Bromont	18/72/6,500
Drummondville	Drummondville G & Curling Club	18/71/6,335
Lennoxville	Lennoxville G & CC	18/72/6,628
Tracy	Club de Golf Sorel-Tracy	18/72/6,566
The Laurentians		
Aylmer East	Glenlea GC	18/71/6,040
Lachute	Lachute G & CC	18/72/6,735
		18/72/6,990
Lake Beauport	Le Manoir St. Castin	18/70/6,300
Montebello	Le Chateau Montebello GC	18/70/6,110
Piedmont	Club de Golf Mont Gabriel	18/72/6,123
Pine Hill	Carling Lake GC	18/72/6,650
St. Adele-en-Hart	Le Chantecler GC	18/70/6,010
St. Jovite	Gray Rocks G & Winter Club	18/72/6,410
Sainte Monique	Green Valley G & CC	18/72/6,700
Montreal-Quebec (St.Maurice Valley)		
Berthier	Club de Golf de Berthier	18/72/6,450
Grand Mere	Club Golf de Grand Mere GC	18/71/6,427
Levis	Club de Golf Levis	18/72/6,789
Loretteville	Club de Golf de Loretteville	18/72/6,694
Charlevoix, North Shore		
Clarke City	Club de Golf St. Marquerito	18/72/6,785
Pointe au Pic	Club de Golf du Manoir Richelieu	18/70/6,110

ONTARIO

Ontario is Canada's largest golfing province. Nine resort districts offer 79 courses. Toronto, a city of 1,500,000, has played host to more major championships than any other in Canada. Superlative tests such as Scarboro Golf Course, Mississauqua Golf & Country Club, Toronto Golf Club, the ultra Boxgrove, Summit, and Lambton rate with the finest. There are in Metropolitan Toronto over one hundred courses, including par-3 and executive course arrangements.

The scenic Thousand Islands region on Ontario's section of the St. Lawrence River has a number of fine courses. In the Muskoka district, Bigwin Inn has long been a summer rendezvous for keen golfers. Far north, in the hardrock mining district clubs such as Sudbury's Idlwylde and the inviting French River Club attract many traveling players.

One of Canada's most famous courses is at the London Hunt and Country Club in London, Ontario. This long par 72, with a championship length of 7,168 yards, in the tradition of Robert Trent Jones–designed courses, has more than a few water hazards. The River Thames (London, Ontario, version) borders the wooded, steeply rolling course and is a factor to be reckoned with on the tenth hole. There is a pond on the par-3 second hole and two more on the par-5 tenth. A deep barranca, or gulley, confronts the players on the 600-yard, par-5 seventh hole and on the eighth, a par 3.

The 550-yard tenth hole is typical of the course and a great par 5. The River Thames runs along the right side of the fairway from tee to green. A large pond eats into the left side of the fairway about where most tee shots land. The area between the river and the pond is not large. The green on this tenth hole is surrounded on the front and left by another pond and guarded on the right by a bunker and the River Thames. The green is long and narrow with difficult pin positions. In designing a par 5, the architect seeks to make all shots from tee to green a test of skill and accuracy. He tempts the long hitters to go for the green with their second shots by giving them a reasonable chance to succeed and makes the third shot a demanding one for shorter hitters.

The following is a rundown of some of the better courses that a tourist can play during a visit to Ontario:

LOCATION	COURSE	HOLES/PAR/ YARDAGE
Agincourt	Brookwood CC	18/72/6,383
Hornby	Hornby Towers GC	18/72/6,700
Hornby	Wydlwood CC	18/72/6,002
London	Fanshawe GC	18/71/6,400
North Bay	North Bay G & CC	18/72/6,458
Port Perry	Sunny Brae GC	18/71/6,160
Pickering	Annandale GC	18/72/6,275
		9/35/2,900
Toronto	Glen Abbey GC	18/72/6,850
Toronto	Glen Eagle GC	18/72/6,950
Toronto	Huntington GC	18/72/6,840

LOCATION	COURSE	HOLES/PAR/ YARDAGE
Toronto	Malton GC	18/72/6,450
Toronto Willowdale	Don Valley GC	18/72/6,456

Ontario Resort Courses

Gravenhurst	Muskoka Sands G & Ski Club	9/35/3,000
Lake Rosseau	Windermere House GC	18/70/6,193
Midland	Midland G & CC	18/72/6,400
Niagara Falls	Whirlpool GC	18/72/6,945
Upper Canada Village	Upper Canada GC	18/72/6,740

MANITOBA

Manitoba has four courses of the resort variety. They are Falcon Lake Golf Course a 6,789-yard Provincial Park course; Wasagaming Golf Course located at Clear Lake in Riding National Park; Minaki Lodge Course (actually in Ontario) right on the Manitoba border; and Victoria Beach Golf Course, situated on the eastern shoreline of scenic Lake Winnipeg.

The private 72-par, 6,757-yard course at St. Charles Country Club in Winnipeg is generally considered one of Canada's best. It is a demanding layout and a score at or near par is *very* well earned. The course has huge fairway bunkers and the trees are just where they should be. The par-5 fourteenth is the most testing hole on this course and typical of the problems faced by the golfer at St. Charles. A dogleg right, the hole plays at 543 yards. There are bunkers down the left side at 200 and 365 yards, a tree on the right edge of the fairway about 270 yards out and a bunker beyond that at 350 yards. The green, almost completely surrounded by trees, opens up to the left side of the fairway. It is guarded by a large trap on the right front, two traps on the left side and one at the rear.

Other interesting courses that the tourist can play in Manitoba are:

LOCATION	COURSE	HOLES/PAR/ YARDAGE
East Kildonan	Rossmere G & CC	18/70/6,250
Falcon Lake	Falcon Lake GC	18/72/6,789
Riding National Park	Wasagaming GC	18/72/6,272
Winnipeg	John Blunbery GC	18/71/6,464
Winnipeg	Kildonan Park GC	18/69/5,556
Winnipeg	Windsor Park GC	18/69/5,367

The view can sometimes be disconcerting when you play golf in Riding Mountain National Park. Here one of the eighteen holes of the course commands a view of well-named Clear Lake.

SASKATCHEWAN

Saskatchewan's Prince Albert National Park, far to the north, has a club known as Waskesiu, dating back to the early 1930's. It is surrounded by good motels and cottages. The golfing visitor may find it interesting to visit some of the Provincial Park Clubs in Saskatchewan, which in many cases still provide the now unusual sand-greens. Here are some of the worthwhile courses in Saskatchewan:

LOCATION	COURSE	HOLES/PAR/ YARDAGE
Duck Mt. Park	Madge Lake GC	18/68/5,544
Moose Jaw	Moose Jaw CC	18/73/6,400
Moose Mt. Park	Kenosee Lake GC	18/69/5,364
Prince Albert	Cooke GC	18/71/6,407
Prince Albert N.P.	Waskesiu Lake GC	18/70/6,059
Regina	Murray GC	18/71/6,640
Saskatoon	Riverside CC	18/72/6,528
Yorkton	Deer Park GC	18/71/5,825

ALBERTA

About 70,000,000 years ago, tremendous internal forces in the earth thrust up a huge chain of mountains from the sea. The sea has long since ebbed away, but the mountains, a part of the Canadian Rockies, still tower massively over the Banff Springs Hotel golf course in Banff, Alberta. The 6,704-yard layout winds along the pine-clad foot of the mountains, capitalizing fully on the gorgeous scenery. Both the golf course and the Banff Springs Hotel, just a hundred yards from the first tee, are owned and operated by the Canadian Pacific Railway. So alluring is the beauty of Banff to vacationers that a quarter of a million people annually flock there and to nearby Lake Louise, forty miles away.

The Banff Springs Hotel originally was a modest hostel for the workmen who laid the Canadian Pacific Railway across Canada during the late nineteenth century. Additions were made over the years, and today it is a sprawling up-to-date 600-room resort hotel offering riding, tennis, swimming, and some of the most breathtaking scenery to be found anywhere in the world.

The stunning par-71 golf course was completed in 1927. Designed by the late Stanley Thompson, a renowned Canadian golf course architect, it was built under enormous difficulties. One hole—the seventh—had to be literally carved out of the face of Mount Rundle. But out of this rocky wilderness arose one of the most splendid golf courses in North America. In the immense space encompassed by the

Saskatchewan's Prince Albert National Park and its Waskesiu golf course is most beautiful and fairly difficult.

mountains distance is quickly swallowed up and one's perspective may be thrown off. Even such a sharp-eyed player as Gene Sarazen found that his eyes played tricks on him when he rejected his caddie's advice to play a long-iron for what looked to be a short approach shot. Positive that he would hit the ball over a mountain if he used the club the caddie suggested, he picked his own club and proceeded to plop the ball halfway to the green.

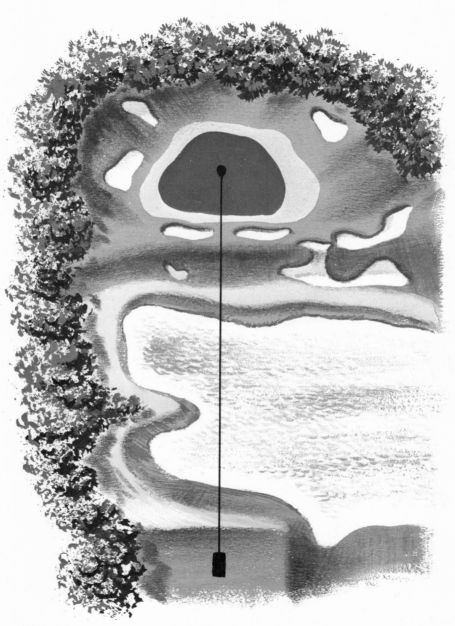

The Devil's Cauldron at Banff golf course.

The par-3, 175-yard sixteenth at Banff is on everyone's greatest 18-hole list. They call this hole "The Devil's Cauldron," because of the twisting winds that blow off the elevated tee overlooking the lake you must carry. About a No. 5 iron should get you across, but you are hitting to a tiny green, and you have to be careful of the wind. There is a slope on opposite sides of the green. This hole proves that you don't have to have 260-yard par 3's to make a great hole.

Some four or five hours of driving, north of Banff, is Canadian National Railways' Jasper Park Lodge. This resort is also a train stop for CN's transcontinental trains. The Jasper Park course is an 18-hole 6,590-yard, par-71 championship layout that attracts tourists from everywhere. Add to this a carefree collection of big, black bears and you have an idea of the kind of gallery you're likely to have while playing golf in Jasper National Park.

The bears are as much a part of the layout as the fairways and the greens. They are also a part of the Jasper Park family; there isn't a man-eater among them. This is not to say the bears are strictly vegetarians, but they are as tame and as genial as the pet you left back home. Behind the Lodge at Jasper National Park, ten to fifteen bears invariably congregate each morning to take inventory of newly arrived guests and to size up the freeloading prospects. On the golf course, the bears are as much at home as the club professional. They betray their playfulness by removing a ball from the trees, or from a bunker, and they love to recline on the velvet cushions of the greens, sometimes to the exasperation of the golfer who hopes to pick up a birdie, not a bear. Still, the bears play a key part in the daily life of the Jasper Park course, and according to the local caddie master, the bears earn their keep by helping greenskeepers pull sprinklers from one fairway location to another. As one visitor to the Jasper course put it: "The bears are great spectators, even if they do pick up a golf ball once in a while. And they're real friendly, often friendlier than the golfers themselves. At least bears don't talk in the middle of your backswing."

Argument rages about which course is best—Banff or Jasper. But this is flagrant hair-splitting. Both are landmarks in the diary of any golfer. And remember that there are other good courses in Alberta, too. Here are some that tourists can play at any time:

LOCATION	COURSE	HOLES/PAR/ YARDAGE
Banff	Banff Springs Hotel GC	18/72/6,704
Calgary	Inglewood G & CC	18/72/6,600
Calgary	Shawnee Slopes GC	18/71/6,700
Edmonton	Riverside GC	18/72/6,375
Jasper	Jasper Park Lodge GC	18/71/6,590
Lacombe	Lacombe G & CC	18/71/5,930
Lethbridge	Henderson Lake GC	18/71/6,359
Red Deer	Red Deer G & CC	18/72/6,743
Sylvan Lake	Sylvan Lake GC	18/72/6,172
Waterton Lakes	Waterton National Park GC	18/71/6,157

BRITISH COLUMBIA

British Columbia golf, played virtually the year round, concentrates heavily around Vancouver, scenically situated against the coastal mountain range. Victoria, a touch of "jolly old England" on Vancouver Island, ninety miles from the mainland, offers, for example, the Victoria Golf Club, known as "Oak Bay."

From the tee of the par-3 seventh hole at the Victoria Golf Club, far above a wildly undulating green, you get a capsule view of some of the wonders of British Columbia. Sailing vessels and great liners pass on the Pacific Ocean, stretching to the far horizon. A scattering of islands forms a breakwater providing sheltered waters for salmon, halibut, cod, and great shoals of herring. In the other direction snowcapped mountains provide a grandeur comparable to the Alps and Himalayas. From the tee of the 215-yard seventh hole you make your shot to a roller-coaster green, with an inlet of the sea tucked in close to the left edge. It is one of golf's spectacular par 3's and one of six par 3's on the distinctive Victoria course.

The seventy-year-old Victoria course, where golfers were once deemed to be using lethal weapons and were obliged to wear bright red jackets easily recognizable to the citizenry at large, has greens that have developed subtle, almost unseen rolls that only age brings. It is a fairly short par 69 playing at less than six thousand yards, but there is rather severe bunkering, both in the fairways and around the greens, and some tight-driving holes. The wind off the ocean is almost a constant factor. A number of tees are small peninsulas overhanging the Pacific.

The Harrison course, while only a 9-hole affair, is one of the most challenging courses in British Columbia.

Other picturesque layouts include Gorge Vale in Esquimalt and Uplands and Royal Colwood in the northern section of the city. The Royal Colwood, for many years the home of the Empress midwinter championships, is a real beauty and open to the public. Gorge Vale, overlooking the Juan da Fuca Straits, offers some of the most exciting scenery of any course in North America.

A short ferry trip across the Strait of Georgia from Victoria brings you to Vancouver, Canada's third-largest city. Golf is a year-round sport here with eight private and six public courses, all within sight of towering, snow-capped mountains. Seymour Golf and Country Club in North Vancouver is 18 holes carved out of the rain forests on the slopes of Mount Seymour. With a 69 rating for its 6,085 yards, the tree-lined fairways make accuracy a must. The greens are excellent and each fairway is isolated so you never feel rushed.

Marine Drive Golf Club was established in 1923 on the Fraser delta. Narrow fairways are surrounded by large trees and a straight shot is a good one . . . no matter how long! At 6,038 yards with a 69 rating, 35 sand traps, and five water hazards, this one challenges any golfer. "Big Bertha," a sand trap on the seventeenth hole, 25 to 30 feet below the green . . . is a real danger zone. Your own club membership card or affiliation credentials will introduce you to most of these private clubs. As the alternative Vancouver's public courses such as McCleery and Fraserview offer excellent play and outstanding views.

There are many fine courses throughout the Province. In the orchard-filled Okanagan Valley, for example, 250 miles east of Vancouver, three 18-hole courses are spaced at convenient intervals in Penticton, Kelowna, and Vernon. Each presents a delightful scenic contrast to the oceanside courses of the west coast. Here are some more of the better courses you can play in British Columbia:

LOCATION	*COURSE*	*HOLES/PAR/ YARDAGE*
Greater Victoria Area		
North Saanick	Glen Meadows G & CC	18/71/7,014
Esquimalt	Gorge Vale GC	18/70/6,351
Nanaimo	Nanaimo GC	18/71/6,570
Victoria	Royal Colwood G & CC	18/70/6,323
Victoria	Uplands GC	18/70/6,228
Victoria	Victoria GC	18/68/5,948
Northern Vancouver Island		
Powell River	Powell River GC	9/34/3,001

LOCATION	COURSE	HOLES/PAR/ YARDAGE
Greater Vancouver		
Vancouver	Fraserview GC	18/69/6,165
Vancouver	Glen Meadow G & CC	18/72/7,014
Vancouver	Langara GC	18/70/6,200
Vancouver	University GC	18/70/6,240
Vancouver	Marine Drive GC	18/69/6,038
Vancouver	McCleery GC	18/69/6,320
Vancouver to United States Border (*and East*)		
Surrey	Hazelmere Valley GC	18/70/6,295
Harrison	Harrison GC	9/35/3,425
Penticton	Penticton G & CC	18/69/6,362
Vernon	Vernon G & CC	18/70/6,555
Trail	Rossland-Trail CC	18/71/6,648 9/35/3,250
Fairmont Hot Springs	Fairmont Hot Springs GC	18/70/6,430

Some rules of thumb when visiting Canada for golf are: (a) make inquiries to provincial tourist bureaus; (b) if moving about, ask for information from leading hotels in the area; and (c) living costs in Quebec and Ontario are the highest in Canada. Everything grades slightly downward from costs in these two regions. Each Canadian province has it own golf association, with the whole fabric well-knit through the Royal Canadian Golf Association.

What about border crossing? A visa or a passport? Forget it. Just bring your clubs.

13

MEXICO AND
CENTRAL AMERICA

The history of golf in Mexico began at the turn of the century when an American named Townsend, who was working there, took spade in hand and dug a few holes in land near San Pedro de los Pinos. Today there are many superb courses throughout the country.

To traditionalists, the idea of playing golf in Mexico may seem incongruous, like holding a bullfight at St. Andrews. But golf in Mexico is no more out of place than it is in Pine Valley or Palm Springs. The game has existed in Mexico nearly as long as it has in the United States, outlasting at least four governments—as noted by bullet holes in the old hacienda at Club Campestre Cherubusco.

To be sure, it is played by only an affluent minority, not unexpected in a nation where a considerable percentage of the population is poor. Nevertheless, Mexico, like so many other countries, is in the middle of a golf boom.

One of the outstanding golf attractions in Mexico is the caddies. The Mexican caddie is a rare breed. Most are older men who depend on their jobs as the only means of income for their families. They take their work very seriously, and will outdo themselves to be the best caddies ever. They will seldom volunteer a criticism, but if your shot is on the pin, the enthusiasm will overflow. And do not worry about understanding gestures, for many golf terms are the same in Spanish as English. Although many of the clubs are listed as private, out-of-country club members may apply for playing privileges through the club professional or secretary. Or just go to the club. While many clubs close on Monday, visitors to Mexico should have no trouble in getting on any course in the country from Tuesday through Friday. It is not that the clubs mean to be inhospitable on Saturdays and Sundays. The problem is that the members themselves can barely squeeze onto the courses on weekends, and there simply is no room for guests. On resort establishments, as in the United States, guests usually can play any time the course is open. But, always remember that when playing on any course—even a resort one—you are not a customer but a guest. The Norteamericano will be more welcome next year if he has invited members to play through and deferred to local custom, including the female threesome who take a plethora of practice swings before each shot.

There are five courses in and about the volcanic topsoil of Mexico City, including Club de Golf Mexico. (Club de golf, as you may suspect, is Spanish for golf club.) The most scenic course of the five is probably Club de Golf la Hacienda, which is almost entirely surrounded by mountains and offers some spectacular views. The course that is usually in the best condition is, surprisingly enough, the newest of the five—the Club de Golf Bellavista, noted for its lush turf, its lightning-fast greens, and its numerous water hazards. A river winds through the course, and the members like to joke that the best ball to use at Bellavista is one that floats.

The oldest club in town is Club Campestre de la Ciudad de Mexico (Mexico City Country Club). It is a fairly flat course, not especially tough except for some trick pin positions and a few traps that guard their greens almost impenetrably. The members of the other four

Homes and a river surround the Club de Golf Bellavista in Mexico City.

Club de Golf Mexico's clubhouse (in the background) is one of the most beautiful in Mexico.

clubs refer to Campestre as the "blue-blood" club. It is an old-guard society preserve, and its immense, Spanish-style clubhouse boasts a magnificent ballroom among other facilities, which include those standard features of Mexico City's better golf clubs, a beauty shop in the ladies' locker room and a barber shop in the men's.

In a modern, "picture-windowed" way, the clubhouse at Club de Golf Mexico is just as much of a showplace as Campestre's. And the course at Mexico is in a class by itself. It is *the* course in Mexico City. There is no question that it is one of the most beautiful courses in the world and a superb test of golf (7,174 yards from the back tees). Club de Golf Mexico also is remarkable for its design. The course is laid out in a series of circles. The back nine runs around the outer rim and is lined with majestic houses, some of which look down on the fairways from steep cliffs. The front nine forms an inner circle, and inside that lies an 18-hole par-3 course known as the campo corto (short course). Another unusual feature at the Club de Golf Mexico is the complete absence of rough. From tee to green you see nothing but fairway, except, of course, for the traps and the trees. And what trees! Club de Golf Mexico is dotted with hundreds of the most beautiful trees that can be found in Mexico. A Mexican cherry tree, for example, looms like a leafy fortress smack in front of the sixth green. And when the jacaranda trees are in bloom in the spring, nature provides an unforgettable target at the 437-yard twelfth hole. From the tee, you aim for a solitary jacaranda tree in a forest of weeping willows off in the distance—an enchanting purple bull's-eye amidst the greenery.

Most of the greens at Club de Golf Mexico are huge and some of the holes seem back-breakingly long—especially the ones that run uphill. When you stagger up the fairway on Hoyo Numero 17, 556 yards and a steady climb from tee to green, console yourself with the thought that it is considered just about impossible to reach that remote green in two. And then remember that Jack Nicklaus twice reached it in two during the 1967 World Cup matches. From the back tee— 575 yards. And with a driver and a 1-iron.

If you are driving from Texas into Mexico, across the border from Laredo is the richest industrial city in the country, Monterrey. The city lies in a lovely mountain valley, cut by the Santa Catarine River. Monterrey boasts two 18-hole courses, the Club Campestre de Monterrey, a 6,563-yard layout, and the 6,450-yard Club de Golf Valle Alto A.C. The city also has two large bullfight rings and a charro arena for Mexican-style displays of horsemanship. After the bullfight, you can stop down at the local Cuauhtemoc Brewery for a tour and a beer on the house.

On the Pacific side of Mexico is its second largest city, Guadalajara. Guadalajara is humidity-free because of its high altitude, and its year-round temperature ranges from 60 to 80 degrees. There are four regulation-size golf courses in the city—the Club Campestre de Chapala, a 9-hole, par-36, 3,142-yard layout, and 18-hole, par-72 layouts at Club Campestre Atlas (7,225 yards), the Guadalajara Country Club (6,330 yards) and the Club Campestre Santa Anita (6,617 yards). There are also two par-3 courses in the Guadalajara area.

Puebla is the center of the area richest in Spanish colonial architecture. Its houses, fountains, civic buildings, and churches, lavish with multicolored Talavera tile, look Andalusian. The cathedral, one of the largest and richest in the Americas, and Puebla's other handsome churches are richly embellished inside and out. The city also has the fine golf course at the Club Campestre de Puebla, a tough 6,591 yard, par-72 layout.

The "Riviera of the Pacific," Acapulco, offers some of the most luxurious tourist accommodations in the world. The government has restricted building so that naturalness will be preserved. Many of the houses and some hotels are built into the sides of the Sierra Madre del Sur range of mountains that form Acapulco Bay.

Acalpulco has a wide range of golf activity and it is on the rise. At present there are five 18-hole courses (two at Tres Vidas), one 9-hole layout, and one 9-hole, par-3 course. It is estimated, if all plans materialize, that Acapulco will have eight golf courses within three to five years.

Pierre Marques has two golf courses, one a 9-hole par 3. The regulation-length course, designed by Percy Clifford—Mexico's leading golf architect—has a feature that is not usually found on American courses. That is, Clifford has built a number of mounds, fitted to the natural contour of the terrain, and covered them with sand. This

The layout of the courses at the Pierre Marques Club de Golf in Acapulco.

technique almost produces an inverted sand trap, and makes for some most interesting shots. Clifford, who has designed over twenty courses in Mexico, has also laid several beautiful water holes and palm-lined fairways at Marques. Although there is a good deal of sand off the fairway, there are no bunkers behind any of the greens. In Clifford's opinion, these would discourage boldness in approach shots.

Of the two courses at Tres Vidas, the East Course is the more challenging. Several of its holes run along the beach area. While the West Course is easier, it is no pushover for the average resort golfer. This course is essentially flat and open, but presents some problems because the contoured greens are well guarded by bunkers and some water.

About forty courses are now available to visiting players, not only in the cities but at resorts like Acapulco, Mazatlan, Tehuacan, Nueva Ixtapan, and others. Most greens fees are reasonable by United States standards although the popular clubs of Mexico City and nearby Cuernavaca must hope to discourage too many visitors with their higher charges. The Asociación Mexicana de Golf, S.A., Copenhague 32, Mexico, D.F., recently listed 35 affiliated clubs but the popularity of the game is growing fast among Mexicans, in the expanding expatriate communities, and in tourist circles. If you want to participate in matches and local events, a letter of introduction from your home club should state your handicap.

We have selected here several of the real tests in Mexico that will challenge any golfer:

LOCATION	COURSE	HOLES/PAR/ YARDAGE
Acapulco	Acapulco GC	18/71/5,950
Acapulco	Pierre Marques GC	18/72/6,702
Acapulco	Acapulco Princess GC	18/72/6,355
Acapulco	Tres Vidas GC	18/72/6,504
		18/72/6,271
Avandaro	Avandaro GC	18/72/6,500
Chihuahua	Chihuahua CC	18/72/6,691
Guadalajara	Club Atlas GC	18/72/6,400
Guadalajara	Guadalajara CC	18/72/6,700
Guadalajara	Santa Anita CC	18/72/6,617
Juarez	Juarez CC	18/72/6,601

LOCATION	COURSE	HOLES/PAR/ YARDAGE
Mexicali	Mexicali CC	18/72/6,400
Mexico City	Bellavista GC	18/72/7,178
Mexico City	Chapultepec GC	18/72/6,415
Mexico City	Ciudad de Mexico CC	18/72/6,800
Mexico City	Hacienda GC	18/71/6,800
Mexico City	Mexico GC	18/72/7,174
Monterrey	Monterrey CC	18/72/7,063
Monterrey	Valle Alto GC	18/72/6,800
Puebla	Puebla CC	18/72/6,591
Queretaro	Queretaro CC	18/72/6,470
Saltillo	Saltillo CC	18/72/6,310
Yucatan	La Ceiba GC	18/72/6,615

TEMPERATURE AND ALTITUDE

City	Feet Above Sea Level	Yearly Temperature Mean	Max.	Min.
Acapulco	10	80	102	62
Guadalajara	5,212	66	99	32
Ixtapan de la Sal	5,428	69	100	49
Mexico, D.F.	7,349	60	88	34
Monterrey	1,765	71	108	50
Puebla	7,052	61	88	30
San Jose Purua	5,904	63	95	45
Veracruz	52	77	99	52

PANAMA

Visitors are welcome to play at the Club de Golf de Panama in Panama City. This is the only real test open to the transient golfer in Panama. The United Fruit Company operates several courses in "banana country" for their employees and should you drop in at one of them, the manager generally will let you play.

The first course in Panama was a few holes strung together in a clearing, and the first clubhouse was a thatch-roofed hut. Now the members enjoy a handsome building and a layout that runs an exacting 6,400 yards and plays to a par 72. The land rolls and tumbles, creating a number of blind shots. The designer, taking advantage of the terrain, made the greens small. A good score depends on pin-point accuracy.

Your score is also helped by an understanding of the climate. The humid air slows the ball. You can almost see it gather moisture as it goes. While the posted yardage seems short, the tropical atmosphere makes the course play noticably longer. In addition, there is the grass. Like other tropical courses, the course in Panama is planted with Bermuda, a tough, wiry cover that does well in the climate but yields little roll. Remember, in sizing up a shot, most of your distance will be carry.

The Panama Country Club is the site of the Panama Open—where Arnold Palmer won his first tournament as a pro in a 6-hole sudden-death playoff with Sam Snead. And here Roberto DeVicenzo—the wonderful "Golfing Gaucho"—shot five birdies on each side and no bogeys for a course record 62. But this course gives away no points. The best player, for example, earns all he gets on the 345-yard, par-4 seventh. The tee is walled in by high tropical grass. Near the middle of the fairway, a high mound and, just beyond it and to the left, a bunker leave a slender tee-shot landing area. The approach is short, to a shelf green. Do not try to bounce the ball onto this surface.

The twelfth, a par 5 of 530 yards, has out of bounds to the left and a fairway that climbs nearly all the way home. Getting there in two is man's work. It is a man's work too, to master the 200-yard sixteenth, the climax of a series of interesting par 3's.

Bright, barefoot caddies, who know the course to the smallest twist and ripple, can give the line of a putt down to "two inches left of the cup." It's a good player who can stroke the ball as precisely as the caddies can see the line.

The wise player gets to this course early in the day, especially during the rainy season, because in the afternoon the warm air, the banyan trees, the royal palms and all the close-packed tropical green are drenched with rain. You need not watch for it, although the darkening skies are hard to miss. Wind precedes the rain, by minutes.

OTHER CENTRAL AMERICAN COUNTRIES

In the Central American countries of Costa Rica, El Salvador, Nicaragua, Honduras, and Guatemala golf is limited to courses operated by United Fruit for their employees and to one private country club, each in Honduras and Guatemala. Of these two, the Guatemala Country Club is by far the best.

This course, in volcanic country, is a 6,617-yard, par-72 layout.

In play are great ravines, or barrancas, which create breathtaking views and hazardous approaches. Plunging at least five hundred feet, these chasms can make you tighten your approach shot considerably, particularly when they slice into both sides of the fairway as they do on the sixth.

Besides the barrancas, you will have to contend with a profusion of trees—pines, cypress, jacarandas—which give shape and character to the course while their grasping branches tighten the fairways. Then there are the greens, soft with heavy grain, which hold approach shots well but give you trouble putting. Finally, the thinner air, about five thousand feet above sea level, gives the short-irons a workout.

14

THE ISLANDS: BERMUDA,
BAHAMAS, AND THE CARIBBEAN

The best time to go to the islands is *anytime*. But for the most enjoyable contrast in weather, the winter season carries the vote. The Caribbean, the Bahamas, and Bermuda offer the wandering golfer some of the most ideal playing conditions to be found anywhere. Everything about the islands is uncomplicated and relaxing. Air service is provided from major U.S. cities by many airlines. Passports are unnecessary and U.S. citizens need only proof of citizenship to return to the United States. Transportation on the islands is varied. Upon arrival in Bermuda, for instance, a visitor may rent a bicycle, a motorbike, or a carriage by hour, day, or week. There are no automobiles for hire, but English taxis are available.

BERMUDA

The surprising thing about the many people who go to Bermuda is that so few of them seem to get there. Most people seem to think they are somewhere off the coast of Florida. Actually, Bermuda is more than a thousand miles from Miami, and less than six hundred from Nova Scotia. It's on approximately the same latitude as Wilmington, North Carolina, and yet is several hundred miles closer to New York City. It's almost equidistant from London and San Francisco. Consequently, Bermuda is nowhere near being a tropical island. (As a matter of fact, Bermuda is not an island, but a chain of more than 150 islands.) Yet it is blessed with near-tropical weather, mainly because the Gulf Stream passes just north of it, cutting off the Arctic winds of the North Atlantic. The average, annual temperature is 70.5 degrees. Frost is unheard of and snow unknown. The air is pollen free, and there is no rainy season as such.

The Bermudas were discovered in 1515 by Juan de Bermudez, a Spanish explorer. Hence, the name. However, they became a British colony almost by accident when, in 1609, Sir George Somers, an

English captain commanding *The Sea Venture* under sail to the Colony of Virginia, ran aground in Bermuda.

Bermuda's islands are divided into parishes: Sandys, Southampton, Warwick, Paget, Devonshire, Smith's, Hamilton, St. George's, and Pembroke, the most densely populated. Pembroke contains Bermuda's only city, Hamilton, on the south side of which is Hamilton Harbour, a deep-water port that can dock large, oceangoing ships directly on Front Street, in the main shopping district. There is another deep water port in St. George, Bermuda's largest town. Tourism is Bermuda's sole industry. There are over 65 places to stay on the islands.

There are ten golf courses open to public play on the islands, of which six are 18-hole. They are the Belmont Hotel and Golf Club, Castle Harbour Hotel and Golf Club, Riddell's Bay Golf and Country Club, The Princess Hotel and Golf Club, Port Royal Golf Course, and The Mid-Ocean Club. All of them are relatively short, very hilly, and invariably windy.

Of the golf courses, the most famous is Mid-Ocean, and justifiably so. It is situated in Tucker's Town, a twenty-minute drive from Hamilton, and was designed not quite a half-century ago by Charles Blair Macdonald, the irascible original amateur champion of the United States, who also built The National Golf Links of America on Long Island and the Chicago Golf Club, the first 18-hole golf course in America. (Mid-Ocean was revised in 1953 by Robert Trent Jones.) Although the course measures only 6,519 yards it plays much longer, partly because so many of its greens are elevated. Then, too, there is the continual wind to contend with and any number of uphill shots. Like so many of the unsolved mysteries of golf, Mid-Ocean seems to present more shots against the wind than with it and more shots uphill than downhill.

By today's architectural standards, Mid-Ocean would be considered old-fashioned, particularly by touring pros. It has a maddening number of blind shots, gigantic greens with all sorts of exaggerated breaks, and what seems to be a superfluous number of bunkers. Mid-Ocean would be considered goat country were it not for its craggy beauty. Indeed, by anybody's standards, the fifth hole, which is called the "Cape," would have to rank among the 18 most beautiful holes in the world. It is that architectural rarity—a hole that is not only superbly pretty but eminently playable. From a tee elevated a hundred feet or more, one hits across an elbow of ocean to an immense fairway that slants to the left on the bias at a miraculously judicious angle. Even from the tiger tee it can be reached by a woman, but can be cut by a leading money-winner only after considerable self-debate. A solid straight-ball will carry any point of the coastline the golfer chooses. Too much draw, and he's in the water. Too much fade, and he's two clubs more away from the green.

Macdonald had a lightsome, almost rococo, style of golf-course architecture. To a point, he copied the classic holes of Scottish linksland much in the way his friend Stanford White copied the classic structures of Greece, and then, like White, modified the style to his own taste, often with superb results. Indeed, the Redan Hole at Mid-Ocean, which is the seventeenth, is superior to the original Redan at North Berwick in Scotland, as is Macdonald's Redan at National Golf Links.

Redan Holes are named after what was once considered to be an impregnable fortress near Sevastopol, Russia. The strategy of the hole is based largely on the slant of the elongated green, which is usually two-level and constructed on the horizontal at a 45-degree angle away from the player. This angle is then protected by a huge bunker, calling—regardless of the flag placement—for a perfectly straight shot or one with a controlled draw, either of which must be played with precise club selection. Any other shot leaves the ball in the bunker or, if on the green, with a huge putt. The original Redan at North Berwick is also blind off the tee, much to the astonishment of knowledgeable Americans who play it for the first time.

At any rate—getting back to Macdonald's fifth hole at Mid-Ocean —he further complicated the hole, by shaping the green so that it is in itself something of a hazard. The putting surface is awesome and is broken into two basic levels, the lower on the left and the upper on the right. While the lower level is flat enough, the upper, which accepts all the faint-hearted and half-hit shots, has the contours of a roller coaster. The result is that any strong second shot, played flush for the flagstick without fear of the ocean on the left, leaves a relatively smooth putt. But any chicken-hearted shot can leave a putt with literally twenty feet of break. And all this strategy has been incorporated into a hole so gorgeous it can't be painted or photographed. It can only be played.

Castle Harbour isn't as demanding as Mid-Ocean, but it's no pushover, either. Here, again, is a roller-coaster type of terrain, which

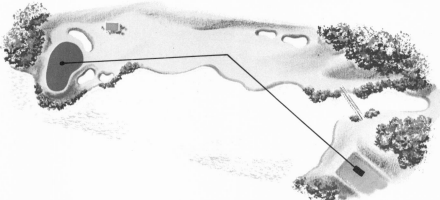

The legendary tee shot on the fifth at Mid-Ocean offers the golfer an option. Short hitters carry Mangrove Lake with a drive of 165 yards, which leaves a second shot of at least a 2-iron. Long hitters can make a 250-yard carry across the widest portion of the lake and be left with a 6-iron or even less on the approach. Babe Ruth walloped eleven straight shots into Mangrove Lake before he cleared this hazard.

provides a succession of spectacular views. All this beauty won't lower your handicap, but it's guaranteed to take the sting out of those triple-bogeys.

With many of its holes exposed to Harrington Sound and Castle

The first green at the famed Castle Harbour course. The second green may be seen at the center rear, and the seventh green at the right foreground.

Harbour, the Castle Harbour Golf Club might be just the spot to get ready for the British Open. The course may not resemble old St. Andrews in many other ways, but it provides the proper atmosphere for anyone intending to test his skill in the winds. Originally built in 1932, it was recently redesigned under the direction of Robert Trent Jones and is now 6,142 yards long and plays to a par 71.

The second hole, a par 4 of 369 yards, is the course's most famous. The elevated tee descends to a fairway sloping toward the ocean on the left, which means that any poorly placed drive ends up a lost ball.

On the right is a line of trees planned to catch a slicing drive. Therefore the best tee shot heads to the right and draws slightly as it catches the downslope of a hill in mid-fairway. The elevated "postage stamp" green is faced with pink, sand-filled traps.

Riddell's Bay Golf & Country Club is the island's most venerable course, constructed in 1922. As is the case on all of Bermuda's courses, with the exception of Mid-Ocean and Port Royal, the greens are about the size of your tablecloth; and with the sea bordering several of the holes, approaches have to kept low and firm. The hole considered to be the toughest on which to make a par is the par-3, 112-yard eleventh. Your tee shot has to carry a deep gully. If you hit short, you can wind up in a bunker or heavy rough. But if you get your ball too high into the wind, it could carry into a bunker or water guarding the rear of the green. Another fine hole is the 411-yard eighth. It is a dogleg to the right, with the dogleg running around an indentation of the bay. Your nerves and courage are sorely tested here, for it's possible to cut almost 200 yards off the hole by hitting a drive across the bay inlet. The course measures 5,560 yards and plays to a par 68.

Blind tee shots, tight, sloping fairways, perverse bunkering, and roller-coaster greens make poor wind play even more hazardous at the 5,717-yard, par-70 Manor course. As is true on most relatively short but cunningly designed layouts, you cannot just stand on the tees and bomb away. Careful placement of shots is imperative, proper selection of clubs even more vital.

On the second hole, for example, a short 326-yard par 4, the fairway doglegs sharply to the left from a raised tee. If you get your ball out to the point of the dogleg, you have to carry a marshy pond fronting the green. This requires a delicately stroked lofted shot, and if the breezes are coming in stiff at you, they could blow your ball into woods on the right.

The fourteenth at Belmont is aptly named "Good Grief." It's a par-3, 115-yarder playing from an angled tee over a sidehill valley to a tiny, sloping green. Bunkers front and rear guard against vacillating players looking for the "safest" club to use. One member recommends playing the hole this way: "Hit your eight-iron into the headwind that occasionally blows here and hope it doesn't quit before your ball comes down." Otherwise, it's "Good Grief" to you, Charlie Brown.

Port Royal is the colony's longest course—a par 71, at 6,631 yards. The nine toughest holes come first and the eighteenth green is a mere step from the clubhouse. The links run alongside a main road, through farming land, past a school, 'round an old fort and along steep, oceanside cliffs. Meantime the golfer must face a range of sand traps, water hazards, doglegs, and prevailing winds. Those who are unnerved by the experience are invited to repair to Port Royal's driving range or 18-hole putting green, to work the kinks out of their games.

The most difficult hole on the Port Royal course is the eleventh, a 458-yard par 4 that plays over a great, high hill, at the summit of which is a breathtaking view. The fourteenth hole, with its surprising stand of pine trees rimming the green, makes you think for a moment that you are at Pinehurst in North Carolina. Number 15 is a rarity among golf holes—one without any rough. What it has instead is clear and present danger—a fairway, set on a high ridge adjacent to old Whale Bay Fort, that is exactly the width of the ridge, about thirty yards. Errant shots to the right slide down an embankment, and shots drawn too far to the left end up in the ocean.

The most diabolical hole on this Robert Trent Jones–designed course is the sixteenth. The tee, fairway, and green are perched on the edge of south shore cliffs. You must hit the green with the first shot or take out another ball. It's a minimum 130-yard carry and it can be accomplished with an 8-iron in calm weather but you'll need a 3-iron when the wind is blowing at you.

The Princess Golf and Beach Club, on one of the island's highest spots, is Bermuda's only executed 18-hole, par-3 course. Designed by golf architect Alfred H. Tull, the 2,563-yard course is a real beauty for variety. Its shortest hole is a wedge shot of about ninety yards. The longest calls for a good drive of 210 yards. In between, nearly every iron in the bag must be used. And when the breezes pick up from the ocean, even the low handicapper needs at least one good wood shot. Skillful iron work and a fine putting touch, rather than power, are what count, and ladies have an equal chance with the men. Rolling fairways, deceptive distances, 64 strategically placed traps, sizable water hazards, and high, elevated tees all add to the interest and challenge. Average playing time is two hours. These high, rolling fairways have magnificent views.

Four 9-hole courses round off the generous selection. The St.

Velvet greens contrast with the shimmering sea at the Port Royal Golf Course's eighth hole. It takes a strong will to keep your eye on the ball amid such scenery. Most of Port Royal's holes have views of the Atlantic and even those that don't are picturesque to the point of distraction.

George Hotel in the oldest part of Bermuda has its own par-35 course measuring 2,455 yards. Slightly longer is the 2,978-yard government-owned course of Queen's Park in Devonshire Parish which boasts the longest hole on the island—the 540-yard fifth. The Holiday Inn and Horizons Hotel both operate 9-hole, par-3 courses.

Since Bermuda is part of the British Commonwealth, the smaller English ball is in wide use here, although the American-size ball is optional. Each has certain advantages and disadvantages. The English ball is smaller, gives more distance, and is more easily controlled, especially in wind. On the other hand, the English ball has a tendency to "bury" in soft sand traps, and is harder to hit if it's sitting lower in the grass. The American ball yields less distance, sits up better on turf, and will not "bury" as much in sand traps. The consensus for playing English ball vs. American ball? The average golfer will benefit by using the American ball. It "sits" better on top of the turf for fairway shots and, since it is larger, it is easier for the average player to hit.

Pros at Bermuda's courses give lessons on playing low shots into the wind to those who have never coped with it before. You can cheat the wind, no matter what ball you use. When playing against it, drop a club or two (instead of a 9-iron use a 7-iron), grip it shorter, play an abbreviated punch shot. With the wind behind you, pick a more lofted club than you would ordinarily. To gain distance off the tee when there's a left-to-right wind, tee the ball high, close your stance, swing inside out and draw the ball. Against a right-to-left wind, tee the ball high, open your stance, swing outside in, and cut the ball. For lower trajectory against the wind, tee the ball lower, grip the club shorter, play the ball farther back in the stance. Keep hands ahead as you release the club-head. Do not follow through completely.

One of the first lessons a newcomer learns is to keep his wedge in the bag. In windy Bermuda, wedge pitches to the green are out. What Bermuda-wise golfers play are 7-iron pitch-and-run shots, and they do it from as far out as 130 yards. They keep the shot low enough not to get caught in the draft, and allow it to run onto the putting surface.

On the greens, remember the break of the grass will normally go toward the water. Greens are usually heavy, thick, grainy. Don't be afraid to hit firmly, after lining up a square stance. Keep the blade square to the line and low.

One thing they won't find in Bermuda is hurricanes. Contrary to some misbegotten notions, Bermuda is not in the so-called Hurricane Belt. The U.S. Air Force has a weather station on the island and sends out planes into the eye of hurricanes emanating from far to the south, in the Caribbean. As a result, many hurricane stories are datelined Bermuda, but none hit the island. That's a good thing to bear in mind when you're trying to keep your ball on its tee on the first hole at Mid-Ocean. It's really mind over matter.

LOCATION	*COURSE*	*HOLES/PAR/ YARDAGE*
Warwick	Belmont Hotel & GC	18/70/5,717
Hamilton	Castle Harbour Beach & GC	18/71/6,142

LOCATION	COURSE	HOLES/PAR/ YARDAGE
Tucker's Town	Mid-Ocean GC	18/71/6,519
Southampton	Port Royal GC	18/71/6,631
Southampton	Princess GC	18/54/2,563
Devonshire	Queen's Park GC	9/35/2,978
Warwick	Riddell's Bay G & CC	18/68/5,660
St. George's	St. George GC	9/34/2,455

BAHAMAS

Regardless of where you go in the Bahamas . . . to Nassau (New Providence Island) . . . to Grand Bahama Island (home of Freeport and West End) . . . to the Out Islands (Eleuthera, Abaco, Berry Island) . . . you'll find challenging courses. Actually with more than a dozen championship golf courses open to public play undulating over verdant terrain on five of the seven hundred islands of the Bahamas, the game commands international attention here.

Golf has been associated with New Providence Island, location of Nassau, capital city of the Bahamas, for almost as long as the time-worn walls of Fort Charlotte, built in 1789.

In the late 1790's, over a hundred years before the first golf course in America was ever planned, Captain Alexander Campbell of His Majesty's Royal Militia wrote a letter to his family in Scotland, telling how he had designed a small golf course during his off-duty hours on the leveled parade ground near his quarters in the shadows of the great fort wall. Captain Campbell, once a caddy as a boy near Glasgow, fashioned a "mashie" and a "putter" out of hammered iron blades. The shafts were made from bamboo shoots cord-tied to the club heads. His golf balls were fashioned from a lignum-vitae tree, a hard wood which provided sufficient resiliency.

The first record of organized golf in Nassau was in the early 1920's when Henry Flagler, Florida railroad and tourist magnate, operated the original Colonial Hotel. A 9-hole layout with rolled sand greens was designed on the Fort Charlotte Parade Grounds.

Late in the same decade, Clyde Munson, owner and operator of the Munson Steamship Line which provided most of the sea transportation to Nassau, leased a tract of land three miles west of Nassau. American golf architect Deveaux Emmette designed and built the 18-hole course which was known until 1969 as the Nassau Golf Club.

At that time it was completely rejuvenated and redesigned and was reopened late 1971 as the Sonesta Beach Hotel and Golf Club.

Another course that was recently rejuvenated is the Paradise Island Golf Club. Formerly Huntington Hartford's Arawak, it underwent complete renovation in the late 1960's. This 6,495-yard par-72 ocean-view course features thick-brush-bordered, rolling fairways, several doglegs and numerous bunkers, deep lakes, and tightly trapped, elevated greens.

The Paradise Island Golf Club boasts of several outstanding golf holes, two of which are virtually unequaled for their staggering beauty. The 466-yard, par-5 fourth hole provides a world of contrast from tee to green. From a dune nestled among the dry natural growth of palmetto palms, a most accurate draw tee shot is required for proper playing position. The hole, a dogleg to the left, is guarded ahead and to the right by a large natural lake at a distance of approximately 220 yards. This water hazard forces play to the left, which is also guarded by a large extremely well-placed bunker. The approach to the elevated green is properly proportioned in width between two deep traps, glaring white against the green putting surface. Upon ascending the green, another world quite suddenly reveals itself. Before your eyes lies an unforgettable sight. Explosions of color take place in the crystal-clear water as far as the eye can see. Bright Hanover Sound, framed by ragged Salt Cay and the rich blue of the ocean's horizon, presents an everchanging picture, its only constancy the inconstancy of its colors and changes of mood.

Along this picturesque shoreline run some of the finest holes on the course, first the short No. 5, 133-yard par 3. The island green, subject to the full force of all the elements, offers a great test of iron play. The bottle-neck green, with huge surrounding traps, plays differently every day with the slightest change of wind or changing of the pin placement.

Designed by a golf pro and architect George Fazio, the sporty Coral Harbour Golf Club course offers wooded roughs, rolling fairways, numerous water holes, and deep sand traps, making it one of the most challenging courses in the Western Hemisphere. A well-known veteran of professional golf, Fazio introduced a course unusual for a flat area. Rivaling any other for beauty, outclassing most in toughness, the 18-hole championship, 6,710-yard, par-70 Coral Harbour is one of the most interesting courses in the Bahamas.

One of the more outstanding holes of Coral Harbour Club, quite indicative of Fazio's disregard for the conventional, is the 195-yard, par-3 seventh. Driving from a choice of two staggered tees, the player is confronted with a choice of entries to a green closely trapped on the right. In the most perfect location, about halfway to the hole, he has left a single tall pine. Standing proudly, straight and strong, it guards the entire left side of the green from entry by a low half-hit shot. This unique and beautiful hazard forces the play either to a very high left-to-right or to a well-hit straight full shot into the rolling green.

The 445-yard, par-4 ninth hole may be played from any of three tees, all of which require a carry over water of varying distances. The play is to a reasonably open fairway, requiring proper position for the most exciting second shot on the course. Over another small water hazard one is confronted by an elevated green heavily guarded by tiers of bunkers. Here again one feels the hand of artistry working freely with carefully selected natural attributes.

The Bahamas longest course, the 7,400-yard, par-73 South Ocean Golf Club located at the southwest corner of New Providence, was opened early in 1972. There is also a sporty, 9-hole, par-3 layout—the Blue Hill Golf Course—located on this island. This course is illuminated for night play.

Grand Bahama. In 1956, Grand Bahama contained nothing but a lumber camp and a bunch of native fishermen. Then, sparked by a piece of legislation known as the Hawks-Bill Creek Act, the island was transformed by a building orgy that produced the bustling city of Freeport and a welter of hotels, golf courses, condominiums and all the other trappings of a resort area.

The principal lures for the visitor are the beaches, which are excellent; the water, which is warm and exceedingly clear (glass-bottom boats do a brisk tour business), and the golf, which is first-class. There also is the International Bazaar, a lovely area created by a Hollywood set designer, who faithfully reproduced small corners of Spain, China, Paris, London, the Middle East, Mexico, Japan, etc., in each of which the food and merchandise are authentic. And then there are the casinos. One of them, called logically enough, El Casino, lies hard by the International Bazaar and looks like something left over from the set of *The Thief of Bagdad*. Down the road a piece, in the Lucayan Beach Hotel, is the other casino, and the dealers there are just as lucky. The Lucayan's casino is the smaller of the two and has more of an intimate, Monte Carlo atmosphere for those who prefer to lose their money on the European Plan.

As far as the golf is concerned, there are many fine courses that you can play. For instance, the Bahamia Golf and Country Club has developed into one of the world's finest golf resorts. Duplicated here are the most interesting holes of the best Dick Wilson courses. Also known as King's Inn and Golf Club, Bahamia offers a new approach to golf-resort design—a golf control center containing 250 golf carts connected directly to the hotel lobby. When a guest is ready to play, he registers at the center where his clubs are placed in a cart and he proceeds to the first tee of whichever of the two courses—the Emerald or the Ruby—he chooses.

The Emerald course was designed by the late Dick Wilson, one of

An aerial view of the start and finish of the 6,859-yard course at Lucayan Golf and Country Club.

the game's outstanding architects, and was opened for play only three years ago. The fact that the course reached peak condition in such a short time is due partly to the fact that there is a virtually unlimited supply of water on Grand Bahama. The course plays at seven thousand yards from the back tees, only moderately long by today's standards, and with its beautifully designed greens and well-placed traps, it is a joy to play. The Ruby was the work of Joe Lee, a long-time associate of Wilson's, and is the same length as the Emerald, although it doesn't seem to be when you play it.

As if the courses weren't testing enough on their own merits, the duffer must face the stern challenge of avoiding the rough, which on Grand Bahama, is really rough. If he is unlucky enough to hit one off line into the wilderness, the golfer's big problem isn't playing the next shot—it's finding the ball. The next problem is finding his way back to the fairway. The ball can be found more often than not, but under almost no conditions is it in a playable lie. Not only is the rough composed of an impressive array of tropical trees, bushes, cactus, and other flora, the ground itself is virtually nothing but coral.

All these delights are also present on the Lucayan Country Club course, another fine Dick Wilson layout that measures 6,900 yards and presents much the same challenge as King's Inn. There may be a few more palm trees and a little bit more elbow room in the fairways, but that rough and that wind are still there and the man who returns with a decent score at the Lucayan has earned it.

The fourth course in the area—Bahama Reef Golf and Country Club—was opened for public play in 1967. This 6,794-yard championship, 18-hole, par-72 course is heavily trapped and has 12 water holes making it a challenge to players. The superb layout is the work of golf architect Byrecton Scott. Adjacent to the championship layout is a 9-hole, par-3 course which is illuminated for night play. In addition, there is an illuminated driving range, the second of its kind in the Bahamas.

Another course with a challenging layout for the keen golfer is the Jack Tar Grand Bahama Hotel and Country Club at West End, Grand Bahama. With the first course built (1960) on this mushrooming resort island, the Grand Bahama Hotel and Country Club has set the pace in making Grand Bahama's West End, Freeport, and Lucaya the world's newest golfing paradise. Designed by Mark Mahannah, this 18-hole, 6,800-yard, championship, par-72 course offers excellent fairways and greens over a fairly even terrain. Mahannah's stratagem includes seven manmade and natural lakes which dot the course—they either cut across or run alongside seven of the 18 championship holes. There are seventy well-placed sand traps and a cultivated rough. An additional nine holes feature seven new water hazards, offer alternate holes and extend the 6,800-yard course to 10,450 yards.

Two of the Bahamas' newest courses are the Fortune Hills Golf Club and Shannon Golf Club. In the Freeport/Lucaya area, the latter course, whose length of 6,810 yards from the back tees makes it shorter than its neighbors, has a par 72 which is no more readily attainable than that of the longer ones. Although Shannon's fairways are lined with the same welter of tropical plants that makes the rough so difficult, there are a tremendous number of pine trees. This gives the course a little less of a tropical and more of a Carolina sandhills look.

The toughest holes at Shannon are the ninth and the eighteenth, both par 4's. The eighteenth features a rocky grotto, complete with waterfall, which makes the approach to the green menacing as well as picturesque. Then there is the thirteenth, a 202-yard, par 3 that has a tree in the middle of the green. This is a great conversation piece, especially if the tree happens to be between your ball and the cup.

Out Islands. Three of the Out Islands have championship courses and they include the famous Cotton Bay Club, situated on the slender resort island of Eleuthera, just a half-hour's flight eastward from Nassau. Once on the course you can see why Cotton Bay is considered one of Robert Trent Jones' finest creations. First there's the unmistakable Jones trademark: the long tees, such as the 150-yard twelfth tee. Then there are the big sprawling bunkers, close to one hundred of them, usually set behind the greens to delineate the target and help you judge the approach shot; and borrowing from the sea, which is never more than a pitch shot away, the greens roll like waves, rising and dipping and changing in shape and size. Finally the entire 7,140-yard, par-72 championship layout is vividly accented by lush green grass and glistening white sand.

On the Great Abaco Island, just sixty minutes by air off the Florida coast, you'll find the beautiful, Dick Wilson–designed Treasure Cay Golf Club, which is built around what is to be a complete residential area, bringing the world of golf right to the doorsteps of guests and residents of this picturesque seaside resort. Tees are longer than usual;

high-rolling fairways are border-spotted with thick brush; and sharp-rising, broad greens are cleverly guarded by nearby lakes and deep sand traps, two characteristic features of a Wilson-built course. In the 6,932 yards of natural landscape there are four par-fivers, the longest a rough 554-yarder . . . and two triple-tees—men's, ladies', and championship. The fifth hole is reputed to be the most difficult to play: the golfer faces a long narrow fairway, bordered by thick brush and vine and two pairs of sand traps. Across this championship, 18-hole, par-72 course, a prevailing crosswind sweeps, adding another challenge.

Cay, pronounced key, means island in Spanish, and that is what Great Harbour Cay is—a small island in the Berry Island group. On this cay there is located the 6,838-yard, par-72 championship course at the Great Harbour Club.

The sixth hole at the Great Harbour Cay course offers plenty of hazards to visiting golfers. This championship course was designed by Joe Lee.

LOCATION	COURSE	HOLES/PAR/ YARDAGE
Nassau	Coral Harbour GC	18/70/6,710
Nassau	Paradise Island GC	18/72/6,495
Nassau	Sonesta Beach Hotel & GC	18/72/6,936
Nassau	South Ocean GC	18/73/7,398
Grand Bahama	Bahama Reef G & CC	18/72/6,794
Grand Bahama	Bahama G & CC	
	(Emerald)	18/72/7,010
	(Ruby)	18/72/7,000
Grand Bahama	Lucayan G & CC	18/72/6,859
Grand Bahama	Grand Bahama Hotel & CC	18/72/6,800
Grand Bahama	Shannon GC	18/72/6,810
Grand Bahama	Fortune Hills GC	9/36/3,280
Abaco	Treasure Cay GC	18/72/6,932
Berry Islands	Great Harbour C	18/72/6,838
Eleuthera	Cotton Bay C	18/72/7,140

THE CARIBBEAN

Twenty-five years ago, golf was not widely known in the Caribbean. Today, there is often fairway greenery where there had once been jungle and underbrush. Golf is beginning to replace swimming and rum-drinking, and the once casual Caribbean golfer is capable now of viewing a sliced drive or an inferior putt with something akin to Yanqui dolor.

Generally, Caribbean courses fall into two categories. First is the resort course operated in conjunction with a hotel; and second is the privately owned golf club operated basically for the permanent residents of the island. Without exception, you will be welcomed at either one. At the present time, only one small course in the Caribbean is operated on a strictly private basis.

Private or resort—each has its advantages. The resort courses are designed with the American tourist in mind. Long, wide fairways, liberally lined with palms, mango, and mahogany trees and abounding in sand and water, are commonplace. On the other hand, the private courses have usually been in existence a great number of years. Fairways are narrow and the greens are exceptionally tight. On most of these courses, a premium is placed more on accuracy than length.

A visiting golfer should not hesitate to arrive at a private club alone, for it is frequently possible to join in play with the locals, and many a lasting friendship has been made this way.

Jamaica. Because of its years of English occupation, Jamaica is the golf center of the Caribbean. The fifty-year-old Constant Spring course in Jamaica is one of the oldest in Latin America. On the island, now, there are enough courses to accommodate everyone, and enough variety of play to satisfy anyone. Rates are generally reasonable, accommodations excellent, and the weather comfortably warm all through the season. (Local enthusiasts claim that the temparature rarely goes above the eighties or below the seventies, but, like everything else, there are exceptions.)

The island is just starting its career as a popular tourist spot, and the emphasis being placed on golf is an encouraging commentary on the game as a major attraction. Six 18-hole courses, four of them of championship length, and four 9-hole layouts are scattered throughout the island, all ready and willing to welcome golfing visitors.

Like everything else for the visitor to Jamaica, golf facilities are concentrated in four areas: Kingston, the capital city, has two 18-hole courses and the 9-hole Liguanea Club; Montego Bay, at the other end of the island, has one 9-hole club in the city, and two others within 15 miles; Ocho Rios, in the center of the north coast, where the trade winds add spice to the game and temper the tropical heat, has a new 18-hole layout (but it is within reasonable distance of Runaway Bay, where one of the longest courses in the islands beckons); to the east, at Port Antonio, there's a fine 9-hole layout; and at Manchester, in the central highlands, nine holes serve the local hotels as well as those in Mandeville.

Big gun of all the Caribbean courses is the Runaway Bay Country Club at Runaway Bay, an awesome 7,145-yard par 74 on the Cardiff Hall Estate in St. Ann Parish on the north coast. (It also can be played less strenuously at 6,819 yards, and par 72). It's a breathtakingly lovely spot, with the blue waters of the Caribbean on one side and the rising foothills of the inland mountains on the other. This Runaway Bay layout offers a genuine golf challenge without reducing the player to exhaustion. Designed by Commander John Harris, world-famous British golf architect, the course has two concentric nines with the first, tenth, and sixteenth tees, and ninth, fifteenth, and eighteenth greens close to the clubhouse. Nothing is "blind" if the player stays where he should be, but the big rolling greens are tightly trapped. The total of seven 5-pars, two of them well over 550 yards long, is a frightening prospect. In addition, there are four 3-pars between 200 and 250 yards long. But these toughies are offset by several reasonably easy fours. Commander Harris has made the trade winds work for him, too, designing his layout so that the wind helps on some of the longer holes, yet adds to the difficulty of the shorter holes.

At Ocho Rios, "the port of swingers," the Upton Country Club was expanded from a 9-hole, 3,340 layout to 18 holes at 6,410 yards. To the west, past the Runaway district, is the famed Montego Bay resort complex. The two ongoing courses in "Mo Bay," as it is sometimes referred to, are the Tryall Golf and Beach Club and the Half Moon Hotel and Cottage Colony. The Half Moon course was built by Robert Trent Jones. This is not one of Trent's best layouts, but we're not sure he can be held fully liable. He had precious little land to work with. The 18 holes are squeezed into a narrow tract between hills and beachside property reserved for homesites. The course stretches over a slice of ground something like that of St. Andrews, without the hook, or the "first golf course's" intrinsic charm. At full length, Half Moon is 7,143 yards long. Par is 72, and it plays almost entirely east-west. No fewer than 15 of its fairways run parallel to another one. Only the short twelfth is entirely off by itself. The course is still not fully grown in with trees so the wind blows freely across it. This means that practically every shot is played in a cross-wind—either right to left, or vice versa. The tees are long and the greens huge (it's a Jones course, remember), the course presents the traditional challenge of its designer's work. You belt it as big as you can off the tee, then judge carefully your second, or third, or fourth shot so the first putt you have is inside one hundred feet. As do all Trent Jones courses, Half Moon offers an ample test of your game.

The Tryall course is, in the opinion of most experts, one of the finest Caribbean resort-type golf courses around. For one thing, it was built on a much more interesting piece of ground than was Half Moon. The natural terrain is in large part hilly and it was used to full advantage in the overall design. With many elevations there are some excellent views from tees and fairways overlooking the blue-green sea.

Tryall's course was started by the late Dick Wilson, a fine course builder, but was finished by Texan Ralph Plummer. The shapes of many of its holes are outlined by full-grown trees, there are more than a few doglegs, and the greens are not excessively big. You have some kind of chance from almost anywhere on the putting surfaces. It's a short course that from the back tees is only 6,398 yards long (par 71), which again proves that sheer length does not necessarily make a "championship" golf course.

At the other end of the island lies the capital city of Kingston, a bustling metropolis of close to half a million people which has the lion's share of the island's golf. Two fine championship courses, Constant Spring and Caymanas, serve the city and its visitors, with the diminutive Leguanea Country Club practically downtown.

In 1935, the Prince of Wales (later the Duke of Windsor) opened the present 18 holes, enlarged from the 9-hole course first built in 1902. Constant Springs' challenging course is snuggled at the foot of the mountains on the northern edge of Kingston. Constant Springs has been one of the leaders in Caribbean golf for sixty years and offers the best in Jamaican hospitality. Each of Constant Springs' 18 holes requires a great deal of thought. Although this is not a long course, each hole can prove tricky, baffling, or both. Local players say that the toughest hole is the eleventh, a par-3 that demands a carry of about 220 yards off the tee. There is a big fall just short of the green. If you hit over the green, you are in serious trouble, because the two heavy grass bunkers on the far side fall abruptly into a mass of tropical growth. Psychologically, most golfers will find the thirteenth more difficult—the first two hundred yards of the fairway being a deep ravine from which it is impossible to play. If you have no nerve, it's possible to play from the elevated tee with a 6-iron to a small plateau about halfway down the canyon. Old-timers of more than thirty years at Constant Springs are still intimidated by this hazard.

Caymanas Golf and Country Club, about 12 miles from Kingston, is often considered Jamaica's premier course. Third in length on the island (6,844 yards, par 72), Caymanas was designed by Canadian architect Howard Watson, and opened for play in 1957. It is regarded as the most exacting test of golf in the Caribbean area, and its layout is one of the most attractive. It abounds in generous, undulating greens, well-placed traps, water, trees. There are no really "big" holes. The longest hole is 532 yards, but it is the sporty character of the play that makes Caymanas a real test for golfers of all categories.

The par-5, 497-yard twelfth hole at Caymanas is one of the

best on the course. The drive is from an elevated tee, affording a superb view of forests stretching out in the middle distance and mountains and forests beyond. The fairway is narrow, with woods and lava rock on both sides and two trees on the left side hiding the green. To reach the green in two shots you must play close to the woods and lava rock on the right side. The pin placement is on the right side of the green with a clear approach between two side bunkers.

If you know a member, and are looking for some restful golf, a visit to Liguanea is a charming interlude, for the tight little downtown club course is beautifully situated overlooking the city.

The south coast has only one golf course, at Manchester, where nine holes have been carved out of tropical jungles to provide a sporty and interesting game. It provides the only highland golf on the island.

LOCATION	COURSE	HOLES/PAR/ YARDAGE
Montego Bay	Montego Bay CC	9/36/2,954
Montego Bay	Ironshore CC	18/72/6,615
Montego Bay	Half Moon GC	18/72/7,143
Montego Bay	Tryall G & Beach C	18/71/6,398
Runaway Bay	Runaway Bay CC	18/73/7,145
Ochio Rios	Upton CC	18/72/6,410
Port Antonio	San San GC	9/35/3,070
Kingston	Constant Spring GC	18/68/5,475
Kingston	Caymanas G & CC	18/72/6,844
Kingston	Liguanea GC	9/32/2,341
Mandeville	Manchester GC	9/35/2,865

Puerto Rico. Golfing on this subtropical island 1,040 miles from Miami is an adventure in contrasts. You can travel west from the city of San Juan and play an exacting seaside course or go east and try a rugged hillside layout. In either case, the luxury and conveniences you'll find leave little to be desired. Accommodations are superb and off-course activities revolve around fiestas, beach parties, and gaming in posh casinos.

Although the island is just 100 miles long and 35 miles wide, it has rain forests and mountains as well as beautiful ocean lagoons to intrigue the golfing tourist. At present there are eleven golf courses in ten locations on Puerto Rico. However, only six are accessible to visitors, the military controlling four and the other being a long way from lodging.

The oldest course on the island is also the most unusual, there or anywhere. The El Morro Golf Club at historic Fort Brooke in Old San Juan was originally built in 1906 as an 18-hole course, but military housing requirements reduced it to 9 holes and 18 tees. It is both ridiculed and loved for its dirt greens; the blind tee shots to the two holes tucked behind the walls of a now-dry moat; the traffic jam on the common fairway used by golfers playing holes No. 1, 6, 7, 8, and 9; and for the cheerful caddies who drag the greens smooth before you can putt, and then either root for you or against you, depending on how they're betting. There is perhaps no other feeling in golf quite like the one the golfer gets when teeing off for the first time on the first hole at El Morro on a busy day. With nothing in sight but other golfers, one will hear a caddie say, "O.K., señor, you can hit." Fortunately for the sport of golf, and one's personal well-being, the youngster is invariably right, and after the first shock wears off, you actually welcome similar challenges as you continue playing. Furthermore, the golfers on the fairway to the right, left, and straight ahead do likewise. They have been just as wary as you, you see. Where else can you get to know strangers and carry on simultaneous conversations with people playing five different holes?

Hitting the short iron to the two greens behind the wall of the moat is another experience that will shake the uninitiated. All you can see is the formidable wall of the castle and you ask your caddie where and what you should hit. "Aim for that spot on the wall," he'll tell you in good English, and, in your best Spanish you say, "Si," Nine iron? you then ask. "Ocho," he replies, and having already visited the gambling casinos, you know he means the eight. So what if you have too much club; it's part of the game to ricochet the ball off the wall. In fact, more holes-in-one have been scored that way than with conventional shots.

Could there be anything else unusual about El Morro, you may ask? Si, señor. On the third hole, a 230-yarder, you must hit *over* the wall from ground level. The wall rises some 30 feet into the air. Any line-drive tee shot may suddenly find you dimple to dimple with your little error. Yes, there's more, but why spoil it? It's a lot of fun playing El Morro, and once you do, you'll want to return again and again. Besides the opportunity to meet interesting people on common ground, pitching to dirt greens which hold shots surprisingly well, and which putt true, you might be about to score your finest round ever. Par is only 66. To play El Morro, check with the Recreation Officer at Fort Brooke.

The second oldest course is the Berwind County Club, which is a 20-minute drive from San Juan, not far from the El Comandante race track. It is a 6,365-yard, par-71 test of skill and skull. A winding brook and a ditch dictate play on no fewer than 11 holes, and trees line most of the fairways. Berwind is a sound challenge.

Berwind members have a high regard for golf and etiquette, are knowledgeable and friendly, and take justifiable pride in their course. The greens are fairly large and hold shots well, but they can get grainy and cause some good putts and almost all weak ones to behave oddly. The golfer who can spot the breaks in these greens at Berwind has a great advantage. The tenth, at 530 yards, and the seventeenth, an elusive green 200 yards from the tee, are two good challenges.

Dorado Beach's classic seaside links is reported to be cooler in summer than many stateside courses, due to the steady trade winds blowing off the Atlantic.

The most renowned course in the entire area, however, is the 27-hole course at Dorado Beach Golf and Tennis Club, the Augusta National of the Caribbean. Immaculately groomed, architecturally sound, scenic beyond description, this Robert Trent Jones creation is considered a milestone in his career. He literally salvaged a swampland overrun by wild tropical growth and converted it into a flat, fertile golf course. Hundreds of coconut palms line lush, Bermuda fairways, and water hazards come into play on at least ten of the holes. Ironically, most of the water is situated on the left, making it virtually a nightmare for hookers.

The par-3 thirteenth, from the back tees, is perhaps the most rugged. Requiring a long tee-to-green shot onto the putting surface that extends out into the lake on the left, it is further protected with traps and trees on the right. Other interesting, challenging water hazards have been included around the Mata Redonda Lagoon and a series of small lakes. The third, for example, is flanked on the left by the lagoon and by trees on the right, with a trap strategically placed about 250 yards from the tee. A wee bit of a dogleg right, where to hit the tee shot? The fourth is one of the prettiest anywhere, a short hole with its green set on the very edge of the beach. The view is breathtaking. The fifth, sixth, and seventh complete the encirclement of the lagoon, with the fifth known as the gambler's hole. A long tee shot puts you in a position to cut the corner via the scenic water route with your second shot. If successful, you're putting for an eagle. If not, you're putting your hand in your pocket for another ball. Most of the greens are large and undulating.

The West nine measure 3,505 yards from the championship tees and 3,290 regular; the Middle nine 3,500 yards from full length and 3,230 regular; and the new East nine 3,581 stretched out and 3,275 regular. All are par 36. But any 18 you choose to play here add up to a formidable round of golf.

Close to the Dorado Beach Golf Club is the Dorado Hilton Country Club. Unlike most seaside courses, this one is rolling with the majority of fairways lined on both sides with tall coconut palm trees. The course is designed to meet all standards of play. The championship course measures 7,300 yards in length, this combined with the rolling terrain, palm-lined fairways and the design of the holes make it a truly championship course. The course from the regular tees measures 6,480 yards, with this big difference in yardage, it allows the player to select the course he would like to play according to his ability. The ladies yardage is 6,087 yards. The course from the championship tees has a course rating of 73. The rating from the regular tees is 70 and the ladies course rating is 73.

Thirty-three miles east of San Juan is Fajardo. Set in one of the most beautiful parts of Puerto Rico, Fajardo is not only a commercial fishing port, but also has become an important center for yachting, fishing and water sports. Nestled in the hillside overlooking this town is another fine Puerto Rico course—the El Conquistador Hotel and Golf Club. It sits majestically surrounded by the sea, bathed in the sun and soft trade winds.

You cannot begin to describe all of the holes at any one of the fine golf courses in Puerto Rico, but the first hole at the new El Conquistador could very well typify golf on the island. This 515-yard par 5 is one of the most beautiful and panoramic opening holes ever designed. Two elevated tees situated on a 380-foot cliff present the golfer with a magnificent view. The first tee overlooks the Caribbean

The El Conquistador Hotel and Club course is a par-70, 6,285-yard layout, designed by Bob Hagge. As you can see, it is well trapped, dotted with trees, has three major water hazards (the ponds serve as home for imported swans), and runs along two streams.

and the Atlantic, with the Virgin Islands in the background. The long winding fairway to a green two hundred feet below the teeing area offers a view of the El Yunque Rain Forest and the Laguna del Convento.

Fort Buchanan, located in Caparra, the first section to be settled after the island was visited by Christopher Columbus in 1493, is a pleasing 9-hole, 18-tee arrangement that looks much easier than it plays. Although it was built for the military personnel at the sprawling base, visitors can make arrangements to play. Most of the greens are at fairway level, making approach shots difficult to pinpoint. But the course plays fast and fair. It boasts a fine finishing hole and the long, tough par-3 third, with its green tucked in a corner, leaves very little margin for error behind or to the left of the putting surface. It is a course one seldom gets tired of playing and if you're there during the late afternoon hours, you'll be treated to a magnificent sunset, a pause in play while the Colors are hauled down (announced by the firing of a cannon), and the happy shouts of youngsters practicing or playing Little League baseball on a nearby plot of ground.

On the south shore of the island, the Ponce Golf Club is generally open for play. It is a good test, a pleasant 9-hole layout, and is the only bona fide course in that part of Puerto Rico. Arrangements to play can be made by contacting the Ponce Intercontinental Hotel. Incidentally, Ponce is also the locale of one of the four excellent institutions of higher learning in the Commonwealth, the Catholic University, as well as the Museum of Fine Arts, which houses some of the masterpieces of the world.

Golfers who have visited Puerto Rico have found it to be a land of glistening, palm-fringed beaches and vivid green mountains, of sun and breeze, of historic fortresses and ancient churches, of towering office buildings, industrial plants, modern highways, a bustling air terminal, and pleasant, hospitable people, most of whom speak English.

LOCATION	COURSE	HOLES/PAR/ YARDAGE
Rio Grande, Loiza	Berwind CC	18/71/6,365
Dorado	Cerromar Beach Club	18/72/6,540
		18/72/6,505
Dorado	Dorado Beach G Hotel GC	18/72/6,425

LOCATION	COURSE	HOLES/PAR/ YARDAGE
		18/72/6,525
Dorado	Dorado Del Mar Hotel and CC	18/72/6,427
Las Croabas	El Conquistador GC	18/71/6,440
Ponce	Ponce CC	9/36/2,975
Catano	Ft. Buchanan GC	9/35/2,964

Virgin Islands. Until 1965, this golfer's dream was more of a nightmare. The one golf course on St. Croix, the largest of the Virgin Islands, was a disaster area, of eroded greens and rock-filled fairways. This has all changed. Visiting golfers now play the 9-hole 2,753-yard, par-36 course at Estate Carleton and the championship Fountain Valley course, sponsored by the Rockefellers and designed by Robert Trent Jones. Estate Carleton's nine holes are laid out around the historic ruins of an eighteenth-century sugar plantation. While this course is not the most difficult by any means, the greens are liberally trapped with sand, and a water hazard figures in two holes. Crumbling sugar mills and giant mahogany trees line the fairways.

Fountain Valley is a 6,870-yard, par-72 championship course in every way and the golfer who demands a difficult course will have to look no further. On what was once a large plantation, the architect and developers of Fountain Valley have created a golfer's paradise. The first hole sets the pace of the remaining 17, right at the start. It is a 510-yard, par-5 hole, with a dogleg to the right, and you must come off an elevated tee as long as possible. Take care on your second wood shot. A pronounced hook will carry you into the tropical growth bordering the fairway and penalities will eat up your game.

There are ten dogleg holes, with sprawling fairway bunkers guarding the corners of every turn. If you found that you were using your sand iron uncommonly often on your round, you will not be surprised to learn that there are over ninety sand traps. Greens are well-guarded with bunkers and water hazards. The designer made excellent use of water on the course, and the par-3, 175-yard fifth hole is a good example. It's over the water all the way to the shelf-green set atop a steep cliff. The green is wide but shallow and two bunkers at the back delineate the target, a design technique used on many of the undulating putting surfaces.

A fabulous "peninsula green," with a horseshoe moat on three sides, undoubtedly makes Fountain Valley's No. 12 one of the famous golf holes in the world. With a sand trap in front, it lies invitingly and deceivingly in front of a theaterlike backdrop of royal palm, mango, and almond trees. It will be one of those holes that always produce excited locker-room chatter after the day's round is over. "You have to hit the green and stay on it," one golfer has remarked. A par 4, it is only 35 yards long from the regulation men's tee, but a bath is certain for any ball hit too strongly for the cup.

Alert golfers playing Fountain Valley will quickly discover that they can use the outlines of several ancient Danish sugar mill ruins which appear on the hills fringing the golf course to zero in for accuracy. On the tee shot from No. 18, the protruding tower of Fountain Mill ruin on the hill just above the pro-shop is directly in line with No. 18 green, 370 yards and a par 4 away. On the dogleg No. 9, the same tower can be used by a good average golfer to line up his second shot toward the green.

On the island of St. Thomas, there is the Herman E. Moore Golf course which is a 9-hole, par-35, 3,398-yard layout. This course has sand greens and is under the jurisdiction of the college of the Virgin Islands. The Estate Carleton, Fountain Valley, the Reef Golf Club (a 9-hole affair), and this course are the only four in the islands.

Dominican Republic. Santo Domingo, the capital of the Dominican Republic, has two 18-hole courses, the Santo Domingo Country Club and Campo de Golf Bella Vista (also known as the Hotel Embajador course). Santo Domingo, although one of the oldest in the islands, had a new course built in the late 1940's, a par-72, 6,672-yard test. The Bella Vista is usually considered the better of the two courses, and from championship tees, plays 7,383, par 72. From the regular tees, it's a 6,862-yard test.

On the south shore of the island, at the resort area of La Romana, we'll find the country's other major golf course. This 18-hole, par-72, 6,790-yard affair was designed by Pete Dye and was opened as a resort course in 1971. Cajuiles Golf Club is literally stunning, the result, some contend, of careful planning, some help from nature and hand labor. Some three hundred Dominican workers piled rocks and planted fairways and shaped greens. "It makes you realize what special equipment hand labor is," said one observer. "All great works of art have been done with hands, not machines."

Haiti. Haiti has one regulation course, the Petionville Club, a 3,010-yard, par-35, 9-hole layout in the hills beyond Port au Prince. There, the air is so light that one can almost drive the downhill, 300-yard first hole with a 2-iron. Although the greens are fair, the fairways are poor. There are layers of limestone on and just below the surface of the turf. It's no place to break in a new set of irons.

Trinidad and Tobago. Trinidad is the home of steel bands and calypso. It is also the home of St. Andrews Golf Club, the dean of Caribbean golf. Located in Maraval, the exclusive suburb of Port-of-Spain, the 5,811-yard, par-68 St. Andrews overlooks the city and the dark blue waters of the harbor beyond. Tourists find a cordial welcome at St. Andrews and there is always someone around the clubhouse to give you a tip or two about the most difficult holes.

Elevated greens, built on coral, are a feature of the Tabago Golf Club course.

St. Andrews differs from the most other Caribbean courses in that the greens are extremely fast. The fifteenth green should be played with a great deal of caution. Its break is extremely deceptive and a too-strong putt will carry you past the cup, where the ball picks up speed on the down slope. Most local players don't even play for the flag from the tee, but rather try to arrive on the green high, so as to roll down into position. St. Andrews is rugged. Electric carts aren't available, but knowledgeable caddies are, and at very low rates. Golf on Trinidad is probably less expensive than at any other major island in the Caribbean. Although St. Andrews is a private club, visitors are always welcome, as they are at the beautiful Pointe-a-Pierre, operated by the Texaco Oil Company for its employees. This lovely 18-hole, 6,398-yard, par-72 course is part of a complete country club, highly unusual in the West Indies where golf clubs tend to have only golf and not the swimming pools and other activities found at many of those in the United States. In addition to golf, Pointe-a-Pierre has tennis, swimming, and squash. Two other courses, both with nine holes, round out golf on Trinidad—the 3,018-yard, par-35 Clifton Hill Golf Club and 2,914-yard, par-36 Brighton Golf Club.

The Tobago Golf Club course, first to be built on the island, was opened in March, 1969. It was the initial project in a proposed resort development expected to include a hotel, cottages, private homes, marina, and at least one more 18-hole golf course. The intention, of course is to attract tourists to Tobago's uncrowded beaches, scenic bays, secret coves, and sleepy villages, and to introduce them to some of the best snorkeling in the Caribbean.

Designed in the American style by British architect John D. Harris, the course is characterized by steep hills, with palm trees on one side, the sea on the other. A good test for all classes of golfers, it stretches to 6,685 yards and a par 72. The front nine, a par 37, has three par-5 holes, the longest measuring 540 yards. The greens, built on foundations of coral, generally hold well-struck approach shots but yield very little to putts.

British Leeward Islands. The most popular of the British Leeward Islands, Antigua has some of the best beaches in the Caribbean and two 9-hole courses in conjuction with the Antigua Beach Hotel and the luxurious Half Moon Bay. The Half Moon Bay Golf Club is par 35, 2,410 yards, while the Gambles is par 34, and 2,550 yards. Another interesting course in this area is the 9-hole, 3,300-yard Cedar Valley Golf Club. You will not find either of these the most challenging in the world, but this will be of little concern, since Antigua, full of beautiful scenery and historic sights, has one of the most pleasant climates in the entire Caribbean. The humidity is low and the winter sun will give you a beautiful tan to bring back home. There is a 9-hole course at the Mill Reef Club, but it is not open to visitors, the only such course in the Caribbean.

The Belham River Golf Club on Monserrat is nine holes of magnificent scenery and one of the most challenging short courses anywhere. Belham River's fairways are air-conditioned by the northeast trade winds blowing through the saddle between a 3,000-foot smoking volcano and a lesser peak. Named by Columbus for the mountain monastery where Loyola founded the Jesuit Order, Montserrat became the home of thousands of Irish families banished by Cromwell, and the contagious brogue was even picked up by the blacks. The story is told of a newly arrived Irishman who, on hearing the Negro dock-worker's familiar accent, inquired how long he had been on the island. "Three years!" exclaimed the Irishman in amazement. "Glory be to God, and ye turned black in that time?"

You won't "turn black" from the sun on the 3,222-yard, par-36 Belham River Valley Course, but your face may be a bit red, unless you find a way to lick a few of its holes.

The second hole—following a conventional four hundred-yard par-4 first dogleg to the right to an elevated green—is a case in point. Your drive must clear 135 yards of tight-rooted marsh grass. Your second shot poses the question—should you take the challenge and play for the island between two branches of the Belham River where it empties into the sea, or play a safe shot to the edge and face a long third shot across the two estuaries to the elevated green of this par-5 575-yard equalizer?

Edmund B. Ault didn't design the one hundred-acre Belham River course for the local color altogether, but your third tee perches by a pit of woods half concealing the crumbled masonry and long-unused boiler of an early lime-juice plant complete with post for tying up ships while loading. From here you drive down 153 yards to a beautiful green bunkered by several traps and the blue Caribbean itself. The short and spectacular fourth with its 100-foot-high green is an easy par 4, a relaxer before No. 5's tough par 4, again crossing the Belham River on a dogleg to the right, to a bunkered green 402 yards away. Numbers 6, 7, and 8 are played straight into the prevailing winds, which seem to add yardage to the 178-yard and 201-yard par 3's, and the 496-yard par 5. Coming back on the ninth with the wind at your back should make the 567-yard par 5 easy but somehow doesn't. It's an exacting hole right to the almond-shaded green surrounded by ubiquitious marsh grass.

The only other courses in the Leeward are the short 2,200-yard, par-30, 9-hole Golden Rock Golf Club on St. Kitts and the Mullet Bay Beach Golf Club, a 9-hole, 2,600-yard, par-35 affair.

British Windward Islands. Grenada is the spice island. An errant drive at the 9-hole, par-35, 2,672-yard Grenada Golf and Country Club is liable to strike the trees lining the fairways and dislodge a shower of mangos and nutmeg. Good caddies are always available to recover balls, and the players behind will be in no rush to play through. They are in no hurry, which is typical of the Caribbees. On this and most of the other islands it is a good idea to bring along a good supply of tees. They are expensive and in short supply in the islands.

On the northern tip of St. Lucia, there is the new 9-hole Cap Estate Golf Course. It is a challenging 3,200-yard, par-36 layout. On St. Vincent, there is the Windward Islands' only other course, the small 9-hole, 2,230-yard par-32 Ratko Mill Golf Course.

Other Islands. Barbados has two golf courses available for the visiting golfer. They are the 18-hole, par-68, 4,759-yard Rockley Golf and Country Club, and 9-hole, par-36, 3,369-yard Sandy Lane Hotel Golf Course. While neither could be classified as truly challenging, they both are fun and rather interesting to play.

In Aruba and Curaçao, there are 9-hole golf courses. The Aruba Golf Club is a par-36, 2,410-yard layout while the Shell Golf Club on Curaçao is a par-36, 3,079-yard course. For those who have their clubs along, these two courses, with their sand greens, make a nice afternoon's exercise.

15

SOUTH AMERICA

South America has some of the best golf courses in the world, and if you plan to visit there, golf should be on your itinerary. Most of the better courses were designed by British and American architects and make full use of the interesting terrain and natural beauty. It might be well to note that in most—if not all—South America golf is played in the British way—no "gimme" putts, no teeing up the ball in the fairway (except as a temporary local rule due to the condition of the course). They also use the British ball. You will probably love it off the tee but hate it on the greens.

Golf in South America is usually played only by the upper classes. As a result, all the courses mentioned in this chapter are private, except for the fine Palermo Park Municipal Golf Course in Buenos

Located in a real "badlands" area of the Bolivian altiplano, some 12,000 feet above sea level, the Mallasilla Golf Club is said to have the highest course in the world with *grass* greens that you can play.

Aires, Argentina. (That was a private club until a few years ago, too.) Membership card or a letter of introduction from the secretary of a North American golf club is usually sufficient to obtain full guest privileges at *most* South American courses. For the nonclub tourist, partial guest privileges generally can be arranged by the local offices of the airlines or steamship companies, hotels, or national tourist bureau. (Several clubs do not give privileges during weekends, so check in advance.) Caddies are well-trained, and while most do not speak English, they can communicate with you very well about golf. At most of the better establishments—especially at the resort areas—language differences are no problem. By the way, while clubs can be rented at many courses, it is a good idea to take your own. Also remember that in South America most clubs are closed on Monday.

As to playing conditions, remember that southern Brazil, Uruguay, Argentina, Chile, and part of Peru have a temperate climate, while the other areas are tropical. However, remember that even in tropical areas, elevation can make a radical difference in the temperature. Golf in Ecuador, Columbia, and Venezuela, because of elevation, is quite pleasant the year round. The dry season, in the tropical areas, is from early December through the middle of April. The tourist bureau of the countries you plan to visit or even your local travel agent can give you advice about your wardrobe.

ARGENTINA

The English brought golf to Argentina at the end of the nineteenth century. The chroniclers of those days remarked with a shade of irony on the wanderings of a few Englishmen devoted to such a strange sort of amusement in the uninhibited locality of San Martin and the surroundings of the metropolitan port.

Those wide extensions of land, of course, served as links. When the Lomas Golf Club was founded in 1892, many Argentines had already taken up the new sport. After this club there came others, that of San Martin and the Fiores Golf Club. In 1900 the Mar del Plata Golf Club was founded, right on the Atlantic coast, and this was followed five years later by the founding of the Golf Club Argentino in the woods and gardens of the district of Palermo in Buenos Aires. Today it is the municipal course.

As a result of the increasing number of players a great many new clubs were founded, and toward 1926 several clubs formed the

Asociación Argentina de Golf. It is worth noting that the outstanding progress and development of the game in Argentina, and the privileged position it occupies among the golf-playing countries of the world, is due mostly to the work of the Association, particularly in the organizing and supervision of important championships and yearly tournaments which attract international figures. There are some twenty thousand active players in Argentina, nearly nine thousand of whom have an official handicap.

Throughout the country there are over a hundred courses, of which sixty-six are affiliated in the Association. In the outskirts of Buenos Aires alone there are twenty golf courses. The leading golf layout in Argentina is generally conceded to be at the Jockey Club. Of the two eighteens, the Red course is considered the more difficult. It was designed by Alister MacKenzie, the architect who made the original plans for the Augusta National Golf Club in Georgia. On the Red course, many of the greens are of the so-called punch-bowl variety, with great mounds, some as high as 15 feet, surrounding the backs and sides of the putting surface. Greens like this can lead to many three-putts.

There are several other excellent courses in the Buenos Aires area that you should consider including: the 6,600-yard Palermo "Wood" Park Municipal course, the 6,986-yard San Andres Golf course, and the 6,885-yard Ranelagh Golf Club. The latter is an interesting layout that has tight, tree-lined driving holes, strategic fairway bunkers, and several water hazards. The course has five par-5 holes and the difficult pin positions on most greens call for well-placed drives and precise approach shots. Ranelagh is similar in its contours to the Wentworth club near London, but its location, Buenos Aires, has more of the flavor of Paris, Genoa, Madrid, or Milan than of London, although British influences are still strong in the city.

Here are some of the courses within one hour's time of downtown Buenos Aires that are considered best to challenge the visiting golfer:

LOCATION	*COURSE*	*HOLES/PAR/ YARDAGE*
Buenos Aires	Jockey Club	
	(Red Course)	18/72/6,383
	(Blue Course)	18/71/6,191
Buenos Aires	Palermo Park Municipal GC	18/72/6,609

LOCATION	*COURSE*	*HOLES/PAR/ YARDAGE*
Buenos Aires	Ranelagh GC	18/73/6,885
Links	Links GC	18/72/6,422
Don Torenato	Hinder Club	18/71/6,342
		18/70/6,154
Hurlingham	Hurlingham Club	18/70/6,212
San Isidro	Club Nautico Isidro	18/71/6,255
San Antonio de Podera	Ituzaingo GC	18/73/6,722
San Martin	San Andres GC	18/73/6,986

BOLIVIA

If you really want to feel like a *big* bettor, you will want to play golf in Bolivia, the home of the biggest golf courses anywhere in the world. Whether you play at 6,369-yard, par-70 La Paz Golf Club or 6,440-yard, par-70 Los Pinos Club (both in La Paz), or at the 6,277-yard, par-72 Oruro Golf Club (near Oruro), you can expect to pick up better than fifty yards on your drives on these mountainside courses. At better than twelve thousand feet, balls carry long distances in this rarefied air. But motorized golf carts are not available at these courses,

It is advisable to keep on the fairways here at the Mallasilla Golf Club, La Paz, otherwise the ball is apt to end up hundreds of feet below in a deep canyon which runs along one side of the course.

so playing them can be most tiring. Since the Bolivian government will not make a statement as to which of the three courses is the biggest—each makes that claim—we will not get into the argument either.

BRAZIL

Soccer is the No. 1 sport in Brazil with 100,000 or more fans regularly jamming stadiums in São Paulo and Rio. But there are golf courses in virtually every major city and some of them, like the Gavea Golf and Country Club in Rio de Janeiro, are considered among the world's most beautiful courses. The front nine was carved out of the hills. While the yardages are relatively short, a straight ball is a must. Slice or hook and you are down a ravine, into a ditch, or surrounded by huge rocks. The back nine is spread along the sea. The whole course is most intriguing with its orchid-bearing trees that line the fairways and the breathtaking view of the Atlantic Ocean, especially from the seventh green.

In fashionable São Paulo, the São Fernando Golf Club is a test for any golfer—even the world's top professionals. This 6,523-yard course is dotted with water hazards and features tight-driving holes. Its many elevated greens with narrow entrances means that the ball must fly onto the putting surface. In keeping with modern course design, greens are flat in areas where the pins are protected by bunkers and rolling where the holes are cut in easier positions.

Remember that your school Spanish will get you around most of South America except in the continent's biggest country, Brazil. This fifth largest nation in the world is the only Portuguese-speaking country in Latin America, but if your grasp of the language is limited to "nao compreendo," you need not rush off to Berlitz. Brazil is a melting pot of many races and cultures and there is usually someone nearby who speaks English, French, Spanish, Italian, Russian, German or even Chinese. And there is no language barrier in the hypnotic beat of the samba or bossa nova.

Leading golf courses that you can play near Brazil's two leading cities are:

LOCATION	COURSE	HOLES/PAR/ YARDAGE
Rio de Janeiro	Gavea G & CC	18/68/6,042
Rio de Janeiro	Itanhanga GC	18/72/6,646
São Paulo	São Fernando GC	18/70/6,523
São Paulo	São Paulo GC	18/71/6,484

CHILE

A painting made in about 1560 indicates that the Indians played a game similar to golf here in Chile. If we painted a picture today we would find the inhabitants playing real golf, since it is a fairly popular sport. While the number of courses is limited, several of the best ones in South America are located in Chile.

The best course in this country is Los Leones, which lies in the lee of the Chilean Andes, a mountain range second only to the Himalayas in height. At first sight, Los Leones looks like an arboretum. You can hardly see the golf course for the trees. Eight thousand trees would be a lot of trees for any golf course; Los Leones has ten times that number, and you would have to be a botanist simply to name the varieties. The fairways snake through this foliage in a series of dog-legs. If you are wild with your drive, you are almost certain to be faced with the bleak prospect of pitching or even chipping safe back to the fairway, for the possibility of discovering a way through the trees is a little like trying to catch lightning in a bottle. Los Leones has only five traps on its fairways, but that is about five more than it really needs. The trees are hazard enough.

Since the course is so heavily planted with trees, the greens at Los Leones have very wisely been elevated. An elevated green calls for a particularly well-controlled second shot, but it becomes almost sadistically penalizing when the green is exposed to the wind. At Los Leones, of course, the wind is almost no factor at all, since the vast foliage on the course screens it off. Thus the raised putting surfaces have been well-advised. They make the approach shots tough, but not impossible, and so the course becomes something more than just a test of the tee shot. This is the sad category into which so many courses that have been carved through trees so often fall. Happily, Los Leones avoids it.

Golf courses of interest in Chile are:

LOCATION	*COURSE*	*HOLES/PAR/ YARDAGE*
Santiago	Club de Golf Los Leones	18/72/6,708
Santiago	Prince of Wales CC	18/72/6,753
Santiago	Club de Golf Sport Francais	18/72/6,652
Rocas de Santo Domingo	Club de Golf Santo Domingo	18/72/6,640
Viña del Mar	Granadilla CC	18/72/6,366

COLOMBIA

The Chibacha legend of El Dorado inspired a group of Spanish conquistadores to brave the Magdalena jungle and discover this 8,600-foot plateau in 1538. There they founded a settlement which is now Colombia's capital with almost two million people—Bogota. It is an incongruously flat place, and at that altitude, a golf ball ripping through the rarefied atmosphere chews up extra yardage. But it is neither the flatness of the terrain nor the thin air that makes the West Course of the Country Club de Bogota a classic example of a tee-shot course.

What does make it one is the constant, relentless demand for accuracy off the tee. The stringbean fairways, almost all of which dogleg gently to the left or right, are bordered by long rows of pine and eucalyptus trees; and they are guarded by deep bunkers and by a series of lagoons that interlace the fairways. The course is 6,914 yards long and plays to a par 72. On the par-4, 463-yard ninth hole, your tee shot must carry one lagoon, but must stop short of a second. To atone for the uniform flatness of the course, the greens have been built up so that their distance from the fairways can properly be gauged, and many of them are of the split-level variety.

The Country Club de Bogota has received all the loving care that can be lavished on a golfing facility. In addition to a glass-encased swimming pool, championship tennis courts and a polo field, it boasts an adjoining layout, the East Course, to make it one of the finest centers of golf and recreation in South America.

Actually, Bogota has three additional fine courses, including El Rincon designed by Robert Trent Jones, as well as several others in various parts of the country that are very worthy of play.

LOCATION	COURSE	HOLES/PAR/ YARDAGE
Barranquilla	Club Lagos de Caujaral	18/72/6,585
Barranquilla	Country Club de Barranquilla	18/72/6,355
Bogota	Country Club de Bogota	18/72/6,914
		18/70/6,536
Bogota	Club de Los Largartos	18/72/6,739
Bogota	San Andres CC	18/70/6,435
Bogota	El Rincon CC	18/73/6,425
Cali	Club Campestre de Cali	18/71/6,860
Manizales	Country Club de Manizales	9/36/3,245
Medellin	Country Club de Medellin	18/71/6,214
Santa Marta	Santa Marta GC	18/72/6,600

ECUADOR

Even the hemispheres get together to enjoy themselves in Ecuador, which is just a half-hour north of Quito, and there you can put one foot in the northern hemisphere while the other is in the southern hemisphere.

Quito, once the capital of the Inca empire, now the capital of Ecuador, is a fascinating city with a rich colonial heritage that recalls the Spanish conquistadores, Simón Bolívar, and General Sucre. It is also the home of the challenging Quito Tennis Y Golf Club course.

This course has a spectacular mountain backdrop and after a golfer plays it the first time he feels like a mountain goat—or in this part of the world, a llama—since the course layout is constantly up and down hills. For such a high course (almost ten thousand feet), the greens and fairways are lush and there are many trees, including olive and eucalyptus.

Two other cities—Ancon and Guayaquil—also have fairly interesting golf courses.

LOCATION	COURSE	HOLES/PAR/ YARDAGE
Ancon	Ancon C	18/70/6,224
Quito	Quito Tennis Y GC	18/71/6,357
Guayaquil	Country Club de Guayaquil	18/72/6,660

The modern clubhouse and putting green at the Country Club de Guayaquil.

PARAGUAY

Paraguay is one of South America's least-known countries. But to the visitor, this country has many interesting things to see and do, including a round of golf on the 6,123-yard, par-70, Asuncion Golf Club. This capital city course, while not of championship caliber, can prove to be a worthwhile challenge if you have included this small country on your itinerary.

PERU

Because of its scenic wonders and great historical significance, Peru occupies a very important position in the overall tourist picture in South America. Of the truly legendary countries in the world, few have a more romantic, swashbuckling appeal than the land of the Incas. It also has some appeal to the golfer, too, because of its several fine courses.

Lima has golf courses all over . . . in the city . . . beside the Pacific . . . and around ruins in the mountains. This means that the type of golfing varies from a lush course to links (i.e., along a shore). The city course is the 6,010-yard, par-72 Lima Golf Club, which has lush vegetation and beautiful flowers to go along with a fairly difficult layout. The 6,475-yard, par-71 Los Incas Club could be considered a South American–links type because of its playing condition, while the 6,233-yard, par-71 Granja Azul course, about a half-hour drive inland from Lima, is located in an arid area in which evidence of Indian occupation still remain.

SURINAM

Located between the British and French Guianas on the northeast coast of South America is the country of Surinam. Here a tourist can find more fun, pleasure, and unusual experience condensed within a few miles than is possible to find in any of the neighboring Carribean

At the Las Incas Golf Club in Lima, Inca ruins run along four fairways.

islands. It even has a 9-hole golf course at the Paramaribo Golf Club
that is different, too. That is, you play nine basic holes, but with a
different number 12 and 17 to make it a very interesting 5,625-yard,
18-hole course.

URUGUAY

Uruguay is the smallest full republic in South America, but in spite
of its size, has three fine 18-hole courses: the 6,337-yard, par-70
Cantegril Country Club; the 6,211-yard, par-73 Club de Golf del
Cerro, and the 6,341, par-72 Golf Club del Uruguay. The latter two
courses are in the capital city of Montevideo.

VENEZUELA

There are approximately twenty golf courses in Venezuela, of which
about half are 9-hole courses. In the Caracas area there are five
courses, four of which are 18-hole and one 9. But golf is a fairly new
sport in Venezuela and additional courses are being built at a fairly

When playing on the Golf Club de Uruguay in Montevideo, you would
imagine that you are back in the midwestern part of the United States. The
trees, course layout, climate, and grass are all similar.

rapid rate. The Lagunita Country Club just outside of Caracas is a basically new one that has achieved remarkable maturity and stature as one of the best courses in South America—in a short while. Transformed from a field of orange groves on volcanic ash, each of its 18 holes has a distinctive character, from the twisting dogleg tenth, a par 5 of 535 yards, with a beautifully bunkered, multilevel green, to any of the five par 3's. The eleventh, a 188-yarder, is especially notable—a deep, undulated green guarded by great pits of sand, and with out-of-bounds skirting the very edge of the left fringe. The fourteenth, a treacherous par 3 of 180 yards, has a boomerang-shaped green, presenting a formidable target nestled among four bunkers.

The picturesque fifteenth, a downhill 405-yard par 4, is literally a valley cut through the volcanic rock. Looking from the tee down this fairway is like peering down a lush, green, high-banked ski-run. You putt on acres of magnificently manicured greens at Lagunita— greens probably as large as any in the world. And when the weather warms up, as it is apt to do in Venezuela, they run as fast as a frightened fox.

For a completely different type of course, you may wish to try the Maracaibo Country Club on the shores of Lake Maracaibo in the city of Maracaibo. The area around the city is like a desert. The air is warm and the terrain is flat and covered with low brush. Yet out of these materials a Scot named James Baird Wilson built a golf course of championship stature, incorporating features reminiscent of St. Andrews and Carnoustie. The bunkers are deep, craggy pits placed in the fairways and around greens. Some traps are hidden behind others that are seen first (a canny Scottish trick). You may rejoice in a shot that seems to have flown free of bunkers, but you may have a rude awakening when you get to the ball. The designer followed the natural terrain in building this course, so it is without great undulation. But it is long. Maracaibo Country Club measures 6,967 yards and plays to every bit of its par 72.

The front nine offers an interesting assortment of tests. It opens on a straight-out par 4 of 445 yards, a hole on which you must be strong, then moves to shorter par 4's calling for careful placement of tee shots, and ends with two imaginative par 5's. The eighth, at 528 yards, demands both power and control. The tee shot is wisely played with a long iron layup short of the water that covers the right corner of the fairway beginning at 225 yards. The second shot, with a fairway wood, must be hit long and straight to a narrow, well-bunkered green.

The ninth hole reverses the requirements of the eighth. Here you can swing away from the tee, banging the drive down into the rough on the right corner to short-cut this doglegging hole, or hit straight out into the fairway. Either way, the second shot must carry a big lake that fronts the green and winds around the full left side of the putting surface.

The greens at Maracaibo Country Club are of two sharply different kinds. The front nine is grown in Uganda grass; the back nine, in more conventional Bermuda. The first, a strain of grass from Central Africa, is as sturdy as a bed of needles. The grass is so tough that the mower blades must be resharpened after each cutting. These greens, virtually without grain, call for a putting stroke quite different from that needed on the Bermuda grass of the back nine.

Other courses that you should try while in Venezuela are:

LOCATION	COURSE	HOLES/PAR/ YARDAGE
Caracas	Caracas CC	18/72/6,700
Caracas	The Junko CC	18/71/6,536
Caracas	Valle Arriba GC	18/70/6,162
Caracas	Lagunita CC	18/70/6,790
Macuto	Carabelleda GC	9/35/3,173
Maracaibo	Maracaibo CC	18/72/6,967
Maracay	Hotel Maracay GC	18/71/3,450

16

THE BRITISH ISLES
AND IRELAND

Ever since the rugged Scotsmen of the fifteenth century began playing their first crude form of golf on the coastal rabbit warrens (thus neglecting their archery practice at the risk of their country's safety), golf in the British Isles has developed in its own quiet way almost as a natural phenomenon. Whether it was on the original links-land (sandy soil amid towering sand dunes reclaimed from the sea), on downland (the springy turf atop the cliffs), on parkland, or heather-covered heathland, the terrain seemed to be right whatever the locale.

Today you can travel the length and breadth of Scotland, England, and Wales, and except for a few mountainous and sparsely populated areas, you will never be more than ten miles from a golf course. And if you stand on the steps of Eros, in London's Piccadilly Circus, it is safe to say that you will have a choice of at least three hundred courses in a fifty-mile radius.

Although the flourishing golfing areas of the United States have grown up around the wealthy winter resorts or expensive residential suburbs, the famous golfing areas in Britain sprang up during the last century without regard to population or economic considerations. Thus, many of Britain's finest courses are concentrated in readily accessible areas.

St. Andrews and half a dozen other fine courses are on the east coast of Scotland in the general area of Edinburgh; on the west coast there are five other first-class layouts near Glasgow. In England, no fewer than seven outstanding courses line the coast of Lancashire and Cheshire, while several in Wales are well worth a visit; the great industrial center of Birmingham boasts two excellent inland tests; and London has so many courses that they are almost impossible to catalogue—from the parkland beauty of Moor Park to the windswept trinity of championship courses on the east coast of Sandwich.

There are approximately 1,700 private clubs and 140 municipal operations in Britain. And the English, Scotch and Welsh private clubs have a liberal policy toward overseas visiting golfers. Members of U.S. clubs should take along a letter of introduction from the club secretary to the secretary of the club to be visited. This will suffice for all but the very exclusive clubs, where you may need to be introduced by a member. The British Tourist Authority, hotels, transportation carriers can usually make the necessary introductions for nonclub members. Greens fees are low when compared to the United States. But, it is wise to write or at least phone ahead to the secretaries of clubs you want to visit, especially if you want to play on a weekend. You can usually hire pull-carts, but there are no gas or electric cars. Rental of clubs is rare.

The visitor to Britain has to be ready for all seasons, which might well occur in a single day. We are inclined to scoff at the Englishman's umbrella. But he needs it! The same holds true for Scotland and Wales. So bring plenty of sweaters—and wet-weather gear. But take along your swimsuit. You never know!

ENGLAND

Because it is traditional for the Royal and Ancient Golf Club of St. Andrews, the ruling body of golf in Britain, to hold the British Open and Amateur Championships on a seaside course (the Ladies' Golf Union has broken with tradition on several occasions), there are a handful of recognized championship courses scattered around the coastline. But grouped with each of these specific meccas is a bevy of satellite courses of hardly lesser interest and renown; so in each particular area there is not just one formidable challenge, but a minimum of three and often more.

These great linksland courses are unlike anything to be found in this country. They are treeless and exposed to the four winds. The close-cropped, undulating fairways are far removed from the lush turf of American country clubs, and bunkers (they do not talk of traps in the Old Country) are deep and foreboding. The rough can range from towering, reed-covered sand dunes to prickly gorse bushes, and the greens are usually large, fast, and tricky. Nowhere else but on a British (or Irish) links can golf be so dependent on the elements. A course bathed in June sunshine one day may be in the path of a raging northeaster the next.

The locals know just how to play these courses in all their various moods, because a stiff breeze (what might well be described as a near gale over here) is par for the course, more often than not. These magnificent tests of golf are to be found on the Kent coast in the southeast corner of England, in Lancashire on England's northwest coast, in Ayrshire, Scotland, looking west to the Isle of Arran, in East Lothian looking north to the County of Fife, and of course, in Fife itself with famous St. Andrews.

The Kent group, dominated by Royal St. George's Sandwich, with neighboring Royal Cinque Ports, Deal, and Prince's on Sandwich Bay, lies some seventy-odd miles southeast of London, and a few miles north of the white cliffs of Dover. All three clubs, from which the French coast can be seen on a clear day, are within a stone's throw of each other.

This particular linksland is steeped in more than mere golf history. It was from this part of the coast that the vast fleet of little ships, immortalized in Paul Gallico's "Snow Goose," set out in their valiant attempt to rescue the remnants of the British forces at Dunkirk; it was overhead that Spitfires and Hurricanes repulsed the Luftwaffe during the Battle of Britain, and from these shores (or slightly southwest) that General Eisenhower launched his combined D-Day invasion.

Though the Sandwich and Deal courses were mined, tangled with barbed wire, and disfigured with concrete blocks, only Prince's was temporarily lost during the war when it was turned over to the army as a battle training ground. Completely relaid after the war, it now offers two courses—the Blue, a long test even from the middle tees and the 9-hole Red course, ideal for a round with the fairer sex. Prince's Golf Club is also the home of the Golfing Society of Great Britain, membership in which entitles you to play 15 of the finest courses in Britain *without* green fees.

Royal St. George's is one of the finest courses in England. Founded in 1887, it is a pretty course of 6,728 yards with splendid if sometimes fearsome bunkers, crisp, sandy seaside turf, and smooth but very fast greens. It is one of the most exclusive clubs in England, so be sure to have your letter of introduction.

Deal is another course of championship caliber. Annually it is the scene of the Halford-Hewitt Tournament, when "old boys" (alumni) of practically every school in Britain meet to renew old friendships and do battle at Scotch foursome.

The Landcashire coast abounds in great courses. On the outskirts

THE ROYAL ST. GEORGE'S GOLF CLUB

Player.. Date..19 ....

S.S.S. 74   Handicap............   Strokes Received............

No.	C Yards	M Yards	Stroke Index	Bogey	Score	Won/Lost/Halved +−0	No.	C Yards	M Yards	Stroke Index	Bogey	Score	Won/Lost/Halved +−0
1	441	429	9	5			10	380	360	10	4		
2	370	358	18	4			11	384	372	8	4		
3	238	222	3	3			12	343	325	17	4		
4	460	436	12	4			13	443	430	2	4		
5	451	436	7	5			14	520	504	14	5		
6	165	155	15	3			15	454	440	6	5		
7	493	469	5	5			16	163	154	16	3		
8	183	175	13	3			17	423	408	4	4		
9	396	382	1	4			18	441	429	11	5		
	3197	3062		36				3551	3422		38		

c. measured from Championship Tees

M. measured from normal Medal Tees

(In Bogey or Stableford Competitions the score at each hole must be noted on the card, except when the hole is given up)

Bogey Result....................................

In
Out

Gross
H'cp

Net

Marker's signature.. Player's signature...

A scorecard from the Royal St. George's Golf Club.

of the resort town of Southport lies the Royal Birkdale links, scene of Arnold Palmer's one-stroke triumph over Dai Rees in the 1961 British Open. It has played host to the Walker and Curtis Cup matches and has been the scene of many British and English championships. It is the most recent club on which the title "Royal" has been conferred, this recognition having been accorded by King George VI shortly after the 1951 Walker Cup matches.

Birkdale is not one of the oldest of the British links but it is one of the toughest and most interesting. Begun in 1889, it has undergone numerous alterations. Only since 1935 has it been recognized as a championship course. Actually it is the backbreaking back-nine that makes this such a tough test. Beginning at the doglegged thirteenth, which measures 517 yards, the drive must be kept as close as possible to two fairway bunkers on the right to open up the approach to the green. With a following breeze, the good hitters should get there with a 5-iron. There is a respite at No. 14, a 202-yard par 3 with an elevated tee and a green surrounded by bunkers, but the long grind resumes at the famous fifteenth, at 536 yards the longest on the course. The terrain is almost flat from tee to green, but well-placed bunkers in the hitting area put a premium on accurate driving. There is a cluster of bunkers at the left and heavy roughs on the right. Because of the prevailing wind, even the boldest of players may not try to reach the closely guarded green in two.

The sixteenth has been christened the Arnold Palmer hole. It was there that Arnie slashed out of the impossible rough and sent an approach rifling to the green in winning the British Open in 1961. Spectators thought the Latrobe, Pennsylvania, muscle man might be headed for a double bogey and a possible blowup before he made his incredible recovery. It is a dogleg right, measuring 401 yards, with a plateau green. Few players will try to take the short cut. They should place their drives on the left and try to loft the ball to the green, because bunkers and heavy grass pose hazards at both the left and the right.

The two finishing holes were made for the strong. No. 17 measures 510 yards. Hills bisect the fairway diagonally. The green is flat and narrow, bunkered on both sides, but most of the belters should be able to reach it with a wood or long iron from a favorable fairway lie. The eighteenth has the advantage of a prevailing following wind, which should cut down its 513 yards. The drive must be placed between a pair of fairway bunkers, one on the left and another on the right. With a good drive, most of the players should get home with a 3-iron.

Birkdale is a course fashioned for the man who can hit his drive on a clothesline. Heavy rough, scrub, and weeds, not to mention the plethora of sand traps, are ready to gobble up any shot that veers from the straight and narrow path. A missed drive almost inevitably brings a penalty. Incidentally, Birkdale has one of the most modern clubhouses in Britain, and from its second-floor balcony you can look out over the entire course and the Irish Sea.

Southport and Ainsdale Golf Club, another championship course in the district, will provide unusual delights (?!) for the unwary visitor. One par 5 demands a long second between two enormous sandhills and over a cavernous bunker lined at its top with railroad ties.

Another fine course a little to the south of Southport is Formby. Stretching just over 6,800 yards, it is as good a seaside course as you will ever see. Other Southport courses include Hillside and Hesketh, in that order of merit.

Directly north, across the estuary of the River Ribble, lies the quiet

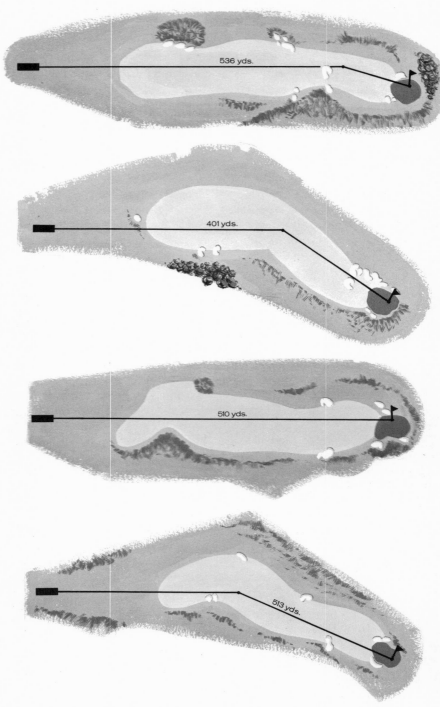

The fifteenth, sixteenth, seventeenth, and eighteenth holes at Birkdale.

little town of St. Anne's, along whose borders stretches the championship course of Royal Lytham & St. Anne's. This test does not seem like a seaside course because it is fully a mile from the sea and is bounded by a railroad and a housing development. But the turf and the wind are certainly seaside and there are enough bunkers for every day of the year. Though not excessively long, it is a good test demanding great accuracy. It was here in 1926 that Bobby Jones won the first of his three British Open titles. A plaque in the face of a bunker on the dog-leg seventeenth hole commemorates Jones' 175-yard mashie-iron shot to the green in the final round which virtually won him the championship.

The eighteenth hole and clubhouse at the Royal Lytham and St. Anne's golf course.

South from the great seaport of Liverpool, and into that part of Cheshire known as the Wirral, stands the Royal Liverpool Golf Club at Hoylake on the Dee Estuary. Hoylake is considered by many experts to be the greatest test of golf in Britain. It also enjoys the reputation of being the best-groomed.

Although Hoylake has been altered since its beginning in 1869, the essential structure of the course is as permanent as the land, and there are a few holes that remain virtually unchanged. Even the modifications worked on Hoylake reflect a sure and certain faithfulness to the original scheme of the course. The simple, uncluttered nature of the challenge has always been left intact. The best example is the run of holes from 14 to 18, a brutal stretch of three par 4's and two par 5's, averaging 487 yards a hole, and with three out-of-bounds possibilities thrown in for good measure. The fourteenth, or The Field, is a 522-yard par 5, with a slight dogleg. The fifteenth, called The Lake, although there is no water anywhere on the course, is an immense 466-yard par 4, littered with eight pot-bunkers, and running into the teeth of the wind. The sixteenth, The Dun, is another par 5, a dogleg 537 yards, requiring a second shot over a dike that extends into the fairway (and that marks the boundaries of the out-of-bounds "Field"), and an extra ounce or two of courage. The 423-yard Royal, the seventeenth, is a "road hole." The long, narrow green (resembling the twelfth green at the Augusta National) sits with its right rear side flush against a fence indicating the out-of-bounds road. The less bold among the players may shoot diffidently short and to the left in order to avoid the road (which fronts the Royal Hotel), but there are four "pots" on that side, so the safe shot must also be exact. At 407 yards, and with the wind, the eighteenth, The Stand, appears to be almost prosaic compared to the thunder of its companions. But the second shot to the greens is all carry because of the series of bunkers that rim the front of the green.

While the course (6,673 yards, par 72) architecture has plenty of character itself, tradition lends some, too. To delve into the history of Hoylake would take a complete book by itself. It was the Hoylake members who instituted both the British Amateur Championship in 1885 and the English Close Championship in 1925. The club negotiated the first amateur international between England and Scotland in 1902 and played host to the first amateur international between Great Britain and the United States in 1921, the prelude to the Walker Cup Matches. It produced such great names as John Ball, Horace Hutchinson, and John Laidlay, who dominated the Amateur in its early years. Harold Hilton, the only Britisher to win the U.S. Amateur (in 1911), was also a Hoylake stalwart. So golf-made were the Royal Liverpool members in the early days that the fabulous John Ball, eight times Amateur Champion and once Open Champion, refused to forego his golf even on his wedding day. After reaching the ninth, not far from the church, he asked his three astonished fellow golfers to accompany him to his wedding. After the ceremony all four returned to the links to complete their round. Incidentally, Hoylake is not only a golfer's haven but a bird sanctuary, too. The flat, muddy Dee Estuary, once a seaport from which William III's troops set out for the Battle of the Boyne, is famous in ornithological circles as a temporary stopover for migratory birds. Many species rare to the British Isles have been seen seeking temporary shelter on the sandy wasteland.

Yorkshire is justly proud of Ganton, some 15 miles inland from Scarborough. And just across the county border from Sheffield into Nottinghamshire is the testing course of Lindrick. Both are heather-covered moorland courses of exceptional quality, each of which has been singled out for international competition.

Due west is the tree-lined course of Mere near the delightfully quaint old town of Knutsford, Cheshire. What could be better than a pleasant round of golf, topped off by an evening's simple entertainment at one of the many excellent "locals"? The historic walled city of Chester is only a few miles away, where the women can window-shop in the "Rows" under cover while admiring the half-timbered buildings.

To the south, Shrewsbury, in Shropshire, is another town of charm and old-world dignity. Ten miles away, the Hawkstone Park Hotel offers a course which may haunt the visitor for many a day. Although it is not considered first-class, it has so many unusual holes that they will stand out in your memory long after championship courses are but names in the back of your mind.

Continuing south, by all means bypass Birmingham, but not before you have stopped off to sample Little Aston and Sutton Coldfield, some ten miles north.

If your route should take you through Lincolnshire, do not be misled by the flat, monotonous countryside. Check the map for Woodhall Spa, and there you will discover a village not unlike Pinehurst, with a course as rich in golfing treasures as you could hope for. But for sheer wealth of golfing gold, nothing can beat the Surrey-Berks-Hants area, due west of London. You can step up to headquarters near Sunningdale, and every day for three weeks you can play a different magnificent course without having to drive more than 15–20 miles. Sunningdale itself has two courses. So do Berkshire, Wentworth, Walton Heath, and Moor Park. Then come Worplesdon, West Hill, St. George's Hill, Woking, Camberley Heath, Coombe Hill, Royal Wimbledon, Swinley Forest, North Hants, Liphook, and Blackmoor.

With the exception of Moor Park, whose courses are parkland in nature, all the courses are true heathland circuits abounding in heather, birch, and pine trees. Worplesdon might be your favorite one day until you played Berkshire Blue or Red the next. They are all basically similar, but different in detail. And then there are Walton Heath's two courses over windswept heather. All these are heathland tests to try the souls of the best golfers. Actually, Walton Health is laid out on the heath about six hundred to seven hundred feet above sea level and exposed to the breezes. The ground is fine and dry and playable after a violent rain. Since Walton Heath lies open to the winds, it has the feel of a seaside links even though it is only twenty miles from London. It is not an easy course, as many expert golfers can testify. The greens are big and the shots longer, the bunkers deeper and steeper; it is golf on a grand scale, although it shouldn't frighten away the less expert player. Golfing here will give him the feel of a large course, where each player is absolutely on his own to play as he sees fit. The accurate player will stand a better chance than the wild swinger who goes strictly for distance. This is true of most English championship courses. If scores are high here, there is no reason for embarrassment. Some of the finest stroke play produces high scores.

Of course, any history of golf must mention the Old Course at Sunningdale. The course derives its fame from the men who have played here, the quality of their play, and the imposing character of its design. Bobby Jones once shot a 66 here while qualifying for a British Open, at the same time establishing a course record that stood for many years. Having taken a liking to the course, Jones proclaimed its virtues at home, and since then Sunningdale has become a regular stop for American golfers visiting England. But is was famous even before Jones. Ted Ray and Harry Vardon played an important match over these 18 holes a long time ago. And two men who became Kings of England were captains of the club. But the ultimate test of character in a golf course is the durability of its interest. This 6,300-yard, par-72 layout is still the challenge it was in 1900, when the famous old pro Willy Park built it.

If club-tangling heather is a measure of strength, Sunningdale is a Goliath. Before this site was a golf course the land was a wilderness of heather, and the plant's lavender blue still dominates the scene. It's on the hills and on the flats, and the shaggy brow it gives the bunkers makes these deep, grasping pits all the more ominous. At the sixth, a par 4 of 392 yards, the wiry little flower surrounds the green patch of fairway. You drive over a field of heather from the tee, and you play your second shot over another disturbingly wide and deep patch. When playing golf at Sunningdale, you sense something of the long life of the game. Like other great old courses, this one has the rugged honesty that comes when the natural features of a place are retained. And indoors, on the fine old wood walls of the clubhouse hang pictures, records, and other memorabilia that tell of a club that enjoys an honored past and looks eagerly to the future.

Golf is available to the visitor of Jersey. Here a threesome putt out at Gorey Common Golf Course.

London, of course, enjoys such golf wealth that it would need a volume to do it justice. Within twenty miles of the city center there are ten thousand acres devoted to golf courses!

Thus there are plenty of challenges for the visiting golfer. To make the task of selection easier, we have chosen the following to be the most testing:

LOCATION	*CLUB*	*HOLES/PAR/ YARDAGE*
Aldeburgh, Suffolk	Aldeburgh GC	18/72/6,479
Ascot, Berks	Berkshire GC	36/Red 74/6,379
		Blue 73/6,244
Broadstone, Hants	Broadstone GC	18/71/6,110
Burnham, Somerset	Burnham & Berrow GC	18/73/6,518
Ferndown, Dorset	Ferndown GC	18/71/6,296

LOCATION	CLUB	HOLES/PAR/ YARDAGE
Freshfield, Lancs	Formby GC	18/74/6,803
Ganton, Yorks	Ganton GC	18/75/6,823
Hunstanton, Norfolk	Hunstanton GC	18/73/6,701
Henley-on-Thames, Oxfordshire	Huntercombe GC	18/70/6,144
Ipswich, Suffolk	Ipswich GC	18/72/6,406
Nr. Sheffield, Yorks	Lindrick GC	18/73/6,526
Sutton Coldfield, Staffs	Little Aston GC	18/74/6,700
Rickmansworth, Herts	Moor Park GC	36/High 73/6,602 West 71/6,013
Fleet, Hants	North Hants GC	18/72/6,392
Hollinwell, Notts	Notts, Golf Club	18/73/6,688
Sandwich, Kent	Prince's GC	27/Blue 74/6,681 Red 36/3,277
Southport, Lancs	Royal Birkdale GC	18/74/6,844
Deal, Kent	Royal Cinque Ports GC	18/74/6,414
Hoylake, Cheshire	Royal Liverpool GC	18/75/6,673
St. Anne's, Lancs	Royal Lytham & St. Anne's GC	18/74/6,657
Richmond, Surrey	Royal Mid-Surrey GC	36/Men's 73/6,380 Women's 73/5,974
Bideford, Devon	Royal North Devon GC	18/72/6,532
Sandwich, Kent	Royal St. George's GC	18/74/6,748
Rye, Sussex	Rye GC	18/72/6,483
Rock, Cornwall	St. Enodoc GC	18/72/6,056
Southport, Lancs	Southport & Ainsdale GC	18/73/6,625
Stratford-on-Avon	Stratford-on-Avon GC	18/72/6,351
Sunningdale, Berks	Sunningdale GC	36/Old 72/6,490 New 73/6,487
Tadworth, Surrey	Walton Heath GC	36/Old 74/6,735 New 73/6,516
Virginia Water, Surrey	Wentworth GC	36/West 75/6,936 East 72/6,209
Pulborough, Sussex	West Sussex GC	18/71/6,211
Woodhall Spa, Lincs	Woodhall Spa GC	18/74/6,822
Woling, Surrey	Worplesdon GC	18/71/6,212
Worthing, Sussex	Worthing GC	36/Lower 71/6,270 Upper 69/5,046

SCOTLAND

Although St. Andrews may not actually be the cradle of golf, as far as the game's disciples are concerned it is Jerusalem, Rome, and Mecca rolled into one, and no one would have it any different. Situated thirty miles northeast of Edinburgh on the North Sea, St. Andrews and its Old Course embody everything that could reasonably be expected of the game's birthplace, and if golf wasn't first played there, it must have been some place quite like it. The ancient cathedral and university town of ten thousand inhabitants originated in the seventh century as the site of a Celtic monastery and developed into the ecclesiastical capital of Scotland. The earliest documented record of golf at St. Andrews was in 1552, but it is known that the game was played there at least a hundred years earlier. The St. Andrews Society of Golfers was founded in 1754 and is the second golf club on record, the Honourable Company of Edinburgh Golfers having been founded in 1744. The club became the Royal and Ancient in 1834 after the king accepted an invitation to become its patron. St. Andrews also was responsible for today's standard round of 18 holes—and quite by accident. The course originally was played as 11 holes out and the same 11 home, but in 1764 two holes each way were combined, making a total of 18. For more than four hundred years the course has been open to anyone and everyone, and only in fairly recent years has a small green fee been charged. Like Mount Everest, it is simply there, the world's heritage just as it has been for centuries.

If your first round on the Old Course seems baffling, don't be discouraged. When Bobby Jones first saw it he called it a "cow pasture." But six years later he described it as "the most fascinating course I have ever played." Actually, the Old Course at St. Andrews is starkly primitive. It is just as nature laid it out and fashioned it with winds and rains and receding seas down through the centuries. There's nothing artificial about it. No bulldozer has ever touched it. Unlike American courses, which are built and molded to an architect's specifications and fitted with manmade hazards, St. Andrews is nature's offspring.

Mastering the Old Course is *not* just a pastime, it is an art. There is no set way to play the course with its rolling fairways and hidden bunkers; that is determined by the elements. And even the wind can be a mean and scheming enemy. Many a player has battled his way out to the seventh in the teeth of the blast, mentally counting the minutes till he completes the four-hole loop to start home with the wind at his back, only to find that with the turn of the tide the wind has veered a full 180 degrees and is still his number one opponent. The fact that it poses such a challenge, that it is a thinker's course, is 75 per cent of St. Andrews' fascination.

Some of the Old Course caddies account for the other 25 per cent. Often they will give you the line without even looking up, as on one occasion when a visitor stood on the twelfth tee, a mile and a half from the town, and was told to play "a foot to the right of the church spire." He looked townward only to see a blanket of mist restricting visibility to a quarter of a mile!

Compared with the lush, tree-lined picturesque courses in America with their multimillion dollar clubhouses, the birthplace of the game seems very drab indeed. Near the first tee of the Old Course stands a square, solidly built stone clubhouse—dirty gray, resembling an old railroad terminal in some Midwestern town. This is the building that houses the Royal and Ancient Club. This is where the first rules of the game were formulated. It is still recognized by many as the supreme authority, although in recent years the United States Golf Association has assumed a strong and independent role in the conduct of the

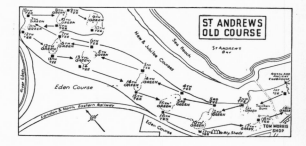

OLD COURSE   ST. ANDREWS

NAME

Hole	NAME	Length	Par	Score
1	Burn - - -	368	4	
2	Dyke - - -	410	4	
3	Cartgate going out -	356	4	
4	Ginger Beer - -	427	4	
5	Hole o Cross going out	530	5	
6	Heathery - - -	367	4	
7	High going out - -	352	4	
8	Short - - -	150	3	
9	End - - - -	314	4	
	Out	3265	36	
10	Tenth - - -	312	4	
11	High going home -	164	3	
12	Heathery going home	314	4	
13	Hole o Cross going home	410	4	
14	Long - - -	527	5	
15	Cartgate going home -	409	4	
16	Corner of the Dyke -	348	4	
17	Road - - -	467	5	
18	Tom Morris - -	364	4	
	Home -	3315	37	

Signed...................................... Out -

Date............................. Total -

"TOM MORRIS" GOLF CLUBS ARE MADE BY GOLFERS AND
WILL HELP TO REDUCE YOUR SCORE.

LARGE SELECTION OF ALL GOLF EQUIPMENT KEPT IN
SALES SHOP FACING 18th GREEN OF OLD COURSE.

DE LUXE, SUMMIT, ACE AND ARIEL WOODS AND IRONS TO
SUIT LADIES AND GENTLEMEN.

TOM MORRIS LTD.,
THE LINKS, ST. ANDREWS.

EST. 1848.   PHONE 499

The scorecard with course layout given to the visiting golfer at Old Course, St. Andrews.

sport. Alongside the course is a stretch of stone buildings, also grayed with age, housing a hotel and small golf shops still bearing the names of the men who hammered out the primitive clubs and molded the gutta-percha balls back in the days when golf was in its infancy. The Old Tom Morris Golf Shop is perhaps the best-known of these.

But as for the course, it's not a bleak, brown, seagirt chain of golf holes. St. Andrews is green, green, green, and not a forbidding-looking course at all. There is nothing very secluded about it, either. The Old Course starts and finishes right in the town. You walk in from the street to the first tee, and the adjoining eighteenth fairway runs alongside another street that is lined with houses, hotels and shops. Both streets, as well as a parking area and a promenade back of the first tee and the eighteenth green, are likely to be crowded with strolling tourists who take in not only the sights and the shops but your brand of golf. Also giving your game a gander from their clubhouse behind the first tee are the members of the Royal and Ancient Golf Club—an organization, incidentally, that does not own the course at St. Andrews. The world's most famous golf course is actually a municipal links that anyone can play for a daily fee of three dollars (but if you plan on playing in the busy season from June to October, be sure to reserve a starting time a day in advance). The R. and A. is simply the best-known and most prestigious of several golf clubs that make their headquarters at St. Andrews.

At a glance, with its open expanse of treeless green turf and its abundance of players—many of them pulling carts—the Old Course looks startingly like some new, well-kept public course in California or Florida. Of course, once you begin playing St. Andrews, you become aware of its special qualities. The turf is truly superb—thick, green, springy, and absolutely made-to-order as a launching pad for a golf ball, whether it's to be struck with a wood or an iron. And this turf is vigilantly maintained; as you play, you see work crews trucking their way around the course, filling in any divots that might not have been replaced by the golfers themselves or their caddies. The greens are flawless. Even the rough, dotted with the purple and gold blooms of the heather and the whin, contributes to the unusual beauty of the course—unusual in our view, at any rate, since we tend to associate the beauty of a golf course with its trees, and yet St. Andrews manages to convey an impression of classic beauty without a tree on the course.

Going home at Old Course—eighteenth tee. The Royal and Ancient Golf Club is in the background.

The Old Course looks a lot easier than it plays. For one thing, the fairways are much narrower to the swing than they are to the eye. They look broad, but that's because one fairway adjoins another without any dividing row of trees. The rough is as tough as it is on any Scottish course—tougher than most, in fact, because the whins (prickly shrubs) are allowed to grow so high. The greens are fast and many of them are stupendously big—big enough to serve for two holes, as a matter of fact, and that's precisely the case. There are seven double greens, one of them nearly an acre in size, and a four-putt green becomes a real possibility if you happen to find yourself on the far edge of the wrong side of a double green, two hundred feet or more from the pin.

The most famous hole on this most famous course is the 453-yard seventeenth, or "Road Hole," which wind and the terrain have made into a "par 4½." It has cost many a golfer a championship. Getting your par calls for hitting a perfect tee shot; if you try to play it safe, it will put great pressure on your second shot. If you're in a good position, you can get home with a No. 5 or No. 6 iron, but you have to guard against hitting over the green. There is nothing but gravel behind, and if you wind up there, you are in deep trouble. No, this is one hole you can't play safe. That's what makes a great hole.

Besides the Old Course there are three other circuits—the New, the Eden and the Jubilee. All are public courses, and in the busy summer months starting times are allotted by ballot the previous evening.

No one can do justice to St. Andrews on paper. The whole atmosphere of the place has to be experienced in person, not just the golf courses but the historic old town itself, where everyone thinks and talks golf. No names need ever be mentioned during a big event.

The Road Hole—the 453-yard seventeenth—at St. Andrews.

Word will spread around the shops that "she's three down" or "he's out in thirty-three." "He" or "she" will refer to whomever the town, in toto, is rooting for.

After the Old Course, almost anything else would be anticlimactic. But as a test of golf, Carnoustie, on the other side of the Firth of Tay, measures up nearly as well. The Championship course, perfected by James Braid, has been ranked by leading professionals as among the best three in the world.

Carnoustie has the seaside course's typical rolling fairways. So bone up on your techniques for hilly lies. But in some ways, Carnoustie seemed the least typical of the seaside Scottish courses. The rough and the traps are not quite as bothersome as they are elsewhere, and you see trees here and there at Carnoustie—a few stands of pine to break the wind. There is also a decidedly different sort of clubhouse from the grim, dark old buildings found on most Scottish courses. Carnoustie's clubhouse is a new and incongruously modern structure with an enormous picture window in the lounge.

If it's luxury you're after, then stop off at the superb hotel at nearby Gleneagles. You'll enjoy its fine cuisine, ballroom, swimming pool, movie theater, and other amenities. And there are two excellent courses, the King's and Queen's. Carved from moorland under the Ochil Hills, with the foothills of the Grampians in the distance, both courses are immaculately kept and provide a change of pace after the rigors of seaside golf.

The Queen's course is rated as the more picturesque of the 18-hole layouts at Gleneagles, but the King's is longer, more challenging, and definitely no slouch when it comes to visual splendor. In fact, from every hole you get a picture-postcard view of the surrounding mountains, trees, and sky—an endlessly stunning panorama. The course was designed by James Braid, one of Scotland's greatest golf-course architects as well as one of its greatest players. It was ingeniously laid out in "compartments," so that every hole is secluded in its own valley or grove, and the privacy is very pronounced.

The King's measures 6,644 yards (and plays to a par 69), but the steeplechasing fairways can deflect even a well-hit ball into rough choked with ferns, heather, and gorse. The greens are elephantine affairs, big enough to force three-putts by even the best golfers; and the bunkers look even more forbidding than most because of their immensity. A hole that perhaps typifies the natural ruggedness of Scotland's inland courses is the 474-yard, par-5 sixth on the King's. It plays to a rolling tree-lined fairway whose rough is guarded by clumps of wild-growing heather. About 325 yards from the tee, the fairway begins to flatten out as it approaches a green whose surface looks as though it had been shaped by the winds.

The best hole of all is probably the thirteenth, a 465-yard par 4 with a difficult carry over a well-trapped ridge, then a superhuman second shot to an elevated green. This hole is known as Braid's Brawest (Braid's Most Beautiful) and was acclaimed by the architect himself as his ideal hole.

The Queen's course, measuring only 6,055 yards (and playing to a par 68), enjoys one feature that is found only rarely on the King's. Many greens are set against an immediate background of dark fir trees so the player can watch his ball dropping from high

The rolling terrain is a major obstacle for a golfer on the King's Course at Gleneagles.

heaven, gleaming white against the dark screen. The very first hole sets the pattern, though in this case, as the hole is 415 yards, the approach shot will probably be played with a big iron or even wood. The fourth, fifth, and sixth greens also have their fir-tree backdrop, in sharp contrast to the third, which is silhouetted against the western sky. As on the King's course, the architect has made subtle use of the dogleg. The first, seventh, and ninth have fairways that bend, the ninth, indeed, curving off to the right behind a hill into a shape that must be nearly that of a fish hook. Accuracy in striking and placing the ball is therefore of the first importance. If this is true of the first nine holes it is even more true of the second nine, even though they are shorter and offer a better opportunity to score. The tenth, for example, is just over four hundred yards but is all downhill and therefore within easy reach in two shots. But the second shot has to be dropped on a green tucked between two hillocks out of sight to the left of the fairway, with sentinel fir trees standing on the hillocks to frame the landscape.

Both courses, however, in the wind and rain—the sort of weather that doesn't at all discourage the Scots from golf—take on an eerie charm that shows them at their best—a hauntingly beautiful expanse of moorland right out of a book by one of the Brontë sisters. In the gloaming, when the winds howl, you half expect to see Heathcliff come marching over the horizon with a brassie in his hand.

Also at Gleneagles, there's the 9-hole Wee course, which almost deserves the dignity of a royal name and perhaps, if it is extended to 18 holes, it will be known as the Prince's course.

Not far from Gleneagles, at Rosemount, Blairgowrie is another course similar in character though not quite so perfectly groomed. It is, perhaps, a better test of golf. The course, like those at Gleneagles, seems to fall into 18 separate channels between pine and fir trees, one channel for each fairway. You have a wonderful sense of being alone, even when the course is busy.

If you have plenty of breath left, then try Pitlochry. Commanding views over the Tummel and Garry valleys with Craiglunie rising to the north, the course has pictorial splendor that defies superlatives. The layout is hilly, but the design offers a challenge.

On the south shore of the Firth of Forth east of Edinburgh is Muirfield, the oldest golf club in the world, according to its owners the Honourable Company of Edinburgh Golfers. For this reason, it doesn't look any too kindly on strangers—you need an introduction from one of its members. Actually, the Honourable Company is so steeped in its own traditions that it shuns some of the conventions of the world of golf. A pro? The Honourable Company wouldn't think of having one. Even something as seemingly basic as par is not for them; at any rate, Muirfield doesn't have any par. There is a scorecard, but it simply lists the holes in numerical order and leaves a blank for your score on each hole. With the Honourable Company in control, Muirfield is not a course that suffers insults lightly—as witness a pair of anecdotes involving Walter Hagen and his British Open victory at Muirfield in 1929. When Hagen turned in a 68 in his opening round, a disbelieving member of the Honourable Company wired him: "Suggest you play rest of championship from back tees." In another round, Hagen saved a stroke by taking a shortcut through the rough on the dogleg eighth—a risky business ordinarily but a worthwhile gamble in the tournament with the rough trampled down by the crowd. As soon as the open ended, the Honourable Company ordered bristling shrubs planted all over the offending area to prevent any repetition of Hagen's sacrilege. In any case, Muirfield is a first-class course and is interestingly laid out so that nearly every hole forms an enclave or pocket of its own, often completely out of sight of the surrounding holes, thanks to the roll of the terrain. But Muirfield's bunkers are what really make the course distinctive and formidable.

Another gem on the East Lothian coast is Gullane, which the natives with some perverseness pronounce Gillan. At least that's what one hapless Englishman believed until he said Gillan to his caddy, who, poker-faced, replied with "Gullan." You just can't win! Anyway, the place has two first-class courses, and a little one for those feeling weak about this time!

Cheek by jowl with the international airport at Prestwick on the west coast of Scotland is the Prestwick Golf Club. It is a seaside course, but it offers no feeling of lying close to the water. Three things about Prestwick impressed most visitors quite strongly. First, the oddity of starting a round of golf in the heart of a busy little town—since the first tee is just off the main street. Second, the sight and sound of the jets landing and taking off at the gigantic airport that adjoins the picturesque old golf course. And third, the character of the course. Prestwick is packed with hazards. It seems to have more and bigger bunkers, more hills and more roll in the terrain, thicker thickets of gorse and heather than most Scottish courses.

Prestwick is one of Scotland's most historic courses. It was where the British Open was played for the first dozen years of the tournament, beginning in 1860. And it can be a ferociously difficult course. Bernard Darwin, the famous British golf writer, once proclaimed: "Prestwick has, I fancy, been the scene of more disasters that have passed into history than any other course—first in point of collective deviltry." The names of some of the hazards are testimony enough to Prestwick's horrors—the Alps, the Himalayas, Willie Campbell's Grave (a bunker named for a nineteenth-century pro who came to grief in it during a British Open). There is also a storied monstrosity known as the Cardinal bunker, which appears to have the dimensions and contours of a moon crater and is unquestionably one of the biggest traps you'll ever see.

Right next to Prestwick is another fine course at Troon. When the rough is grown for a tournament, the course sets a high premium on

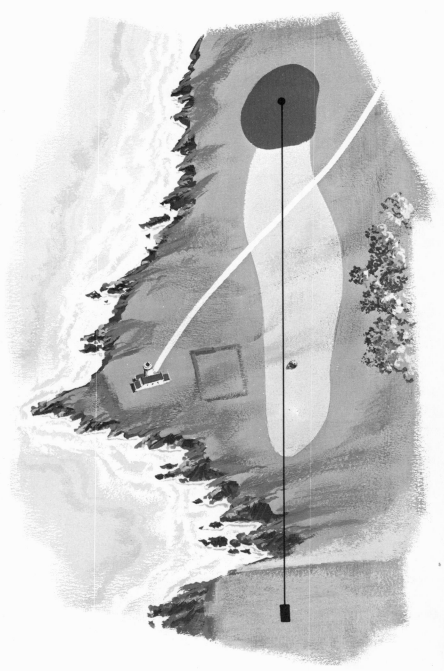

The famed ninth hole (475 yard, par 4) at Ailsa (Turnberry) (*left*) and the

125-yard Postage Stamp hole (eighth) at Troon (*right*).

straightness and accuracy. The sixth hole at Troon, 580 yards, has the distinction of being the longest hole on the British championship circuit—just as the eighth, 125 yards, is the shortest. This same eighth hole, known as the Postage Stamp, is Troon's most famous hole. What faces you here when you stand on the tee is very small, long, narrow green, with a high mound guarding the left side and a deep drop into a bunker on the right. Depending on how the wind is blowing, you can use anything from a wedge to a wood here. The trick is to land on the green and to hold. Otherwise, you might wind up having a game of ping-pong. If you hit the mound, your ball is very likely to run off the other end into the bunker. Blasting out, you can again hit the mound and come back.

Three other courses within a few miles of Prestwick are Western Gailes, Barassie, and Turnberry—all of them well up to championship class. Especially recommended is Turnberry both for its two fine courses and its palatial hotel.

A golfer on holiday at Turnberry steps out of the hotel door and descends the stairs past a putting green and a pitch-and-putt course to his choice of two great 18-hole layouts: Arran, with its gorse-lined fairways and view across the Firth of Clyde to the island of Arran; or Alisa, seven thousand yards long, par 72. For all the nearness of the sea, Turnberry's turf is touched by neither sand nor salt. You play on fairways as soft and full-grown as those on many inland courses and to greens that hold the longest, hardest wood shots. But the sea winds blow, and their changing direction and velocity make golf a new experience every round.

Play at Ailsa opens with a relatively uncomplicated par 4. Then the price rises. From the championship tees, the second and third are bruising par 4's. The fourth is a treacherous par 3 along the sea. And the seventh is a swinging dogleg lined on both sides by extremely thick rough, which is often wet. Shortcuts are out of the question. Ailsa keeps a man honest all the way. But it is this course's ninth that makes golfers talk in their sleep. Few holes in the game can compare with this 475-yard par 4. It plays over a corner of land that was once part of the castle grounds of a Scottish king, and it is still majestic. The tee is on a peninsula. The drive must carry two hundred yards of ocean and rock to the fairway. As if the drive were not enough, the second shot demands another masterpiece. Here it's a long iron—quite often a wood—over a domed fairway to a green falling off to deep rough on the right. This is more than a hazard, it is a peril, and few come out of it in par. Every golfer who knows

Turnberry knows that this hole is heroically demanding yet typically—Scottishly—fair. He can hardly wait to get at it.

Of Scotland's many courses, the following are considered the most challenging that you can play:

LOCATION	CLUB	HOLES/PAR/ YARDAGE
Blairgowrie, Perthshire	Blairgowrie GC	18/72/6,490
Carnoustie, Angus	Carnoustie GC	36/74/7,103
		74/6,398
Cruden Bay, Aberdeenshire	Cruden Bay GC	18/71/6,280
Gleneagles, Perthshire	Gleneagles Hotel Golf Courses	36/King's 69/6,644
		Queen's 68/6,055
Gullane, E. Lothian	Gullane GC	45/No. 1 72/6,461
		No. 2 70/5,592
		No. 3 68/5,008
Muirfield, Gullane, E. Lothian	Hon. Company of Edinburgh Golfers	18/74/6,806
Nairn, Nairn	Nairn GC	18/71/6,342
N. Berwick, E. Lothian	North Berwick GC	18/71/6,321
Pitlochry, Perthshire	Pitlochry GC	18/69/5,687
Prestwick, Ayrshire	Prestwick GC	18/72/6,571
Bridge of Don, Aberdeenshire	Royal Aberdeen GC	18/72/6,384
St. Andrews, Fife (Also Eden and Jubilee courses)	Royal & Ancient GC	36/Old 73/6,936
		New 73/6,612
Barnton, Edinburgh	Royal Burgess GC	18/72/6,448
Dornoch, Sutherland	Royal Dornoch GC	18/72/6,505
Troon, Ayrshire	Troon GC	36/Old 72/6,533
		Portland 72/6,113
Turnberry, Ayrshire	Turnberry Hotel Golf Courses	36/Ailsa 73/7,025
		Arran 71/6,653

WALES

Wales boasts more than a hundred golf courses. Nowhere are you far from a golf course and no resort is without one. What's more, no family man need feel guilty about escaping to the nearest golf course at the expense of his "widow" and "orphans," as most seaside courses adjoin glorious stretches of golden sand, while the inland courses are invariably placed just where they make the most of Wales' incomparable scenery.

North Wales courses have a particular appeal to the visitor and many of them are of championship standard. Wales' largest resort—Llandudno—boasts four 18-hole courses within a similar radius of miles, Pwllglas, near Ruthin, is typical of the many small, 9-hole inland courses where as consolation for a "fluffed" shot you have a breathtaking panorama of the Vale of Clwyd and its row of sentinel hills. For exciting golf in the North there is nowhere better than the superbly situated course at Nefyn—provided you have an adequate supply of golfballs with you, for playing the second nine holes, located on a small peninsula, "is like playing off the upper deck of an aircraft carrier!" to quote a local sage.

In Mid Wales the two golfing gems of Cardigan Bay are undoubtedly the superb links of the Royal St. Davids Club nestling at

The Royal St. Davids Club in Mid Wales is built around the foot of King Edward I's castle at Harlech.

the foot of Edward I's castle at Harlech, and Aberdovery immortalized by Bernard Darwin in his writings, a little farther south. But for complete contrast and for springy mountain turf at its best try the course perched high above lake and town at Llandrindod Wells right in the heart of Wales.

In South Wales, Cardiff, the capital city, has six courses on its doorstep. The same is true of Swansea. Southeast Wales has some fine parkland courses, while inland, high above the valleys, there are dozens of similar courses with its own individual challenge and special brand of welcome to visiting golfers. Of course, in South Wales at least five of the layouts—Tenby, Ashburnham, Pyle, and Kenfig. Porthcawl and Southerndown come into the championship category and regularly attract top professional and amateur tournaments.

Southerndown represents one of the three kinds of courses on the British isles. There are the inland courses such as Sunningdale or Walton Heath; the links, such as St. Andrews or Carnoustie; and courses on the "downs" like this par-70 layout of over 6,500 yards.

A "downs" is a gently rolling terrain within sight and sound of the sea, but not truly part of the seashore. This means a sea wind, but no sandy base. The combination provides for absorbing golf. There are no trees, but fairways are linked by clutching, sharp-needled gorse; one trip off the fairway emphasizes the need for accuracy from the tee. This is a natural golf course, its basic design dictated by the essential character of the land. The eighteenth hole, a 437-yard par 4, has a two-level fairway with a high grass ridge running on the same line as the hole itself. You can play up to the left, the high road, or to the right, the low road home. Making the player decide is the mark of a good hole, a good course. And that is Southerndown, as lilting and colorful as the fun-loving, friendly Welsh.

LOCATION	CLUB	HOLES/PAR/YARDAGE
Aberdovey Merionethshire	Aberdovey GC	18/73/6,515
Harlech, Merionethshire	Harlech GC	18/73/6,290
Llandudno, Caernarvonshire	Llandudno GC	18/74/6,465
Porthcawl, Glamorganshire	Royal Porthcawl GC	18/74/6,658
Southerndown, Glamorganshire	Southerndown GC	18/72/6,493
Tenby, Pemrokeshire	Tenby GC	18/71/6,131

IRELAND

Whether you fly to Dublin, Shannon, or Belfast, there are over two hundred fine golf courses awaiting your arrival. One of the wonderful things about golfing in Ireland is the almost bewildering variety of courses from which to choose. Geographically speaking, this island terrain offers such rich and rare contrast that a round of golf can mean a rural ramble over a 9-hole gem of gently undulating greenery or a massive battle with a hazard-packed layout of craggy mountains and ferocious windswept fairways. Whether you tackle one of the great courses or settle for a quieter passage, it only remains for us to remind you to keep your head down and follow through.

Let's start our tour of the great Irish courses, which are yours for the playing, in the north, where the Irish accent is less pronounced and even occasionally mistaken for a Scottish one in its mildest form. On the northern tip stands the resort town of Portrush, and along its shores stretch 45 holes of wild seaside beauty. A mile or two east is the famous Giant's Causeway—great columns of black basalt jutting out to sea. And who is to say that they weren't built by giant leprechauns in this land of make believe?

The first professional tournament ever held in Ireland was run by the Royal Portrush in 1895—seven years after its establishment. It was won by the famous Sandy Herd who beat Harry Vardon in the final. In July 1951, this famous County Antrim Club had the distinction of being the first Irish course to house the British Open Championship.

Royal Portrush today has three courses—the Dunluce course being the championship links. With a total length of 6,809 yards, it provides a relentless test for the best of golfers. The narrow curving fairways allow no room for errors with great sandhills always looming near and the roughest of rough an additional hazard. Portrush is laid out in a marvelous stretch of true golfing country. A remarkable feature of the links is the formation of the dunes in two, and sometimes three, distinct levels, from which the prehistoric sea receded, leaving parallel lines of high sandhills with plateaus and valleys between. The course begins with a hole that is almost too stiff—with an out-of-bounds area in the center (as at Hoylake) and a risky second to a double-terraced plateau green. Ridges and saddles abound through the course with a sheer drop to the beach beyond the fifth green—a fine dogleg-type hole, incidentally. The eighth is real tiger country with an armchair green set in sandhills. The fourth—well-named Calamity Corner—is a graveyard for many golfers—a par 5 that doesn't allow for mistakes in an inch of its 478 yards. The seventeenth (520 yards) is the longest hole of the round with bunkers on all sides and the typical Portrush narrows. Portrush is truly a championship course—spectacular in parts—subtle in others. Accurate driving is essential, with the undulating greens offering a rare test of pitching and putting skill.

In the Belfast area, there are such courses as the Royal Belfast, Balmoral, Belvoir Park, and Clandeboye, and within an hour's drive the Royal County Down at Newcastle.

At Royal County Down, there are two courses—the No. 1, or Championship Course, and the No. 2, or Ladies Course. The No. 1 course is in two loops of nine holes and nearly every great golfing personality has struggled here. If you plan to pay a visit, take the advice of the veterans and bring your sand blaster. You'll play with the Mountains of Mourne sweeping down to the sea beside you, for Newcastle is laid out on the shores of Dundrum Bay, and sand, heather,

Newcastle, County Down, nestles at the foot of the Mourne Mountains.

and sea are major features. Newcastle is a stiff test even for the top-class golfer. Though tees are built up on the top of ridges and greens are wonderfully true (they say that the man who can't putt on Newcastle greens can't putt!) the course is a subtle one. Sandhills are an ever-present hazard, ridges and valleys mean trouble for a crooked shot. The third hole is as demanding a par as one is ever likely to meet—468 yards. The eighteenth at 530 yards is the longest hole and builds up to a tremendous finish. The approach shot to the ninth green has been described as the "second best shot in the world." Newcastle is craftily bunkered and calls for very accurate playing. Blind drives are a feature and at the thirteenth (419 yards) a blind second shot is also necessary. This hole, by the way, is a splendid example of the delayed dogleg strategic problem. It has caught the fancy of many visitors from across the Atlantic and has been carefully copied in one of the holes of the Cincinnati Country Club in Ohio. The sixteenth (267 yards) is the only hole of the drive-and-chip type in the round and very unusual one it is. From the tee, the ground drops steeply into a valley below where an island in the middle of an ornamental pond offers a unique hazard to carry with the drive. Playing Newcastle helps you keep to your figure. In addition to two 500 yarders, there are two 470 yarders, and half a dozen or so 415–430 yarders. There are four par-3 holes and the shortest of the par 4's are the three holes between 370 and 380 yards. Newcastle has a handsome clubhouse, well equipped with bars, lounges, dining rooms, and lockers.

Portmamock is to Irishmen what St. Andrews is to the rest of the golfing world. The fabulous course, a few miles along the coast from Dublin, is like a Jekyll and Hyde. On a calm day it can present a gentlemanly exterior, stern, unrelenting, but courteous. But in the fury of a gale, it drops its mask and becomes the wildest layout in the British Isles. Actually, Portmamock is that rare type of golf course—a true links. Although in America the term "links" has become today a synonym for any acreage on which the game of golf is played, in its strict sense a links is a golf course laid out on links-land, those sandy deposits left on shorelines by centuries of receding oceanic tides. The really genuine examples of this type of golf course to be found in America can be counted on the fingers of one hand. Almost all of the world's championship specimens are located on the British Isles; notably Troon, Carnoustie, and St. Andrews in

Scotland; Hoylake, Birkdale, and Sandwich in England; and Port-rush and Porthcawl in Ireland. Portmarnock is Ireland's classic ex-ample of a true "links," jutting into the Irish Sea from a peninsula 26 miles south of Dublin.

Unlike American courses, many of which have been bulldozed and dynamited into "championship" condition to fit some architect's ghoulish scheme, Portmarnock and other links in the British Isles get their distinctive championship quality from their very lack of planned construction. Nature has given them many of the features that make them great. Their lush bent grasses, for instance, were fertilized by the droppings of birds of the region and were kept cut by cows, sheep, and hordes of wild rabbits. Many of their bunkers were formed by animals that burrowed their way into the turf as protection against the frigid seawinds, which, in turn, filled the bunkers with sand.

At Portmarnock, foul weather is the rule and fair the exception, so golf becomes not so much a game against tricked-up landscape as a struggle against the elements. So inseparable has this type of wind-swept, rain-whipped terrain become from the British idea of the game

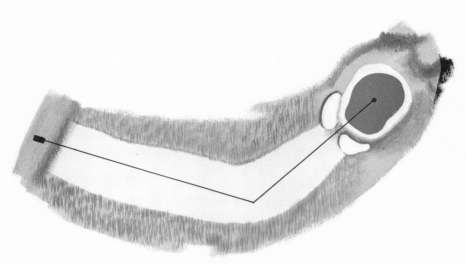

The fourteenth (a par-4, 385-yard) hole is considered the greatest at Port-marnock.

that the British Open and British Amateur, the oldest, most prestigious contests in golf, have traditionally always been played on a seaside links similar to Portmamock. In over a hundred years there has never been an exception to this unwritten rule.

As though its weather did not make the course stern enough, Portmamock presents narrow fairways lined with fierce rough, made all the more fierce by thick growths of bracken. Portmamock is, furthermore, one of the world's most thoroughly trapped courses. It sports 120 bunkers, or nearly four times as many as Augusta National, a course that is generally regarded as one of the finest nonlinks in golfdom. In addition, at Portmamock, there is a subtle change of direction at almost every hole with the wind always a variable factor. Rough swooping hills, seamarsh, and sand traps have all been utilized with an uncanny course craft. The third, considered to be one of the best holes on the links, is a typical example. Water laps the tee, and the hole winds in a semicircle with dunes on the left and the shore on the right. The fourteenth, considered to be the greatest hole of all, is also a left-hand dogleg. The sixth, longest at 579 yards, is a par 5 and a formidable enemy in a northeast wind. In spite of its length Portmamock is a fair course—its greatness lies in the problems it presents, the decisions needed at almost every hole. The very choice of club can make or break a round and you'll never know till you've played the ball.

While in this area, a stop at the Royal Dublin Golf Club is a must. It is probably the only championship course in the world that is situated within the boundaries of a capital city. The oldest golf club in the Republic of Ireland, it is built on the Bull Island, four miles from the center of Dublin city. Bull Island, which did not exist until 1816, came into being after a wall was built to stop the erosion in Dublin Bay. The wall was designed and the work supervised by Captain Bligh of *The Bounty,* who was, prosaically enough, on the staff of Dublin Corporation at the time.

The Club was founded in 1885 by Sir Arthur Lumsden, a Scotsman living in Dublin. Sited originally in Phoenix Park, it moved to its present location four years later, and now boasts one of the finest clubhouses in Ireland. The links are 6,657 yards in length and the course layout bears a marked resemblance to St. Andrews. Red fescue grass provides an ideal basis for greens and fairways with, as in all Irish seaside courses, a wandering wind to add that extra hazard. Fine bunkers, close lies, and subtle trapping are all features of Royal Dublin, and inaccuracy on approach shots can prove fatal to low-scoring ambitions. The four famous short holes—the fourth, sixth, ninth, and twelfth are fine examples of skillful layout, calling for a keen eye and precision play. The fifth, or Valley Hole—hardest hole of the course—is a par 4 (428 yards). A narrow fairway with fierce rough on both sides, it demands absolute accuracy. Danny Kaye, when he played at Royal Dublin, took one look at the hole and asked his caddy for a rifle! The eleventh, at 535 yards (par 5) is the longest hole. Played from an out-of-bounds position, it is uphill all the way and, with a wind of any strength, can take three woods to reach the green. Possibly the most controversial golf hole in Ireland, the eighteenth (478 yards, par 5) is known as the Garden hole. It provides a grandstand finish with the largest green of the links situated in front of the clubhouse verandah. From the tee, the player drives to a spacious fairway with a drain on the right hand side. Inside the drain is the "garden" or practice ground, which is out-of-bounds. The second shot can be played over or around the "garden." Failure to carry has been the death of many a good score, triumph the glorious finale to a great round. Whichever you attempt, you'll find Royal Dublin a worthwhile course to play.

In the northwest corner of Ireland, you'll find the County Sligo Golf Club—or Rosses Point, as it is internationally known. Golf at Rosses Point is a red-blooded sport and holes which appear to be reasonable par 4's demand powerful hitting. Set on the Atlantic seaboard, near Sligo town, it is a tremendously testing course. The links are laid out so that holes are played in every direction and the breeze comes from all angles. The links, as played from the Championship tees, measures 6,435 yards. It is natural golfing country with natural hazards abounding. From the fifth tee, you look down the side of cliff to a breathtaking panorama of holes spreading into the distance below you. Mountains on one side, sea on the other, all add to the wild grandeur of the majestic rolling surroundings. You'll find it a tough course to tackle. Dogleg holes are frequent with a double dogleg at the fourteenth (440 yards, par 4)—the hardest hole on the course. The twelfth (495 yards) is the longest hole, the ninth (152 yards) the shortest. In all, there are four par 3's, twelve par 4's, and two par 5's. Rosses Point is not exceptionally long but it plays long, and calls for a wonderful variety of shots and a great degree of accuracy.

South along the west coast of Ireland, the next "great" course we'll reach is Lahinch. Like so many of the Irish courses, it is rugged in character, wild and wonderfully beautiful in scenic layout, with sandhills, sandpits, grassy hollows, and rough hills providing a fierce challenge. In 1907, the course was lengthened considerably, and in what looked like impossible golfing country, the greenskeeper, assisted by fourteen men and two horses, worked for almost two years to convert the mountains into fairways. In 1928, the course was reconstructed, and the great days of Lahinch and the great golf began. Perhaps the most famous holes on this superb course are the Klondyke fifth (488 yards, par 5, with a blind second shot) and the Dell sixth, (151 yards, par 3). The lofty Lahinch tees give a breathtaking view of some of the finest golfing country that Nature has ever provided—and some of the loveliest scenery.

Driving the twelfth (353 yards, par 4), your straight line is the

Lahinch, County Clare, is often called the "home of Irish Golf" because everyone in this holiday resort talks golf and plays golf.

O'Brien castle on the other side of the road, with, on the left, the vast golden beach waiting for you to pull the shot. But many assert that the sixteenth (196 yards, par 3) is the best hole on the links, with the wind from the sea taking your tee shot where it will. Many a championship hope has gone with this same wind. Lahinch now has 27 holes—the new nine being also of championship standard. Special features of the new course are extra large greens and tees and a unique dogleg across the loop of a river. You can't afford to relax at Lahinch—you can only determine to return—as most golfers do, because there is something magical in the attractions of this wonderful Irish course.

No help is needed from the Blarney Stone (not far down the road) to describe the beauty of Killarney Golf Club. The many shades of green that proliferate here confer the gift of eloquence upon any golfer who plays or even sees—the course. The 6,600-yard, par-74 course, built by Sir Gordon Campbell with the assistance of Henry Longhurst, one of England's best-known golf writers, is the work of men who know and love the game. And what materials they had: water, meadowland, woods, and the air and sky of Ireland. They left standing many fine old trees that add strategic elements to the play even as they help preserve the beauty. At the par-3 eighteenth, cypress trees frame the green with a windswept look reminiscent of the Monterey Peninsula in California.

Killarney Golf Club is unique in Ireland, since it's the only true "lakeside golf," having many of the attributes of the seaside and the inland. Lower Lake, largest of the Killarney chain, lies beside the course and becomes a perfect part of it. Two par 3's must be played over blue, mist-shrouded water. Killarney is a deceptively open course. You feel as if you could hit the ball full out as you look down the fairways, but you'd better think twice, because every hole is bordered by thick, deep rough. When the grass is wet, you practically need the strength of a blacksmith to hack the ball out. There's a saying around Killarney that when you can't see the mountains across the lake, it's raining. When you can see them, it's going to rain. The moisture gives the soft fairways some of the finest turf in the world from which to hit a golf ball.

To talk of Killarney Golf Club is, inevitably, to talk of Killarney. The course is a jewel of beauty—the panoramas intoxicating in their sheer perfection. It has been called "the most majestic golf course that has ever been conceived." You will be hard put to concentrate on your golf as you play a round, though holes such as the tricky sixth, the eighth green, which has a concealed stream in the foreground, the eighteenth—the finest par 3 in the world—all present problems. Killarney is a memorable experience—with everything to be said already said—and none of it doing sufficient justice.

The list of fine Irish courses is lengthy—Baltray, County Louth; Rosslare, County Wexford; Galway, County Galway; Bundoran, County Donegal; Rosapenna, County Donegal—to name just a few. Remember that whether staying in the city or touring the Irish countryside, there's always a course within calling distance. Every golf course in Ireland, including clubhouse and other facilities, is open to visitors. Waiting is virtually unknown during the week and even when the members turn out in force at the weekend, delays are minimal. In Dublin city however, Saturday and Sunday golf is out, as club competitions are nearly aways a standard weekend feature. Ireland being a small country, distances are no problem, so your hotel is probably only a few minutes' drive from the course, with the exception of Dublin where you may have a twenty- to thirty-minute drive from the city center.

The Irish climate is responsible for the idyllic golfing conditions. Winters are generally mild and summers relatively cool, so that you'll rarely suffer from slow greens or fast fairways with your game at the mercy of the grass. Courses are in good playing condition all year round, though naturally, more golf is played from March through October. With the long summer evenings, you can play golf as late as 10:30 p.m. with light to spare. At this time of year also, there is an extensive list of "open" competitions in most clubs and visitors are especially welcome.

The visiting golfer to Ireland may or may not want to travel light. But bringing your own clubs is a better idea than playing with borrowed ones—as many a golfer with a torn-up card can testify. But the pro at any Irish club will be able to fix you up with a set if you decide against bringing your own. If your golf bag is a prized possession, you might consider investing in a light vinyl plastic cover which envelops clubs and bag and sells for about eight dollars in North America. As to clothes—a couple of sweaters will be very useful in the salty breezes you'll probably encounter on the various seaside championship links. Lahinch or Ballybunion—the west winds on these Atlantic shores can be boisterous—and if you slice far enough, the next stop is Long Island. A light rainproof jacket is also a good idea for protection against those sudden Irish "showers." Bring your own golf shoes—preferably your heaviest pair, because the rough on most Irish courses is just that—*rough*. Do not bring golfballs. The top brands—British and American sizes—are sold in all pro shops. On the other hand, a small sponge will prove useful, as ball-washing gadgets are few and far between on Irish courses.

Before leaving the subject of Irish golf, we must say a word about Ballybunion Golf Club. It has a special distinction among Irish—or, for that matter, any—golf courses. Not only does it offer a tremendous golfing challenge—it also startles the visitor with its famous "Vision of Killsaheen." On a rare calm day, this vision appears in the sea near the long Clare Peninsula, not far from Loop Head. The phenomenon

From this green at the Ballybunion Golf Club you can see the famous "Vision of Killsaheen." But if you don't see this rare vision, you will have plenty of good golf.

lasts for about 15 minutes before it fades into nothingness, leaving the sea clear and blank as it was before. What is the vision? Go to Bally-bunion and you may even see it for yourself.

Every golf club in Ireland, of course, has its own legends, and most of them are true. In fact, certain golf writers who have played only one round of golf in Ireland have returned to America to write books on their experiences. This is not surprising, because a day at an Irish golf club combines all that is best in the Irish way of life—good golf, excellent talk, some drinking, relaxation, some more drinking, singing galore, and maybe some more drinking. That's what you need after facing such challenges as:

LOCATION	*CLUB*	*HOLES/PAR/ YARDAGE*
Ballybunion, Co. Kerry	Ballybunion GC	18/71/6,417
Bundoran, Co. Donegal	Bundoran GC	18/72/6,360
Cork, Co. Cork	Cork GC	18/71/6,134
Baltray, Co. Louth	Co. Louth GC	18/72/6,605
Rosses Point, Co. Sligo	Co. Sligo GC	18/70/6,435
Killarney, Co. Kerry	Killarney Golf and Fishing Club	18/72/6,714
Lahinch, Co. Clare	Lahinch GC	18/71/6,434
Portmamock, Co. Dublin	Portmamock GC	18/72/7,093
Rosapenna, Co. Donegal	Rosapenna GC	18/70/6,044
Newcastle, Co. Down	Royal Co. Down GC	18/71/6,647
Dollymount, Co. Dublin	Royal Dublin GC	18/71/6,657
Portrush, Co. Antrim	Royal Portrush GC	36/Dunluce 73/6,809 18/Valley 72/6,641

17

THE EUROPEAN CONTINENT

The next time you take a golf vacation, try paying those green fees in francs or lire. For years, the American golfer has largely ignored the many fine courses and resorts on the European continent, but with increased jet travel, the Atlantic Ocean is no longer the water hazard it once was. Many of the golf tours offered by the airlines would make Marco Polo look like a homebody. Imagine starting your trip by driving from the first tee at the Royal Golf Club de Belgique in Brussels, then traveling on to France and Golf de Saint-Nom-la Breteche, at the edge of Paris. If the season is spring, a stay in this fabled city will be irresistible. Next on the itinerary, head south to Italy and the shores of Lake Como or to the eternal city of Rome and the Circolo Golf Olgiata, 27 holes of championship golf. Then, there's the Glyfada Golf Club in Greece, the Monte Carlo Golf Club at Monaco, or the Clube de Golf da Penina in Portugal. Of course, Gibraltar is visible from several holes of the new Robert Trent Jones course at Sotogrande del Guardiaro in Spain. If 18 of these challenging holes don't satisfy you, there's an additional 9-hole, par-3 layout. As in the United States, Canada and the British Isles, because golfing facilities in Europe are so extensive, we've only been able to touch on some of the more significant courses that you can play.

AUSTRIA

Austria's golf courses are situated in beautiful and charming surroundings, which give golfers not only a chance for playing under ideal conditions but also that inspiring feeling of being linked with Nature, which is one of golf's principal attractions.

All Austrian golf courses are simple to reach by rail or road and invariably have a good selection of inexpensive hotels close at hand. They also offer fine chances for excursions as well as for sporting and social attractions of every kind. The golf season in Austria generally runs from April through October, except in Vienna, where it is now being played year round.

Since Austria is the land of the Alps, many of the country's 16 courses are above 2,500 feet. Most of them have a natural appearance, with very few sand traps and other manmade hazards. As in many European countries, Austrian courses are usually not as meticulously groomed as those in the British Isles and the United States. But Austria's golf courses have all the facilities and amenities which make a game an unforgettable experience. The following courses will provide sufficient challenge:

LOCATION	COURSE	HOLES/PAR/ YARDAGE
Badgastein	Golf Club Gastein	9/36/3,087
Dellach	Karntner GC	18/70/6,214
Enzesfeld	Enzesfeld G & CC	18/72/6,773
Innsbruck-Igls	Golf Club Innsbruck-Igls	9 (18 tees)/ 65/5,291
Kitzbuhel	Golf Club Kutzbuhel	9/36/3,215
Murhof	Golf Club Murhof	18/72/6,588
Seefeld	Golf Club Seefeld-Wildmoos	18/72/6,965
Vienna	Golf Club Wien	18/70/6,011
Wiener Neustadt	Golf Club Fohrenwald	18/72/6,649

BELGIUM

There are ten golf courses in Belgium and they all have similar qualities. For instance, tucked away in the emerald lushness of a Belgian forest just outside Brussels is the 6,628-yard, par-73 Royal Golf Club de Belgique, a course of breathtaking beauty and chilling demands. Golf here is played in an atmosphere of regal splendor, perhaps echoing the days when kings and dukes and other royal guests, such as the Archduke Maximilian of Austria, hunted game on the land. Indeed, it was King Leopold II of Belgium who in 1906 turned the land over to be converted into a golf course. Because the land came from the king, the name "royal" was affixed to the club.

The most distracting features of the Royal Belgique are the more than fifty varieties of trees—everything from elms and firs to willows and chestnuts—that border the narrow fairways, and the violet-hued rhododendrons clustered here and there in the woods. The most distinctive features of the course are the abrupt doglegs that funnel into bottleneck fairways, which at times seem no wider than the waist of a Gibson Girl. One characteristic of the Royal Belgique that is typical of many European courses is the cross-bunkering—that is, a series of two or three bunkers that bisect the fairways, as one would expect, just where a miscalculated drive is apt to land. The approaches to the greens are in the main unprotected, and they invite pitch-and-run shots, which are more in vogue in Europe than are the lofted wedges played in the United States. The greens hold shots well, and while they are relatively flat, it takes a firm stroke to master the tricky rolls in less than three putts. It's been years since anyone has tried to will the ball into the hole with a royal scepter.

The following "royals" will offer plenty of good golf while in Belgium:

LOCATION	COURSE	HOLES/PAR/ YARDAGE
Antwerpen	Royal Antwerp GC	18/74/6,542
		9/35/2,394
Brussels	Royal Golf Club de Belgique	18/73/6,697
		9/32/2,033
Brussels	Royal Waterloo GC	18/74/6,789
		18/69/5,041
Ghent	Royal Golf Club les Buttes Blanches	18/70/6,431
Liège	Royal Golf Club du Sart-Tilman	18/74/6,676
Knokke-Het Zoute	Royal Zoute GC	18/72/6,626
Mons	Royal Golf Club du Hainaut	18/71/5,958
Spa	Royal Golf Club des Fagnes	18/74/6,353

CZECHOSLOVAKIA

There is very little golf behind the "Iron Curtain." Soviet-government sports officials say positively there are no courses in their country. This is also true in China, Mongolia, Tibet, Albania, Poland, and East Germany. Six holes of the old Romanian Golf Club at Bucharest are in use by members of the diplomatic corps from Western European and American nations. The diplomats play under the name "Diplomatic Golf and Country Club." They go around the course three times, giving them 5,409 yards of golf and a par 69 to compete against.

Golf is a disease, the Romanian government says, and the natives are not allowed to play. But some of them have played a bit. The old Bucharest course was a good 18-hole layout before World War II, but the players came only from the upper classes.

For a time there was—and it may still be there—a small course near Sofia, the capital of Bulgaria. The Bulgars have been pushed around for so long by so many people it is no wonder they have had little time for niceties such as golf.

In Czechoslovakia, golf is making a comeback. There is a connection between the game and the government's plans for luring in Western tourists, and there is also a certain number of Czech golfers.

Actually golf enjoys an old tradition in Czechoslovakia. Its cradles were the spa Karlovy Vary (Carlsbad) and Marianske Lazne (Marienbad). Other golf courses were created in the Slovak spa Piestany and in the High Tatra Mountains, but they deteriorated during World War II and have not been reestablished because of lack of interest. There was also a picturesque golf course at Svratka in the Bohemian-Moravian hills and a course at Klanovice near Prague that is used for other sports today. At Lisnice, near Prague, there is a 9-hole course still in use.

Marianske Lazne (Marienbad) has two golf clubs, Slovan at Marianske Lane and Dynamo at Zadub, totaling about sixty members. Altogether, there are about three hundred golfers registered with the various golf clubs in Czechoslovakia.

There are a number of handicap competitions for which the prizes are sports cups of Bohemian cut glass. Each year, there are further championships in medal and match play held alternately at Marianske Lazne and Karlovy Vary.

Besides the older established golf clubs at Marianske Lazne, Karlovy Vary, and Prague, new sections have been created at Podebrady-Lazne and Jablonec n/N, the center of the well-known Czechoslovak jewelry industry.

There is no lack of golf enthusiasts in this picturesque country, but growth of the game is impeded by the fact that golf clubs and balls must be imported. To provide them is always difficult, so the visitor is well-advised to bring his own. To compensate, the sport enjoys a great advantage in Czechoslovakia—playing fees are very low. The courses are opened from May 15 to October 31.

News reports of bygone times tell us about the foundation of the golf courses at Marianske Lazne. According to these reports, an English professional then at Karlovy Vary designed the course, and Edward the VII, King of England, inaugurated the links and signed his name into the chronicle of the club at the opening ceremonies in August 1905. At that time, only nine holes were opened. Many prominent persons joined the club. For seven years, until his demise, Edward the VII was guest of this spa. Considering the possibilities at the disposal of the King of England for his recreation, his sojourn there constituted the highest praise for Marianske Lazne. At the first tee, there still remains a memorial stone inaugurated in 1933. On the stone, there is a bronze relief of the king, and on the desk, engraved in English: "In memoria the opening of Marienbad golf links his Majesty King Edward VIIth. August, 1905."

The Slovan course at Marianske Lazne is surrounded by coniferous woods and bushes and is actually in the midst of a natural park of about 120 acres. These grounds are at an elevation of about 2,500 feet above sea level and the actual turf is said to have healthful radioactive emanations. One treads upon ground as soft as Persian carpets,

The sixteenth tee of the Slovan Course at Marianske Lazne (Marienbad).

the smell of the trees pervades the air, and the quiet is disturbed only by the twittering of the birds. The course is 6,012 yards and plays to a par 71.

During World War II, the course at Karlovy Vary deteriorated. Afterward, members of Slovan and Karlovy Vary rebuilt it, and in 1960 it was solemnly reopened. Now it covers 125 acres and is a 6,253-yard layout that plays to a par 71. The fairways are sloping, descending and some have an inclination toward the sides. The soil is a little harder and proves excellent in rainy weather. This course requires physical fitness. The scenery, with its view of the Krusne Mountains in the distance, is memorable and the view from the Golf House on the eighteenth fairway is enchanting. Some fairways, placed in the frame of coniferous and deciduous trees, show a pageant of all colors and their various shades are most resplendent in autumn.

DENMARK

You don't need to miss your daily round of golf when you visit Denmark—the country has over two dozen courses all situated in beautiful surroundings and visitors are always welcome. But, as most clubs hold tournaments on various days during the season, you would be wise to contact the club secretary before calling on the course of your choice. This is a good rule to follow throughout Europe. Incidentally, the golf season in Denmark usually runs from March through late November.

The Rungsted Golf Klub is generally considered Denmark's finest course. An easy drive from Copenhagen on excellent roads, this layout adds a special kind of pleasure to the resort area along the Danish coast. In fact, the excitement begins with banked fairways that line the course, forcing a careful placement of tee shots to allow for the roll-off. There are 13 holes with out-of-bounds. At Rungsted, the sporting Danes have a demanding golf course. And to add to the excitement, in the stands of beech that mark this course, there are many water hazards. The thin strips of water are rarely seen from the tee, but they become apparent as you enter the trees.

Major C. A. MacKenzie laid out this 6,300-yard, par-70 test just before World War II. He was obviously a man who understood the value of fairway bunkers, both as directional markers and as threats to the off-line hitter. On the 405-yard third hole, for instance, three big bunkers along the right side of the fairway show the way you must go from the tee—left.

The par-3 sixth is another example of the architect's faculty for bunker placement. A trap in front of the green and two more to the left appear from the tee to be separated by no more than their respective collars as they enclose the putting surface. Actually, the front bunker is some twenty yards short of the green. But the gap is no great help on this 205-yard one-shot hole. Another trap at the right corner of this green helps form one of the best par 3's in the game.

While most golf courses in Denmark are easy to play—except for Rungsted—the following can provide an interesting entertainment:

LOCATION	COURSE	HOLES/PAR/ YARDAGE
Copenhagen	Copenhagen GC	18/71/6,315
Rungsted	Rungsted Golf Klub	18/70/6,284
Elsinore	Elsinore GC	9/35/3,112
Korsor	Korsor Golf Klub	18/71/6,146
Nyborg	Sct. Knuds Golf	18/71/6,562
Aberra	Sonderjyllands GC	18/73/6,960
Resenbro	Silkeborg GC	18/71/6,593
Ebeltoft	Djursland GC	18/70/5,542

FINLAND

There are 12 golf clubs in Finland, with some 1,350 members. While membership in a golf club at home is desirable, it is not essential for playing Finnish courses.

The end of May to the beginning of October is the golf season in Finland. The best courses are:

LOCATION	COURSE	HOLES/PAR/ YARDAGE
Homeenlinna	Aulangon (Anlanko) Golf Klubb	9/35/2,623
Helsinki	Helsigin Golfklubb	18/70/6,199
Tampere	Tammer Golfklubb	18/70/6,104
Turku	Aura GC	9/36/3,193

FRANCE

Golf is not as popular in France as it is elsewhere on the Continent, but there are over one hundred courses in the country and many of

In Finland, you have a choice of girl caddies at such courses as Aulanko (*above*) or, in northern country, the colorful Laplunders (*opposite*). In Finland,

these could be classified as excellent. Green fees, by European standards, are quite high in France, especially on weekends and holidays. Incidentally, many of the clubs are closed Tuesdays, a few on Mondays.

All courses in France are private, but playing privileges are not too difficult to obtain, especially on weekdays and if you are a member of a golf club at home. Hotels and transportation company representatives are also helpful in getting you permission to play.

The Paris vicinity, of course, has the most and some of the finest layouts in France. For example, a stroll through the trees and over the dales of the parklike 6,700-yard, par-71 Golf du Racing-Club de France à la Boulie golf course rivals the joys of a visit to nearby Versailles. But playing La Boulie is something else. The challenge is dramatically clear on the tee of the 345-yard, par-4 fifth hole. This hole has everything. The elevated tee overlooks a big fairway bunker and a long, ascending fairway that bends slightly left as it climbs to

Norway, and Sweden it is possible to play golf north of the Arctic Circle in the light of the Midnight Sun.

a huge green. To the right of the putting surface are four bunkers hacked from a sloping bank, over which is out of bounds. To the left is extremely fast fall-away to rough. Tall trees and bushes all down the line round out a hole typical of La Boulie's fine layout. Its many narrow fairways and clever bunker placement have created tight openings to the greens.

Then there are the par 3's, five all told, each a gem of short-hole construction. Short hole? The tenth is 210 yards long; only a strong and accurate shot succeeds. The tee is at least one hundred feet above the green, and the panoramic view is delightful—except, perhaps, for the four mammoth bunkers that almost entirely surround the green.

Two other well-known courses in the Paris area are ones at Saint-Nom-la-Breteche and Saint-Cloud. Both are rather long and the par 5's are rather difficult because of the long approach shot needed to get home.

Here are the better courses you play in France:

LOCATION	CLUB	HOLES/PAR/ YARDAGE
Boulonge s/Mer	Golf Club d'Hardelot	18/74/6,552
Cannes	Cannes Golf Club	18/73/6,063
Cannes	Cannes Country Club	18/72/6,149
Chantilly	Golf de Chantilly	18/71/6,688
Chantilly	Golf de Lys	18/73/6,475
Compiegne	Golf Club de Compiegne	18/72/6,016
Coudray-Montceaux	Golf du Coudray	18/72/6,233
Deauville	New Golf Club, Deauville	18/72/6,217
Divonne-les-Bains	Golf Club de Divonne	18/72/6,353
Etretat	Golf Club d'Etretat	18/70/6,026
Evian	Golf d'Evian	18/72/6,223
Fontainebleau	Golf de Fontainebleau	18/69/5,890
Granville	Golf Club de Granville	18/72/6,124
Marseille	Golf Club de Marseille-Aix	18/73/6,326
Monte Carlo	Monte Carlo Golf Club	18/65/5,400
Ozoir-la-Ferriere	Golf Club d'Ozoir-la- Ferriere	18/71/6,129
Saint-Germain-en-Laye	Golf de Saint Germain	18/72/6,364
Pau	Pau Golf Club	18/70/5,830
Rouen	Golf Club de Rouen	18/71/6,039
Saint-Jean-de-Luz	Golf de Chantaco	18/72/6,035
Senlis	Golf de Morfontaine	18/72/6,606
La Teste	Golf Club d'Arachon	18/71/6,870
Le Touquet	Golf Club du Touquet	36/No. 1 72/6,137 No. 2 74/6,408
Vaudreuil	Golf du Vaudreuil	18/74/6,957
Versailles	Golf de Saint-Nom-la- Breteche	36/No. 1 74/6,704 No. 2 73/6,704
Versailles	Golf du Racing Club de France	18/No. 1 72/6,721 18/No. 2 72/6600

GERMANY

There are approximately a hundred golf courses in Germany and visiting golfers are welcomed at almost all of them. Green fees are reasonable and club rentals are readily available. The golf season depends on the part of Germany you are visiting. In certain regions it's a year-round sport.

The German courses are varied, and there is no set pattern to their design. The Frankfurter Golf Club in Frankfurt-am-Main, for example, is a spacious course of nearly 6,500 yards, with a par 72, that presents good golf in an expansive environment. A rugged elegance and solidity are appropriate to its situation and age—more than fifty years. Towering evergreens are ever-present sentinels for the fairways. The tenth, for example, is a 360-yard, par-4 straightaway between walls of forest to an angular green guarded by four sand traps. Another outstanding feature is the formidable bunkering. The 150-yard, par-3 fourth, for example, has four deep sharply sculptured pits clearly delineating the target, a shapely, well-textured putting surface. Many bunkers are high-walled, and afford that challenging rarity, a blind sand shot, with no sight of the pin.

Length off the tee is very helpful. The plush soft fairways give up little roll, and holes like the eighteenth, a fine finisher of 435 yards, par 4, call for a cannon shot off the tee. Two bunkers at 220 yards on either side of the fairway demand accuracy, and it takes a big approach to reach the long, narrow green which is superbly bunkered, as usual.

Another championship course that presents a different type of layout is the Hamburger Golf Club. Except for the par 3's, all but two holes dogleg on this 6,648-yard, par-72 course. You can't cut the corners unless you cannonade the ball over the tall trees that guard the turns. And as for the par 3's, each is a specialty of the house. On the fifteenth, you play from a tee so high you feel as if you were in a plane coming in to land on the narrow, runwaylike green below.

Although the height of that tee is unusual, elevated tees are common at Hamburg. They are all demanding; but the height gives a view of what lies ahead—a bit of assistance that often proves welcome. For instance, on the 550-yard second hole you see first the heather that your drive must carry just ahead of the tee and, beyond the heather, hemmed in by tall pines and thick oaks, a gradually narrowing fairway that swings right and takes a long, sweeping, uphill course to a deeply trapped green. It's a sight to see—and a fine hole to play.

Here are some of the better courses that you can play while in Germany:

LOCATION	CLUB	HOLES/PAR/ YARDAGE
Baden-Baden	Golf Club Baden-Baden	18/68/4,978
Bad Ems	Mittelrheinischer Golf Club	18/73/6,226
Berlin	Berlin Golf & Country Club	18/70/6,346
Cologne	Golf-und Land-Club Koeln	18/74/6,710
Duesseldorf	Duesseldorfer Golf Club	18/72/6,451

LOCATION	CLUB	HOLES/PAR/ YARDAGE
Duesseldorf	Land-und Golf-Club	18/72/6,842
Feldafing	Golf Club Feldafing	18/72/6,201
Frankfurt	Frankfurter Golf Club	18/72/6,497
Fuerth in Bayern	Monteith Golf Club	18/70/5,873
Hamburg	Hamburger Golf Club	18/72/6,648
Hamburg	Hamburger Land-und Golf-Club in der Lueneburger Heide	18/74/6,369
Hamburg	Golf Club Hamburg-Walddoerfer	18/73/6,358
Hanau	Golf Club Hanau	18/73/6,809
Hanover	Golf Club Hanover	18/71/6,332
Heidelberg	Heidelberger Golf Club	18/72/6,352
Nuermberg	Golf Club Am Reichswald e.V.	18/72/6,562
Ramstein	Woodlawn Golf Club	18/70/6,215
Stuttgart	Stuttgart Golf Club	18/73/6,895
Wiesbaden	Rheinblick Golf Club	18/72/6,100

GREECE

Get up—or stay up—and see the Parthenon at dawn. Pick a tiny restaurant on the quay in Piraeus, drink coffee, and watch the boats with Tourkolimanon Harbor at your elbow. Drive to Sounion and see the statue of Poseidon at sunset. Or play golf in a clean Mediterranean light that works miracles with color.

While there are only three courses in Greece, the Glyfada Golf Club, near the Athens airport, is one of the finest courses in Europe . . . or the world. This 6,643-yard, par-72 layout appears flat, but it is not. The soil seems stony and grudgingly fertile. It is. Every yard of top-soil was hauled in and artfully graded for the rich fairways and fine big greens of this first 18-hole course in Greece. The grass is excellent and predictable.

Although sharp challenges arise from details of design, Glyfada's basic tests depend on three main traits. First, planting. Hundreds of young trees and stretches of new grass make roughs tricky yet create fairways unequivocally defined. The sixth hole, a par-4 beauty, 435 yards long, plays through pines that line the rough and, in places, reach 10 or 15 yards into the fairway. Add out of bounds to the left

The view from first green toward the clubhouse at Glyfada, in Greece.

and you get a hole worth the best you can give it. Second, topography. Glyfada lies between the Hymettus Mountains and the Aegean Sea. Putts tend to break from the ridges toward the sea. But do not take too much for granted. Extra breaks built into the greens make study pay. Third, bunkers. Fairway traps are well-placed, always sternly exacting. But the surprise is a bit of consistency. Of 18 greens, 17 have traps at the right front corner.

Greece's two courses are the 9-hole, par-34, 2,906-yard Hellenic Golf Club, near Athens, and 18-hole, par-72, 6,800-yard Corfu Golf Club on Corfu Island. The latter is a new layout—it opened in 1972 —and is located near a complete resort complex.

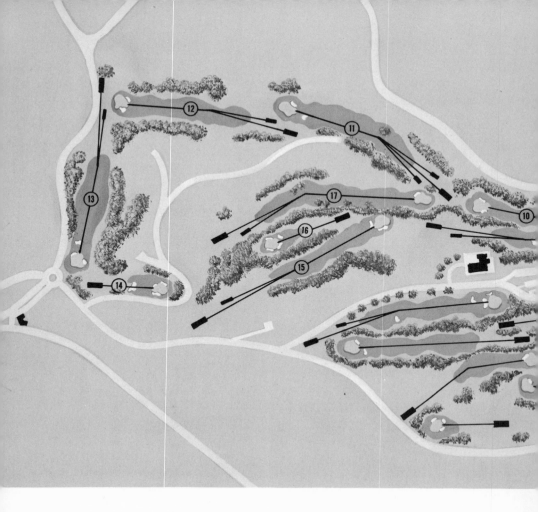

The layout of holes at the Olgiata Club near Rome.

ICELAND

This island country has four 9-hole courses that are worthy of mention and play if you should visit there. They are as follows:

LOCATION	COURSE	HOLES/PAR/YARDAGE
Akureyri	Golfklubbur Akureyrar	9/34/2,730
Keflavik	Golfklubbur Sudurnesja	9/36/3,303
Reykjavik	Golfklubbur Ness	9/35/2,655
Vestmannaeyjar	Golfklubbur Vestmannaeyja	9/33/2,616

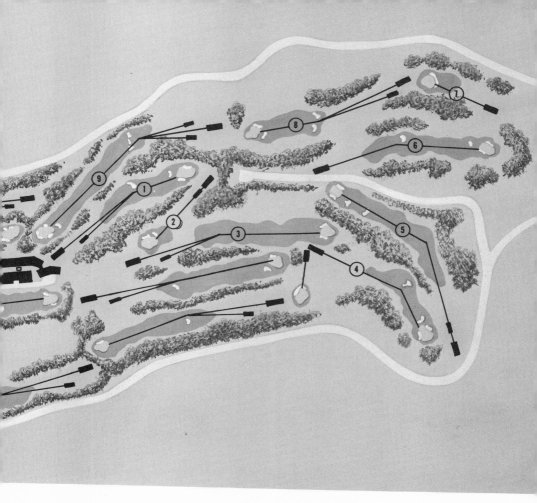

ITALY

Early in this century two British diplomats, strolling along the Via Appia, and observing the hills of Rome, the pines, the ancient ruins, decided that this was a good place for a golf course. Thus in 1903 was founded the Golf Club of Rome, first in the city and in the country.

The visionary gentlemen were right. The setting is beautiful, and the course matches it. The 18 holes measure a total of nearly 6,400 yards. Par is 71, and rolling terrain provides a completely honest test of golfing skill. The existing topography is superbly used in holes such as the ninth, a 432-yard par 4. This fairway lies in a canyon with a needle-thin outlet, perhaps two yards wide, that leads to the green. Making the approach here is like playing through a keyhole. Then there is the seventeenth, a smashing par 4 of 412 yards that usually plays into the wind, and always plays to a narrow, rough-bordered fairway, and over two—not one, but two—creeks crossing the fairway close to the green. This beautifully conditioned course hugs the hills and stretches across the valleys like green velvet. Taking a divot seems sacrilegious. The greens might be the envy of a carpet maker.

Another fine course in Rome is at the Olgiata Club. The 18-hole West course—there is also a 9-hole East course—measures a sufficiently long 6,800 yards and plays to a par 72. Six of the par-4 holes are near the extreme legal length (470 yards), thus putting an emphasis on accurate long-iron and fairway wood shots. This emphasis becomes even more important when it is noted that the Italian course's par-5 holes have been designed to yield birdies, since a good drive and a strong second shot will, in most cases, get you from tee to green.

There are many other excellent locations for golf in Italy. For instance, the green, rolling Brianza, or small-lake region, or northern Italy, dominated by Lake Como and encircled by the misty "Little Alps" mountain range, are some of the world's truly natural spots for a golf course. Again, men of foresight noted this in 1926—when the course was built—and since then golfers who came here from all over the world have learned to prize the 18 holes of the Villa d'Este Country Club. It was designed by James Gannon, an Irishman, a left-handed golfer, and an architect of the old school. To overcome this course, a player needs more than power. Accuracy off the tee is a prime concern, and the shrewd player will swallow his pride and use a 3-wood, or even a 2-iron from the tee of a par-4 hole.

The 364-yard, par-4 twelfth is a case in point. A huge mound in the center of the fairway at the driver distance will take even the straightest of shots and send the ball rolling either left or right into deep grass, trees, or bushes. While not extremely long—the course measures 6,070 yards, and plays to a par 70—Villa d'Este has soft fairways that give up little roll, so you get exactly the distance your shot deserves. Because each hole is different, interest is sustained throughout the round. You never get two shots alike. The course winds through acacias, chestnuts, and Scotch firs. From every tee the golfer must carry yards of bush, tall grass, and small trees before finding the fairway. The heavy rough that is left to grow serves to highlight the proper path to take. Soft, spongy grass surrounds the greens; you don't putt from the edges here. Sometimes you must slug a wedge just to get the ball out onto the putting surface. Even so, this is not an unfair golf course. It just makes you play a little better. It rewards the golfer with fairways peerless in the quality of their turf, with greens that putt true blue, and with the satisfaction of knowing he has been tested to the full.

Well-organized golf clubs and courses are available in the the major Italian tourist centers. While there are no public courses in Italy, the traveling golfer can usually play almost anywhere without difficulty. If you don't have a letter of introduction from your home club, arrangements can usually be made by hotels and transportation concerns. Here are some of the most challenging courses in Italy:

LOCATION	CLUB	HOLES/PAR/ YARDAGE
Barlassina	Barlassina Country Club	18/71/6,562
Bergamo	Golf Club Bergamo L'Albenza	18/72/6,600
Biella	Golf Club Biella Le Betulle	18/73/6,462
Bologna	Golf Club Bologna	9/34/3,033
Fiuggi Fonte	Golf Club Fiuggi	9/35/3,225
Grosseto	Golf Club Punta Ala	18/72/6,639
Milan	Golf Club Milano	18/72/6,318
Mogliano Veneto	Golf Club di Villa Condulmer	9/34/2,804
Rome	Circolo Golf Olgiata	27/West 72/7,100 East 34/3,097
Rome	Golf Club Roma	18/71/6,457
Turin	Golf Club Torino	18/72/6,656
Venice	Circolo Golf Lido di Venezia	18/71/6,081
Villa d'Este	Villa d'Este Golf Club	18/70/6,554
Vittorio Veneto	Golf Club Vittorio Veneto	9/36/2,730

LUXEMBOURG

When you think of Luxembourg you may think small, but the people who built the Golf-Club Grand-Ducal de Luxembourg, where Shell played its match, thought big. This is the only course in the country, and it's a good one. Tall pines and white birches border the course from tee to green. Sighting the long, rolling fairways is easy. You need only look between the lines of the forest. But note this: if you get into the trees you have only one choice—take an iron and chip the ball back out to open spaces.

The sand traps on this course are obviously the work of designers who took a large view of their job. The bunker fronting the par-3 fourth hold, for example, may well be one of the biggest in the game. And—as if size were not hazard enough—the builders filled this vast trap with a fine, powdery sand. An unlucky golfer can work up quite a thirst playing out of it.

The greens are big, too. They can be hit in regulation figures, but getting close to the hole requires well-considered club selection. A three-putt green can come up quickly from seventy feet. While it may seem appropriate to use the small European golf ball at Luxembourg, your best bet is to throw away your maps and preconceived notions and be ready for a rigorous test. This par-72 course, playing to a little more than six thousand yards, puts a premium on well-controlled drives and accurate approaches. The country is small, but its golf course offers every big challenge in the book.

MONACO

The past is very much present around the course of the Monte Carlo Golf Club at Monaco. The steeply terraced fairways take their contours from vineyards planted by Roman legions that occupied this part of the Mediterranean coast two thousand years ago. A flowering plant whose yellow petals brighten the edges of the course is called *genêt;* it is the source from which the Plantagenet dynasty took its name.

This is a mountain course, over three thousand feet up in the Alpes Maritimes, and it has the characteristics of mountain courses. For example, it is compact. The course measures 4,829 yards and plays to a par 66. But don't be misled. There are eight par 3's, and every golfer knows you get only one chance to hit the ball straight on the short holes. The course provides a good test of your wood and iron game.

No test is better than that offered by the 175-yard twelfth. This hole plays from a high tee over white mountain rock to a postage-stamp green sitting on a precipice. Over the back and down to the left is a steep fall-away. As the saying goes around Monte Carlo, pull the ball on this hole and it may end up on the high road to Nice. The hills and stepladder terraces lead to many blind shots, and you need a billiard player's sense of angles to bounce the ball off the hills into the best position.

Another bit of local lore: when you line up a putt, look for the biggest mountain. No matter how flat the green appears to be, the putt will break away from that high point. Back in 1910, when this course was first opened for play, people used to come up the long, twisting road by horse and carriage. It was a three-hour trip, with a stop for lunch, and with each turning in the road the view of Monaco and the Mediterranean became more and more beautiful—and the height a bit more striking.

NETHERLANDS

The game of golf as we know it today was played as early as the fourteenth century in Scotland. From there it conquered the world. But there are many reasons to believe that the cradle of this noble game was the "low countries by the sea" where "kolving" was in the most early times a typically national game.

In those days one had to have plenty of space for the game of "kolf." It was played on church squares, village greens, in churchyards, on highways, and during the winter, on ice. In the paintings of Van der Meer and Avercamp, Dutch painters whose favorite subjects were winter landscapes and gay skating scenes, it is often claimed that there are kolvers in action on the ice.

In 1398, Duke Albrecht of Bavaria officially gave permission to the population of Den Briel (South Holland) "to hit the ball with kolven outside the city walls." Several years later the same sporting duke presented the citizens of Haarlem with a large plot of land for the purpose of "kolven and other games."

Most courses in the Netherlands are not too long but are very tricky. The Haagsche Golf en Country Club is typical. At first, the layout at The Hague comes as something of a disappointment to American golfers, accustomed as most of us are to the meadowland type of course. From the first tee at The Hague, you see few of the hazards you would expect to see on a golf course: no lakes or streams, only scattered trees, and very few sand traps. In fact, there are only 19 bunkers on the entire course. (Some American courses flaunt more than 100.) What you do see is a vast stretch of sand dunes reaching clear over the horizon to the North Sea, lying about two miles away. Carved out of these dunes are patches of fairway, winding their bumpy ways to terraced greens tucked between huge mounds of beach that are covered with grass as thick as asparagus.

The large number of dunes allows you little margin for error, for they leave no alternate routes to the green. If you play a hole any other way than straight down its own fairway, you will be in the rough. It consists largely of unraked sand as thin as sugar, in which your ball often half buries itself. All of this is overrun with tangled bushes as though to get out of as barbed wire.

Added to the confusion of this hellishly frustrating rough are biting sea winds off the North Sea that seldom blow the same direction two days in a row, or for that matter, throughout the same day. Combined with the severity of the rough and the course's serpentine fairways, the winds make The Hague one of the most exacting tests of driving in the entire world of golf. After a bad day with their drivers, lots of golfers walk off the eighteenth green at The Hague exhausted, looking as though they had spent the day climbing mountains.

Inland courses in the Netherlands are a little different. Trees are the number one obstacles and they are placed strategically along the fairways—and sometimes in them—making shot placement a most important part of Dutch golf. To further emphasize this point, the roughs are very tough and the greens are small. The Golf Club de Pan (or the Utrechtse Golf Club as it sometimes is called) is a fine example.

Like most Dutch courses, this layout is a thinking man's golf course. Every shot must be well thought out and carefully positioned so the next one can be easier. Make a mistake and you play off a sidehill lie, out of thick heather, from the trees, or to a blind green. It's a course of doglegs, like the 514-yard, par-5 eleventh, a great driving hole, with a narrow, twisting fairway turning right between high mounds, rough, and trees. There are straightaways, like the par-4 tenth, a 345-yarder that narrows at one point like an hourglass. And there are robust par 4's like the 427-yard fourth, with its banked and turning fairway flanked by trees and rough, calling for great power all the way. Beautifully molded par-3 holes round out this excellent test.

The majority of the courses in Holland are 9-hole affairs, but they are located near major cities and are easy to reach. At most clubs— including the following—visitors are welcome, even without a letter of introduction.

The Bagstad at the Olso Golf Klubb is a challenge to any golfer.

LOCATION	COURSE	HOLES/PAR/ YARDAGE
Amsterdam	Amsterdam GC	18/68/5,376
Arnhem	Rosendaelsche GC	9/35/3,025
Breda	Toxandria GC	18/70/6,189
Diepenveen	Sallandsche GC	9/35/3,061
Eindhoven	Eindhovensche GC	18/70/6,322
Hattem	Hattemse GC	9/34/3,165
Hengelo	Twentsche GC	9/36/3,024
Hilversum	Hilversumsche GC	18/71/6,425
Hummelo	Keppelse GC	9/31/3,509
Utrecht	GC De Pan	18/72/6,315
Wassenaar	Haagsche G & CC	18/72/6,627
Wittem	Wittem G & CC	9/37/3,163
Zandvoort	Kennemer G & CC	18/71/6,290

NORWAY

Golf and scenery always go together in Norway. The season is probably shorter than anywhere else—from May to the end of September

—but in Norway you can play golf around-the-clock during the summer season. That is, in the northern twilight you can see the pin two hundred yards away at 10:30 p.m. For about 23 weeks a golfer with the time and stamina can play 18 holes early in the day and 18 more before dark.

The most famous course in Norway is the Bagstad at the Oslo Golf Klubb. This par-72 layout measures 6,366 yards, but the hills make the challenge equal that of a longer course. On the rugged fifteenth, a short par 4, you work uphill from tee to green. Even the strongest driver may see his ball land—and roll toward him.

Other fairways plunge toward trouble. The route to the fourth green banks and twists into a deep depression, where only the ablest show a profit. A tip from the experienced: lay up short from the tee on this par 4. But not all fairways meet the slopes head on. Several curve around the hills to produce tricky downhill lies. The tumbling forested country gave the architect materials for doglegs that cannot be defied. Oslo's sixth makes a 90-degree turn to the left. Don't try to short-cut or you'll be as lost as the babes in the woods.

Water helps shape the course. A lake borders all the left side of the fifth fairway and circles close behind the green. The eighth demands a crisp iron shot over water to a neat two-level green.

Incidentally, the Ibestad Golf Club is the northernmost course in the world, located at a latitude of 69 degrees on Rolla island, halfway between Narvik and Harstad. The golf club was started in 1967 and has around fifty members. Golf is a compartively new sport in Norway. The first club was started in Oslo in 1924. But, whether you wish to compete in one of the open championships or you just drop in for a round of golf at a local course, you will be warmly welcomed.

LOCATION	*COURSE*	*HOLES/PAR/ YARDAGE*
Bergen	Bergen Golfklubb	9/32/2,514
Ibestad	Ibestad GC	9/32/2,368
Oslo	Oslo Golf Klubb	18/72/6,366
Oslo	Oustoen Golfklubb	9/36/3,060
Sarpsborg	Borregaard GC	18/34/2,827
Stavanger	Stavanger Golfklubb	18/68/5,653
Trondheim	Trondheim Golfklubb	9/34/2,935

PORTUGAL

The traveling golfer will find some of the best courses in Europe in Portugal. Less than 15 miles from the capital city of Lisbon, for example, is the Clube de Golf do Estoril.

Looking as if it had been engraved on the hill overlooking the international playground of Estoril, with its luminescent beaches and clear blue ocean, the Estoril Golf Club is as beautiful to see as it is exciting to play. But visitors should not be distracted by the scenery. This course requires the closest attention. The finely molded contours of this course—much of it has been worked over a base of solid rock—stretch a modest 5,451 yards and play to a par 69, but the demands of the course are anything but modest. Estoril's narrow, pine-tree-lined fairways (reached in most cases from elevated tees) don't begin until at least one hundred yards out. Moreover, bunkers creep in on the tight fairways, just hungering to catch a careless drive, and the heather and gorse that make up the rough seem as tough as barbed wire. More often than not, the course is whipped by strong breezes blowing in off the ocean; selecting a club can be like solving a problem in aerodynamics.

The most fearsome hole on the course is the par-4, 265-yard thirteenth. From an elevated tee, your drive must thread a narrow corridor of trees flanked on both sides by stone walls marking out-of-bounds. Members of the club call it "The Valley of Fear," and it's a good idea to allow oneself to be led through it by one of Estoril's caddies. Bright-faced youngsters in blue coveralls and dark blue berets, they seem to have an uncanny talent for knowing the best way home, the right line on the greens—and for coming up with a lost golfball in the woods. And at Estoril, there's nothing like local knowledge.

Two hundred miles to the north of Lisbon is the Oporto Golf Club, the oldest in Portugal. Set amidst sand dunes at Espinho, at the mouth of the Douro River, it has been dubbed a miniature Carnoustie—but instead of being long, is rather short. So is another nine holes at Miramar, slightly nearer to Oporto. Yet another 9-hole club is at Vidago, one hundred miles due east of Oporto, and so, rather off the beaten track. Lying in the foothills bordering Spain, it is noted for its beauty and for the fact that many of Portugal's best players learned the game there.

Of course, the big resort golf area is in the Algarve, Portugal's southernmost province. Some two hundred miles from Lisbon, the

DISTANCES IN METERS   S. S. S. 72

MARKERS SCORE	HOLE	CHAMPION-SHIP	CHAMPION-SHIP PAR	MEN'S	MEN'S PAR	STROKE INDEX	PLAYERS SCORE	+ — 0
	1	442	5	436	5	11		
	2	340	4	329	4	15		
	3	377	4	366	4	7		
	4	368	4	357	4	3		
	5	366	4	355	4	5		
	6	447	5	438	5	9		
	7	182	3	176	3	13		
	8	376	4	370	4	1		
	9	310	4	302	4	17		
	OUT	3208	37	3129	37			
	10	430	4	393	4	12		
	11	90	3	87	3	18		
	12	495	5	480	5	4		
	13	177	3	169	3	16		
	14	393	4	370	4	2		
	15	402	4	390	4	10		
	16	541	5	496	5	8		
	17	163	3	155	3	14		
	18	384	4	373	4	6		
	IN	3075	35	2913	35			
	Total	6283	72	6042	72			

PLAYER :..

MARKER:..

DATE :..

A scorecard from the Club de Golf at Vale de Lobo. Note, as in many European countries, distances are given in meters. To convert to yards, multiply by 1.2.

Golden Coast, as it's often called, has unbeatable golfing weather. An ever-present breeze, combined with extremely low humidity, makes the high temperature relaxing and pleasant.

Presently—several are in the planning or construction phase— there are three excellent 18 holes in the Algarve: Clube de Golf de

Vilamoura, Clube de Golf de Valo do Labo, and Clube de Golf da Penina. The latter is possibly the best and most interesting.

Golfers of all types can feel at home on this course. Each hole boasts three sets of tees for men and two sets of tees for ladies, stretching the course's length from 6,250 yards with the "orange" tees to approximately 7,200 yards with the "tiger" tees. It's even possible to play Penina at 7,400 yards, making it one of Europe's longest.

Many said it was the course that couldn't be built, because designer Henry Cotton's plans called for the course to be hewn from former rice fields. Today, a quarter of a million trees and 25,000 flowering shrubs later, Penina continues to attract the golf and luxury conscious from everywhere.

The par-3 thirteenth hole is often cited as Penina's most beautiful with a winding stream forming a lateral water hazard on the right as it meanders around to the back of the green, curving inward and away in a lazy fashion. Boldness is called for on this 220-yard hole, even though most golfers first think a faded shot is their ticket to the green. The most-advised route is over the water, with a slight draw, ensuring a positive landing.

Another of the picturesque water-hazard holes is the tenth, which opens the back nine on a note of difficulty and precision. Measuring 570 yards, the course kicks off with a drive over a water hazard that

The famous duck lake at the twelfth hole at Penina Golf Course in Portugal. Incidentally, the green is over 1,000 square yards—most greens in the Algarve region are big.

The famed cliff seventh hole at Vale de Lobo.

needs a 220-yard carry for initial success. More water greets the golfer on his second shot, where he witnesses the fairway's sharp right turn. And the wide, large open green for this par-5 hole is typical of the scenic splendor of Penina.

Rather than give the impression that this fabulous course is one to scare off the average golfer, it should be noted that Penina's par-73 course has these hazards placed fairly. And the number of returning golfers attests to its challenge and reward.

There are several golf courses on Portugal's adjacent islands—the Azores and Madeira—that the visitor may play. Here are the most challenging courses in Portugal:

LOCATION	CLUB	HOLES/PAR/ YARDAGE
Estoril	Estoril GC'	18/69/5,556
		9/35/2,931
Espinho	Oporto GC	18/71/5,272

LOCATION	CLUB	HOLES/PAR/ YARDAGE
Lagos	Palmares GC	18/73/7,000
Madeira Islands	Santo da Serra GC	9/35/2,867
Terceira (Azores)	Terceira Island GC	18/70/5,688
Madeira	British CC	18/68/5,398
S. Miguel (Azores)	Clube de Golf de S. Miguel	9/33/2,616
Montes de Alvor	Clube de Golf da Penina	18/73/6,889
Quarteira	Clube de Golf de Vilamoura	18/73/6,914
Faro	Clube de Golf de Vale Do Labo	18/73/6,930

SPAIN

In Spain, fine courses can be found around the country's leading cities of Madrid and Barcelona and along the Costa del Sol and the northwest coast. In the Madrid region, the Club de Campo is considered one of the finest in the world. In an ideal subtropical climate with views across parklike country toward the city, the university, the Guadarrama Mountains, and the brown-gold fields of Spain, this course is a golfer's dream. The men responsible for this layout planned with vision and worked with skill. They also thought big. This place is vast. Besides the 7,000-yard-plus course, par 72, Club de Campo has polo fields, steeplechase courses, soccer fields, picnic grounds, and a play area for members' children, a rambling, graciously elegant clubhouse —and another 9-hole course.

The architect never ran out of ideas, and everything he thought of gives the golfer food for thought. Elevated tees are among the highest you'll find anywhere. On the 495-yard, par-4 first the tee shot must carry two hundred yards over full-grown trees to the fairway far below. On the fifth, a par 4 of 365 yards, it is uphill all the way. The climb increases the actual playing yardage. Trees and traps, tightening the fairway from both sides, make this one of the most fearsome driving holes of all. There is not a pickup hole in the lot.

Although water hazards are relatively insignificant at Club de Campo other features are spectacular. Bunkers, enormous, high-walled caverns, protect the greens with an authority that forbids an inept approach. Fairways fan out to a tempting breadth, only to close in again, demanding a sniper's accuracy. The big greens are superbly conditioned, subtly contoured—and many are blind, their charms hidden from the approaching golfer until that moment of truth when he tops

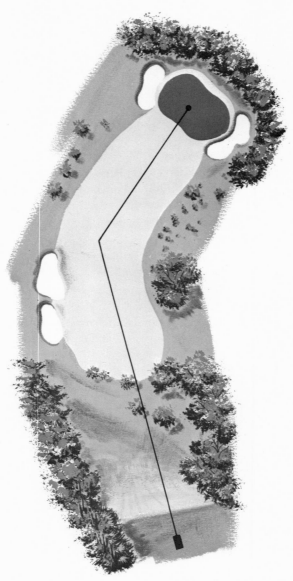

The thirteenth hole at Club de Campo in Madrid is a par-4, 446-yard affair. The trick on this hole is to cut the dogleg by aiming your drive down the right side from the elevated tee. But if you push it too far to the right, you are in the trees and bad rough, and it will cost you an extra shot. There are bunkers at 200 and 230 yards out on the left, at the point of the dogleg. You hit your approach with anything from a 6- to an 8-iron. The green is good-sized and undulating, and it is guarded by two large bunkers at the right front and the left rear.

a rise to find his ball. The grace and strength that are so much a part of Spanish tradition show strongly in this course, which challenges every golfer to show that they are also part of him.

Just outside of Barcelona is the Real Club de Golf "El Prat"—a par-72 layout of over 6,400 yards. It won't take you long to realize that El Prat has some of the most demanding holes you'll find anywhere.

Take the tight fairways, hemmed in by pines and palm trees. Here the premium is on control, accuracy, straight-arrow drives. A wind from the sea can play havoc with drives. Even after you hit the narrow fairways the pressure does not let up: you face severe bunkering around greens that seem to be sculpted into the terrain, favoring precise hitting on the approaches. Interestingly shaped and covering a lot of ground, many of the traps have high front walls that force you to explode the ball. They guard well-contoured greens that are as fast as lightning, demanding a firm but delicate touch.

You will agree that El Prat's architect, Javier Aranas, who has built a number of great courses in Spain, has designed a superb layout, a challenging course in surroundings that are altogether breathtaking. If you tend to look up on a shot from time to time, it is understandable, since several holes border the sea, and a beautiful lagoon provides the only water hazard.

Even before the Costa del Sol took up golf, you could tell it was going to be a natural. Stretching along the Mediterranean coast of Spain, this golden strip lies poised between tropical sun and cool sea. Manicured courses, fiendishly plotted to test any handicap, are everywhere you look. But when you birdie the eighteenth on the Costa del Sol, the fun is just beginning. Instead of marching back to the clubhouse for a beer and a round of poker with the boys, you can stretch out on the beach and watch the bikinis saunter by. Or take in a bullfight. Or step into the shade of a medieval cathedral.

The focus of golf on the Costa del Sol is the Marbella-Torremolinos area. The two best courses to play are Nueva Andalucia and Rio Real. The other courses are the Atalaya Park (whose hotel is the destination point of most of the United States golf tours to Spain), the El Candado and the 9-hole course of the Hotel Guldalmina. Most exclusive is Sotogrande, which is not on the teeming Marbella seacoast tourist strip at all, but rather an hour's drive west to the farthest uncrowded extremity of the Costa del Sol where the clubhouse, apartment compound, and the first tee are within view of the Rock of Gibraltar.

The Costa del Sol is one of the most beautiful courses in the world and offers plenty of challenges to the touring golfer.

Nueva Andalucia is an irrigated pocket valley, a small green gem set in the colorless, dry Sierra, slotted like a V toward the Mediterranean, with a round, stone bullfight arena standing like a sentinel above the entrance. The scene must have been an inspiration to Robert Trent Jones, who has shaped and manicured the land into what must be counted one of his finest pieces of golf architecture. The entire 18-hole Nueva Andalucia is contained in this tiny valley, but Trent Jones has created two 9-hole layouts so distinctly different that somewhere around the eleventh or twelfth hole you begin to marvel that you are in the same place where you played the first nine. Although the two layouts apparently interlace on another, the first nine is played almost entirely down in the bottom of the valley, following charming streams and ponds with swans, then entering into fairways narrowed by rows of olive trees.

Nueva Andalucia's second nine, by contrast, is a hill course that takes you high up in the open spaces of the Mediterranean sky. The tenth green is a low-lying fortress encircled by a moat. The sixteenth green demands the most careful approach shot, because its steep gradient to the left can easily carry a ball into a trap. Equally memorable is the seventeenth hole, which offers a true option to hit your second shot via the left or right route.

The clubhouse at the Rio Real Golf Club is a gem among the world's resort golf facilities—great high-ceilinged rooms decorated with Spanish tapestries, an expansive stone veranda surrounded by flowering shrubbery and looking high over the 18-hole layout. Rio Real's hilly first nine is tricky and full of seeming injustices to the golfer, including a thread-the-needle, slope-away par 3 and a 475-yard, par-4 ninth hole. By contrast, the second nine is relatively flat, down in the valley and easy. Incidentally, there are no golf cars yet in Spain, either because the Spanish are traditionalists who believe the player should walk, or there is never enough crowding to make it necessary to speed play, or because the golf entrepreneurs there have not yet been informed about all the profitable windfalls and tax write-offs to be gained from a fleet of electric cars. The main reason, though, is that caddies are cheap and plentiful, although Rio Real surely must have the worst caddies in Spain.

For many Americans, the ultimate golf destination is Sotogrande, ten-million-dollar 3,000-acre resort carved out of sand dunes and hillside at the farthest extremity of the Costa del Sol, within easy smuggling distance of Gibraltar. It should be said at the outset that organized tours are not welcome at Sotogrande. If you want to stay and play at the golf hotel, the best approach is to write in advance for reservations (Sotogrande, Cadiz, Spain), giving your country-club affiliation in the States. These formalities presumably have not been imposed on certain dedicated Sotogrande golfers such as the Duke of Windsor, Guy de Rothschild, Sean Connery, the Duke of Lerma, the Biddles, and the Patinos. At Sotogrande, one thinks twice about the foursome ahead before asking permission to play through. And one dresses for dinner.

The par-72, 18-hole Sotogrande course was Robert Trent Jones' first layout in Europe and for those familiar with Trent Jones methodology, it holds few surprises. It is tough going for the short hitter off the tee, the greens are closely trapped, and water hazards abound. A trip into the forested Spanish rough is a frightening affair, enough to make a man revert to using his irons off the tee in places. But then there is solace in seeing all those expensive houses built along the fringes of the fairways. For relaxation, Sotogrande also has a delightful 1,320-yard, par-3 course that can be played in less than an hour.

Spain's Canary Islands have several fine golf courses and they are especially recommended for winter playing because of their mild climate. The better courses of Spain are as follows:

LOCATION	CLUB	HOLES/PAR/ YARDAGE
Barcelona	Club de Golf de San Cugat	18/68/5,632
Barcelona	Real Club de Golf El Prat	18/72/6,529
Bilbao	Sociedad de Golf de Neguri La Galea	18/72/6,759
Costa de Azahar	Club de Golf Costa de Azahar	9/37/3,390
Guadiaro	Sotogrande del Guadiaro	18/72/6,800
		18/72/6,296
		18/72/6,211
Madrid	Real Sociedad Hipica Espanola Club de Campo	18/74/7,164 (also 9-hole course)
Madrid	Real Club de la Puerta	18/72/5,961
Malaga	Golf Club Guadalmina	18/72/6,786
Las Palmas (Canary Islands)	Club de Golf de Las Palmas	18/71/6,211
Los Monteros	Rio Real Golf Club	18/71/6,130
Marbella	Atalaya Park Golf Club	18/72/6,900
Marbella	Nueva Andalucia Golf Club	18/72/7,080
Puigcerda	Real Golf Club de Cerdana	12/72/6,562 (for 18 holes)
San Rogue	Club de Golf Campamento	9/35/2,961
Santander	Real Golf de Pedrena	18/70/6,255
Tenerife	Club de Golf de Tenerife El Penon	18/72/6,133
Torremolinos	Parador Nacional de Golf Club	18/70/6,060
Malaga	Club de Campo de Malaga	18/72/6,442

LOCATION	CLUB	HOLES/PAR/ YARDAGE
Zaragoza	Zaragoza Golf Club	9/35/3,100
Murcia	La Manga Campo de Golf	18/72/6,455
		18/72/6,855
El Escoril	La Herreria Club	18/72/6,615
Playa de Pals	Club de Golf de Pals	18/73/6,490
Valencia	El Saler Club	18/72/6,600
Torrevieja	Club de Golf Villa Martin	18/72/6,700

SWEDEN

From an inconspicuous beginning in 1888 when an English landscape architect constructed a 9-hole course on a private estate, golf in Sweden has grown rapidly to the point where Sweden now ranks second (after England) among Europe's golf nations. Presently there are more than 135 courses.

The greatest increase has come in the last decade. As a result municipal authorities have begun to set aside land for golf courses and to grant direct financial support so that everyone can afford to play. The visitor who wishes to play golf in Sweden will be admitted as a guest player. In some instances a membership card or letter of introduction from his home club would be helpful.

The season is relatively short, but you can make up for lost time by playing almost around the clock in June or July. Most courses open in May and close in September. When Arnold Palmer toured Sweden in 1970 he discovered one difficulty: "Playing in Sweden presents a special hazard: they have the world's most beautiful girls over there and it's tough to concentrate on one's game!"

One of the best and most interesting courses in Sweden is the Halmstad course at Tylosand, a New England–type resort on the shores of the Kattegat, that bay of the North Sea which separates the west coast of Sweden from Denmark. One of the most appealing things about Tysoland is how naturally the Swedish countryside lends itself to golf-course architecture. The main road into town cuts through the Halmstad course. As you drive along, you can see patches of fairway through the spruce and the birches and the firs. The grass isn't just green; it's emerald, its color accented by the whiteness of the sandy soil from which it grows. Bramble bushes are planted in strategic spots, and are allowed to grow wild in the rough, which is

The first tee of the Delsjo course, the site of the Volvo Open and other international events. The 18-hole, par-71 layout winds through a natural park and features narrow fairways.

laced with azalea, dogwood, and rhododendron. For a little while you are back in the sandhills of the Carolinas when, in point of fact, you are hardly ten degrees from the Arctic circle.

Like the No. 2 course at Pinehurst, which it very much resembles,

Halmstad is a tight test of the tee shot. Its skinny fairways are made to appear even narrower by thick growths of pines bordering each hole almost from tee to green. On several of the par-4 holes these pines trespass directly across the fairway, like fences, two hundred yards or more from the tee, or just about where you hoped to hit your drive. Hence you are faced not only with the considerable problem of getting to these trees but with getting through or over them. Because of the often torrential rains that blow in off the Kattegat, the greens at Halmstad usually putt on the slow side. Since they are not exceedingly large, nor severely sloped, they are not difficult greens to calculate. At Halmstad—to summarize the situation—you putt for show and *drive* for dough.

Of the more than 135 courses, here are a few that should prove of special interest to the traveling golfer:

LOCATION	COURSE	HOLES/PAR/ YARDAGE
Haljarp	Bastads Golfklubb	18/71/6,065
Ostra Vik	Boras Golfklubb	18/70/5,850
Gothenburg	Delsjo Golfklubb	18/71/6,154
Djursholms	Djursholms Golfklubb	18/72/5,740
Stockholm	Drottningholm Golfklubb	18/71/6,544
Falsterbo	Falsterbo Golfklubb	18/73/6,354
Falsterbo	Flommen Golfklubb	18/73/6,235
Tylosand	Halmstad Golfklubb	18/72/6,482
Jonkoping	Jonkoping-Huskvarna Golfklubb	18/72/6,075
Karlstad	Karlstad Golfklubb	18/72/6,560
Lidingo	Lidingo Golfklubb	18/72/6,598
Linkoping	Linkopings Golfklubb	18/72/6,365
Malmo	Ljunghusens Golfklubb	18/74/6,490
Lund	Lunds Akademishka Golfklubb	18/74/6,586
Orebro	Orebro Golfklubb	18/74/6,470
Rya	Rya Golfklubb	18/72/6,250
Danderyd	Stockholms Golfklubb	18/72/6,355

SWITZERLAND

After machine tools, you are the most important cog in the Swiss economy, contributing a share of about $300 million deposited by tourists in Switzerland each year. Although you are sure to buy their products—watches, cameras, lace, embroidery, woodcarvings—you visit the country for other reasons: the unforgettable scenery; the gracious Swiss hotels with their impeccable service and superb cuisine; and the skiing, the mountain-climbing, and the golf. Not the least of these is the golf. You would have to travel far to find so many fine courses within a 30–40 mile radius of every major city. Once you've played there you will agree that the Lausanne Golf Club, surrounded by hills and forests with panoramic views of Lake Leman and the Alps, is a must for visiting golfers. The 2,800-foot-high course, playing just over six thousand yards, is seven miles from the center of Lausanne, a lively, cosmopolitan city with attractive boulevards, sophisticated shops, and an interesting nightlife.

It is doubtful whether you've ever played an approach shot on a fairway chopped out of hills that narrow to ten yards just before reaching the green. But you face this needle-threading shot on the par-4, 325-yard twelfth hole at Lausanne. It plays from an elevated tee high above the fairway, which has high walls on the left side. There's a fairway bunker on the right about 175 yards out, then a steep fall-off on the right to trees and out of bounds. The fairway climbs uphill slightly and narrows to ten yards between a high hill on the left and a cliff on the right. The green is high-walled at the back left and falls abruptly to the right.

At all times at Lausanne you are confronted with lush, deep roughs produced by winter snows and summer rains and greens that are elevated and steeply banked. This means very delicate chips and pitches if you miss the green even by a few feet. There are fine par 3's, including the 126-yard third hole. It plays from an elevated tee beside a meadow where cowbells jangle gently on your backswing. The play is over a deep valley filled with trees and long grass to a steeply elevated plateau green that drops off sharply on three sides.

Several Swiss courses are in resort areas that combine skiing and golf. One of these is the Crans-sur-Sierre Golf Club, Switzerland's best and biggest layout. The hazards that distinguish this course, which measures 7,088 yards in length and plays to a par 73, can be readily ascertained by stepping onto the first tee. For here the player meets virtually all the challenge that has been built into the Crans course. The starting hole, a par-5, 585 yards, presents the first of ten blind tee shots and puts him immediately at the mercy of the typically wide and cruelly convoluting fairway.

It's more than coincidence that the direction markers look like so many lonely slalom poles, for these same rolling fairways that can catch a good drive and send the ball careening wildly into rough or bunkers are also ski slopes that will topple the boldest of schuss-boomers during the winter months.

The greens at Crans are as smooth as carpets, but they are not made any more accessible by the evergreen trees that stand sentinel on several holes right in the middle of the fairway. And while the fairways may be shaped to the natural terrain, the bunkers here were created by human cunning; they are well-placed and filled with tiny pebbles and a coarse sand that make explosion shots an adventure. The rough gets cut just once a year. The land is owned by several hundred farmers; each fall, just before the playing of the Swiss Open at Crans, they mow the grass and use it to feed their cattle. It's just as well that they do, since, by that time, you almost need a machete to hack your way out.

The golf in Switzerland usually runs from April through September, except in the southern portion, where it starts a month or so earlier, and continues to the end of October. Also, remember that Swiss golf is generally high-altitude golf. Watch your clubbing in the thin mountain air.

LOCATION	CLUB	HOLES/PAR/ YARDAGE
Ascona	Golf Club Patrizale	18/72/6,375
Bad Ragaz	Golf Club Bad Ragaz	18/71/6,408
Berne	Golf and CC Blumis- berg	18/73/6,615
Crans	Crans Golf Club	18/73/7,088
		9/34/2,849
Davos	Golf Club Davos	9/36/2,876
Geneva	Golf Club de Geneve	18/73/6,326
Gstaad	Golf Club Saanenland	9/36/3,094
Lausanne	Golf Club Lausanne	18/72/6,744
Lenzerheide	Golf Club Lenzerheide- Valbella	18/70/6,282
Lucerne	Lucerne Golf Club	18/70/5,994
Lucerne-Burgenstock	Golf Club Burgenstock	9/31/2,300
Zurich-Zumikon	Golf and CC Zumbikon	18/72/6,485
Niederbueren	Ostschweizerischer GC	18/72/6,261
St. Moritz	Engadine GC Sameda	18/72/6,281

18

AFRICA AND
THE MIDDLE EAST

In Africa and the Middle East, good golf can usually be found in former British colonies or territories, or regions under their influence. The major exception to this is Morocco, where golf flourishes under direct leadership of their king.

Like the continent itself, golf in Africa offers a great many contrasts. In Kenya or Rhodesia, for example, your playing partners may be lions, while in the Middle East or Egypt, there are excellent green courses in a part of the world where sand is prevalent. In South Africa, on the other hand, there are championship layouts that are similar, and as challenging as those in the British Isles or the United States.

One good rule to follow if you plan a golf game in Africa or the Middle East is to bring your own clubs. Club rentals are available at only a few locations, mainly in South Africa, Egypt, and Morocco.

SOUTH AFRICA

South Africa, because of its moderate sunny climate, its wide open spaces and its all-year-round way of outdoor life, is an ideal sporting country. And for few other sports are facilities more abundant and more attractive than for golf.

Golf first came to South Africa by way of Britain in 1882, when the first course was laid out at Wynberg with the assistance of the British garrison. This was the beginning of the Cape Golf Club, which held its first competition in 1886, and encouraged the spread of golf to Mafeking and Kimberley, the Eastern Cape and the Transvaal, where the first club was established near Johannesburg in 1890.

There are now over three hundred golf courses spread throughout South Africa. Within easy reach of every city, town, or holiday resort there are several first-class courses and at least one of championship standard.

South Africans play golf all the year round and, to keep their courses in tip-top condition in areas of scanty rainfall, they use millions of gallons of water. Today all greens are turfed—a far cry from the days when most had surfaces of Kimberley blue ground (the soil from which diamonds are extracted), mine tailings, and other unusual sandy substances. The clubhouses, too, have often grown from small huts to near-hotels.

The layouts of South African golf courses are interesting and imaginative. International planners and local devotees have displayed remarkable ingenuity in using the attractive hazards which nature has so generously provided. Most courses are set amidst such magnificent veld, mountain, or coastal scenery that visitors at times find it hard to keep their eyes on the ball. Others find that the sunny climate engenders a healthy thirst at the nineteenth hole.

The Royal Durban Country Club is a fine example of the infinite variety of a South African championship course. The original first hole prompted Sam Snead to ask: "Where's the other half of the fairway?" Today, reconstructed to permit passage of the national road to the north, the mythical "other half of the fairway" still lures the

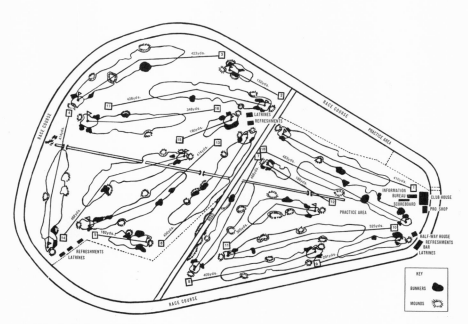

The hole layout of Royal Durban Country Club.

sliced tee shot over an out-of-bounds fence. The overcautious or fearful, flinching from the thought of "three off the tee," may find it hard to recover from thickish rough with a view of the green blocked by a steeply risking hillock on the left. The green is set up by a hollow in front and backed by a huge, bush-filled dune, a cavernous receptacle of many golf balls thought by their strikers to be perfectly played. In fact, to ensure a morale-lifting, opening par 4, the second shot has to be one of great merit.

The short second is played from one high ridge to another over a deep-grassed hollow; possibly all is plain sailing on a calm day but this hole can be a nervy affair when it blows.

No. 3 calls for special mention—a fine long 2-shotter played from an elevated tee on the same level as No. 2 green. From this commanding position on the sand-dune ridge you look down on a valley, which after a flat stretch, gradually rises through mounds and undulations to a green in the shadow of a tree-covered dune. As the great Tom Simpson, doyen of British golf architects, would say, here is a perfect example of "suppressio veri" because the hollow in front of the green provides deceptive dead ground, and it is even-money that on the first time around you'll be short. The large green falls away on both sides into grass hollows from which you'll need a very deft chip to get near the pin.

Regular players select the 4th as an outstanding one-shot hole. This hole has had a "face lift"—literally so—because the mound formerly hiding most of the green is now pushed away to give almost complete visibility. From the height of the tee on the dune ridge the green lying below looks very small. You should probably select a stronger club than seems necessary, because there is still some dead ground left in front of the green. It may all look a little frightening at first but this hole is deceptive; it is made to look difficult by a subtle arrangement of slopes and mounds.

This string of four holes has often proved to be the downfall of aspiring champions. But now for a little relief as we descend into lower levels after carrying a ridge of flattish sand hills at No. 5. Nos. 5, 6, and 7, all good and interesting holes in the "Parklands" make a pleasant prelude to the more dramatic No. 8—a great hole in our book. The tee is in line with the dune ridge, which marches on the left with the fairway, and the player, looking for the shortest line, must closely skirt the bush-covered slopes or he will either finish in a bunker on the right edge of the fairway or find a hanging lie on the side slopes.

The second shot here to a green perched high among the dunes compares with those great seconds in South Africa like the seventeenth at Maccauvlei, the thirteenth at Humewood, the fourteenth and sixteenth at Scottburgh, and the third at East London.

The No. 9 fairway is flat until you reach a wide hollow. Well left, risking the bunker, the green is open; from the right, the approach to the angled green over the guarding bunkers is not easy.

No. 10 is a man-sized hole, the longest, the fairway dipping and then rising to a mounded green well guarded by "spectacle" bunkers. The contrast of gleaming white sand with the green of the fairway makes this hole quite spectacular.

A longish 4, No. 11, has also had a facelift which included landscaping of the fairway with an artificially made hollow of deceptive width fronting the green.

The next hole, a one-shotter, is famous as the scene of the humiliation of the Duke of Windsor—then Prince of Wales. According to the legend he took a 17 here. If one misses the putting surface the ball finishes up at the base of steep slopes and many stories are told of well-known golfers being nearly sent round the bend as they crossed and recrossed the green.

After the Parkland 13 and 14, interesting short and long two-shotters respectively, No. 15 is a short hole, unfortunately lacking natural features but with a well-guarded green, which is a necessary link with the spectacular sixteenth with its green high up on the ridge.

Now you are back near the sea again and in sand-dune country. Most people always remember No. 17 as a hole "that is different." A clever tee shot to a flattish area on the right rim of the valley and you can see the green. Otherwise from the base of the deep basin of the fairway the second shot can be a bit of guesswork. On a calm day a good drive may reach the home green but it must be placed leftish to allow for a side slope. The fairway drops steeply on the right down to the practice area; a long pull finds the end of the protecting ridge and finishes well below fairway level.

It's a great sensation standing on the eighteenth tee, the green in full view, with the imposing clubhouse as background. Good resolutions are likely to go by the board here as we have visions of a possible eagle; you hit that little bit too soon, too hard, or too late, and then suffer the anguish of a ruined score as the ball slides away off the fairway. A little longer and this hole would be mediocre—just another drive and pitch, but at this awkward and tempting distance, it is just the finish needed for a course which rewards good golf but ruthlessly exposes all weaknesses.

A golfing tour of South Africa is well worth planning, for in addition to playing the grand old game, the visitor has a chance to see wonderful sights and to enjoy the sunny climate. No matter whether you are visiting a game reserve, a gold or diamond mine, a Bantu area, a coastal or mountain resort, or traveling along the famed Garden Route, there is sure to be a good golf course close at hand.

As South Africa's biggest city, and the commercial and industrial hub of Africa, it is not surprising that Johannesburg has more golf clubs than any other center in the country. There are few places in the world which have sixteen golf clubs virtually within walking distance of the city, and another twenty or so within a radius of 35 miles. The best known 18-hole courses are:

CLUB	PAR/ YARDAGE	CLUB	PAR/ YARDAGE
Bryanston CC	73/7,191	Maccauvlei GC	73/7,011
Glendower GC	72/7,060	Royal Johannesburg	
Houghton GC	72/7,115	GC	72/7,283
Kensington GC	72/6,774		71/6,946
Killarney GC	72/6,791	Wanderers GC	72/6,832
Kyalami CC	73/7,060		

Thirty-six miles north of Johannesburg lies Pretoria, the charming and dignified administrative capital of South Africa. Pretoria's parks, trees, and public gardens are its greatest pride, and its six 18-hole golf courses worthy companions. These include:

Defence GC	72/6,846	Waterkloof CC	71/6,741
Irene GC	71/6,690	Wingate Park CC	72/7,127
Pretoria GC	72/7,026	Zwartkop CC	72/6,838

Many gold mines have established excellent courses along the Witwatersrand, and the visitor will also find good 18-hole golf clubs in all the tourist areas of the Transvaal. Such clubs include:

Benoni CC	72/6,843	Reading CC	72/6,708
Germiston GC	71/6,997	Springs CC	73/6,957
Nelspruit GC	72/6,545	Standerton CC	72/6,672

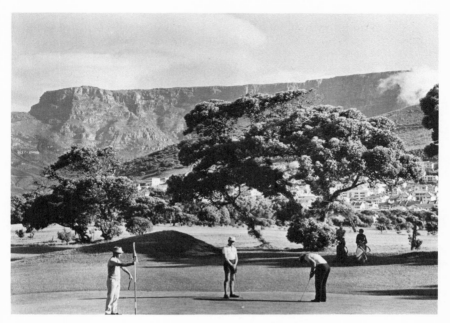

The beautiful Metropolitan Golf Club in Cape Town.

At Kimberley, the Diamond City, there is the Kimberley Golf Club, a 6,843-yard championship layout that plays to a par 73.

Cape Town, the historic Mother City, was also the birthplace of golf in South Africa, where turf greens were first introduced in 1907. There are 11 fine courses in Cape Town and on the Cape Peninsula, seven of 18 holes and four of 9 holes, set amidst delightful coastal and mountain scenery. The best 18-holers are:

CLUB	PAR/ YARDAGE	CLUB	PAR/ YARDAGE
Clovelly CC	73/6,246	Royal Cape GC	71/6,433
King David CC	74/6,776	Westlake GC	74/6,368
Mowbray GC	71/6,646		

The countryside surrounding Cape Town to the north and west is known as the Boland, in which there are plenty of fine courses, such as:

Hermanus GC	73/6,341	Strand GC	72/6,810
Stellenbosch GC	71/6,725		

Lying between Cape Town and Port Elizabeth is the lovely Garden Route, a popular resort area where visitors can play golf at many courses against a backdrop of mountains, forests, rivers, lagoons and beaches. Some of the 18-hole clubs in this area are:

CLUB	PAR/ YARDAGE	CLUB	PAR/ YARDAGE
George GC	72/6,476	Oudtshoorn GC	72/6,489
Mossel Bay GC	73/6,423	Plettenberg Bay CC	69/6,136

Port Elizabeth on the eastern Cape coast has six golf courses, two of which are of championship standard unsurpassed in South Africa. The main 18-hole links are:

Port Elizabeth GC	73/6,665	Wedgewood Park CC	72/6,494
Walmer GC	73/6,746	Aliwal North GC	71/6,289
Grahamstown GC	70/6,342	Royal Port Alfred GC	70/6,136
Nitenhage GC	71/6,515		

East London, a charming holiday center at the mouth of the Buffalo River on the east coast, has three good 18-hole courses. They are:

Alexander CC	71/6,151	West Bank GC	70/6,165
East London GC	72/6,530		

Top holiday playground of Southern Africa on the subtropical Natal coast, Durban is geared to give enjoyment to thousands of visitors, including golfers. There are at least 11 courses within easy reach of the city and these include:

Athlone GC	73/6,439	Royal Durban GC	72/6,554
Circle CC	73/6,477	Scottburgh GC	71/5,984
Beechwood GC	73/6,405	Southbroom GC	71/5,728
Durban CC	72/6,456	Umbogintwini GC	71/6,141
Kloof CC	70/6,264	Umkomaas GC	71/6,199
Port Shepstone	71/6,372		

There are a number of good 18-hole golf courses in the Orange Free State, centered mainly around the goldfields and the inland holiday resorts. These include:

Bethlehem GC	72/6,749	Oppenheimer Park	
Bloemfontein GC	71/6,938	GC	71/6,892
Defence GC	72/6,633	Sand River GC	71/6,856

CLUB	PAR/ YARDAGE	CLUB	PAR/ YARDAGE
Harrismith GC	72/6,867	Schoeman Park GC	72/6,702
Kroonstad GC	73/6,890		

RHODESIA

Rhodesian golf was born in Bulawayo in November 1894, just 13 months after the European occupation of Matabeleland—a mere two years after the completion of the Chicago Golf Club, the first 18-hole course in the United States. Salisbury followed Bulawayo in 1899, nine years after the entry of the Pioneer Column.

There are now nearly seventy golf courses in Rhodesia, seven being of recognized championship standard. The virtual absence of frost ensures that greens are maintained in tip-top condition throughout the year. Because of the early sunrise and bright sunshine, daylight hours are long, enabling a golfer to play 54 holes or more in a single day.

In Rhodesia's beautiful capital city, Salisbury, there are now 12 golf clubs within a twenty-mile radius of the city center. Of these, Royal Salisbury is perhaps the most widely known, and has acted as host to such famous golfing "greats" as Walter Hagen, Bobby Locke, Sam Snead, Tommy Bolt, Dai Rees, Gary Player, Arnold Palmer, and Billy Casper. The title "Royal" was conferred on the club when the Prince of Wales visited Rhodesia and enjoyed playing there in the early 1920's.

Royal Salisbury differs from most of the other championship courses in Rhodesia in being a relatively flat, parklike course, with no water hazards. Its chief obstacles are an abundance of trees and strategically placed bunkers.

Another very interesting course in Salisbury is the Henry Chapman Golf Club—a difficult, undulating, well-treed course, with an abundance of water hazards. The first nine has a tiger finish, the last three holes providing the most testing sequence of the entire course.

Over five thousand pines and other trees grace the fine Wingate Park Golf Club, ten miles from the center of Salisbury. Reported to be an easy course to play, the fact remains that no visting professional or leading amateur has managed to tame it. The par-3 hole with water protecting the front and left side of the green is particularly challenging.

Other good courses in the Salisbury area include Rhodesia's

longest course (7,290 yards), Warren Hills Golf Club, said to have some of the finest greens in South Africa; the picturesque Salisbury South course with numerous impressive rock hazards; and Ruwa Country Club, east of Salisbury, where a water-reticulation system has recently been installed.

At Bulawayo, Rhodesia's second largest city, the Bulawayo Golf Club course can hold its own with any in South Africa. A comprehensive water-reticulation system ensures championship conditions throughout the year, and a new clubhouse has just recently been completed. Its greens have been favorably mentioned by many of the famous golfers who have played here. The Matsheumhlope River meanders through the course and provides a formidable hazard at a number of holes, notably the double hazard on the twelfth, which has been described by a world-famous professional as worthy of inclusion in the makeup of an "ideal" course.

Umtali, one of the loveliest towns in Rhodesia, combines an impressive display of exotic flowering trees and shrubs with some fine architecture and a slight but unmistakable continental atmosphere derived from her Portuguese neighbor. While the golfer enjoys the championship Hillside course in Umtali, the nongolfer can derive equal enjoyment from a spectacular twenty-mile drive to the Vumba Mountains. Here, at Leopard Rock, in a gentle Constable-like world of lush green meadows and luxuriant vegetation, he can cheerfully pit his resources against the 9-hole (18 tees) course in the hilly grounds of a picturesque hotel. Nearby are the magnificent gardens of the Vumba National Park.

Those who fancy a combination of excellent trout fishing and golf should travel north to the rarefied air of Inyanga, where the mountains are laced with swift-flowing streams, waterfalls, and picturesque lakes. Troutbeck Inn at 6,600 feet offers an undulating, attractively treed 9-hole (par 34) course with imposing water hazards. The sixth hole (downhill, par 3) is another one of the best holes in South Africa. The carry to the green across a swift-flowing mountain stream has to be precise; bunkers trap any fall away to the right, rocks intercept an approach from the left. Annual spring and autumn tournaments include a "long drive" competition from a special tee overlooking Troutbeck Lake, with a water carry of 181 yards, and an uphill finish. The present record is 297 yards.

Interesting water hazards are also encountered on the Rhodes-

A view across the eighteenth green at the Hillside Golf Club in Umtali. The beautiful Vumba Mountains are in the background.

Inyanga National Park course, situated among stately pines and conifers within easy reach of an attractive hotel, the Inyangombe, and Nyamziwa Falls, Nyangwe Fort, and the mysterious "Slave Pit" structures. The Mare and Inyangombe rivers, particularly, form interesting hazards on the fourth, fifth, sixth, and seventh fairways, while the Mare River, bordering the second, third, and fourth fairways, is "out of bounds."

Another popular golfing spot in the Inyanga area is Brondesbury Park. This fine 9-hole course, under full water reticulation, offers superb views of the surrounding mountains, and winds its way through picturesque peach and apple orchards. The back four holes, with many natural hazards, form a peninsula one thousand feet above the valley below, and the tricky eighth hole (par 3) plays to a taxing uphill finish.

All the main courses in Rhodesia welcome visitors. Some of the best courses are as follows:

LOCATION	CLUB	HOLES/PAR/ YARDAGE
Bulawayo	Bulawayo GC	18/72/7,055
Bulawayo	Bulawayo CC	18/72/6,765
Salisbury	The Country Club	18/72/6,718
Gatooma	Eiffel Flats GC	9 */72/7,009
Gatooma	Gatooma GC	9 */72/6,812
Gwelo	Gwelo GC	18/71/6,933
Bulawayo	Harry Allen GC	18/72/7,005
Salisbury	Henry Chapman GC	18/71/6,941
Umtali	Hillside GC	18/73/6,811
Inyanga	Brondesburg Park	9/36/2,990
Inyanga	Inyanga National Park	9/35/3,105
Inyanga	Troutbeck GC	9/34/2,846
Umtali	Leopard Rock GC	9 */69/6,110
Salisbury	Royal Salisbury	18/72/6,855
Salisbury	Ruwa CC	18/72/6,851
Salisbury	Salisbury South GC	18/71/6,747
Salisbury	Sherwood CC	18/72/6,828
Salisbury	Warren Hills CC	18/72/7,290
Salisbury	Wingate Park GC	18/72/6,916
Shabani	Roland Park GC	18/72/6,495
Umtali	Umtali GC	18/72/6,532

* with alternate tees for 18 holes.

KENYA

Lying astride the Equator on Africa's east coast, Kenya is a big, wide-open country of palm-fringed, coral beaches; inland bush; grassland plains, and the rich highland plateau with its warm, sunny days and cool, crisp nights. It offers an immense diversity of peoples and cultures, welding together nearly one hundred different tribes. Sightseers will be fascinated by such groups as Mount Kenya's famed Chuka drummers, wearing headdresses of wild Colobus monkey skins; the Luo dancers on the shores of Lake Victoria; the hardy plains people with their eight-foot, double-edged spears and colored shields; the Masai, the Kikuyu; the Kisii; and the Wakamba.

It is a land where animals live as they always have lived, which sometimes means they can be found grazing on golf courses. For instance, outside the sedate old clubhouse at Nairobi's Karen Country Club a large notice may warn: "Beware of the lions on the course today."

The Karen Country Club course—generally considered Kenya's best—is a picturesque layout situated, as most courses in the country, at over five thousand feet above sea level. It plays shorter than its 6,750 yards because of the thin air. In addition, the fairways are usually hard and dry except during the period from March 15 to early May, when there are long rains. These factors, plus the strategic fairway bunkers and numerous doglegs, require some precise judgments by visiting golfers.

There are 34 courses presently in Kenya and all are rugged and rather hilly. There are no golf carts or club rentals available at any of the clubs. However, all welcome visitors except on weekends when tournaments are held. Here are several of the better courses in the vicinity of Nairobi which you can play:

CLUB	HOLES/PAR/ YARDAGE	CLUB	HOLES/PAR/ YARDAGE
Karen CC	18/72/6,750	Railway GC	9/35/3,112
Kiambee GC	9/35/3,292	Royal Nairobi GC	18/72/6,819
Limuri CC	18/71/6,561	Sigona GC	18 71/6,759
Muthaiga GC	18/70/6,531		

Another interesting championship course is at Kitale—about 250 miles from Nairobi at the foot of Mt. Elgon.

OTHER COURSES IN CENTRAL AFRICA

In the capital city of the independent Republic of the Congo, Kinshasa, there's a fine 18-hole, par-72, 6,235-yard course at the Golf Club de Kinshasa. While golf can be played here the year round, June through September is considered best, since it's the driest time and evenings are cool. Arrangements can usually be made to play at Kinshasa without difficulty.

Senegal, Nigeria, Liberia, and Ghana all have 9-hole courses available to tourists near their capital cities, but none can be considered overly challenging. The Achimota Golf Club near Accra, Ghana, however, is one of the most beautiful in Africa. Its fairways are lined with poui trees, frangipanis, flame trees, yellow elder, and other bright tropical flowers and plants.

MOROCCO

Morocco can be called the "golf capital of Northern Africa." It is particularly well endowed for golfers because European players can get a game in Morocco at times of the year when the climate makes it impossible in their own countries. There are courses in Mohammedia Marrakesh, Rabat, Casablanca, Ketama, Kenitra, and Tangier. The first three are the largest and they attract large numbers of golfers.

The Mohammedia (Golf Club de Fédala) course is world-renowned, and an International Moroccan Golf Week (sponsored by His Majesty King Hassan II) is held here and in Marrakesh during the first week in March. The Mohammedia course is an 18-hole test of golfing skill that measures 6,369 yards and plays to a par 73. The course is close enough to the Atlantic to be affected by it. Cypress trees shaped by years of sea winds and the pounding of waves nearby are reminders that the ocean is an ever-present element in the play. As expected, a sandy subsurface gives up very little roll in the fairways and makes it imperative that iron shots be struck evenly—the ball first and divot after.

The generally flat terrain in no way detracts from the challenge of the layout. Take the seventh hole, for example. This is a par 5, 495 yards, that doglegs left. The tee shot is over a vast expanse of bushes, sand and rough. The wind blows left to right across the fairway, and the approach is to a green well guarded by deep bunkers. Immediately following is the par-3 eighth hole, a 195-yarder that plays from an elevated tee to a small green bunkered in front and at the sides. It takes one fine and well-played iron to reach this putting surface.

The Marrakesh course is a par-72, 5,745-yard, 18-hole layout located on the Ait Ourir road about three miles from Marrakesh. The greens are irrigated by submersion because of the dry climate, but the course is open—as are all Moroccan courses—all year. Incidentally, during the winter months you can combine golf with skiing in the nearby legendary Atlas Mountains.

The Marrakesh course is the one best known in all Africa.

The newest golf course complex in Morocco is the 45-hole layout designed by Robert Trent Jones. Located some six miles from the Government City of Rabat, it contains two 18-hole and one 9-hole course. The championship layout, called the Rouge course, is 6,947 yards, par 72, while the other (Blue) course is 6,336 yards, par 71. The 9-hole affair is 2,947 yards and plays to a par 35.

The courses are typical of Jones design—large greens, big tees, and plenty of well-placed bunkers. A fully automatic sprinkler system is installed to provide a completely green course year round. This beautiful course with Bermuda-grass fairways and lush greens makes for a perfect setting.

Here's a rundown of the Moroccan golf courses—all of which welcome visiting golfers:

LOCATION	COURSE	HOLES/PAR/ YARDAGE
Casablanca	Anfa GC	9 */67/4,770
Casablanca	Fedala (Mohammedia) GC	18/73/6,369
Kenitra	Kenitra GC	9/35/2,574

LOCATION	COURSE	HOLES/PAR/ YARDAGE
Ketama	Parador GC	9/36/2,707
Marrakech	Marrakech GC	18/72/5,745
Rabat	Royal Rabat GC	18/72/6,947
		18/71/6,336
		9/35/2,947
Tangier	Tangier CC	9/35/2,702

* with alternate tees for 18 holes.

EGYPT

There are five golf courses—two of which are 18-hole layouts—available to touring golfers in Egypt. While they are private courses, there's no problem to play on them. As a matter of fact, when diplomatic relations between Egypt and the United States are good, you'll be very welcome. Club rentals are available at all courses, and all courses are kept in fairly good condition for this part of the world.

Egyptian courses are quite flat, but are challenging mainly because of sand traps, which are plentiful and must only be played with a sand wedge. Because of the condition of the sand, it's wise to get out of the sand first, then work toward the green.

While golf is a year-round sport in Egypt, most visiting golfers prefer the winter and early spring months when the climate is warm but not hot and humid.

LOCATION	COURSE	HOLES/PAR/ YARDAGE
Alexandria	Alexandria Sporting Club	9/35/2,866
Alexandria	Smouha Club	18/72/6,293
Cairo	Gezira Sporting Club	9/69/5,803 (18 tees)
Cairo	Heliopolis Sporting Club	9/34/2,736
Cairo	Mena House GC	18/72/6,010

TURKEY

Turkey can't be considered a "real" golfing nation. There are only a few courses outside the major cities, and of these, just two or three are worthy of mention. Turkish golf courses are rather difficult to play because of rocky terrain, but local rules are quite liberal. They permit improvement of your lie anywhere on the course, even on the greens. Visitors are always welcome at all Turkish golf clubs.

LOCATION	CLUB	HOLES/PAR/YARDAGE
Ankara	Ankara GC	18/71/6,121
Istanbul	Istanbul GC	18/72/5,570
Izmir	Bornova GC	18/71/5,684

ISRAEL

While there is only one course at present in Israel, more are on their way. The one existing course, like so many things this little nation has created in its brief history as a republic, was not an easy acquisition. The Rothschild foundation tackled the gigantic task of conquering the 365 acres of sand dunes and scrubby growth. There was almost endless experiment with mixtures of seed and fertilizer. Ultimately, seed from Arizona and plants from Georgia helped Israel to win another uphill fight. Today, the 6,671-yard, par-72 Caesarea Golf and Country Club course has carpetlike greens and challenging, landscaped fairways—a green miracle in the desert.

Caesarea, located on the shore of the Mediterranean, bids to become a choice Israeli resort. Ideally situated between Tel Aviv (32 miles to the south) and Haifa (25 miles to the north), hotels and villas are already springing up around the Caesarea club. The course is open to the visiting golfer, but is frequently crowded.

LEBANON

This small Arab country has four of the finest courses in the Middle East. Although all are only 9 holes, the courses are all grass, including very respectable greens.

The Golf Club of Lebanon course, near the Beirut International Airport, measures 3,204 yards and includes a standard assortment of two par-5 holes, five par 4's, and two par 3's. Alternate tee and green arrangements permit back-9 variety and brings the 18-hole yardage to 6,289, par 72. While this course frequently is crowded, there's generally sufficient room to accommodate tourists, especially during the week and in the morning.

The other course open to tourists is the Delhamyah Country Club, 15 miles south of Beirut. This 3,265 yard par-36 nine is laid out in

Natural sand traps and hazards, as well as a few man-made ones, are legion at the Rolling Hills course in Dhahran.

foreboding sandy and rocky terrain. If you manage to keep the ball in play on the Bermuda fairways, which slant sharply in all directions, and stay out of the rocks, you'll be in good shape until reaching the green. Here strange things begin to happen. Sown with a strain of *Zoysia japonica,* the putting surfaces break so sharply toward the sea that the ball often turns *uphill*. It's incredible, but it's true.

The other two Lebanese courses—the Zahrani Country Club and Ras El Lados Golf Club—are oil-company owned and operated for employees. Visitors are welcome, but they must play with a member. The best time to play golf in Lebanon is from March to December.

IRAN

There are, at present, two golf courses in this country. The first was the par-72 Field Golf Club near Abadan, which is open only to oil-company personnel and their guests. The other is the new 7,188 yard, par-73 Imperial Country Club in Teheran. This is a difficult course, with two of the pars over six hundred yards. The fairways

Golfers confronting a pipeline on the Rolling Hills course in Dhahran.

are of Kentucky Blue, while the greens are of Pentcross Bent. The club has a complex of first-class facilities, including an elaborate clubhouse, swimming pool, tennis courts, stables, restaurant, bar, and nearby hotels. Tourists are welcome at all times at the Imperial Country Club.

OTHER MIDDLE EAST COURSES

There are other courses in the Middle East, but most of them are very private (owned by sheikhs) or company operated. While most of the company courses will accept outsiders, their locations are remote and generally far from any resort area. For example, the Arabian American Oil Company has built three country clubs in Saudi Arabia. They are the 27-hole Rolling Hills at Dhahran, the 18-hole Rahinah at Ras Tanura, and the 18-hole Ain Nakl at Abqaiq. Par is 72 and the course rating 71 for all three.

Though the USGA regulations governing golf are virtually the same for Americans in Saudi Arabia as they are in the United States, geographically, the sport is different. In the desert, the golfer is fighting two rivals—his competitor on the course, and the sand. The fairways are white sand instead of green grass. The greens are black oil mixed with sand instead of emerald velvet. Tees, covered with Celotex, are built several feet above the desert to avoid the sand. A well-hit ball may carry more than two hundred yards into the sand and stop dead. There is no bounce, no roll. Red balls are used in place of white because, at a distance, they are easier to spot in the sand.

To a newcomer in Saudi Arabia, a golf course looks like one big sand trap. The fairways are so much a part of the surrounding desert that, sometimes, the golfer finds it necessary to take a second look in order to locate them. Strips of oil and lengths of pipe mark the fairway every fifty yards. A ball landing on the other side of these boundaries is considered in the rough and is played as it lies.

Bulldozers carved these fairways out of the desert. They dug down to a hard, clay base, scooping up rock and sand. Although the

Saudi Arabia's golfers have one advantage over most golfers—they can smooth out putts as they like with a steel drag.

substratum is excellent for driving, the golfer may have less control over his shot. To aid him, a local exception to the USGA rules is allowed, and he is permitted to tee up his ball on a tiny mound of sand. Because there is always some breeze stirring in this desert land, flying sand drifts over the green, ruffling the surface. To meet this situation, a steel drag was devised for the players to smooth a path from the lie on the green to the cup. As their play would disturb the green again, it's the custom of golfers before leaving to drag the green a second time so it will be level for the next group's approach shots.

The steel drag, solution of one problem, led to the beginning of another. In smoothing the green, the drag dumped sand into the cup. Using Yankee ingenuity, a bright Aramco engineer invented an inner, removable cup from which the sand can be easily emptied.

While a breeze can disrupt sand on a green, a full-scale shamal can devastate an entire golf course. Although Arabian sandstorms don't give scheduled performances, they usually arrive during the months of May, June, and July, and blow sometimes as long as forty days at 35–50 miles an hour. Driving the sand before it, this terrifying wind builds up dunes on the fairways, rakes the toppings from the greens, and completely buries the links. Saudi contractors must shovel out the sand with bulldozers and wrestle the golf course back from the desert.

Though the weather is always hot in this region, it is more bearable for golfers during the cooler months, October to May. The more daring players, including some of the newcomers, golf all year 'round. Starting at the crack of dawn, they get in 18 holes before the heat builds up. The adventurous ones go still further. Tempting fate, they play in temperatures up to 114 degrees. Every now and then, someone suffers sunstroke. Once, a foursome, just arrived from the States, golfed on an August afternoon, all warnings to the contrary, and passed out before reaching the fifth hole.

In such heat, a golfer can develop a terrific thirst. To keep their players from getting dehydrated, the company keeps ten-gallon jugs of ice water at each tee. It's estimated that the average golfer drinks two to three quarts of water during a round:

19

ASIA AND THE FAR EAST

For four and a half centuries golf was a game played almost exclusively in Scotland. Then, in a short space of years, it became a game of international proportions as the British Empire girdled the globe during the reign of Queen Victoria. Even before there were courses in America, it was possible to play at clubs in Calcutta, Bombay, Rangoon, Bangalore, and Colombo, most of which had been started by Scottish jute traders with extensive interests in the Far East.

While golf has been played in Asia and the Far East for quite some time, its popularity was until recently limited to a great extent to players from Great Britain and the other colonial powers. But, after World War II, the natives took up the game and golf became universally popular in Asia and the Far East. In Japan, for instance, there were only 17 courses in operation at end of the war. Today there are well over six hundred. This is the greatest percentage increase in popularity of golf anywhere on the face of the earth.

One of the reasons for increased interest in golf in this part of the world is the Far East Tour. Similar to the PGA one in the United States, this tour is a series of golf open championship in the Philippines, Singapore, Malaysia, Thailand, Hong Kong, Formosa (Taiwan), Korea, and Japan. In addition to professional golfers from the nations involved, players from Europe, Australia, New Zealand, and the United States participate. The caliber of play is excellent and the interest of the people is high.

INDIA

Since India is so steeped in British influence, it is not surprising to learn that the game of golf has flourished in this ancient land for more than a century. Scottish troops garrisoned in Calcutta built a golf course there in the 1830's; it is believed to be the oldest in the world outside Scotland.

The Delhi Golf Club—followed closely by the Royal Calcutta Golf

Club—is reportedly the best among India's 16 first-class courses and best of the country's eight true championship courses. (It is estimated that there are over fifty courses in India, but only the ones mentioned here would really interest the traveling golfer.) The Delhi Golf Club derives its character and charm from the geography, climate and culture of the country. The course is situated on what was once a Mogul burial ground and is spotted with several Mogul tombs. The Moguls were the Moslem dynasty that ruled India untl British times. It was under these Moslem leaders that the great architecture of India flourished, represented today in its finest form by the Taj Mahal. The course, which plays to slightly more than seven thousand yards consists of 18 holes, par 74, with six par-5 holes and four par-3's. The atmosphere of the club is mostly Indian except for its international flavor of Britishers, a few Americans and foreign embassy personnel from all over the world. The practice green is tucked in under the shadow of one of the larger Mogul tombs, where members can sip drinks and have food served as they watch players play the eighteenth green.

The entire Delhi course is as still as the primordial jungle in which it was built some forty years ago. On some of the holes, thickets of trees must be carried by the tee shot in order to reach the fairways, which are relatively wide. But the width can be more a curse than a blessing; it tempts you to be bold with your tee shot, so that even scrupulously careful players find drives penetrating the jungle growth that borders the course.

The course is still visited by wildlife. It is years since anybody has spotted a cobra, but jackals leave tracks in the bunkers filled with a soft, powdery sand. The more than three hundred species of birds in the area make the club one of the biggest sanctuaries in northern India. But the most prominent residents of the course are the 25 families of rhesus monkeys that live in trees behind the fourteenth green, locally called the "Monkey Hole." The monkeys used to steal the flagstick from the hole, until club officials wound barbed wire around the pin. The monkeys also like to steal golfballs, chew off the covers, and try to eat the rubber. It is tough enough trying to putt those wavy greens without having to fend off a larcenous monkey.

Foreign tourists who hold tourist introduction cards (issued automatically with visas) can make arrangements for temporary membership (which is very inexpensive) directly with the club before arrival.

Or, once in India, they can make arrangements through any of the Government of India Tourist Offices in 11 major cities. Guest privileges at the Delhi club include full use of the clubhouse and all facilities such as locker rooms, bar, and restaurant. Electric golf carts are not available. The club does not rent golf clubs, but the use of a set of clubs could be arranged through the local professional. Actually, it is a good idea to carry all necessary equipment if you plan to play golf in India. Balls and tees especially are in very short supply throughout the country. However, caddies are readily available, and instead of one, you use two. That is, each player uses a caddy to carry his clubs plus an "agewalla," or forecaddie, who runs ahead and spots the ball when it stops rolling or finds the ball in the rough. He also guards the ball from thieving birds and animals—remember balls are scarce. Thus, a foursome in India is actually a twelvesome— four golfers, four caddies, and four agewallas.

The championship Royal Calcutta Golf Club is 6,827 yards with a par 73. Built on flat land with many water hazards, it is close to first-class hotels in the city. Bombay's championship course is the Chembur Golf Club & Willingdon Sports Club. The best time of the year to play at these courses as well as at Delhi are October, November, and December (also the most favorable season for tourists).

In southern India, Madras boasts two first-rate clubs. The Gymkhana Club, founded in 1886, has a par 72 for its 6,282 yards. The Cosmopolitan Club is the site of the South India Amateur Championship Tournament. Best months for golfing in Madras are July to March. In most courses in this region and in the mountains, the golfer finds a putting surface of sand and oil. Sweeping a smooth path from ball to the hole is quite legal, and makes the surface similar to grass.

In South India's Nilgiri Hills is Ootacamund's Gymkhana Club course, laid out on undulating ground 7,500 feet above sea level. Also in cooler South Indian country is the Bangalore Golf Club, Bangalore. This beautiful course lies at 3,000 feet above sea level.

Probably one of the highest golf courses in the world is the one at Gulmarg in Kashmir. The 18-hole course, with a yardage of 6,460 feet and a par 70, is laid out in a rolling mountain meadow area at an altitude of 8,700 feet. Flanking the course boundaries are forests of pine, and towering above the pine slopes are snowcapped Himalayan peaks. Gulmarg is about 28 miles by car and then four or so by pony from Srinagar, tourist center of Kashmir. Srinagar itself has a flat 18-hole double flagged course (and nine holes).

Here are India's most challenging courses:

LOCATION	COURSE	HOLES/PAR/ YARDAGE
Agra (facing Taj Mahal)	Proforma	18/71/5,898
Bombay	Bombay Presidency GC	18/71/6,127
Bombay	Chembur GC & Wellingdon Sports C	18/73/6,349
Calcutta	Royal Calcutta GC	18/73/6,827
		18/71/6,217
Faridabad	Country GC	18/71/6,044
New Delhi	Delhi GC	18/74/7,079
Kashmir	Gulmarg	18/70/6,460
Saidapet	Cosmopolitan C	18/72/6,030
Guindy	Gymkhana C	18/72/6,282
Ootacamund	Gymkhana C	18/72/6,110
Bangalore	Bangalore GC	18/70/5,913
Wellington	Gymkhana C	18/72/6,326
Srinagar	Srinagar GC	9/35/3,011
Trivandrum	Trivandrum GC	9/36/3,775
Munnar	High Range C	9/35/2,874

SINGAPORE

The Singapore Golf Club, which received the title "Royal" from George VI in 1938, was formed in 1891. It was laid out on the grounds of a local hospital and jail. As was the custom then, the individual holes were given names rather than numbers, and because of the odd location of the course, they received such morbid designations as Cholera, Smallpox, Mortuary, Gallows, and Gaol.

In 1924 the club moved to its present site in Bukit Timah, seven miles from the center of the city. Under the expert eye of James Braid—who with Harry Vardon and J. H. Taylor formed the Great Triumvirate of British golf—18 holes were hacked through 275 acres of Malayan jungle. Another 18 holes were added six years later. Then, in 1963, the Singapore Island Country Club was founded in 1963 by the merger of the Royal Singapore Golf Club and the Royal Island Club. The club has all four courses in Singapore. They are: the Island Course, 18 holes, 6,470 yards, par 71; Bukit Course, 18 holes, 6,584 yards, par 71 (this was the famous "Old Course" of the Royal Singapore Golf Club); Sime Course, adjacent to the Bukit, 5,997 yards, 18 holes, par 68; and the recently added course designed by C. K.

Cotton & Company, 18 holes, 6,745 yards, par 72. Incidentally, tourists may use the facilities of the Singapore Island Country Club provided they are introduced by a member (most local hotel managers and travel agency managers are members).

The courses are generally considered to be among the most beautiful in Southeast Asia, with greens bordered by lush jungle vegetation. Although the land was once primitive jungle infested with cobras, monkeys, tigers, and wild boars, it looks today like an English park, largely because the course has been carefully planted with trees selected from the British Isles, giving the membership an Occidental retreat from the Oriental bustle of downtown Singapore. For instance, on the first, second, third, seventh, and eighth holes of the Bukit Course, which overlook a manmade lake known as MacRitchie Reservoir, the scene lacks only a nanny helping a four-year-old feed breadcrumbs to the ducks to take a Londoner back to a summer's day on the banks of the Thames.

The designers of all four courses made excellent use of a large water area and natural contours to test the skills and temperaments of the players. On the Island Course, the 460-yard, par-4 sixth hole is a good example. It plays from an elevated tee to a tight fairway sloping steeply to the left. The lake runs much of the way down the left side and there are trees on both sides of the fairway and a bunker in the middle. The green, guarded by left and right bunkers, is perched on a knoll, with the ground sloping to the left toward trees and the lake at the rear.

Because Singapore gets more than one hundred inches of rainfall a year, the fairways are rich and soft, and yardage on any shot must be got almost entirely by carry. You'd expect this to be true on the greens too, but actually, most of the greens have been built up in such a way that the putting surfaces are spread out, like wet sheets, purposely exposed to the equatorial sun. As a result, their subsurfaces have been broiled crisp. A pitch or a chip to a green often runs much farther than even the most perceptive player might imagine.

MALAYSIA

Scattered throughout Malaysia, within commuting distance of the larger cities, are some thirty golf courses. Of these, five are fine courses with full clubhouse facilities. All are private clubs but guests may be introduced as visitors if arrangements are made in advance through the secretaries of the various clubs. Golfing in Malaysia is year round.

The Royal Selangor Golf Club, outside Kuala Lumpur about 250 miles northwest of Singapore, is considered the best in Malaysia. It has a tropical complexion and a professional toughness. For example, the tee shot on the 542-yard, par-5 sixth must carry a row of grass mounds ironically named the Himalayas. Although the course is fairly flat, it is no pushover. Its heritage is the knowledge and love of golf brought east by Europeans who came to the Straits of Malacca for tin and rubber and tea.

The northern-bred player should note the grass. Chosen to stand up under year-round heat, it is stiff and sturdy, and gives up little roll. Distance off the tee is carry all the way.

Another note on distance: you do not drill a ball as far through the air in the tropics as you can in the Alps, the Rockies, or the Andes. Greens, reflecting the old school of design, are relatively small, interestingly shaped, and nicely guarded. The par-3 eighth, of 153 yards, requires an iron shot over a pond to a short narrow green on a rise between two bunkers. There is a sharp fall-away to more water behind and to the right. The green of the par-4 third, a narrow, T-shaped surface, practically sticks its tongue out at you from between two bunkers.

Trees also require careful aim. The drive on the 428-yard, par-4 tenth must needle through an aisle of trees in the tee-shot landing area. Hook your tee shot on the 378-yard, par-4 fourth and you will find a big rain tree on your line to the green. At Selangor the charm of the tropics joins the character of Western tradition to make golf a treat and golfers thoroughly at home.

Here are the fine courses you should consider if planning a trip to Malaysia:

LOCATION	COURSE	HOLES/PAR/ YARDAGE
Penang	Penang GC	9/36/3,150
Ipoh	Perak Turf & Sports C	18/73/6,418
Kuala Lumpur	Royal Selangor GC	9/35/2,954
Cameron Highlands	Tanah Rata GC	9/35/2,954
Pahang	Fraser's Hill GC	9/36/3,284
Malacca	Ayer Keroh GC	18/36/6,988

THAILAND

The growth of golf in Thailand over the past few years has been little short of phenomenal. In 1964, this country was accepted as a member of the Far East Golf Circuit; the sport has snowballed into becoming one of the most popular in the country, with more than three thousand active golfers using some dozen courses.

Thailand's courses are plush and rich in vegetation. Caddies are usually available (at some courses, caddies are girls). In addition to the regular caddie, most players have a forecaddie (who marks any ball hit into the water) and a "klong-boy" (who dives into the water to retrieve the ball). As in India, golf balls are scarce and labor is cheap. Also visitors should plan on supplying their own equipment as rental is difficult. Visitors will see six, seven, or more golfers playing together. Foursomes have priority, but larger groups, called "alligators," are allowed.

The best time for golf is the cold season, December through February, when temperatures are in the seventies and eighties, but humidity is low. March through May is the hot season and uncomfortable for golf except in the early morning or late afternoon. From June through October, monsoons prevent play.

The Royal Thai Air Force Club, laid out between the military and civil runways of the Don Muang Airport, and the Bank Pra Golf Course, a fairly new layout, are the only full-size 18-hole courses in the capital city of Bangkok. However, the most interesting is the par-66, 5,010-yard Royal Bangkok Sports Club. Weaving in and out of the club's racetrack, bordering cricket and field-hockey grounds, and veined with "klongs," or canals, this course has eight par-3 holes. While this mini-length course lacks size, the twenty-foot-wide klongs which came into play on nearly every hole, and the tee-to-green out-of-bounds pattern that tightened a number of fairways are tests of strategy as well as control.

Outside of Bangkok, the seaside resort at Hua Hin has a fine 18-hole golf course. Green fees are low at all Thai course and visitors are welcome as guests of members, usually easily arranged. The following courses are worth trying:

LOCATION	*COURSE*	*HOLES/PAR/ YARDAGE*
Bangkok	Bank Pra GC	18/72/7,070
Bangkok	Dusit GC	18/66/5,050

LOCATION	COURSE	HOLES/PAR/ YARDAGE
Bangkok	Royal Bangkok Sports C	18/66/5,010
Bangkok	Royal Thai Air Force GC	18/72/6,875
Bangphra	Bangphra GC	18/72/6,417
Hua Hin	Hua Hin GC	18/72/6,760

HONG KONG

Hong Kong has five golf courses of varying difficulty which attract visitors the year round. Of these, four are maintained by the Royal Hong Kong Golf Club, the other by Shek O Country Club.

Three of the Royal Hong Kong Golf Club courses are located at Franling (45 minutes from Hong Kong) in the New Territories and are set among green rolling hills. Their lengths are as follows: Old Course, 18 holes, par 72, 6,378 yards; New Course, 18 holes, par 71, 6,324 yards; Eden Course, 9 holes, par 35, 2,226 yards.

Shek O Country Club at Shek O (across the island from Victoria) on Hong Kong Island is an 18-hole mini-course of 5,120 yards, par 65, and is beautifully sited on the headland between two beaches. The Royal Hong Kong Golf Club's Deep Water Bay course is a 9-hole, 2,200-yard layout also located on Hong Kong Island. A visitor golfer is welcomed at all Hong Kong's facilities if he is introduced by a member or carries a letter of introduction from the secretary of a golf club which has reciprocal arrangements with the Royal Hong Kong Club.

All of Hong Kong's courses are good despite the fact that they are difficult to maintain in Hong Kong's variable climate. Courses are maintained entirely by hand by groups of local women; to complicate the problem, cattle are allowed by law to graze at will over the courses. Local rules permit the golfer to smooth out hoofprints before he putts.

Speaking of the greens, most are planted in Gezira grass from Egypt and can be rather difficult to putt on. In addition, during the summer months they are apt to become patchy and too hard to hold approach shots. Actually, only a small circle around the hole is manicured to the perfection usually expected of the entire putting surface. Fairways are wide and there is little trouble from the tee, although if the golfer ventures too far off in the rough, he is likely to find ancient Chinese burial sites.

For the golfer the best time to visit Hong Kong is from September to March, when the courses are in their best condition and the temperature is in the mid-seventies.

TAIWAN

Taiwan's best course is the Taiwan Golf & Country Club at Tamsue near Taipei. The course, one of the oldest and best in the Orient, is site of the China Open, one of the events in the Far East golf circuit. This 18-hole, par-72, 6,684-yard layout is open to visitors without advance arrangements or starting time. Green fees and caddie rates are low, but no clubs are available for rental. However, a set can usually be found for the visitor.

Other fine courses in the Taipei area include: Paipei Golf Club, not far from downtown Taipei, 9 holes, 3,200 yards, par 72; new Linkou International Golf Club, 18 miles north of Taipei, 18 holes, 7,150 yards, par 72, overlooking Taiwan Strait.

Elsewhere in Taiwan you wish to try one of the following good courses: Feng Yuan Golf Club at Feng Yuan, 13 miles from Taichung, 9 holes; Tsoying Navy Golf Club, 9 holes; Kaohsiung Golf Club, 18 holes, 6,500 yards, par 72.

KOREA

Korea has two fine 18-hole golf courses for visitors, one in Seoul and the other in Pusan. The Seoul Country Club, on the outskirts of Seoul adjacent to the Walker Hill Resort, is an 18-hole, 6,855-yard, par-72 layout. Visitors are welcome at all times on this scenic, hilly course.

The Pusan Country Club at Haeundae Beach, about 12 miles east of Pusan, is near the resort area of Tongnae Hot Spring and is a good 18-hole, 6,175-yard, par-72 layout. Visitors are welcome. Remember that the best time for play in Korea is from spring to autumn.

JAPAN

The first golf course in Japan was built in 1901 by Arthur Groom, a British tea merchant. It was a private four-hole course on Mt. Rokko, in back of the bustling port city of Kobe. Groom invited friends of the foreign community to join him in games. As more foreigners from the international port used the course, it became too small. On February 27, 1903, the Kobe Golf Club, the first golf club in Japan, was formed by these foreigners and Groom's course was formally opened as an expanded 9-hole layout. The greens were of sand with a gutter around them to prevent the ball from falling off. In October 1904, the course was expanded to 3,576 yards and 18 holes. It had a "bogey" of 78. In those days, a bogey was a term initiated by the English and meant a score that an ordinary player might shoot, depending on conditions.

At that time there were no cable cars up Mt. Rokko. The players were carried up the mountain from Kobe by porters bearing litters. The devotion of the foreigners to the game astounded the natives. Kanichi Nishimura wrote in his history of the sport in Japan: "The Occidentals played this strange game in rain and sunshine, in cold and heat, in complete engrossment. Seeing this, one could only suppose that the play was for gain. They were probably betting."

For years, the game was confined to foreigners. In 1946 there were

Devotees of golf in Japan find this three-tiered driving range to their liking. The unique range is located in the heart of midtown Tokyo on the grounds of a Buddhist temple. Each platform has fifty stations.

only 17 courses in operation. Today there are 619 courses and some three million players. The game's boom can be traced to Japan's victory in the Canada Cup in 1957 at Kasumigaseki. At that time, there were only one hundred courses in the country. When little Pete Nakamura and Koichi Ono defeated America's Sam Snead and Jimmy Demaret as well as the stars of some thirty other nations, interest skyrocketed. It was actually an Oriental version of Ouimet's triumph at Brookline. But, whereas Ouimet's victory popularized the game in America among the midddle classes, the boom in Japan has remained confined largely to wealthy business men and politicians.

Of the over six hundred existing courses, only about 10 per cent are open to the general public. Their rates are fairly high. However, the public interest is being whetted by driving ranges, and municipal authorities may find it necessary to provide additional public facilities. There are seven hundred driving ranges in Tokyo alone, some with as many as three tiers.

Except for Britain, Japan has more golf facilities than any country of comparable size. Some 129 courses are accessible in one or two hours by car from the center of Tokyo, and about 80 courses are located in the Kyoto-Osaka area. All of the courses are laid out according to regulations and there are none in finer condition on any continent. One of the major reasons for the excellent condition is the exceptional care taken by the girl caddies. These efficient girls not only replace divots, but carefully reseed them from small bags they carry. Caddie fees are very low.

The visiting golfer is welcome at all times almost everywhere and arrangements can readily be made by the hotel management. If he wishes to go further afield, the local Japan National Tourist Organization will help to make arrangements. Some clubs restrict the number of guests on weekends and holidays and others require introduction by a member, but the welcome mat really is out in Japan and the season is year-round.

As the golf fever has spread, a new industry has grown in the manufacturing of golfing equipment and wearing apparel. The golfing tourist no longer will find it necessary to tote along his heavy equipment, for all his requirements can be easily filled and at relatively low rental cost. Lunch is served at most clubs, and tipping, where it is permitted, is modest. It is wise to check with the manager before dealing out gratuities.

A typical example of the rate of growth of the game is the membership at the Kasumigaseki Country Club, a pine-studded, 36-hole course situated in Kawagoe, just outside of Tokyo. Twenty-five years ago membership at Kasumigaseki numbered 250. Today, it is only one of many courses in the Tokyo vicinity with a membership of well over 2,000. This championship layout has a par 72 on both the East course, stretching 6,913 yards, and the West course, measuring 6,590 yards. The greens are composed of korai grass, similar to but coarser than Bermuda and requiring a more solid whack when putting. Incidentally, most Japanese courses have two greens on each hole, which may be alternated at any time.

Ninety miles north of Tokyo in the city of Nikko, one may enjoy the natural beauty of the Nikko Country Club, an extensive 18-hole, par-72 private course located on the Daiya River. The city is just a two-hour trip from Tokyo by Japanese National Railways, on the newly introduced electric train, "Nikko." The course can be reached in ten minutes by car from Nikko Station. Nikko City is situated in the heart

The Fuji Course at Kawana is one of Japan's most difficult. Note the size of the green.

KAWANA OSHIMA COURSE

COMPETITION   PLAYER

HOLE NO.	He'p	NAME	YARDS	PAR					+ − ○
1	7	KUMAGAI'S ADVENTURE	354	4					
2	17	TAMETOMO PROMENADE	199	3					
3	1	KAIGAN-DORI	373	4					
4	5	GOOD-BYE	351	4					
5	13	MIKAERI-ZAKA	262	4					
6	15	S. O. S.	147	3					
7	9	OHTANI'S SMILE	282	4					
8	3	OCHUDO-MAWARI	464	5					
9	11	TOKAIDO	408	4					
OUT			2840	35					
10	14	TERRACE	380	4					
11	2	LINKS LAND	363	4					
12	4	NORTH COL	360	4					
13	12	VENI VIDI VICI	286	4					
14	18	TWIN	117	3					
15	8	HODOGAYA	330	4					
16	16	JIGOKU-DANI	180	3					
17	6	CHAMPSELY-SEES	494	5					
18	10	W. &. D.	361	4					
IN			2871	35					
TOTAL			5711	70					
			HANDICAP						
			NET SCORE						

6 INCHES

LEVEL SAND IN BUNKER

DATE

PLEASE REPLACE DIVOTS

ATTESTED BY

The scorecard for Oshima Course (*above*) and local rules for the Fuji Course (*opposite*).

of Nikko National Park, the most famous of Japan's tourist resorts. Scores of spas throughout the park, each surrounded by lovely scenery, have a plentiful supply of hot mineral water, fine accommodations and well-developed modern facilities. They have become favorite stopping places for visitors.

ローカル・ルールス（富士コース）

一　アウトオブバウンヅの境界は白杭にて標示す。

二　ペナルテイ無くして球を拾い上げ得る場合
　　イ　球が境界棚・境界石標・梯子段・杭・切株・砂入・溝・道路
　　　　垣根・金網・岩・モグラの揚土・又は穴・水道栓等に接近し
　　　　て其の距離一クラブレングス以内なる時は球を拾い上げて、
　　　　之を二クラブレングス以内にドロップする事を得。
　　ロ　グリーン上に限り球を拾い上げて、球に附着せる泥等を拭い
　　　　再び原位置に置く事を得。
　　ハ　球が樹上に止り地上よりの高さ一クラブレングス以上なれば
　　　　其の樹の根元より二クラブレングス以内にドロップする事を
　　　　得。（但し一ストロークの罰打を課す）

LOCAL RULES (Fuji Course)

1. The boarder lines for "Out of Bounds" are marked by white posts.

2. In the following cases the ball may be lifted without penalties :
   a. A ball lying within one club length against the boundary fence or stone, road, draining pit, wire-netting, heap of soil done by the mole, hole, water taps, rock, etc., may be lifted and dropped within two club lengths at the side of the green and not nearer the hole.
   b. A ball on putting green may be lifted, cleaned and replaced on the same spot.
   c. A ball lodged in a tree over than one club length may be lifted and dropped within two club lengths from the tree not nearer the hole. Penalty in this case is one stroke.

KAWANA
Fuji Course

Kawana Hotel
Tel Ito 37-3191

The Aobayama Golf Course, a tree-lined, 18-hole public layout, is ten minutes from Sendai Station, in Sendai city, the cultural center of the island of Honshu. Though over two hundred miles from Tokyo, the distance is covered in less than five hours by limited express train. Aobayama has a par 72 for 6,820 yards. It is interesting to note that although the Japanese are mostly short hitters, they like their courses long. The average course in Japan averages a little under 7,000 yards in length, compared with a little over 6,400 yards in America. In addition, the heavy fairway turf on most Japanese courses discourages bounce and roll and makes them play even longer.

On Hokkaido, northernmost of the four main islands of Japan, is the Sapporo Golf Club, a well-conditioned 18-hole, 7,100-yard layout with a par 72. This private course is located in the educational and commercial center of the island, Sapporo, a comparatively new city easily reached by train, ferryboat or plane. The course has bent-grass fairways and greens of Kentucky blue grass; thus, play is similar to those in major portions of the United States.

Two hours to the south of Tokyo is the famous Kawana Golf Club.

The twin layouts here were built in a pine forest overlooking Sagami Bay. The flat light coming off the water, accentuating the shapes and patterns of the trees, creates a scene resembling a delicate painting.

On the championship Fuji Course, the fairways tumble and roll from a procession of steeply elevated tees, and they have the manicured look of only the best-maintained golf courses. Wiry-textured korai grass, a species of amazing durability, makes it almost impossible to get a bad lie in the fairways, while making it imperative that you stroke your putts firmly into the back of the cup on the greens. The thick-tufted grass allows for no leeway at all around the hole. This course is 6,970 yards long and plays to a par 70.

The Oskima Course at Kawana has a par 70 for 6,662. Golf at Kawana came about by accident. A little more than 35 years ago, Kishichiro Okura, a prominent Japanese businessman, decided he wanted a meadow built on some land he owned in the Kawana-Lto area. The man he hired to build his meadow told him that the sub-surface predominantly of lava made it more suitable for a golf course than for a meadow. Mr. Okura accepted the remark as whimsy. But when he returned to his property about a year later, he found that a golf course had been laid out. The explanation of the man in charge was right to the point: "The whole ground was unsuitable for a meadow," he explained, "and I let myself make a golf course." Thus was born the Oshima Course. The Fuji Course was built in 1936, after Mr. Okura decided that as long as he was going to have a golf course, he might as well have one that offered a view of his beloved Mt. Fuji. The two courses at Kawana, then, remain his legacy to Japan, which now has more golfers in relation to population than any other country in the world.

For those interested in the relics of the civilization of old Japan, Kyoto is a city rich in historic associations and legendary lore. It was the capital of the country for more than ten centuries and its imposing shrines, temples, and palaces with elaborately designed gardens remind visitors of the glory and splendor of days long past. Within a short driving distance of the city are four outstanding membership courses.

The Tanabe Country Club is a top 18-hole, 6,677-yard layout with a par 70. The Joyo Country Club and the Kyoto Golf Club, are both 36-hole courses easily reached by auto within a half-hour from Kyoto Station. Joyo's East course is a challenging par 72, 7,131 yards, and the West course is par 70 for 6,162 yards. The East course at Kyoto is 6,015 yards for a par 68, and the West course measures 5,200 yards for a par 66.

Iboraki Country Club is also not far from Kyoto. This club has a very demanding course, 6,638 yards long, par 72. Trees, hills, and water provide the basic challenges. Delicately silhouetted pines or full stands of woods reach out to increase the penalty of errant shots. Fairways slant, twist, climb, and roll. Water comes into play on several holes, testing ability and creating picture-postcard scenes. Manmade features are expertly blended with terrain. Bunkers thoughtfully placed and artfully shaped, serve especially well in defining greens and nowhere better than on the 156-yard, par-3 fifteenth. Good planting and grading enhance topography. The course is impeccably kept in the best tradition of Japanese gardening.

For an exciting test and exquisite view, it is hard to beat Ibaraki's 498-yard, par-5 fifth. The line off the tee is a huge aluminum ball topped by a needlelike spire, a monument to war dead. At 225 yards the fairway dives toward a green protected on the left and front by bunkers, on the right by a lake, and to the rear by trees.

The eighteenth, a par 4 of 464 yards, ranks among the best finishing holes in Asia. The drive should cut the corner of a pond that lines the left side of the fairway to three hundred yards. The second shot must cope with bunkers on the right and, beyond them, another pond.

The following courses are all 18-hole layouts. They are listed by the name of the club; the city it is in; then the general area; yardage/par; and whether it is public (p), semiprivate, (sp), or membership (m). Although there are often restrictions in the membership clubs on weekends and holidays, visitors may be able to play on other days. In some cases, it may be necessary that the visitor be accompanied by a member. Here are the most challenging courses that you can play in Japan:

Sopporo GC, Sopporo city, Hokkaido, 7100/72 (m)
Aobayama GC, Sendai city, Miyagi Pref., 6820/72 (p)
Hanno GC, Hanno, Saitama Pref., 7135/73 (m)
Kasumigaseki CC, Kawagoe city, Saitama Pref., 6913/72, 6590/ 72 (m)
Musashi CC, Musashi, Saitama, 6735/72 (m)
Sayama GC, Iruma-gun, Saitama, 7060/72 (m)
Tokyo GC, Sayama, 6805/72 (m)

Takasaka CC, Higashi-matsuyama city, Saitama Pref., 6740/72, 3410/36, (m)
Ukima Golf Links, Kawaguchi city, Saitama Pref., 6700/72 (p)
Abiko GC, Abiko, Chiba Pref., 6690/72 (m)
Chiba CC, Noda, Chiba Pref., 6940/72 (m)
Keiyo Kokusai CC, Chiba-gun, Chiba Pref., 7005/72 (m)
Sodegaura CC, Chiba Pref., 7050/72, (m)
Takanodai CC, Chiba, Chiba Pref., 7070/72 (m)
Fuchu CC, Minamitama-gun, Tokyo, 6470/72 (m)
Hachioji CC, Hachioji, Tokyo, 6880/72 (m)
Koganei CC, Kitatama-gun, Tokyo, 6755/72 (m)
Sakuragooka CC, Minamitama-gun, Tokyo, 6760/73 (m)
Tokyo Tomin GC Fuji Course, Adachi-ku, Tokyo, 5430/67 (sp)
Daihakone CC, Hakone Sengokubara, Kanagowa Pref., 7123/73 (m)
Hakone CC, Hakone Sengokubara, Kanagawa Pref., 7100/73 (m)
Hodogaya CC, Hodogaya, Yokohama city, Kanagawa Pref., 6724/72 (m)
Kawasaki Kokusai CC, Kawasaki city, Kanagawa Pref., 6495/72 (m)
Sagamihara GC, Sagamihara city, Kanagawa Pref., 7255/74, 6805/71 (m)
Nasu GC, Nasu, Tochigi Pref., 6650/72 (m)
Nikko CC, Nikko, Tochigi Pref., 6995/72 (m)
Oarai GC, Oarai, Ibaraki Pref., 7190/72 (m)
Otone CC, Sarujima-gun, Ibaraki Pres., 6718/72, 6397/72 (m)
Ryugasaki CC, Ryugasaki city, Ibaraki Pref., 7012/72 (m)
Ota GC, Ota City, Gumma Perf., 6877/72 (p)
Karuizawa GC, Karuizawa, Nagano Pref., 6890/72 (m)
Fuji CC, Gotemba, Shizuoka Pref., 6970/72 (m)
Kawana Hotel GC, Ito city, Shizuoke Pref., 5711/70, 6691/72 (p)
Aichi CC, Nagoya city, Aichi Pref., 7150/74 (m)
Forest Park Golf Assoc., Higashikasugai-gun, Aichi Pref., 7005/72 (p)
Miyoshi CC, Nishikamo-gun, Aichi, 7030/72 (m)
Nagoya GC, Nagoya, Aichi Pref., 6550/70 (m)
Nara Kokusai GC, Nara, Nara Pref., 7155/72 (m)
Joyo CC, Kuse-gun, Kyoto, 7131/72, 6162/70 (m)

Tanabe CC, Tsuzuki-gun, Kyoto, 6677/70, (m)
Ibaraki CC, Ibaraki, Osaka, 6756/72, 6950/72 (m)
Osaka GC, Sennan-gun, Osaka, 6435/72 (m)
Takatsuki GC, Takusuki, Osaka, 6000/72 (sp)
Ashiya CC, Ashika, Hyogo Pref., 6520/72 (m)
Hirono GC, Miki, Hyogo Pref., 6950/72 (m)
Kakogawa GC, Kakogawa city, Hyogo Pref., 6294/72 (m)
Naruo GC, Kawanishi, Hyogo, 6875/70 (m)
Nishinomiya CC, Nishinomiya, Hyogo, 6630/72 (m)
Takarazuka GC, Takarazuka city, Hyogo Pref., 6393/72, 6613/
    72 (m)
Fukuoka CC, Fukuoka, Fukuoka, 6700/72 (m)
Koga GC, Kasuya-gun, Fukuoka, 6790/72 (m)
Moji GC, Moji, Fukuoka Pref., 6700/72 (m)
Wakamatsu GC, Wakamatsu, 6700/72 (m)

Okinawa. The Okinawa Country Club in the suburbs twenty minutes from Naha City, is operated by the New Okinawa Tourism Development Company and is open to visiting golfers the year around. The course has 9 holes, 3,085 yards, and a par 35. Visitors are welcome and have all the privileges of the club. Okinawa also has three military courses on which guests of military personnel members may play.

PHILIPPINES

Although golf has been played in the Philippines for more than sixty years, it has become a game of national concern only since the end of World War II. Before the war, the country had only five courses. Today, it sports 46 and has half a dozen others on the drawing boards. The enthusiasm of the Filipinos for the game is perhaps matched only by those who play the game over the "public links" near major American cities.

One of the most beautiful courses in the Pacific is the Wack-Wack Golf and Country Club, about a half-hour drive from Manila. But a this club members often arrive at the club at four o'clock in the morning on weekends to await their starting times at one of the club's two courses, the East and the West. By half past five it is not uncommon to have two hundred members eating breakfast in the dining room as the sun peeks over the horizon.

The East Course at Wack-Wack may not be the longest course in the world, although it is long enough, and it may not be the toughest, although it is tough enough, but it can easily lay claim to being the wettest. It is laid out over land that was formerly used as rice paddies. Creeks, which zigzag throughout the entire area, come into play on 13 different holes. On three other holes are artificial ponds, leaving a grand total of only two holes free of water hazards. To contribute to the dampness, the course is often subjected to rainstorms of monsoon proportions. At this time, the fairways are as thick as glue underfoot, and the heavily matted Egyptian grass on the greens has the consistency of chewing gum. Like the Augusta National, Wack-Wack gets its championship qualities not from the narrowness of its fairways—which, in point of fact, are very wide—but from the strategy that is needed in skirting its labyrinthine groves of trees and approaching its wisely trapped greens, some of which are banked so steeply that it is not uncommon to find several inches of break on a putt that is only two feet long.

The Philippines' second important course is the Manila Golf Club. This par-70 course in the heart of Manila plays at only 6,238 yards but is a difficult test, with rather severe bunkering, both in the fairways and around the greens, and many wasp-waisted driving holes. Sloping greens, heavy bunkering, and difficult pin placements test the players' putting skills and the delicacy of their chips and pitches. The wind can require some thoughtful selection of clubs.

The 341-yard, par-4 twelfth hole is typical of this challenging layout. The drive is from a slightly elevated tee, with out-of-bounds all the way down the right side. On the left side, cutting into the fairway at the length the players drive, is a deep depression with a big tree growing out of the middle. Farther left, the fairway falls away into a barranca and a stream. The pin placement is on the right front of the green, guarded by a bunker.

An hour's drive from Manila and another five minutes along a winding private road take you to the Valley Golf Club—and one contrast after another. The encompassing bowl of the Marikina Mountains is dry and scrub-covered. The course is an oasis of grass and quiet water. The elegantly modern clubhouse is built of glass and concrete. Its roof sweeps up with the line of a native thatch. Greens, which look like velvet and putt mathematically true, are done in grass imported from the Champions Club at Houston, Texas. They are groomed by native women.

Only first-rate golf makes par 72 on these formidable 7,054 yards. Yet the effort is a joy. The clubhouse stands invitingly in sight from most of the holes. Service bars offer welcome breaks at several points along the course. The architect studied the topography and used it well. High tees give views of doglegging, boldly banked fairways bordered and crossed by water. The tenth stands above a fairway that banks right-to-left and doglegs the same direction. To the left are trees and, beyond them, swamp and open water. To the right a bunker at 260 yards makes precision off the tee essential. Great sinuous bunkers, knowingly placed, are lined with gray sand almost as coarse as gravel. The coarseness resists packing under the downpours of the rainy season; it also demands close attention from the player. And the color contrasts dramatically with the green. The Philippines have taken to golf with a zeal unsurpassed even in Japan. The Valley Golf Club concentrates eagerly on the game and every delight it offers. Even the water tower is shaped like a ball on a tee.

For play, the best months are June through December. It is usually no problem for the visiting golfer to play the Philippines' courses. The following are top courses for you to play while there:

LOCATION	COURSE	HOLES/PAR/ YARDAGE
Antipolo	Valley GC	18/72/7,054
Manila	Manila GC	18/70/6,138
Mandaluyong	Wack-Wack G & CC	18/72/6,872
		18/71/6,386
Makati	Fort Bonifano GC	18/72/6,445

FIJI

Golf has been played in Fiji for more than sixty years and there is a fine series of 9-hole (18-tee) courses conveniently sited around the main island of Viti Levu and on Vanua Levu. The Fiji climate is suitable for year around golf—the driest period and the best for golfers is usually from June to October—and green and caddy fees are very low.

All clubs welcome visitors and a letter of introduction from the secretary of a golfer's home club usually is enough to ensure full privileges.

LOCATION	COURSE	HOLES/PAR/ YARDAGE
Suva	Fiji GC	18/72/6,245
Nadi	Airport GC	9/71/6,066 (18 tees)
Lautoka	Lautoka GC	9/69/5,464 (18 tees)
Nadi	Ba GC	9/69/5,701 (18 tees)
Vatukoula	Vatukoula	9/69/5,600 (18 tees)
Lambasa	Lambasa	9/69/5,675 (18 tees)

INDONESIA

Covering an area as large as the European continent or the United States, a string of three thousand islands big and small extends across the waters connecting the great Pacific and Indian oceans, between Australia and the Malay Peninsula, in the form of a huge arc along the Equator; this is Indonesia. But this large land mass has only twenty courses, of which only five have 18 holes.

While the courses of Indonesia don't reach the high standard of some of their counterparts in Thailand, the Philippines, Singapore, and Malaysia, they are interesting and can be quite testing. The Djakarta and Senajan Golf Clubs—both in Djakarta—and the Jani Golf Club in Surabaya can give your golfing skills a good workout.

OTHER FAR EAST AREAS

Other Pacific and Far East countries with limited facilities for the visiting golfer include Guam, Nepal, Tonga, Western Sama, Tahiti, Sri Lanka (formerly Ceylon), and Pakistan.

The Windward Hills Golf Course is the only nonmilitary course on the island of Guam, and has 18 holes which will challenge anyone's ability. It is a privately owned club and no more than a thirty-minute drive from downtown Agana. It is almost never crowded, and has an airport for small planes within walking distance of the clubhouse. All golfers are welcome and the charges are nominal.

Royal Nepal Golf Club, Nepal's only golf course, is built on a ragged plateau outside Bhotahiti, Katmandu. The 9-hole course has a par 32 but newcomers to the 1,900-yard links sometimes are lucky to finish in the 90's. The fairway consists of a canyon with natural traps and ravine-type hazards some fifty feet deep. Green fees and caddie rates are nominal and the course is always available to visitors, but members have priority on competition days.

The Tahiti Country Club is a par-72, 6,250-yard course which is only slightly hilly. The greens and fairways have been entirely planted with seed from the Hawaiian Islands and are lush and true. There is a river running through the course and two artificial lakes have been formed. The largest of the lakes is the practice driving range; floating golf balls are used. The natural vegetation provides some challenging rough and three of the holes are bordered by grapefruit trees. Pros who have played the course describe it as fair and say that it keeps you honest at all times.

Tonga's 9-hole golf course (par 34) in Nukulalofa is located in the royal burial grounds inside the city. Western Samoa's Apia Golf Club, three miles from Apia, has a well-kept 18-hole course which is open to visitors if arrangements are made in advance through the secretary.

The golf course at the Tahiti Country Club (Atimanono Golf Club) is 18 holes, 6,950 yards, with a par 72. Situated along a picturesque blue lagoon, the rolling fairways are lined with lush grapefruit trees, spotted with small lakes, and vibrantly colored tropical flowers flourish everywhere. While Atimanono is not the toughest, trickiest, or longest course in the world, it has to be one of the most beautiful.

In Sri Lanka, there is the famed Royal Colombo Golf Club, in Colombo, a championship layout of 18 holes, 6,286 yards, par 70. In addition to this excellent course, there are two 9-hole layouts at Colombo (Havelock Golf Club) and at Nuwara (Eliya Golf Club) that are available for visiting golfers.

In West Pakistan, several of the leading cities—Karachi, Rawalpindi-Islamabad, Lahore—have small golf courses, but on the whole most of them do not rate too highly.

20

AUSTRALIA AND NEW ZEALAND

If you are prepared to negotiate such uncommon hazards as stray kangaroos, steaming thermal blowholes, and sheep on the fairway, on some of the world's best championship layouts, go to Australia and New Zealand.

Tucked away Down Under in the South Pacific, they are becoming two of the hottest stops on the tourist trail and are more accessible each year as airlines and steamship companies step up their services. Here, in a temperate climate that allows year-round play, golfing tourists can be assured of a warm welcome, greens and service fees so low as to be almost nominal, and a selection of courses bristling with excitement and good golf. Golf, in both countries, has long been a leading sport and the number of players that tee-off each Saturday and Sunday in quest of the elusive par is impressive.

The most notable contrast in comparing American–New Zealand–Australian golf, however, is the number of players in the latter countries that belong to private clubs. The public courses are fairly crowded, but most of their clientele are absolute beginners, and once a player can break one hundred, he generally seeks membership in a club. Annual membership subscriptions are low, ranging from around $30 to a little over $150 a year.

AUSTRALIA

All major Australian courses are playable the year round, for Australia is in the same latitude (10–40 degrees south) as South Africa and mid-South America. Brisbane is best during April to October, while on the southern coast, springtime (September to November) and autumn (March to May), when daytime temperatures seldom exceed the mid-70's, are recommended. May and September may be rainy.

Golf is a good way to meet and mix with Australians, because despite the current following for the champions, most Australians still play for pleasure. There is a sociability about the game Down Under

that seems to suit the local temperament. Hospitality is always assured. Australians always try, and usually succeed, in making fellow
golfers from overseas feel as if they have never left their home links.

Public courses are usually available, but it is wise to book a starting
time, because the public courses in the capital cities handle an aston-

Australia's symbol, the kangaroo, rubs shoulders with golfers in Victoria.
The animals live in a wild state in the coastal bush country around the course
and feed on the appetizing green grass on the fairways, unperturbed by golfers
playing past them. Humans can approach to within a few feet before the
animals hop away—and then only a few feet.

ishing amount of traffic. For example, Melbourne's Yarra Bend and Sydney's Moore Park average three thousand rounds of golf each week, and often report more than five hundred rounds daily. Residential or country clubs will quote a tariff on presentation of a visiting golfer's membership credentials, and some will require a letter of introduction from the home club, especially leading clubs like Royal Melbourne and Royal Sydney. It is wise to check with the club secretary or even to write ahead to avoid disappointment. But even without the proper credentials, golfers will find many outstanding public courses to enjoy. Clubs, buggies, golf shoes, balls, and lockers may be hired at public as well as private courses. Many public courses have showers, and some have restaurant and bar facilities, though these are usually only available at private clubs.

Australian courses range from the immaculate sandbelt courses of Melbourne to the slag-heap greens of mining towns like Port Pirie, from Bourke (Western, New South Wales), where six-foot-deep cracks open up during droughts, to oiled sand greens. Ashes, sand, even metal dust are used as playing surfaces in some areas where there is little or no natural grass cover.

Hazards include crows, rabbits, kangaroos, water buffalo, and even crocodiles. Australian courses also boast such distractions as lyrebirds and bowerbirds nesting in secluded scrub near fairways, and kangaroos, including one friendly fellow at Melbourne's Kingston Heath who obligingly stands motionless when shots are being played. Golf clubs may be found from northern tropical Queensland, where fairways may be lined by fragrant hibiscus and frangipani shrubs and fruit-laden banana, mango, and pawpaw trees, to the attractive country mountain areas of southeast Australia, where the fairways are tightly bounded by great eucalyptus and thick bush that spells disaster for a straying ball. As a rule, roughs are thick, much coarser than those found in the United States. Greens on courses in the metropolitan areas generally use bent grass and it is usually cut quite close so that even the longest putt will travel a true line. Outside of the metropolitan regions, many of the courses use sand. Sometimes the sand is rolled to provide a flat putting surface; in other instances it is mixed with oil to offer a very slick surface.

Golfers planning a systematic tour of Australia's courses have one *big* decision to make—whether to begin or end their stay by playing the famous sand-belt courses near Melbourne. One of America's leading tour pros, after visiting Melbourne recently, summed matters up by saying that Melbourne was the "city with more golf widows than any other in the world."

On the ten-mile stretch of sand just outside Melbourne there is Royal Melbourne, Metropolitan, the Commonwealth, the Victoria Heath, Woodlands, and Huntingdale. All are magnificent year-round, 18-hole courses that require a minimum of effort to keep in first-class condition. Probably the most difficult is the 6,456-yard, par-73 West course at Royal Melbourne, whose spacious bunkers have made more than one international player wish he had never heard the word "sand." Royal Melbourne also has a par-74, 6,546-yard East course and full clubhouse facilities.

The Victoria is a par-73, 6,665-yard layout that has dense rough calling for extreme accuracy off the tee. Lining the fairways at the Commonwealth, a 6,616-yard test, are gum trees, Australia's own eucalyptus. These tall trees, bearing hard nuts and scraggy bark look

The fifth tee at the Royal Melbourne Golf Club. The course has no water hazards, but formidable bunkers keep golfers wary.

A golf match at the Koojonga course in South Australia. Eucalyptus trees are the typical course vegetation in this region.

most impressive, and in spite of the absence of lower limbs and foliage, can cost strokes if you tangle with them. The Kingston Heath is a championship course with first-class amenities. It is a par 74, 6,807 yards.

Apart from the "big four"—Royal Melbourne, Kingston Heath, Victoria, and Commonwealth—there are others like Yarra Yarra, Riversdale, and further down the coast, Peninsula and Patterson River (both exclusive residential country clubs), and Long Island. Among the newer courses are Keysborough (set in a particularly attractive bushland setting), Cranbourne, and Southern.

If Melbourne lays claim to the title of Australia's golfing capital, Sydney, the largest city, with a population of two and a half million, has the most golfers. To accommodate them, there are numerous private and public courses, many with magnificent views of the city's justly famous harbor. One of the best private courses in the Royal Sydney at Rose Bay on the Harbor. Founded in 1893, it has a sand base and a testing 72-par, 6,651-yard layout. Alongside the main course is a subsidiary 9-hole test.

Eleven miles southeast of Sydney on the coast at La Perouse is the New South Wales. This 6,667-yard, links-type course is set right on the sea, and cliffside holes, exposed to the winds that sweep in from the Pacific, make for a challenging test. Some of the La Perouse holes provide shot-making as thrilling as anything in the world. For example, a short outward hole where the player can look down from the tee at huge Pacific breakers rolling over an old wrecked hull on jagged rocks. On the short seventeenth, an 8-iron will get you onto the green on occasions while at other times, a full-blooded driver shot is held up by a gale and falls short. Another unique feature of the course is that the four par 3's face each of the four main directions of the compass. Other courses in Sydney are the Australian at Kensington, one of Australia's oldest clubs, and The Lake at Kingsford, where no fewer than ten of the course's 18 holes are bordered by natural lakes.

Adelaide's neat square mile of city area is surrounded by a 1,700-acre parkland that includes three public courses—a 9-holer and two 18-holers, which allow businessmen to play an early round before going to the office. But the two best courses in this region are the Royal Adelaide and Koojonga, both ranking with the best in the country, with a combination of seaside and inland characteristics.

Perth's smaller population is well endowed by such courses as the Royal Perth, Cottesloe, Lake Karrinyup, and nearby Royal Fremantle.

In Brisbane, the Royal Queensland course, situated at Eagle Farms, with its swaying palms lining each fairway, lends a tropical appearance, and coarse grass greens provide true putting surfaces. Some holes of this 74-par, 6,784-yard course run alongside the Brisbane River, and the golfer can pause to watch passing ships. The city's other main club, which goes by the wonderful name of Yerongpilly, was founded in 1896 and has a par-73, 6,613-yard layout on undulating ground.

Now comes the test of a real golfer in Australia. Almost due west of Brisbane, in the heart of the great Australian desert, is legendary Alice Springs, the jumping-off place for tourists visiting massive Ayers Rock, some three hundred miles further west. Water, to put it mildly, is scarce in Alice. Rain for most of the year is unknown. Golfers, however, are determined people, and a full-size course has been built out of desert. Grass is the only missing ingredient. Hazards are rocky outcrops, while the greens are sand, liberally mixed with oil to keep it from blowing away.

Rivaling Alice Springs in overcoming adversity is the course in Cook, midway between Adelaide and Kalgoorlie on the Nullabor Plain. Many of the nine holes are stretched to incredible distances— they have to be, as the average drive on the rock-hard ground is around five hundred yards. The greens are sand, of course, and the traps are surrounded by sheets of corrugated iron to keep them from blowing away. To add to these distractions, the caddies do not wear a stitch of clothing—they are Aborigines, million-year inhabitants of Australia's interior.

Members of the golf club at Port Hedland in the tropical iron-rich Pilbara district of Western Australia, 1,300 miles north of Perth, believe their links is probably the worst in the world. For most of the year their 9-hole course shows a dead flat surface of rocky, cracked, iron-hard earth covered with spinifex. During the mid-summer cyclones it becomes a red steaming quagmire. Par for the course is 71. The members, keen golfers all, display great affection for their do-it-yourself links.

Golf is even played on the islands of the Great Barrier Reef. For example, South Molle Island (linked by air with the Queensland mainland) has a 6-hole course which is the site of an annual Tropical Golf Tee-Off, with a cash purse for professionals. This year's tournament, which included a pro-amateur championship, offered water-skiing, skindiving, and beach barbecues as unusual fringe attractions for competitors.

Away from the big cities there are many courses in Australia that come close to matching city standards—for example, in Horsham, Victoria, and Orange, New South Wales—both readily accessible to the visitor. However, the following courses are considered the most challenging in Australia:

COURSE	HOLES/PAR/ YARDAGE	DESCRIPTION
Australian Kensington	18/72/6,667	Founded 1882—one of Australia's oldest clubs. Treeless, suburban layout. Subsidiary 9-hole course.
Royal Sydney Rose Bay	18/72/6,651	Founded 1893. Testing course overlooking Sydney harbor. Sand-based. Subsidiary 9-hole course.
New South Wales La Perouse	18/72/6,667	Challenging, links-type course, with testing, cliffside holes, rugged winds. Four par-3's face each direction of the compass.
The Lakes Kingsford	18/72/6,618	Features include par 3, 355 yards. 16th with double water carry. Automatic watering. Subsidiary 18-hole (par 72, 6,492 yards).
VICTORIA		
Royal Melbourne Black Rock	36/E 74/6,546 W 73/6,456	Founded 1891. Undulating, sandbelt courses, both of top caliber, with natural tea-tree cover, expert bunkering on West course.
Kingston Heath Mentone	18/74/6,807	Championship course with first-class amenities.

COURSE	HOLES/PAR/ YARDAGE	DESCRIPTION
Metropolitan Oakleigh	18/74/6,602	Championship course on sandbelt, with extensive tree and shrub cover. Fine amenities.
Victoria Cheltanham	18/73/6,665	Championship, classic sand-belt, naturally drained, with lush growth, excellent.
Commonwealth Oakleigh	18/74/6,616	Sandbelt, with fast greens, attractive gum-lined fair-ways. Features 150-yard lake flanking 3rd and 16th (dogleg) holes. All facilities in clubhouse, including "long" bar with fine views.
Yarra Yarra Oakleigh	18/73/6,563	Championship course on sandbelt, with exacting, heavily trapped short holes. Heavy cover of native growth, with fairways lined by gums. Full clubhouse facilities.
Kingswood Dingley	18/74/6,669	Attractive semi-country course of championship caliber. Founded 1937. 16 miles from city.
Huntingdale East Oakleigh	18/75/6,941	Sandbelt course. 10½ miles from city. Full clubhouse facilities.

QUEENSLAND

COURSE	HOLES/PAR/ YARDAGE	DESCRIPTION
Royal Queensland Eagle Farm	18/74/6,784	Gently undulating cham-pionship course with sandy soil. Palms, other tropical growth lines fairways. True putting greens, well-trapped. Strong winds pro-vide good test. All amenities including bar, dining room.
Brisbane Yerongpilly	18/73/6,613	Founded 1896. Undulating course with two creeks.

COURSE	HOLES/PAR/ YARDAGE	DESCRIPTION
Gailes Gailes (Public)	18/73/6,722	Subsidiary 9-hole course. Bar in clubhouse. Championship rated. Easy undulating course. Feature its steep hill on 2nd. Bar, etc., in clubhouse.
TASMANIA		
Kingston Beach Hobart	18/74/6,488	Overlooks Derwent River. 11 miles from city. Well-wooded natural sand. Steep 1st, 18th holes, remainder flat.
SOUTH AUSTRALIA		
Koojonga Lockleys	18/73/6,525	Semiwooded, sandy course of championship caliber, with interesting hilly holes, well-groomed greens. Excellent amenities.
Royal Adelaide Seaton Park	18/73/6,714	Founded 1893. Flat course with tricky rough. Feature is "crater" hole 11th. Venue of 1962 National Open.
WESTERN AUSTRALIA		
Royal Perth South Perth	18/72/6,543	Founded 1895. Flat, championship standard course overlooking Swan River.
Cottesloe	18/72/6,400	Undulating, championship course near ocean beach.
Lake Karrinyup Balcatta	18/72/6,507	Lakeside course, with undulating terrain, natural water hazards.
Royal Fremantle Fremantle	18/72/6,488	Undulating, championship, links-type course.

Note: There are also golf courses of high standard and in luxuriant, tropical settings, at Port Moresby, Goroka, Madans, and Lae in the Territory of Papua-New Guinea.

NEW ZEALAND

The first thing the traveler notices as he wings his way over New Zealand, after visiting Australia, is the greenness of the countryside. With a climate similar to that of northern California, this pocket wonderland in the South Pacific offers everything to the tourist from the thermal activity of Yellowstone, to the grandeur of the Swiss Alps, to the white sand beaches of Hawaii. It would be difficult to end up more than a few miles from a golf club in any part of the country.

Of course, if you end up far enough out in the backblocks, the layout may be only nine holes, sheep may graze peacefully on the fairways, and an additional hazard may be barbed-wire fences around the green. But nevertheless, it is possible to play, and it is on these fairways that some of the most serious and exciting matches for the honor of being the "Waimaungataroto champion" are fought out.

New Zealand, with a golfing population of approximately eighty thousand players using 325 registered golf clubs, boasts some of the finest greens and fairways found anywhere. Golf in New Zealand has a year-round appeal as a sport and recreation, and has provided an ideal training ground for its young players of promise. In fact, in New Zealand golf is more than just a game. It is an accepted fact of life. New Zealanders have been playing golf for a hundred years and can currently boast one golf course for every eight thousand citizens, a per capita rating that not even Scotland can claim. More than 20 per cent of the country's active golfers are less than 18 years old. Caddies are never used and electric carts are unheard of. Instead, New Zealanders use hand carts—or "trundlers" as they call them—which are pulled by friends or members of their family whenever they play in major competitions. In some parts of the country, greenskeeping is left entirely to sheep herds and putting surfaces have to be fenced off to protect them from deer.

As in Australia, a visitor, with a letter of introduction from his home-club secretary or pro, can be assured of a warm welcome and all club privileges. It is advisable to contact the secretary or president of the club you plan to visit beforehand to arrange partners for a game. While golf is a year-round sport in New Zealand, the top seasons are the spring (September, October, and November) and the fall (March to June).

The choice of the best course in New Zealand is a difficult one. As a stern test of golf for the scratch player, overseas professionals are impressed by Paraparaumu Beach Golf Club, near Wellington, the capital city. A 6,472-yard course lying on a sand belt six hundred yards inland from the Tasman Sea, was laid out 14 years ago by an Australian architect named Alex Russell, who was once a player of championship stature. The course reflects a profound knowledge of the game. Russell bulldozed a quarter of a million yards of sand to form a links that has been favorably compared to the classic courses over which British championships are traditionally played. Towering sandhills dictate the line of play on practically every hole. The fairways tumble and toss in every direction, with the result that a level stance is a rarity. The perimeters of the greens are steeply banked, and these banks, in turn, are potted with bunkers with deep overhanging lips which can snare a trap shot that is not played authoritatively. And then there is the wind, always the wind.

The Paraparaumu Golf Course in Wellington is considered one of the toughest tests in New Zealand.

When it is not blowing off the sea, it whistles down from the treeless slopes of the Tararua Mountains, hanging over the course in the background. The course at Paraparaumu Beach is not the sort you would want to play with anything short of your best game.

The Arikikapakapa Golf Course, in Rotorua, is one of New Zealand's most picturesque courses. Situated near the heart of the North Island's thermal region, the course has the added attraction of hissing steam fumaroles.

Auckland, the largest city in New Zealand, has many courses. Vying for consideration are Titirangi, a shorter course (only 6,294 yards) which makes up for its lack of distance with astute layout, set amid beautiful native bush; the Auckland Golf Club, a beautifully manicured course, 13 miles south of the main city area; and Muriwai, a new 18-hole course, which is separated from the crashing breakers of the Tasman Sea by only a narrow row of dunes.

For the golfer who wants something a little different, undoubtedly the course to play in New Zealand is the Roturua Club's Arikikapakapa course at Whakarewarewa in Roturua. Local legend has it that if a tourist can pronounce the aforementioned correctly, without help from New Zealand's native Maoris, he will break par by seven strokes. Arikikapakapa is set in the heart of New Zealand's extremely active thermal area, and smoking blowholes, geysers, and boiling mud pools surround the golfers on every side. The fairways are wide, but if your ball disappears into a patch of titree (local underground) which is emitting clouds of wispy smoke, you would be well advised to leave it alone and drop another one.

Another resort club in the vicinity is at Taupo. Some ten thousand rounds were played last year on this course, which is situated by Lake Taupo, a mecca for trout fishermen. Taupo and Arikikapakapa are two high-grade courses in New Zealand which do not require any credentials to play.

New Zealand's South Island is seldom lagging behind North Island in providing facilities for tourists and the field of golf is no exception. The first stop for most travelers after crossing Cook Strait is Christchurch. This city has two fine courses—Shirley and Russley. Both are 18 holes, six thousand yards plus layouts, and if on the flat side, make up for it with an abundance of trees. Further south is the Scottish settled city of Dunedin. The 6,380-yard St. Clair course, which is only ten minutes from the center of the city by car, is set in rolling country. This course has been the scene of many New Zealand championships and provides harbor and ocean views from many of the tees and greens. Further south again, the nearest city of any size to the Antarctic, is Invercargill. Scottish in origin, it has an excellent golf course at Otatara, only four miles out of town.

Here are some of the best courses of New Zealand for the tourist to play:

COURSE	HOLES/PAR/ YARDAGE	DESCRIPTION
NORTH ISLAND		
Paraparaumu Beach GC Wellington	18/71/6,472	Visitors welcome if they telephone day before they want to play so partners can be arranged. The best day of week for visitors is Wednesday. Greens always in excellent order.
Titirangi GC New Lynn	18/72/6,161	The course is very beautiful and has many natural difficulties.
Wanganui GC (Belmont Links) Wanganui	18/71/6,244	It is mostly undulating with one or two fairly steep holes.
Aukland GC Middlemore	18/71/6,226	Has parklike layout in flat to gentle undulating country. The Tamaki estuary borders several holes, and course is heavily bunkered.
Wairaki Resort GC Wairaki	18/72/6,903	The 14th, appropriately named "The Rogue," is the longest hole (608 yards) on the course.
Roturuna GC (Arikikapakapa Course) Wakakarewarewa	18/70/6,012	In addition to natural thermal hazards and the customary sand traps, some holes are guarded by crater-like chasms with a seemingly uncanny magnetism for the loose ball.
Taupo GC Taupo	18/72/6,145	Course is dominated by Mt. Tauhara; nearby are thermal baths, and the Wairakei Geothermal Power Project.

COURSE	HOLES/PAR/ YARDAGE	DESCRIPTION
The Grange Club Papatoetal	18/72/6,316	Scenic, but rather difficult.
Wellington GC Heretaunua	18/71/6,217	Contains five par-3 holes ranging in length from 123 to 202 yards. The shortest —15th hole—is the most celebrated on the course.
SOUTH ISLAND		
St. Clair GC Dunedin	18/72/6,380	Seaside course with fairway between well-grassed gently rolling sandhills. Excellent views of city, harbor, and ocean.
Nelson GC (Tahunanui Links) Nelson	18/70/6,700	The undulating fairways call for accuracy and good judgment.
Invercargill GC Invercargill	18/71/6,719	One of the longest courses in the country.
Otago GC Dunedin	18/72/6,401	Rather interesting layout that can give trouble.

Appendix A
THE MOST CHALLENGING
AMERICAN COURSES YOU *CAN* PLAY

The selection of the most challenging courses that you can play in the United States is almost as difficult as it would be to play them. The staff of *Golf* magazine, from the suggestions of the professional golfers who contribute to our magazine has compiled the following listing of one hundred of the most difficult courses in the United States. Sure, we may have left out your favorite "tough" course (sorry!), but here are the ones selected by our experts:

LOCATION	*COURSE*	*YARDAGE/PAR/ RATING* *
Alabama		
Dauphin Island	Isle Dauphine CC	7,000/72/73
Point Clear	Lakewood GC	6,429/70/73
Arizona		
Carefree	Desert Forest CC	6,929/72/72
Litchfield	Goodyear G & CC	7,220/72/74
Arkansas		
Cherokee Village	Cherokee Village GC	7,051/72/72
Hot Springs	Hot Springs G & CC (#3)	6,915/72/72
California		
Apple Valley	Apple Valley CC	6,765/71/71
Carlsbad	La Costa CC	7,013/72/73

* Course rating is the evaluation of the playing difficulty of a golf course compared with other rated courses, for the purpose of providing a uniform, sound basis on which to compute handicaps. This rating is based on yardage and the ability of a scratch player to play the hole, since handicaps are used to adjust players' scoring ability to a scratch level. Incidentally, courses are rated by golf associations, not by individual clubs.

LOCATION	COURSE	YARDAGE/PAR/ RATING *
Carmel	Carmel Valley G & CC	6,756/72/72
La Jolla	Torrey Pines GC	7,011/72/72
Ojai	Ojai Valley Inn & CC	6,426/70/70
Palm Desert	Del Safari GC	7,002/72/72
Palm Springs	Canyon GC (South)	6,700/71/72
Pebble Beach	Pebble Beach Golf Links	6,747/72/75
Pebble Beach	Spyglass Hill GC	7,035/72/76
Colorado		
Evergreen	Hiwan GC	7,114/70/70
Florida		
Boca Raton	Boca Raton Hotel & CC	6,777/71/71
Fort Meyers	Cypress Lake CC	7,048/72/72
Miami	CC of Miami (West)	6,927/72/73
Miami	Doral CC (Blue)	7,028/72/74
Miami	Miami Lakes CC	7,030/72/72
Pompano Beach	Palm Aire Lodge & CC	7,120/72/73
Ponte Vedra Beach	Ponte Vedra CC	6,786/72/72
Sarasota	DeSoto Lakes GC	6,927/72/73
Tarpon Springs	Innisbrook G & CC	6,745/72/72
West Palm Beach	West Palm Beach G & CC	6,475/72/72
Georgia		
Sea Island	Sea Island GC	6,873/71/71
Hawaii		
Kaanapoli	Royal Kaanapoli GC	7,179/72/75
Kamuela	Mauna Kea Beach GC	7,016/72/74
Kona	Keauhou-Kona CC	6,814/72/72
Waianae	Makaha Inn & CC	7,252/72/75
Idaho		
Boise	Plantation GC	6,522/72/72
Sun Valley	Sun Valley GC	6,227/70/71
Illinois		
Lemont	Cog Hill GC (#4)	7,224/72/73
Iowa		
Davenport	Emeis Park GC	7,000/72/72
Iowa	Finkbine GC	6,905/72/72
Waterloo	Gates Park GC	7,210/72/72

LOCATION	COURSE	YARDAGE/PAR/ RATING *
Maine		
Bar Harbor	Kebo Valley GC	6,709/70/70
Maryland		
Baltimore	Mount Pleasant GC	6,730/71/74
Massachusetts		
Bolton	International GC	7,040/72/74
Mashpee	CC of New Seabury	7,122/72/74
Sulton	Pleasant Valley CC	6,713/71/74
Montana		
Billings	Yellowstone CC	7,000/70/70
Nevada		
Incline Village	Incline Valley CC	7,116/72/72
Las Vegas	Desert Inn CC	7,209/72/73
Las Vegas	Paradise Valley CC	7,069/72/72
Las Vegas	Sahara-Nevada CC	6,581/71/71
New Jersey		
Tuckerton	Atlantis CC	7,085/72/73
New Mexico		
Albuquerque	Paradise Hills G & CC	7,185/72/72
Albuquerque	University of New Mexico	7,246/72/75
New York		
Farmingdale	Bethpage GC (Black)	6,873/71/73
Grossinger	Grossinger's GC	6,758/71/71
Kiamesha Lake	Concord Hotel & CC	
	(Championship)	7,205/72/76
	(International)	7,062/71/72
Monticello	Kutsher's GC	7,157/72/72
South Fallsburg	Tarry Brae GC	7,180/72/74
North Carolina		
Pinehurst	Pinehurst CC (#2)	7,051/72/73
Southern Pines	Pine Needles CC	6,905/72/72
Whispering Pines	Whispering Pines CC	7,151/72/74
North Dakota		
Fargo	Fargo CC	6,627/72/72
Grand Forks	Grand Forks CC	6,980/72/72

LOCATION	COURSE	YARDAGE/PAR/ RATING *
Oklahoma		
Checotah	Fountainhead State Park GC	7,023/72/72
Oregon		
Hillsboro	Meriwether National GC	7,042/72/72
Pennsylvania		
Bushkill	Tamiment GC	7,110/72/73
Hershey	Hershey CC	6,928/73/74
Pocono Manor	Pocono Manor Inn & GC	6,855/72/72
	(West)	6,720/72/72
Shawnee-on-Delaware	Shawnee CC	6,720/72/72
South Carolina		
Hilton Head Island	Palmetto Dunes GC	7,207/72/74
Hilton Head Island	Harbour Town Links	6,885/72/74
Myrtle Beach	Dunes G & BC	7,180/72/74
South Dakota		
Sioux Falls	Elmwood Park GC	7,100/72/73
Texas		
Houston	Memorial Park GC	7,122/72/73
San Antonio	Pecan Valley CC	7,007/70/72
Vermont		
Warren	Sugarbush Inn & CC	6,741/72/73
Virginia		
Williamsburg	Golden Horseshoe GC	6,750/71/73
West Virginia		
Morgantown	Lakeview CC	6,850/71/71
White Sulphur Springs	The Greenbrier Club	
	(Old White)	6,534/70/70
	(Greenbrier)	6,473/70/70
Wisconsin		
Milwaukee	Brown Deer GC	7,030/71/73
Wyoming		
Jackson	Jackson Hole G & TC	7,045/72/73

LOCATION	COURSE	YARDAGE/PAR/ RATING *
Puerto Rico		
Dorado Beach	Cerromar GC (North)	7,070/72/73
	(South)	7,130/72/72
Dorado Beach	Dorado Beach GC (East)	7,005/72/72
		6,913/72/73
Las Croabas	El Conquistador GC	6,285/70/70
Virgin Islands		
St. Croix	Fountain Valley GC	6,909/72/72

Appendix B

THE MOST INTERESTING
GOLF HOLES IN THE
UNITED STATES AND THE WORLD

After making a survey of the outstanding golf courses of North America, the staff of *Golf* magazine next chose the most interesting holes that you can play in the United States. These holes were not selected on difficulty alone, but rather because they offered a colorful panorama of grass, water, trees, bunkers, sand, and other features to rest, refresh, and challenge the golfer. The holes listed here meet these tests and the intent is not to compare but to give the reader a cursory introduction to some of the finest and most interesting golf holes in the United States. While several of the great courses of the United States have more than one interesting hole, only one was selected from a club.

PAR 3'S

STATE	*COURSE*	*HOLE*	*YARDAGE*
Arizona	Camelback GC	17	220
Arizona	Scottsdale Inn & CC	17	208
California	Carmel Valley G & CC	17	160
Florida	Ponte Vedra GC	16	134
Georgia	Callaway Gardens (Lake View)	5	152
Hawaii	Kuilima GC	2	180
Hawaii	Mauna Kea	3	215
Idaho	Sun Valley GC	15	235
North Carolina	Mid Pines CC	2	181
Tennesse	Gatlinburg CC	12	152
Vermont	Basin Harbor Club	13	195
Virginia	Golden Horseshoe GC	3	215

PAR 4'S

STATE	COURSE	HOLE	YARDAGE
Alabama	Lakewood GC (Magnolia)	9	381
Arizona	Arizona Biltmore GC	14	455
California	Alisal GC	8	410
California	Canyon CC (South)	5	410
California	Indian Wells GC	10	464
California	Silverado CC (South)	6	390
Colorado	Broadmoor GC	7	470
Florida	Breakers GC (West)	9	447
Florida	Doral CC	18	437
Florida	Innisbrook G & CC	10	435
Hawaii	Keauhou-Kona CC	8	450
Hawaii	Makaha Inn & CC	5	427
Hawaii	Royal Kaanapoli CC	3	438
Georgia	Sea Island GC (Seaside)	7	435
Illinois	Cog Hill CC	16	383
Massachusetts	New Seabury CC	16	402
Massachusetts	Pleasant Valley CC	17	402
Montana	Yellowstone CC	11	430
Nevada	Paradise Valley CC	18	424
Nevada	Sahara-Nevada GC	6	442
New Hampshire	Wentworth Fairway GC	14	415
New York	Concord Hotel & GC	8	399
New York	Kutsher's GC	13	455
Oregon	Salishan Lodge GC	7	417
Pennsylvania	Shawnee Inn GC (White)	8	380
Pennsylvania	Skytop Club	18	355
Pennsylvania	Taminent GC	6	450
South Carolina	Harbour Town Golf Links	18	330
Vermont	Sugarbush Inn GC	15	445
West Virginia	The Greenbrier (Old White)	16	407

PAR 5'S

Arizona	San Marcus GC	9	635
Arizona	Goodyear GC (Gold)	10	610
California	LaCosta GC	17	573
California	Pebble Beach Golf Links	18	530
Florida	Boca Raton GC (West)	6	630
New York	Grossinger's GC	4	512
North Carolina	Beaver Lakes GC	13	690

PAR 5'S

STATE	COURSE	HOLE	YARDAGE
North Carolina	Pinehurst CC (#2)	10	596
South Carolina	Dunes G & BC	13	535
South Carolina	Palmetto Dunes CC	9	540
Virginia	The Homestead (Upper Cascades)	16	534
Virginia	Tides International 18	3	535

INTERESTING HOLES ON WORLD COURSES

The following are the most interesting holes you can play on courses other than in the United States:

HOLE	COURSE	YARDS/PAR	COURSE	YARDS/PAR
1	Crans-sur-Sierre GC (Switzerland)	585/ 5	Royal Lytham & St. Anne's GC (England)	208/ 3
2	Walton Heath GC (England)	445/ 4	Valley GC (Philippines)	460/ 4
3	Gleneagles Hotel GC (Scotland)	393/ 4	Prestwick GC (Scotland)	505/ 5
4	Doral Beach GC (Puerto Rico)	205/ 3	Royal Johannesburg GC (South Africa)	476/ 4
5	Mid-Ocean GC (Bermuda)	433/ 4	Royal Portrush GC (Northern Ireland)	392/ 4
6	Glyfada GC (Greece)	435/ 4	Cotton Bay GC (Bahamas)	539/ 5
7	Club de Golf Mexico (Mexico)	575/ 5	Royal Dublin GC (Ireland)	352/ 4
8	Banff Springs Hotel GC (Canada)	175/ 3	Troon GC (Scotland)	125/ 3
9	Royal County Downs GC (Northern Ireland)	426/ 4	Turnberry Hotel GC (Scotland)	475/ 4
	Out	3,672/36		3,532/36

HOLE	COURSE	YARDS/ PAR	COURSE	YARDS/ PAR
10	London Hunt & CC (Canada)	350/ 5	Royal Cinque Ports-Deal-GC (England)	385/ 4
11	Laguneta CC (Venezuela)	188/ 3	Fuji CC (Japan)	550/ 5
12	Kooyogan GC (Australia)	391/ 4	Monte Carlo GC (Monaco)	175/ 3
13	Club de Campo (Spain)	466/ 4	Wentworth Club (England)	437/ 4
14	County Sligo GC (Ireland)	440/ 4	Portmarnock GC (Northern Ireland)	385/ 4
15	North Berwick CC (Scotland)	203/ 3	Royal St. George's CC (England)	435/ 4
16	Royal Liverpool GC (England)	532/ 5	Royal Melbourne Club (Australia)	215/ 3
17	Carnoustie GC (Scotland)	423/ 4	St. Andrews (Scotland)	453/ 4
18	Wack Wack G & CC (Philippines)	422/ 4	Capilano G & CC (Canada)	575/ 5
	In	3,615/36		3,610/36
	Total	72	Total	72

Appendix C

THE WORLD'S GOLFING NATIONS

The following tabulations of a number of golf courses in the following countries have been provided by national golf organizations and tourists offices. In many cases it does not include so-called "company courses." This is especially true in Central America and the Middle East.

NORTH AND CENTRAL AMERICA

Canada	1,216	Mexico	49
Guatemala	2	Panama	1
Honduras	1	United States	10,494

BERMUDA, THE BAHAMAS, AND THE CARIBBEAN

Antigua	3	Montserrat	1
Aruba	1	Nassau and the Bahamas	16
Barbados	2	Puerto Rico	11
Bermuda	10	St. Kitts	1
Curaçao	1	St. Lucia	1
Dominican Republic	3	St. Martin	1
Grenada	1	St. Vincent	1
Haiti	1	Trinidad and Tobago	9
Jamaica	12	Virgin Islands	4

SOUTH AMERICA

Argentina	106	Guyana	1
Bolivia	5	Paraguay	2
Brazil	29	Peru	19
Chile	31	Surinam	1
Columbia	21	Uruguay	7
Ecuador	3	Venezuela	25

EUROPE

Austria	16	Ireland	214
Belgium	13	Italy	37
Bulgaria	1	Luxembourg	1
Canary Islands	1	Malta	1

Czechoslovakia	2	Monaco	1
Denmark	24	Netherlands	21
Finland	12	Norway	6
France	101	Portugal	15
Germany	94	Romania	1
Gibraltar	1	Spain	36
Great Britain	1,697	Sweden	136
Greece	3	Switzerland	28
Iceland	9	Yugoslavia	1

AFRICA

Angola	1	Morocco	7
Congo	4	Nigeria	3
Egypt	5	Rhodesia	68
Ghana	7	Senegal	2
Guinea	2	South Africa	322
Kenya	34	Uganda	14
Liberia	2		

THE MIDDLE EAST

Iran	2	Lebanon	4
Iraq	3	Turkey	7
Israel	1		

ASIA

Burma	44	Malaysia	31
Ceylon	2	Nepal	1
Hong Kong	5	Pakistan	24
India	52	Singapore	6
Indonesia	20	Taiwan	9
Japan	639	Thailand	12
Korea	4		

THE PACIFIC

Australia	1,274	Papua–New Guinea	5
Fiji Islands	7	Philippines	42
Guam	1	Samoa	1
New Zealand	325	Tahiti	2
Okinawa	4	Tonga	1

Appendix D

SOURCES OF
GOLF TRAVEL INFORMATION

UNITED STATES
To obtain further information on golfing—as well as travel data—in a particular area, write the state agency mentioned below:

ALABAMA Alabama Bureau of Publicity and Information, State Highway Building, Montgomery, Alabama 36104

ALASKA Alaska Travel Division, Department of Economic Development, Pouch E, Juneau, Alaska 99801

ARIZONA Travel Development Section, Department of Economic Planning and Development, 3003 North Central Avenue, Suite 1704, Phoenix, Arizona 85012

ARKANSAS Arkansas Department of Parks and Tourism, 149 State Capitol Building, Little Rock, Arkansas 72201

CALIFORNIA State of California, Office of Tourism and Visitor Services, 1400 Tenth Street, Sacramento, California 95814

COLORADO Travel Development Section, Colorado Division of Commerce and Development, 602 State Capitol Annex, Denver, Colorado 80203

CONNECTICUT Connecticut Development Commission, Vacation-Travel Promotion, State Office Building, Hartford, Connecticut 06115

DELAWARE Bureau of Travel Development, Division of Economic Development, Department of Community Affairs and Economic Development, 45 The Green, Dover, Delaware 19901

FLORIDA Bureau of Tourism, Florida Department of Commerce, 107 West Gaines Street, Tallahassee, Florida 32304

GEORGIA Tourist Division, Georgia Department of Industry and Trade, P.O. Box 38097, Atlanta, Georgia 30334

HAWAII Hawaii Visitors Bureau, 2270 Kalakaua Avenue, Suite 801, Honolulu, Hawaii 96815

IDAHO Department of Commerce and Development, State Capitol Building, Room 108, Boise, Idaho 83707

ILLINOIS Division of Tourism, Illinois Department of Business and Economic Development, 222 South College Street, Springfield, Illinois 62706

INDIANA Division of Tourism, Department of Commerce, State House, Room 336, Indianapolis, Indiana 46204

IOWA Iowa Development Commission, Tourism and Travel Division, 250 Jewett Building, Des Moines, Iowa 50309

KANSAS Travel Division, Kansas Department of Economic Development, 122-S State Office Building, Topeka, Kansas 66612

KENTUCKY Department of Public Information, Advertising and Travel Division, Capitol Annex Building, Frankfurt, Kentucky 40601

LOUISIANA Louisiana Tourist Development Commission, P.O. Box 44291, Baton Rouge, Louisiana 70804

MAINE Maine Department of Economic Development, State House, Augusta, Maine 04330

MARYLAND Division of Tourism, State Office Building, Room 404, Annapolis, Maryland 21401

MASSACHUSETTS Division of Tourism, Massachusetts Department of Commerce and Development, Leverett Saltonstall Building, Boston, Massachusetts 02202

MICHIGAN Michigan Tourist Council, 300 South Capitol, Suite 102, Lansing, Michigan 48926

MINNESOTA Vacation Information Center, Minnesota Department of Economic Development, 51 East 8 Street, St. Paul, Minnesota 55101

MISSISSIPPI Travel Department, Mississippi Agricultural and Industrial Board, State Office Building, Room 1504, Jackson, Mississippi 39205

MISSOURI Missouri Tourism Commission, P.O. Box 1055, Jefferson City, Missouri 65101

MONTANA Department of Highways—Advertising Unit, Helena, Montana 59601

NEBRASKA Tourism Division, Nebraska Department of Economic Development, P.O. Box 94666, Lincoln, Nebraska 68509

NEVADA Tourism-Travel Division, Department of Economic Development, Carson City, Nevada 89701

NEW HAMPSHIRE New Hampshire Division of Economic Development, P.O. Box 856, Concord, New Hampshire 03301

NEW JERSEY New Jersey State Promotion, Department of Labor and Industry, P.O. Box 400, Trenton, New Jersey 08625

NEW MEXICO Tourist Division, New Mexico Department of Development, 113 Washington Avenue, Santa Fe, New Mexico 87501

NEW YORK   Travel Bureau, New York State Department of Commerce, 112 State Street, Albany, New York 12207

NORTH CAROLINA   North Carolina Department of Natural and Economic Resources, Travel and Promotion Division, P.O. Box 27687, Raleigh, North Carolina 27611

NORTH DAKOTA   North Dakota Travel Department, State Capitol Grounds, Bismarck, North Dakota 58501

OHIO   Travel and Tourist Division, Ohio Department of Development, P.O. Box 1001, Columbus, Ohio 43216

OKLAHOMA   Oklahoma Tourism & Information Division, 500 Will Rogers Memorial Building, Oklahoma City, Oklahoma 73105

OREGON   Travel Information Section, Oregon State Highway Division, Salem, Oregon 97310

PENNSYLVANIA   Pennsylvania Department of Commerce, Bureau of Travel Development, 402 South Office Building, Harrisburg, Pennsylvania 17120

RHODE ISLAND   Tourist Promotion Division, Rhode Island Development Council, Roger Williams Building, Providence, Rhode Island 02908

SOUTH CAROLINA   Division of Travel and Tourism, South Carolina Department of Parks, Recreation and Tourism, P.O. Box 1358, Columbia, South Carolina 29202

SOUTH DAKOTA   South Dakota Department of Highways, Travel Division, Pierre, South Dakota 57501

TENNESSEE   Tennessee Department of Conservation, Division of Information and Tourist Promotion, 2611 West End Avenue, Nashville, Tennessee 37203

TEXAS   Texas Tourist Development Aegncy, P.O. Box 12008, Capitol Station, Austin, Texas 37203

UTAH   Utah Travel Council, Council Hall, Capitol Hill, Salt Lake City, Utah 84114

VERMONT   Information/Travel Development, Vermont Development Agency, 61 Elm Street, Montpelier, Vermont 05602

VIRGINIA   Virginia State Travel Service, 911 East Broad Street, Richmond, Virginia 23219

WASHINGTON   Tourist Promotion Division, Department of Commerce and Economic Development, General Administration Building, Olympia, Washington 98504

WEST VIRGINIA   Travel Development Division, West Virginia Department of Commerce, State Capitol, Charleston, West Virginia 25305

WISCONSIN   Bureau of Vacation and Travel Services, Department of Natural Resources, P.O. Box 450, Madison, Wisconsin 53701

WYOMING   Wyoming Travel Commission, 2320 Capitol Avenue, Cheyenne, Wyoming 82001

DISTRICT OF COLUMBIA (WASHINGTON, D.C.)   Washington Convention and Visitors Bureau, 1129 20th Street, N.W., Washington, D.C. 20036

COMMONWEALTH OF PUERTO RICO   Puerto Rico Tourism Development Company, G.P.O. Box BN, San Juan, Puerto Rico 00936

GUAM   Guam Visitors Bureau, P.O. Box 3520, Agana, Guam 96910

VIRGIN ISLANDS   Tourist Bureau, Department of Commerce, P.O. Box 1692, Charlotte Amalie, St. Thomas, Virgin Islands 00801

World Golfing Nations. Sources of golfing and tourist information from the various golf nations, write:

ARGENTINA   Embassy of the Argentine Republic, 1600 New Hampshire Avenue, N.W., Washington, D.C. 20009

ARUBA   Aruba Information Center, 576 Fifth Avenue, New York, New York 10036

AUSTRALIA   Australian Tourist Commission, 1270 Avenue of the Americas, New York, New York 10020

AUSTRIA   Austrian National Tourist Office, 545 Fifth Avenue, New York, New York 10017

BAHAMA ISLANDS   Bahama Islands Tourist Information, 30 Rockefeller Plaza, New York, New York 10020

BARBADOS   Barbados Tourist Board, 801 Second Avenue, New York, New York 10017

BELGIUM   Official Belgian Tourist Bureau, 720 Fifth Avenue, New York, New York 10019

BERMUDA   Bermuda Department of Tourism, 610 Fifth Avenue, New York, New York 10020

BOLIVIA   Embassy of Bolivia, 1145 19 Street, N.W., Washington, D.C. 20036

BRAZIL   Brazilian Government Trade Bureau, 551 Fifth Avenue, New York, New York 10017

BURMA   Embassy of the Union of Burma, 2300 S. Street, N.W., Washington, D.C. 20008

CANADA   Canadian Government Travel Bureau, 150 Kent Street, Ottawa, Ontario, Canada

CARIBBEAN   Caribbean Travel Association, 20 East 46 Street, New York, New York 10017. (Aruba, Barbados, Bonaire, British Virgin Islands, Cayman Islands, Colombia, Curaçao, Dominican Republic, Guadeloupe–St. Barthelemy–St. Martin, Haiti, Martinique, Montserrat, St. Kitts–Nevis–Anguilla, St. Maarten–Saba–St. Eustatius, Turks, and Caicos Islands.)

CEYLON   Ceylon Tourist Board, 609 Fifth Avenue, New York 10017

CHILE   Embassy of Chile, 1736 Massachusetts Avenue, N.W., Washington, D.C. 20036

COLOMBIA   Colombia Government Tourist Office, 140 East 57 Street, New York, New York 10027

CURACAO   Curaçao Tourist Board, 604 Fifth Avenue, New York, New York 10020

CZECHOSLOVAKIA   Cedok-Czechoslovak Travel Bureau, 10 East 40 Street, New York, New York 10016

DENMARK   Danish National Tourist Office, Scandinavia House, 505 Fifth Avenue, New York, New York 10017

DOMINICAN REPUBLIC   Embassy of the Dominican Republic, 1715 22 Street, N.W., Washington, D.C. 20008

ECUADOR   Embassy of Ecuador, 2535 15 Street, N.W., Washington, D.C. 20009

EGYPT, ARAB REPUBLIC OF   Egyptian Government Tourist Office, 630 Fifth Avenue, New York, New York 10020

FINLAND   Finnish National Tourist Office, Scandinavia House, 505 Fifth Avenue, New York, New York 10017

FRANCE   French Government Tourist Office, 610 Fifth Avenue, New York, New York 10020

GERMANY   German National Tourist Office, 500 Fifth Avenue, New York, New York 10036

GHANA   Embassy of Ghana, 2460 16th Street, N.W., Washington, D.C. 20009

GREAT BRITAIN   British Tourist Authority, 680 Fifth Avenue, New York, New York 10019 (England, Scotland, Wales, and Northern Ireland).

GREECE   Greek National Tourist Organization, 601 Fifth Avenue, New York, New York 10017

GUATEMALA   Embassy of Guatemala, 2220 R Street, N.W., Washington, D.C. 20008

REPUBLIC OF HAITI   Haiti Government Tourist Bureau, 30 Rockefeller Plaza, New York, New York 10020

HONG KONG   Hong Kong Tourist Association, 548 Fifth Avenue, New York, New York 10036

ICELAND   Embassy of Iceland, 2022 Connecticut Avenue, N.W., Washington, D.C.

INDIA   Government of India Tourist Office, 19 East 49 Street, New York, New York 10017

INDONESIA   Embassy of the Republic of Indonesia, 2020 Massachusetts Avenue, N.W., Washington, D.C. 20036

IRAN   Embassy of Iran, 3005 Massachusetts Avenue, N.W., Washington, D.C. 20008

IRAQ   Press Information Office, 14 East 79 Street, New York, New York 10021

IRELAND   Irish Tourist Board, Ireland House, 590 Fifth Avenue, New York, New York 10036

ISRAEL   Israel Government Tourist Office, 574 Fifth Avenue, New York, New York 10036

ITALY   Italian Government Travel Office, 630 Fifth Avenue, New York, New York 10020

JAMAICA   Jamaica Tourist Board, Pan Am Building, 200 Park Avenue, New York, New York 10017

JAPAN   Japan National Tourist Organization, 45 Rockefeller Plaza, New York, New York 10020

KENYA   Kenya Tourist Office, 15 East 51 Street, New York, New York 10022

LABANON   Lebanon Tourist and Information Office, 527 Madison Avenue, Suite 304, New York, New York 10022

MALAYSIA   Embassy of Malaysia, 2401 Massachusetts Avenue, N.W., Washington, D.C. 20008

MEXICO   Mexican National Tourist Council, 677 Fifth Avenue, New York, New York 10020

MONACO   Monaco Government Tourist Office, 610 Fifth Avenue, New York, New York 10020

MOROCCO   Moroccan National Tourist Office, 597 Fifth Avenue, New York, New York 10017

NETHERLANDS   Netherlands National Tourist Office, 576 Fifth Avenue, New York, New York 10036

NEW ZEALAND   New Zealand Government Tourist Office, 630 Fifth Avenue, New York, New York 10020

NORWAY   Norwegian National Travel Office, Scandinavia House, 505 Fifth Avenue, New York, New York 10017

PAKISTAN   Embassy of Pakistan, 2315 Massachusetts Avenue, N.W., Washington, D.C. 20008

PANAMA   Panama Government Tourist Bureau, 630 Fifth Avenue, New York, New York 10020

PARAGUAY   Embassy of Paraguay, 2400 Massachusetts Avenue, N.W., Washington, D.C. 20008

PERU   Embassy of Peru, 1320 16 Street, N.W., Washington, D.C. 20036

PHILIPPINES   Philippines Tourist and Travel Association, 15 East 66 Street, New York, New York 10021

PORTUGAL   Portuguese Tourist Information and Trade Office, 570 Fifth Avenue, New York, New York 10036

RHODESIA   Rhodesia National Tourist Board, 535 Fifth Avenue, New York, New York 10017

SCANDINAVIA   Scandinavia National Travel Offices, Scandinavia House, 505 Fifth Avenue, New York, New York 10017 (Norway, Sweden, Denmark, Iceland).

SENEGAL   Embassy of the Republic of Senegal, 2112 Wyoming Avenue, N.W., Washington, D.C. 20008

SINGAPORE   Singapore Tourist Promotion Board, 251 Post Street, San Francisco, California 94108

SOUTH AFRICA, REPUBLIC OF   South African Tourist Corporation, Rockefeller Center, 610 Fifth Avenue, New York, New York 10020

SPAIN   Spanish National Tourist Office, 589 Fifth Avenue, New York, New York 10017

SWEDEN   Swedish National Travel Office, Scandinavia House, 505 Fifth Avenue, New York, New York 10017

SWITZERLAND   Swiss National Tourist Office, The Swiss Center, 608 Fifth Avenue, New York, New York 10020

TAIWAN   Chinese Embassy, 2311 Massachusetts Avenue, N.W., Washintgon, D.C. 20008

THAILAND (SIAM)   Tourist Organization of Thailand, 20 East 82 Street, New York, New York 10028

TRINIDAD AND TOBAGO   Trinidad and Tobago Tourist Board, 400 Madison Avenue, New York, New York 10017

TURKEY   Turkey Tourism and Information Office, 500 Fifth Avenue, New York, New York 10036

URUGUAY   Embassy of Uruguay, 1918 F Street, N.W., Washington, D.C. 20006

VENEZUELA   Venezuela Government Tourist and Information Office, 485 Madison Avenue, New York, New York 10022

GUIDE TO GOLF TOUR AGENTS

These firms offer organized preplanned golf-travel holiday packages:

Alice Travel, Inc., 446 Pleasant Valley Way, West Orange, New Jersey 07052

American Airlines, 633 Third Avenue, New York, New York 10017

Braniff Airlines, Exchange Park, Dallas, Texas 75235

CIE Tours, 564 Fifth Avenue, New York, New York 10036

Thomas Cook, 587 Fifth Avenue, New York, New York 10017

Delta Airlines, Inc., Atlanta Hartsfield International Airport, Atlanta, Georgia 30320

DiCarlo, 151 West 40 Street, New York, New York 10018

Eastern's Flying Golfer's Club, P.O. Box 71, Farmingdale, New York 11735

Fun-Tyme Tours, 1824 Kings Highway, Brooklyn, New York 11229

Gogo Tours, 353 Lexington Avenue, New York, New York 10016

Golf Club America, Suite 360, 24300 Southfield Road, Southfield, Michigan 48075

Golf Tours International, 49 West 57 Street, New York, New York 10019

Haley Corp., 11 East 44 Street, New York, New York 10017

ITP, Suite 631, 11 West 42 Street, New York, New York 10036

Pacific Golf Enterprises, P.O. Box Q, Honolulu, Hawaii 96815

Tortuga Express Tour Company, P.O. Box 4002, Anaheim, California 92803

TWA Golf Tours, 605 Third Avenue, New York, New York 10017

United Airlines, P.O. Box 66100, Chicago, Illinois 60680

Wide World of Golf Tours, 98 Post Street, San Francisco, California 94104

Grateful acknowledgment is made for pictures used from the following sources:

Australian News and Information Bureau, pp. 382, 384, 385, 387
Bermuda News Bureau, pp. 221, 222, 225
Braniff International, pp. 258, 259, 260
The British Tourist Authority, pp. 281, 288
The British Travel Association, pp. 269, 273, 278
The Bunting Co. Ltd., p. 230
Leo A. Cohen, p. 156
Cowley Photos, p. 173
Finnish Tourist Association, p. 308
Harry W. Graff, Inc., p. 343
Graphic Industries Ltd., p. 206
Hawaii Visitors Bureau, p. 178
John G. Hemmer, pp. 12, 74
Irish Tourist Board, p. 269
Fred Kuehn Studio, p. 110
Taylor Lewis and Associates, p. 71
Dom Lupo, pp. 20, 221
L. McNally, p. 50
Manley Commercial Photography, p. 149
Ministry of Information, Salisbury, Rhodesia, p. 347
B. H. Moody, pp. 354, 355, 356
Northern Ireland Tourist Board, pp. 273, 291, 299
Norwegian Information Service, p. 321
Panagra, pp. 250, 253
Parrott Photography, p. 96
Reuterphoto, p. 4
Julius Shulman, p. 163
Hal Rumel Studio, p. 141
Swedish National Travel Office, p. 309
Watson Bros. Photography, Inc., p. 164
Wide World Photo, p. 367

INDEX OF GOLF COURSES